Iran and the Challenge of Diversity

Iran and the Challenge of Diversity

Islamic Fundamentalism, Aryanist Racism, and Democratic Struggles

Alireza Asgharzadeh

First published in 2007 by
PALGRAVE MACMILLAN™
175 Fifth Avenue, New York, N.Y. 10010 and
Houndmills, Basingstoke, Hampshire, England RG21 6XS
Companies and representatives throughout the world.

PALGRAVE MACMILLAN is the global academic imprint of the Palgrave Macmillan division of St. Martin's Press, LLC and of Palgrave Macmillan Ltd. Macmillan® is a registered trademark in the United States, United Kingdom and other countries. Palgrave is a registered trademark in the European Union and other countries.

ISBN-13: 978–1–4039–8080–9
ISBN-10: 1–4039–8080–2

Library of Congress Cataloging-in-Publication Data

Asgharzadeh, Alireza.
    Iran and the challenge of diversity : Islamic fundamentalism, Aryanist racism, and democratic struggles / by Alireza Asgharzadeh.
        p. cm.
    Includes bibliographical references.
    ISBN 1–4039–8080–2
        1. Iran—Ethnic relations—History—20th century. 2. Pluralism (Social sciences)—Iran. 3. Pan-Iranism. 4. Iran—Politics and government—20th century. I. Title.

DS268.A75 2007
305.800955—dc22   2006033080

A catalogue record for this book is available from the British Library.

Design by Newgen Imaging Systems (P) Ltd., Chennai, India.

First edition: June 2007

10 9 8 7 6 5 4 3 2 1

Printed in the United States of America.

For Təyibə Sadə

Bülbüllər eşqinə yandı   *Hamısı ehdini dandı*

CONTENTS

PREFACE

This study is a multidisciplinary work that draws on fields of history, sociology, literature, politics, anthropology, and cultural studies to explore the origination, development, and continuation of racist ideas in Iran. It analyzes the relationships among European racist ideas, the creation of the Indo-European language family, and the emergence of modern racism in Iran, interrogating the construction of notions such as Aria, Aryan race, and Aryanism in an Iranian context. By situating Iran within the Orientalist discourse and by exploring its cultural, linguistic, and ethnic developments in light of Orientalist/Aryanist reconstruction of Iran's history, the study examines various levels of nation building, identity construction, and aggressive nationalism in Iran. It shows the way in which nationalism and racism worked to place the Indo-European-speaking Persian ethnic group in a position of advantage vis-à-vis Iran's non-Persian nationalities, ethnic groups, and communities. In so doing, it challenges conventional notions about Iran's history, culture, and language by privileging the multinational, multicultural, and multilingual character of Iranian society.

Employing multiple perspectives and theoretical frameworks, the study analyzes issues of ethnic inequality, exclusion, and oppression in Iran from antiracist and anticolonial standpoints. It establishes the existence of racism in Iran as a salient determining factor in creating social inequality, oppression, and unequal power relations. Surveying select works of history, literature, religion, politics, and various official and nonofficial publications, the research examines how the dominant group uses sites such as literature, history, language, and the education system as strategic spaces from which to justify its privileged position in society. Through a critical exploration of the dominant discourse, the study suggests the possibility that the minoritized can also use their own discursive sites to resist acts of racism, colonialism, and oppression. To this end, it offers an analysis of a "counterhegemonic" discourse created by the marginalized to resist and combat racism. The study points to obvious limitations of these sites for the colonized and offers ways to improve their effectiveness. By way of a conclusion, the study highlights future directions for research and possibilities for democratic transformations in an Iranian as well as a Middle Eastern context.

In completing this study, in addition to benefiting from other experiences in the form of existing narratives on the topic, I also draw on my own personal experience and knowledge. As a member of the minoritized Azerbaijani ethnic group in Iran, from early childhood I learned the pain and agony of not being able to communicate, read, and write in my own mother tongue. Shortly after the establishment of the Pahlavi dynasty in 1925, all non-Persian ethnic groups and nationalities in Iran were denied the right to education in our own languages. Notwithstanding the fact that we Azeris, Kurds, Arabs, Baluchs, Turkmens, and others constituted the numerical majority in the country, the government sought to supplant our languages, cultures, and histories with those of the Persian minority. As non-Persian citizens of Iran, we were subjected to open and shameful acts of linguicide, cultural annihilation, and forced assimilation.

I completed my primary and secondary education in a schooling system where I was not allowed to read, write, and even speak my own mother tongue. The education system in Iran promoted and enforced a superficial sense of nationalism based on Persian language and identity. The richly multicultural, multiethnic, and multilingual character of Iranian society was explicitly denied. The school environment, textbooks, curricula, extracurricular activities, teachers, and school administrative personnel all subscribed to and served the view that saw Iran as one nation with one language and one identity. In essence, monoculturalism and monolingualism became the official doctrine of nation-building processes in the country. As a result, the Iranian education system itself came to function as a huge engine for linguicide, deculturation, and assimilation.

Like millions of non-Farsi-speaking Iranians, I grew up longing for an education system where difference and diversity were valued, where students were encouraged and felt proud to talk in their own language, to read their history along with other histories, to see that their people's contributions were registered in textbooks alongside other contributions, to feel proud of who they were and where they came from. However, achievement of these aims and goals in my birthplace remained an ideal for me and millions of other students, teachers, and educators. I left Iran in my early twenties with a vision of aspiring to live in a society where difference and diversity were respected. Later on when I finally found my way into Canadian learning centers, I was really impressed to see the level of attention, discussion, and analysis that went into conceptualization, theorization, and realization of difference and diversity in these institutions of learning and education.

It was in Canada where I learned to read and write in my own mother tongue. For a period of three years I closely worked with a bilingual magazine published by the Azeri-Canadian Community Center in Toronto. Shortly after, I became the editor of another Azerbijani-Persian journal titled *Qurtulush*. Working with these journals opened up new ways of learning about issues of power, cultural hegemony, and linguistic repression. The mere fact that these journals were partly written in the Azeri language was reason enough for members of the dominant language to brand me and my colleagues as traitors, secessionists, and separatists. Without even reading the journal and knowing its content, former friends and acquaintances began to isolate me, considering me a dangerous, radical element disloyal to Iran's territorial integrity. It was due to this painful experience that I came to realize the degree of shortsightedness and narrow-mindedness that a reactionary sense of nation, nationalism, national boundaries, and nation-statism can generate. Experiencing the oppressive conduct of members of the dominant group made me conscious of the degree to which being positioned in a place of privilege due to one's language and ethnicity can blind one to the viciousness of injustice and oppression. The repressive actions and behaviors of some members of the dominant group resulted in my deeper understanding and appreciation of such basic rights and freedoms as the freedom of expression, democratic rights, and the right for self-determination at both individual and collective levels.

The experience of writing for, and running, a minority-language journal placed me at the center of various nationalistic, ethnic, and linguistic encounters. More and more I came to an understanding that, given the history of Oriental despotism, arbitrary incriminations, persecutions, and marginalizations in an Iranian and Middle Eastern context, any notion of a democratic system in a society such as ours must be grounded in a clearly articulated principle of "the right for self-determination." What this means is that any democratic system for us should be based on a voluntary desire and willingness of various nationalities to come together and form a federal or a confederative political system. A most essential requirement of such a system is both the acknowledgment and realization of the individual and collective freedom of Iran's various nationalities and ethnic groups to choose and to determine in a democratic manner their own destiny.

For an antiracist and antioppression activist, working on issues of difference and diversity is not and cannot be an exclusively academic matter. It is, first and foremost, a matter of working toward the larger ideals of social justice, human rights, inclusivity, and democracy. Such ideals may have a chance of being realized in a Middle Eastern context, only if and when the right to be different is properly acknowledged and implemented. The time for denying difference and diversity, for ignoring ethnic, cultural, linguistic, and religious plurality in our Iranian society has long passed. It is high time to embrace an inclusively representative democracy in line with universal principles of human rights and freedoms.

OUTLINE OF THE BOOK

The book is divided into four main interconnected parts: (1) theoretical and methodological issues; (2) Iranian diversity in historical contexts; (3) dominant discourse and counternarratives; (4) conclusions, implications, and future directions. Chapter 1 establishes the boundaries of the study, providing a comprehensive introduction to the book. This chapter also gives an overview of current state of difference and diversity in the Islamic Republic of Iran, the way the government deals with this phenomenon, and the way this phenomenon challenges the totalizing and totalitarian Islamic state.

Chapter 2 provides an overview of discursive/theoretical frameworks that inform and influence this study. They include the anticolonial discursive framework, antiracism theory, critical discourse analysis, and postcolonial theory. The chapter discusses the main tenets of these theories and outlines their relevance to the present work. The chapter also covers the literature review, methods of research, data analysis, and related research tools and issues that have been used throughout the study.

Chapter 3 contextualizes the construction of the "Iranian nation" in a historical setting. It interrogates the paradigm of "Aryan myth" and its implications for the current racism in Iranian society. The chapter surveys various methods and genres of historical investigation on and about Iran. In particular, the chapter looks into the construction of images of Persia, Cyrus, and the Achaemenids through such sources as the Old Testament as well as in certain Greek and Islamic writings. A study of the construction of the image of Persia in ancient texts is important because of its relevance to issues of ethnic domination, cultural appropriation, and denial of diversity in the present. The chapter also investigates the Orientalist reconstruction of Iran's history which sought to find an original homeland for the white Nordic race. In order to establish the existence of such an origin, Orientalists had to fabricate various myths crafted by way of misinterpretations and misrepresentations, which culminated in, among other things, the elevation of the Persian minority to the status of a "superior race" with superior culture and language while excluding non-Persian ethnic groups from Iran's history. An interrogation of the Aryanist paradigm illustrates the extent to which Aria based racism is still relevant and functional in contemporary Iran.

Chapter 4 looks into the rise of Reza Khan to power, the establishment of the Pahlavi dynasty, and the implications that it has had for Iran's non-Persian communities. Brought to power in 1921 through a British-engineered coup d'état, Reza Shah's regime gave birth to the infamous doctrine of "one nation, one language, one country." This doctrine was faithfully followed by his son, Mohammad Reza Shah and has had detrimental consequences for non-Persian ethnic groups. In essence, a main concern of the Pahlavi regime was to create a monolithic Iranian nation based on the Persian language and culture. The chapter explores the stifling of diversity in this era and its implications for the present. The chapter also explores the current state of difference and diversity in Iran by exploring salient aspects of the politics and policies of the Islamic Republic toward minoritized communities. Deviating from conventional methods of research on the subject, the chapter highlights the historical continuity of struggle for equal treatment and equal rights on the part of such major ethnic groups as Azeris, Kurds, Arabs, Baluchs, and Turkmens.

Chapters 5 and 6 focus on the role of the dominant literature and the marginalized discourse, respectively. In addition to official documents produced by the governing bodies, the literature in these chapters also include works of elites as well as "ordinary" writers, poets, and intellectuals. Allocation of an independent space to explore this genre of work was necessary in that many dominant bodies contend that acts of racism and exclusion are committed only by the governing apparatuses and that ordinary intellectuals and writers are "innocent" in the oppression of minoritized communities. An investigation of samples of the dominant literature in chapter 5 shows that the majority of writers, poets, and intellectuals producing work in the dominant language are not so "innocent" as we are led to believe that they are. For the most part, they are at least accomplices in perpetuating feelings of superiority complexes for the dominant, while inferiorizing the others.

When it comes to articulating various linguistic and ethnic/national demands, the dominant group promotes the position that the majority of members of non-Persian communities are quite happy with the subordinated status of their language and culture; and that it is only a few elite who raise the banner of ethnic equality and equal treatment. An exploration of works of various genres produced by the marginalized in chapter 6 shows that, contrary to the dominant claims, the excluded communities indeed do want realize their ethnic, cultural, and human rights and that they do resist acts of racism and xenophobia directed against them. Moreover, the allocation of an independent space to the marginalized literature serves to decolonize the spaces traditionally considered as the exclusive domain of the dominant.

And finally, chapter 7 brings together the thrust of various arguments pursued throughout the book. It also elaborates on a number of democratic possibilities that may have a positive impact on the status of diversity and its management in contemporary Iran. This chapter highlights the importance of education in initiating change and transformation in society. Likewise, it explores the functioning of such democratic bodies as civil society, the need for transparency, and freedom of expression as significant stepping stones on the path to equal treatment and full inclusion. Moreover, the section highlights the importance of acknowledging difference and diversity in dismantling such totalizing ideologies as Islamic fundamentalism in the Middle East generally, and in Iran in particular.

As already noted, this study is very important because as of yet, no similar work has been done on issues emerging from race, racism, monolingualism, and monoculturalism in Iran. This is a first decolonizing research of its kind in an Iranian context. It is decolonizing because of the following:

- It deconstructs the dominant Eurocentric ideas of nation, nationalism, nation-statism, and Aryanism in an Iranian context.
- It implicates the dominant members of Farsi-speaking community in their capacity as writers, poets, and intellectuals in producing, reproducing, and maintaining unequal ethnic, cultural, and linguistic relations in Iran.
- It provides a space for marginalized communities in Iran to articulate their condition through their own voices, in their own languages, and by way of their own literatures, as opposed to being exclusively represented through the dominant Persian language and literature.
- It redefines and rearticulates the question of citizenship based on equal cultural, linguistic, and human rights of each citizen, each collectivity, and each community. This rearticulation challenges the dominant notion of citizenship, which presently seeks to grant the ownership of the country to certain group(s) based on their "Aryan-ness."

The study is also important in its treatment of difference and diversity as a significant sociopolitical issue that will determine the future course of social, cultural, and political development in Iran. A look at the neighboring countries of Afghanistan and Iraq illustrates the degree to which difference and diversity are detrimental in a Middle Eastern context. It is hoped that this book will clear the way for future researchers to continue the work on issues of difference and diversity and their democratic realization not only in Iran but also in the wider Middle East.

Acknowledgments

This work has grown out of a doctoral dissertation that was completed at Ontario Institute for Studies in Education of the University of Toronto. Many friends, colleagues, and mentors have helped me through this process. In particular, I would like to thank Bijoy Barua, George Dei, Stan Doyle-Wood, Rose Folson, Farideh Hakimi, Budd Hall, Zabeda Nazim, Paul Olson, Brenda Shaffer, Njoki Wane, and Margot Wilson, without whose guidance and help this work would have not materialized.

A number of important Azeri and Iranian online journals, newspapers, and discussion groups provided a space for me to discuss some of the ideas in this book with a wide variety of audiences and benefit from their valuable feedback. In particular I would like to mention Azer-Dialogue, Tribun, Shams Tabriz, Durna, Baku Today, and Achiq Söz. Thank you all for your generosity, for sharing your passion, your ideas, your stories, and your knowledge.

I would also like to thank Farideh Koohi-Kamali and Gabriella Georgiades, the two invaluable editors at Palgrave Macmillan and their assistants, Julia Cohen and Joanna Mericle. From the very beginning they realized the importance of this work and helped me every step of the way to make the publication of this book possible. Kristy Lilas and Katie Fahey of Palgrave Macmillan superbly coordinated the preparation of the manuscript. I thank them for their diligence and professionalism. Finally, I wish to express my appreciation to Maran Elancheran of Newgen Imaging Systems, for his valuable assistance with the preparation of the manuscript, his unfailing dedication, and his extraordinary attention to details.

NOTE ON TRANSLITERATION

The transliteration of personal and place names follows a simplified version of the standard set by the International *Journal of Middle East Studies.* With the exception of (') for hamzeh and (') for ayn, all other diacritical marks have been omitted. All local and indigenous names are transliterated as they are pronounced in Arabic, Azeri, Farsi, Kurdish, or Turkish. The only exception is the Azeri (ə), which is represented with the Turkish (e) to make the transliteration uniform and easy to follow. Unless otherwise stated, all translations are my own.

CHAPTER 1

Introduction: Establishing the Boundaries

My idea in Orientalism is to use humanistic critique to open up the fields of struggle, to introduce a longer sequence of thought and analysis to replace the short bursts of polemical, thought-stopping fury that so imprison us. . . . Our role is to widen the field of discussion.

(Edward Said, August 7, 2003, p. 3)

ORIENTALISM AND ARYANISM

Edward Said's Orientalism (1978) ushered in a new genre of scholarship and narration that sought to explore various aspects of the impact of Western colonialism and Orientalism on Eastern societies, particularly in realms of culture, literature, and discursive representation. Although Said confined his work to mainly British and French Orientalism in and about Moslem societies, his visions and ideas culminated in the development and evolution of a large body of scholarship that focused on various aspects of Orientalism, colonialism, neocolonialism, nationalism, and so forth (Hulme, 1986; Behdad, 1994; Harlow, 1999; Edwards, 2000; Jersild, 2002; Benjamin, 2003; Bohrer, 2003; Yoshihara, 2003; Lockman, 2004; Kalmar and Penslar, 2005). Thus works were developed around such notions as Japanese Orientalism (Tanaka, 1993), Asian Orientalism (Hay, 1970), German Orientalism (Murti, 2001), Italian Orientalism (Schneider, 1998), and American Orientalism (Little, 2002), which looked into the imperial/Orientalist approach of these societies to their surrounding world—to their "Other," as it were.

Notwithstanding the growing body of works exploring Orientalist relationships in recent decades, there is still an urgent need to study the impact of Orientalism, Aryanism, and similar European discursive constructs on various levels of nation building, nationality construction, overt nationalism, and racism not only in Western countries but more importantly in Oriental societies themselves. In other words, there is a need for studies to focus on power configurations, ethnic relations, linguistic/racial hierarchies, religious issues, cultural appropriations, and the like within Oriental societies, particularly those affected by the Orientalist/Aryanist paradigm. Evidently, this is an area that has hardly received any scholarly attention. This study explores this area by situating Iran within the Orientalist discourse and by exploring its cultural, linguistic, and ethnic developments in the light of the Orientalist and Aryanist discursive reconstructions of Iran's history. By investigating such a reconstruction, this study challenges the privileged place of Farsi and its speakers, the Persian ethnic group, in contemporary Iran.

Described as "the land of Aryans," Iran has a unique position within Indo-Europeanist and Aryanist discourses. Along with India, it has served as a source of primary material for European racism and particularly for the construction and formulation of the Indo-Europeanist/Aryanist project. At the same time, certain ethnic groups in Iran have used the European construction of "Aryan race" and "Iran" to dominate other groups perceived to be "non-Aryan." This fact has motivated my focus on the socioeconomic, educational, and psychological ramifications of Aryanist racism in contemporary Iran, an Oriental society that has been influenced in a peculiar way by Europe's Aryanist discourse. However, to date, there has been no significant research focusing on the existence of racism in Iranian society.

In view of Iran's unique position in Indo-Europeanist and Aryanist discourses, a study of various socioeconomic, educational, politicocultural, and psychological ramifications of Aryanist racism in contemporary Iran represents much needed research that can throw considerable light on overall racist projects. This study explores the pattern of development of "Indo-Europeanist" ideology from the point of its inception in Europe down to its utilization in Iran from the beginning of the Pahlavi era (1925–1979). It analyzes the relationships among European racist ideas, the creation of the Indo-European language family, and the emergence of modern racism in Iran. In so doing, it challenges conventional notions about Iranian history, culture, and civilization by highlighting the multinational, multicultural, and multilingual character of Iranian society.

It is important to note that Iran was never directly colonized in the classical sense of the word. Unlike Africa and India, Iran's colonization was indirect, through covert control of governing bodies and natural resources, a situation that did attract the full attention of Western colonial powers. More significantly, as an imaginary space perceived to be the original homeland of the Aryan race, Iran engaged the imagination of Western scholars, writers, travelers, and literary figures. Initially the Orientalist and Indo-Europeanist adventurers began their journey in discourse, languages, literatures, narratives, and texts. These Europeans wanted to discover their prehistoric origin and their original homeland. But there was no record of such an origin and such a homeland. The term prehistory first and foremost meant that those histories and stories that existed prior to the text were in fact excluded by textuality, by discourse, by text, and by language. So the Europeans had to invent an imaginary homeland, a protolanguage, and a prehistoric race for themselves; this they had to do in discourse and in language. However, in order to construct a discursive reality and a reality in discourse, one would still need some primary material. Hence, the necessity and significance of ancient Persian and Sanskrit texts and sources.

Partha Chatterjee (1993) has correctly noted that Western Orientalism paved the way for the emergence of nationalism and nation-statism by unearthing histories and symbols of the Oriental society that were previously unknown to Orientals themselves. When the Orientalists constructed a history—whether real or imaginary—for Orientals, they also provided them with a sense of origin, continuity, and temporal/spatial consciousness. Such a consciousness in turn served to foster a sense of nationalism among the Orientals. Jadunath Sarkar, a Bengali nationalist, has noted with gratitude the service that Orientalists have done in unearthing certain Indo-Aryan texts:

> In the nineteenth century we recovered our long lost ancient literatures, Vedic and Buddhistic, as well as the buried architectural monuments of Hindu days. The Vedas and their commentaries had almost totally disappeared from the plains of Aryavarta where none could interpret them; none had even a complete manuscript of the texts. The English printed these ancient scriptures of the Indo-Aryans and brought them to our doors. (Sarkar, 1979, p. 84)

Similarly, in *The Multiple Identities of the Middle East*, Bernard Lewis maintains that a rediscovery of Iran's past became only possible in the third-quarter of the nineteenth century, when "Iranian intellectuals read European scholarship and literature, and began to realize that they too had an ancient and glorious past to which they could lay claim" (1998, p. 71). These statements confirm Chatterjee's observation that the "evidence from Orientalist scholarship was extremely important for the construction of the full narrative of nationalist history" (1993, p. 98). Chatterjee's observation is a very valid one, as far as the crafting of a history for Orientals is concerned. However, the crafting of a history is only one side of the story. There is another side to the story, which has to do with the unfolding of Orientalist fabrications among the Orientals themselves. Orientals were definitely not a homogenous community. Countries such as India and Iran contained very diverse populations who came from very different ethnic, linguistic, religious, and cultural backgrounds. Therefore, it was only logical that certain ethnic groups would be in a position to take advantage of the Orientalist reconstruction while others would automatically be placed in a disadvantaged position. The present study seeks to shed light on this aspect of Orientalism and colonialism in Iran, that is, on its being extremely advantageous to certain groups and gravely disadvantageous to others.

The racist ideology that Europe's colonial order created went far beyond the European borders and deeply affected other people in distant lands. In their scramble to "scientifically prove" the "inferiority" of other races, the colonizers had to come to terms with the ancient civilizations of Africa, Sumeria, Babylonia, and Assyria, among others. They sought to achieve this by inventing other European races in areas other than Europe. The result was "the discovery" of Indo-European linguistic fragments in Iran and India, followed by the invention of the "Aryan myth"—the assumption that civilization on earth originated from the Aryan race. The Aryans are said to be the blonde, blue-eyed, white-skinned Europeans who speak a Vedic Sanskrit or an Indo-European language. Further, the Aryan myth promotes the idea that the Aryan race is both biologically and culturally superior to all other races. As a result, Aryans should, wherever and whenever possible, subjugate other peoples and prevent these peoples from mixing with them, thus causing the degeneration of the superior Aryan race. This work examines the ways through which notions of Aryan race, Aryan myth, and Aryan superiority are played out in an Iranian context.

RESEARCH AND LEARNING OBJECTIVES

This study analyzes issues of ethnic inequality and racial oppression in Iran from an antiracist standpoint. It establishes the existence of racism in Iran as a salient determining factor in creating social inequality, oppression, and unequal power relations. It also establishes the existence of strong connections and causal relationships among Western racist discourses and the ongoing Aryanist racism in Iran. The study provides a critical antiracist examination of the ways in which the Persian ethnic group has made use of eighteenth- to twentieth-century European racist discourses to consolidate its political, cultural, and linguistic hegemony in Iran. At the same time, it explores various ways and strategic sites through which the ongoing racism can be effectively resisted and eventually eliminated in Iran.

The study uses select works of history, literature, religion, politics, and various official and nonofficial publications to meet its general learning objectives. The material is surveyed in accordance with the author's racial/ethnic background, language, and gender-whenever applicable. Moreover, attention is paid to the texts' dates of publication and their relevance to the subject matter. More specifically, the study analyzes the following as its concrete research objectives:

1. First is Construction of the image of "Other" and the processes of "othering" and "otherization" in classic Persian texts. The two important texts to be studied in this regard are the book of Avesta (the holy book of Zarathustranism), and the *Shahnameh* of Ferdowsi (1010/1960). These two texts are important in that they were among the primary sources for Western scholars' interpretation, imagination, analyses, and discursive reconstruction of not only a history for Iran but more importantly an origin as well as a homeland for what came to be known as the Aryan race. Additionally, important ancient sources such as the Old Testament and Herodotus's *Histories* are consulted whenever necessary.

2. Second is literature produced by European writers from the eighteenth century onward as they reconstructed notions of Aria/Arya, Aryanism, and Indo-Europeanism using ancient Persian and Indian texts as primary material. Here the study explores the ways words such as Aryan, Aria,

and even symbols such as the swastika were dug out from ancient Persian and Indian texts, reinvented, and completely reconstructed in a new format and reproduced discursively for wider economic, racial, colonial, political, cultural, and historical implications. The aim in this section is to investigate the necessary connections among these discursive formations and a host of material, historical, and social conditions in an Iranian context.

3. Third is literature produced by the government apparatuses starting from 1925 during both the monarchic and Islamic regimes in Iran. Through this literature, the coercive role of government as an agent of the dominant group is examined to look at the ways in which the government reinforces the subservient status of minoritized groups through its oppressive linguistic, educational, and ethnic policies. More concretely, the research analyzes how the government uses its economic power to promote a single language; how it uses its military force to suppress other languages; how it uses its education system, publishing, and propaganda organs to justify its actions, to marginalize other cultures, and exclude other ethnic groups from the processes of social, cultural, and economic development. Through this literature, issues emerging from relations of power, of inferiorization and superiorization by way of language, discourse, and voice are explored to shed light on the processes of production, reproduction, validation, and legitimation of racism in Iran.

4. Fourth is literature produced by the dominant Farsi-speaking group to reinforce the status of the Persian language as a superior tongue that deserves to supplant all the other languages. Here too the study seeks to uncover power relations, notions of misrepresentation, privilege, identification, and the context within which the dominant discourse is produced, maintained, and reproduced. The study reveals that those possessing a privileged linguistic and ethnic background try to maintain the privileged status of their mother tongue at the expense of excluding and annihilating other languages. From this revelation we learn that in order to be an accomplice to acts of colonialism and racism, one does not necessarily need to be a member of the governing political administration. There are numerous other bases of power such as language, ethnicity, and religion that position one in places of privilege, influence, and authority that are denied to those who are marginalized. In the words of Michel Foucault, power seeps through the web of all human interactions and social relations down to the "very depth of society" (Foucault, 1977, p. 27). In order to maintain their privileged space, elites of the dominant group implicate themselves in acts of racism, exclusion, and othering.

5. Last, but not the least, literature produced by members of minoritized communities either in their own language or in the language of the dominant group. Through this literature, the important role of language as a means of creative expression, intellectual and psychological development, self-identification, and, more importantly, resistance vis-à-vis the imposed order is analyzed. This part of the study is extremely significant in that it privileges the voices that traditionally have been excluded from the dominant discourse. When minoritized bodies and groups are represented in the dominant media and by way of the

dominant voice and language, such representation is never an impartial act but is in essence "misrepresentation." By privileging the marginalized voices and proscribed languages, a more authentic and objective picture is presented of the relationship between the colonized and the colonizer, of how acts of resistance are taking place, and how the marginalized voices are engaged in processes of decolonization.

One of the overall objective of this study is to show how the above-mentioned tendencies have come together to maintain the privileged status of the Persian ethnic group and its language while at the same time minoritizing, foreignizing, and vilifying all the other ethnicities, nationalities, and languages. The study shows that, in order for racism to be defeated in Iran, it is imperative that its discursive bases and linguistic/textual foundations are challenged, deconstructed, and rendered ineffective. To this end, the study highlights the central role of language in producing and maintaining the racist order in Iran. Simultaneously, it illustrates the effective role of marginalized languages in the process of resistance and decolonization. Other important areas such as history, historiography, the education system, along with the role of intellectuals and intelligentsia are also explored as important factors in maintaining the status quo—and in resisting it.

The study is based on the following three objectives:

1. establishing the existence of racism and its detrimental ramifications for social, political, economic, and educational developments in Iran;
2. examining the role of Europe and the West in general in the origination and development of modern racism in Iran; and
3. exploring possible mechanisms, ways, and sites through which racism can be eliminated in Iran, for example, empowering the marginalized languages, providing space for the expression of indigenous histories, and reforming the education system.

The Existence of Racism

Racism is a universal phenomenon. It can exist in Europe and North America, just as it can exist in the Middle East and Iran. From the outset, this book sets out to establish the fact of the existence of racism in Iran in defiance of the dominant group's insistence that racism does not and cannot exist in Iran. This book provides sufficient documentation to prove once and for all that racism does exist in Iran. In so doing, the study situates racism as both a concept and praxis, right at the heart of issues of exclusion, oppression, domination, and internal colonialism in an Iranian context. By avoiding any mention of the term racism, the dominant discourse in Iran has provided a completely upside-down picture of social and ethnic inequality in the country, while labeling antiracist activists as traitors, foreigners, agents of foreign governments, and so forth. This study situates the concept of racism in its proper theoretical, sociocultural, epistemological, and practical place within

Iranian society by exposing various acts of the dominant group, including its labeling of antiracist activists. The study shows that without including racism as a legitimate category at the center of issues of justice, democracy, and equality in Iran, it would be impossible to provide a comprehensive analysis regarding social and ethnic relations in an Iranian context.

The Role of Western Racist Discourses, Aryanism, and Orientalism

This book offers an analytical model for the understanding of current Iranian racism by investigating its origination in European paradigms. It examines the connections among race, language, nationality, and the formation of the Indo-European language family as these influence the reconstruction of a notion of Arynism and Aryanist racism in Iran particularly from the beginning of the Pahlavi period (1925–1979) up to the era of the Islamic Republic (1979–present). The thesis interrogates the implications of Orientalist reconstruction of Iran's national history particularly in light of existing ethnic and cultural diversity in the country. It provides a critique of Orientalist notions such as Aria, Aryan race, Aryanism, and Indo-Europeanism in the works of scholars such as William Jones, Freidrich von Schlegel, Count Joseph-Arthur Gobineau, and Friedrich Max Müller. The objective is to illustrate the existence of strong causal relationships between the Orientalist/Aryanist constructs and a plethora of material, historical, social, national, cultural, political, and racial/ethnic conditions in an Iranian context. In so doing, the research emphasizes on various discursive and practical ways in which the Orientalist/Arayanist discourse has influenced racism in Iran through describing Iran as the Land of Aryans; redefining and reconstructing such absurd notions as Aria/Arya, the Aryan race, and Aryanism; fashioning a history for Iran and its inhabitants with an emphasis on Iran's supposedly superior Aryan/Persian heritage; and so forth.

Ways of Resisting Racism in Iran

How can racism be eliminated in Iran? The study offers some practical solutions for this question primarily through democratization and reforming of the education system, provision of spaces for expressions of marginalized identities, histories, cultures, literatures, and voices, along with concentration on principles of human rights, and the right to self-determination. The research addresses these issues by identifying two distinct discourses developed in the country: the dominant discourse and the resistant counterhegemonic discourse. The research examines the ways through which the dominant discourse uses fields such as literature, history, language, and the education system as strategic spaces from which to justify its privileged position in society. By way of its critical exploration of the use of these strategic sites by the dominant group, the study suggests the possibility that the minoritized can also use these same fields to resist acts of racism, colonialism, and oppression. To this end, it offers an analysis of a counterhegemonic discourse created by the marginalized to resist and combat racism. The study points to obvious limitations of these sites for the colonized and offers ways to improve their effectiveness.

IRANIAN DIVERSITY IN A HISTORICAL CONTEXT: AN OVERVIEW

The history of what is now known as Iran is a history of various ethnic groups, languages, and cultures coexisting amongst one another from time immemorial. For as long as history can remember, ever since the establishment of the first Elamite civilization around 5000 BC, Iran has been a multiracial, multicultural, and multilingual society (Ghirshman, 1954; Zarrinkoob, 1957; Pirnia, 1983; Dandamaev, 1989; Zehtabi, 1999; Poorpirar, 2000, 2001a, 2001b). According to historians, the first major government was established in the region by the emergence of the Elamite dynasty around 2250 BC (Field, 1939; Zehtabi, 1999). An indigenous people to the region, the Elamites were founders of a rich culture and civilization. They had their own unique alphabet, and they spoke an agglutinative, non-Indo-European, non-Semitic language. They ruled in the region for 2,210 years, until their dynasty disintegrated in the year 640 BC (Diakonov, 1965; Sadr, 1997). Alongside the Elamites, other cultures having agglutinative, Afro-Asiatic, and Semitic languages are documented to have coexisted (Biruni, 1879; Field, 1939; Istakhri, 1961).

About 4,000 years after the formation and flourishing of various cultures in the region, a new ethnographic development took place in the Iranian Plateau, and it was the arrival of waves of nomadic groups to the plateau who later came to be known as Aryans or Indo-Europeans. There is no uniform consensus on the exact points of origination and departure of these nomadic groups. While some have identified their origins in India, others have cited such places as Central Asia, southern Russia, and Caucasia (Ghirshman, 1954; Poliakov, 1974). According to one dominant view,

> The majority of the Aryans left their homes in southern Russia for the plains of central Asia; only the near-Iranian Scyths and a few genuine Aryans remained there. The Hyrcanians settled along the northern slope of Alborz and the coastal plain below, south of the sea to which they gave their name. (Olmstead, 1948, p. 19)

The first wave of these Indo-European immigrants arrived in Iran around 2000 BC. Finding the area extremely rich and resourceful, they encouraged other Aryan nomadic groups to join them. Around 1200 BC these new immigrants had reached western and central parts of current Iran. The first Indo-European state was created in Iran in 550 BC through the disintegration and subsequent replacement of the Median dynasty by the Achaemenians (see also Dandamaev, 1989; Dandamaev and Lukonin, 1989). After ruling for 220 years, the Achaemenid dynasty was put an end to through the invasion of

Iran by Alexander the Great in 330 BC. After the death of Alexander in 323 BC, three of his officers divided his empire amongst themselves. Each ruled over a segment of the empire and its population. Ever since then, Iran has continued to be ruled by the Greeks, Arabs, Turks, Persians, and others.

In the year 637 CE, Arab-Islamic forces defeated the Sasanid regime in the famous battle of Qadisiyya and started spreading the Islamic faith throughout the region. The new faith spoke of the equality of all individuals before God and promised the establishment of a society with more equitable living conditions. With their high taxes and never-ending internal strifes and external wars, the Sasanid rulers had all but lost any popular power bases within and among the masses. In the course of their rule, class divisions had increased incredibly and had become overtly visible even to the unconcerned and politically unconscious masses. Signs of discontent and dissatisfaction were evident all over the plateau, so much so that when the Islamic-Arab forces attacked the country, the people showed no interest in defending the decaying Sasanid regime (see also Zarrinkoob, 1957; Lambton, 1969; Pirnia, 1983).

The introduction of Islamic civilization to Iran fundamentally transformed the existing political, cultural, linguistic, and of course religious landscapes of the region. Zarathustrianism lost its status as an important religion in the country and was gradually replaced by Islam. This replacement, however, was not total and adherents to the faith of Zarathustra still continued to live in some parts of the country, while a large segment migrated to India. On the cultural front, perhaps a most significant development was the establishment of the modern Farsi language with a new Arabic alphabet. Soon after the Islamic conquest, the Arabic language became the major language of science, philosophy, literature, and governance. Such important Iranian scholars as Al-Razi (d. 932), Al-Khawrizmi (780–850), Al-Biruni (973–1048), and Ibn Sina (Avicenna) (973–1037) produced their major works in Arabic. After about two centuries, the modern Farsi language gradually developed that not only used the Arabic alphabet but also relied heavily on the Arabic language and Arabic traits in its structure and vocabulary. Even the style and form of poetry writing in Iran fundamentally changed, following the Arabic style of rhythm, rhyming, and form.

For nearly two centuries the Umayyad caliphs ruled the Islamic world from the center of their power in Medina and Damascus. Rulers and governors were assigned to different territories, regulated the running of their provinces, and responded to the caliph directly. Around the middle of the eighth century, the Umayyad caliph was defeated and the Abbasids took the reins of power. They transferred the capital city to Baghdad and ruled from there until 1258, when the Mongol invasion put an end to their rule. The disintegration of the caliphate in Baghdad culminated in the emergence of local dynasties throughout the region. Tribal dynasties and local kingdoms such as the Samanids, Ziyarids, Deylamites, Ghaznavids, and Kharazmis continued to rule over territories and localities. This long period also witnessed various invasions such as that of the Mongols and Tamerlane's.

In the year 1501, Shah Ismail Safavi of Ardabil was able to bring together the local dynasties of Qaraqoyunlu and Aqqoyunlu and found the Safavid dynasty. The Safavid succeeded in establishing Shi'ism as the national religion of Iran and uniting the country from the Caspian Sea to the Persian Gulf, and from Mesopotamia to India and Central Asia. Under the Safavids, various tribes and ethnic groups remained relatively autonomous in practicing their traditions, cultures, and languages within the loosely governed empire (Mazzaoui, 1972; Woods, 1976; Savory, 1980).

While Orientalists and the dominant Fars-centered literature attempted to present the Safavids as Persians, the fact remained that they were of Turkic origin and Azeri-Turkic was the main language of Shah Ismail's court, followed by Farsi and Arabic, respectively. Moreover, Shah Ismail was a great lover of poetry and literature. Under the pen name Khatayi, he produced his famous "Divani Xetayi" in Azeri-Turkic (see Birdoğan, 2001). A unique literary style known as Qoshma was also introduced in this period, utilized, and developed by Shah Ismail and later on by his successor Shah Tahmasp. In 1722, the Qandhar-based Afghan tribes, adhering to the Sunni branch of Islam, defeated the ill-equipped and increasingly weakened Safavid army and brought to an end the central rule of the Safavid dynasty that had persisted for over two centuries. Thus, the central authority yet again collapsed and various regional powers and local dynasties emerged as important power bases, negotiating the running of their own territories and kingdoms. A period of civil unrest, ethnic rivalry, and racial tension ensued (Lockhart, 1958).

In 1779, the Turkic-speaking Qajars of Azerbaijan managed to defeat a number of mainly regional rulers and extend their rule all over Iran as early as the beginning of the nineteenth century (see also Bakhash, 1978). In their official documents, the Qajars frequently referred to the name of the country they ruled as Mamalek-e Mahruseh-ye Iran (the Protected Countries of Iran) signifying the federalist and confederative geopolitical structure of the country. Aside from other transformations, two important developments took place in the Qajar era that continued to influence issues of difference, diversity, and ethnic pluralism in Iran up to present day. In the geopolitical sphere, the Qajars lost on two occasions large segments of Iranian territory to the Russian Empire. In 1813, the year of the Golestan Peace Treaty, the Iranian government handed over Qarabagh, Genje, Shirvan, Sheki, Baki, Derbend, Kuba, and other territories to the Russian emperor. And again in 1828, by way of Turkmen-Chay Treaty, Nexchivan, Ordubad, and other territories were handed over to the Russians (Kazemzadeh, 1968).

In terms of religious developments, the Qajar period saw the emergence of a religious movement under the leadership of Sayyid Ali Muhammad (1819–1850), better known as Bab (The Gate). Otherwise known as the Babi movement, this religious movement grew out of Shia Islamic thought and found some followers in the country (Bosworth and Hillenbrand, 1983; Amanat, 1989). The Babis did not play a significant social and political role in Iranian society. However, they inspired another religious movement—Bahaisim—that definitely had far more religious, social, cultural, and political consequences. Initially founded and led by Mirza Hussein Ali (1817–1892) "Baha'u'lllah" (Glory of God) Bahaisim continued to survive and attract followers in Iran up until the Islamic Revolution of 1979. After the establishment of Islamic rule in Iran, Bahaisim became an outlawed religion, with its practitioners being persecuted openly. This case added another category of religion-based racism, exclusion, and oppression to the already existing racist order. Meanwhile, the Bahai faith spread quickly beyond Iranian borders, having acquired considerable followers in Europe, India, Asia, and North America. Currently the Bahai faith has developed into a world religion, completely independent from Islam.

The early twentieth century marked the beginning of a new national and social consciousness in Iran. Influenced by various literary and sociopolitical trends in the wake of the Russian Revolution of 1905, many writers, intellectuals, and poets began to revolutionize the Iranian sociocultural landscape. Fathali Akhundzadeh introduced drama into Iranian literature. Taliboff and Zeynal-Abedin of Maragheh were promoting their modern genre of imaginative prose, social criticism, and literary realism hitherto unknown in Iran. At the same time, Jalil Memet-Quluzadeh and Aliakbar Saber were attacking the oppressive authority of feudal lords, religious despotism, and reactionary ruling elite by way of their merciless social and political satires, widely spread through the paper *Molla Nesred-Din*. In Tabriz, Mirza Hasan Roshdiyyeh had laid the foundation of modern schooling and pedagogy. He had written the first ever modern textbooks in the history of Iran, entitled *Ana Dili* [The Mother Tongue] and *Veten Dili* [The Language of Homeland] to be used in Azerbaijani schools (see also Berengian, 1988, p. 47). Moreover, the ideals of social justice, equality, and humanism vis-à-vis the struggle against colonialism, despotism, and religious bigotry were being promoted through the works of many writers and intellectuals in Farsi, Azeri, Kurdish, Arabic, and other languages.

All these cultural, literary, and social activities culminated in the birth of a politicointellectual movement in 1906 that came to be known as the Constitutional Revolution (Browne, 1910; Bayat, 1982; Afary, 1996). This revolution had its popular bases in Azerbaijan, being led by such Azeri leaders as Sattar Khan, Baqer Khan, and Heydar Amuoglu. Aside from the Azerbaijanis, other ethnic groups such as the Bakhtiyaris, Armenians, and Persians took active parts in guaranteeing the victory of the movement. At this time, the country was ruled by the Azeri-speaking Qajars, whose language and ethnic policies were not discriminatory and exclusionary, based on language or ethnicity. Under the Qajars, no single language was elevated to the status of official/national language of the country, nor was any language or ethnic group vilified and demonized for not being Aryan. The Qajar era of "Mamalek-e Mahruseh-ye Iran" (independent kingdoms of Iran) was a recognized multiethnic, multicultural, and multilingual society governed through a loose form of federalism where all ethnic groups were free to use, study, and develop their languages, literatures, cultures, traditions, and identities.

Ervand Abrahamian (1979) has provided an excellent picture of linguistic diversity during the Constitutional Revolution:

> The geographical barriers were compounded often by linguistic differences. Persians, Bakhtiyaris, Qashqayis, Arabs, and Lurs lived in the Central Plateau. Small groups of Baluchis, Afshars, and Arabs were scattered in the southern deserts. Kurds, Lurs, Arabs, Afshars, and Mamesenis inhabited the western mountains. Azeris, Shahsavans, Kurds, together with scattered settlements of Armanians and Assyrians, lived in the northeastern districts. Gilakis, Taleshis, and Mazandaranis populated the Caspian provinces. Finally, Persians, Turkomans, Kurds, Shahsavans, Afshars, Timurs, Balushis, Tajiks, and Jamshids resided in the northeastern regions. Iran, thus, was a land of linguistic diversity. (Abrahamian, 1979, p. 389)

As the movement's title suggests, constitutionalism was one of the obvious aims of this revolution. The leaders of the movement demanded that the monarch should not enjoy absolute power but should rule based on a constitution adopted by the people's representatives. This debate was immediately followed by the introduction of new concepts to the political lexicon of the country. Prominent among these concepts were terms such as secularism, nationalism, and the role of religion. The religious segment of intellectuals and elites under the leadership of prominent clerics such as Ayatollah Sheikh Fazlollah Nouri vehemently opposed secularism, nor did they approve of the idea of a secular state detached from Shia religious doctrines and the teachings of sharia.

In contrast to the religious trend, a more confrontational secularist trend emerged that increasingly came to find its expression in both democratic and nationalist views and slogans. This "nationalism," which was initially envisioned based on the rights of the individual/citizen, failed to define itself in an inclusive fashion. More and more, the term Irani (to be an Iranian) came to be equated with Fars/i (to be Persian). This nationalism was thus articulated in terms of an ethnic nationalism based exclusively on Persian language and identity. Such reactionary nationalism sought to glorify Iran's pre-Islamic past by blaming Islam and the Arabs as responsible for all the ills of the country, where Iran's backwardness and lack of progress were blamed on Islam and the Arabs, who were portrayed as destroyers of Iran's supposedly superior civilization.

A Fars-centered ethnic nationalism failed to include in a democratic manner the non-Persian groups and nationalities within an emancipatory discourse. In spite of this, the non-Persian ethnic groups and their representatives in the parliament managed to insert in the constitutional text a very important article regarding the formation of "Anjomanha-ye Ayalati va Velayati" (the local and provincial councils). Although such councils were not permitted to take form, this clause served to affirm that non-Persian ethnic groups were fully aware of their ethnic and national identity and the rights to which their distinct identities entitled them vis-à-vis the dominant Persian group.

In recent history, it was during the reign of Reza Shah Pahlavi (1925–1941) that the name Iran was officially adopted to refer to the country (see also Vaziri, 1993; Kashani-Sabet, 1999). The country currently known as Iran was initially called Elam or Elan (see, e.g., Biruni, 1879). During the reign of two Persian dynasties of Achaemenid and Sasanid, occasional references were made to "Iranshahr" and "Iranzamin" (Olmstead, 1948; Ghirshman, 1954), and until the reign of Reza Shah it was mainly referred to as Protected Countries/kingdoms of Iran, signifying thus the autonomous status of various regions (Vaziri, 1993; Kashani-Sabet, 1999).

Abroad, the Orientalists and foreign governments continued to call the area Persia (and its different variations such as Peres, Peresa, and Persiana) until Reza Khan issued a decree to all foreign embassies in Tehran, demanding the use of the name Iran instead of Persia. Reza Shah went so far as to threaten the foreigners that mail bearing the name Persia would be returned back to the senders (see also Wilber, 1981; Kashani-Sabet, 1999). At any rate, what was known in Western courts, and their literature, as the Persian Empire or Persia had no meaning for diverse populations inhabiting the plateau. Persia was an elitist designation used only and exclusively by outsiders. In subsequent chapters, I will discuss in detail the meaning and significance of the name-change during the Pahlavi era. At this stage, it is enough to say that such activities followed an exclusionary project well in line with the Orientalist/Aryanist enterprise whose ultimate aim was to deny the existence of ethnic and linguistic diversity in Iran and replace it with the absurd notion of "one country, one nation, one language."

Ethnic pluralism, difference, and diversity have always been a defining characteristic of what used to be called Elam, Elan, Protected Countries of Iran, and finally Iran. Peoples of various ethnic origins, such as the ancestors of contemporary Azeris, Kurds, Baluchs, Turkmens, Arabs, Gilaks, and others have lived in Iran for centuries. These diverse ethnic groups have always constituted the numerical majority in Iran, from ancient times up to present. However, the continuation of the Pahlavi regime's monolingual and monocultural agenda for Iran has brought the country to the brink of ethnic discontent and nationalistic tensions since 1925, the year of Reza Khan's coronation as the king of Iran.

After the fall of Pahlavis, the Islamic Republic has continued to emphasize the importance of Shia Islam and the Persian language as the two tenets of Iranians' national identity. However, the conventionally dominant view of a national identity based on the Persian language and Shia Islam is increasingly wearing thin, particularly in the face of growing demands for the recognition of various ethnic, national, cultural, linguistic, and religious rights and freedoms. The current Islamic Republic's response to the growing challenge of diversity has been dismally inadequate. Moreover, the fall of the Soviet Union has led to the creation of a number of important nation-states such as Azerbaijan and Turkmenistan in which the Azeri and Turkmeni tongues have become official and national languages. The ruling elite in Iran has been using polemics such as the inadequacy of non-Persian languages to become languages of instruction and correspondence. How can they explain this lame excuse now that these languages are the languages of instruction, learning, and teaching in neighboring countries? Formidable challenges are also coming from recent developments in the neighboring countries of Afghanistan and Iraq, where multiple languages have been officially recognized as languages of instruction, communication, media, education, and so on. All these developments are seriously threatening the continuation of monolingual and monocultural policies of the Islamic government in Iran. It is against such a backdrop that the search for practical democratic solutions to manage diversity in Iran becomes crucial.

CURRENT STATE OF PLURALISM, DIFFERENCE, AND DIVERSITY

There has never been a government-sponsored census in Iran based on language or ethnicity regarding the country's population composition. All the available figures and numbers alluding to the linguistic, ethnic, and religious composition of Iranian society are based on secondary sources and unsubstantiated estimates. The latest national census conducted in 1996 showed Iran's total population to be 60,055,488, of which 50.81 per percent were men and 49.19 percent were women. According to this census, about 61 percent or 37 million of the population resided in urban areas and 39 percent or 23 million in rural areas, with a small percentage living as nomadic tribes. Of the total population, 39.56 percent were below the age of 15; 56.12 percent were in the 15–64 age group; and 4.32 percent were in the age group of 65 and above. Life expectancy was 69 for women and 66 for men. The census indicated nothing about the diverse linguistic and ethnic backgrounds of Iran's peoples.

Among the various ethnic groups inhabiting Iran, there are no visible physical markers such as the skin color distinguishing different groups and individuals. The people who constitute this diverse population, however, are distinguishable from one another through easily identifiable cultural characteristics such as language, religion, ethnic affiliation, and, to some extent, geographical location. Among various characteristics, language is the most salient marker serving to distinguish various ethnic groups and communities from one another. While the religious factor has also become quite important in recent years, particularly pertaining to Bahais, Sunni Muslims, and Jews, language still remains a most powerful marker of ethnicity and identity.

Notwithstanding the country's multilingual character, only one language—Farsi—is acknowledged by the authorities as the legitimate "official" and "national" tongue of all Iranians. While the government apparatus and members of the dominant Persian group have tended over the years to shrink the number of non-Farsi-speaking populations, members of non-Persian communities have vigorously rejected the official accounts of their numbers. In spite of all the propaganda around the "national status" of the Persian language, and despite over 80 years of forced assimilation, out of Iran's total

Table 1.1 Linguistic Composition of Iran's Population (Percentage to the Total Population of 65,758,000; Literacy Rate—70–75%)

Ethnic group	Language	%	Religion	Area of residency
Arabs	Arabic	3.17	Shia/Sunni (Islam)	South
Armenians and Assyrians	Armenian/Assyrian	.50	Christians	Northwest/Central
Azeris (including Qashqayis, Shahsevans, Afshars, and Qaragozlus)	Azeri (Turkic)	37.3	Shia (Islam)	North/Northwest
Baluchis	Baluchi	2	Sunni	Southeast
Kurds	Kurdish	7	Sunni	West/Northwest
Lurs and Bakhtiyaris	Bakhtiyari/Luri	4	Shia	Central
Mazandaranis and Gilakis	Gilaki/Mazandarani	7	Shia	Northwest
Persians	Farsi	35.92	Shia	Central Iran
Turkmens	Turkmeni (Turkic)	2	Sunni	North
Others		1.38	—	—

Sources: The above estimates are taken from a variety of sources, including Ethnologue, (2002); HRW (1997); Hassanpour (1992a); Aghajanian (1983); Nyrop (1978); Abrahamian (1970); and Aliev (1966).

population of 66 million (approximate figure), no more than 22 million speak Farsi as their mother tongue (Ethnologue, 2002). Table 1.1 above illustrates some general characteristics of Iran's population.

Speakers of Iranic Languages

As table 1.1 illustrates, Iran's Farsi-speaking population constitutes a little below 36 percent of the total population and is mainly concentrated in central and eastern Iran in such major cities as Isfahan, Shiraz, Mashhad, Kerman, Tehran, and Yazd. The Persian language belongs to the Indo-European language family that, along with Kurdish, Gilaki, Mazandarani, Lori/Luri, Sistani, Bakhtiyari, and also Tajik and Pashtun, constitute what are called the Iranic languages. According to the latest estimates, the Farsi speakers and those speaking very close dialects of Farsi such as Luri, Bakhtiyari, Lak, Gilaki, Taleshi, and Mazandarani make up around half of the total population, while the other half is composed of speakers of non-Iranic languages such as Turkic, Arabic, Assyrian, as well as independent Indo-European languages such as Kurdish, Baluchi, and Armenian.

It is important to realize that belonging to an Iranic language group does not, in and of itself, imply solidarity and cooperation with the dominant Farsi-speaking community. The recent history of such major Indo-Iranic-speaking groups as the Kurds and Baluchs indicates that these communities have not been content with the dominant status of Farsi in Iran. On the contrary, they have time and again challenged the legitimacy and authority of Fars-dominated Iran both historically and in the present. The Farsi-speaking community also differs from other Iranic-speaking groups such as the Kurds and Baluchs through religious affiliations in that a vast majority of the Persians are Shia Muslims, whereas the Kurds and Baluchs mainly adhere to the Sunni branch of Islam.

Ever since the establishment of the Pahlavi monarchy in 1925, Persian-populated towns and cities have been the main centers of government attention, receiving the lion's share of investments, industry, infrastructure, and development projects, while other areas have remained significantly underdeveloped. The same trend has continued, and even intensified, under Islamic rule. In the words of a well-known Iranian Arab scholar, Yousef Azizi-Banitorof,

> during the 8 years of the Rafsanjani presidency investment in Kerman province (the president's home province) was 300 times of that in East and West Azerbaijan, Zanjan and Ardebil—all with Azeri majorities. Official figures show that investment in Khuzistan is lower than before the revolution or even before the Iran-Iraq war. Yet the majority of the wealth of the region (even non-oil wealth) is exported to other regions. This is a province that from the point of view of industry, agriculture, services, and excise duty income is rich, and the oil extracted from its soil accounts for 80–90% of the national income. Yet, according to the deputy from Abadan and Khorramshahr, only 20–30% of the ports of these two cities have been reconstructed after the war. Before the war they were the most active ports in the country. (Azizi-Banitorof, 2003, p. 6)

Next to Persians, the Kurds are another Iranic-language-speaking ethnic group comprising about 7 percent of Iran's population. They are mainly concentrated in the province of Kurdestan in north and northwest Iran, in western Azerbaijan, in the province of Bakhtaran (Kermanshahan), and northwest Khorasan. There are also large Kurdish communities in neighboring countries of Turkey, Iraq, Syria, as well as the ex-Soviet republics. Unlike the Persians, the majority of Kurds are Sunni Muslims, which makes them a religious minority in addition to being an ethnic/linguistic minority.

Similar to other non-Persian populated regions, the Kurdish-populated areas have not fared well economically. Mustafa Hijri is the current secretary general of Democratic Party of Iranian Kurdistan, one of the oldest Kurdish parties that has been fighting for "the attainment of Kurdish national rights within a democratic federal republic of Iran" since 1945 (see http://www.pdki.org/index.php). In an interview he notes,

> In comparison with Kurd-populated areas, cities on the outskirts of Kurdistan such as Zanjan, Ghazvin and Tabriz and towns in the Eastern Azerbaijan Province are full of large workshops, factories and industrial and manufacturing centers. Yet you will not find a single factory in the entire Kurd-populated areas—only tiny workshops—and even these have been erected with local capital. The facts of economic discrimination are so blatant that it strikes an outsider leaving Kurdish territories for other areas. A delegation from the Socialist International who entered Iraqi Kurdistan via Iran wrote in their report that when you enter the Kurd-populated areas from outside you are struck by the obvious economic discrimination. (Hijri, 2001, p. 2)

Throughout modern history, the Kurds have been involved in continuous and persistent political struggles not only in Iran but also in neighboring countries of Turkey, Iraq, and Syria. Their struggle is centered around the demand for cultural, political, and national rights in each and every country where they live as a major ethnic/national group. In recent years, their situation has changed considerably in Iraq, following the U.S. occupation of Iraq and subsequent removal of Saddam Hussein from power. The improved situation of Iraqi Kurds, on the one hand, and the pressure from the European Union to improve Turkey's human rights records, on the other, are expected to positively affect the status of Turkey's Kurdish community. In turn, these new developments are influencing the situation of Iran's Kurdish population. While hopes of improved living conditions under an Islamic regime have faded away, as one researcher has observed, Kurdish politics continue to be "an integral part of the bigger political picture in Iran" (Koohi-Kamali, 2003, p. 215).

Baluchs or Balochs are the third comparatively distinct Iranic-language speaking ethnic group that inhabit the far southeast of Iran, comprising approximately 2 percent of the total population. In terms of religious affiliation, the Baluchs are Sunni Muslims who form a part of a larger ethnic group living in the neighboring Pakistan and Afghanistan. Despite their linguistic similarities with other Iranic-speaking groups, the Baluchi community of Iran has vehemently resisted various assimilatory policies and actions orchestrated by central governments throughout Iran's modern history. Like the Kurds, due to their adherence to the Sunni branch of Islam, the Baluchs have become subjected to religious discrimination in the Islamic Republic. Again, this new found discrimination is added to the already existing class-, ethnic-, language-, and region-based discrimination. Economically, the Baluch-inhabited province of Sistan va Baluchistan is one of the poorest in the country. As a result of dire economic conditions, lack of employment and unbearable poverty level, some members of the community have turned to drug trafficking and similar activities. At the same time, the community's demand for equal rights and equitable treatment has continued to live on and get stronger with the passage of time. A document posted on the Baluchestani National Movement Web site rightly observes,

> Despite the failure of numerous Baloch rebellions over the past decades in Pakistan and Iran, Baloch nationalism continues to be a source of deep concern to the governments of these countries. Aroused by the success of surrounding nationalisms—the Indian, the Persian, and the Turkish—and goaded into desperation by its own failures, Baloch nationalism in the sixties and seventies became increasingly radical and uncompromising. For these reasons, the Baloch have come to play an increasingly significant role in South-west Asian affairs. Their behaviour is one of the important factors in the future stability and security not only of the Baloch-inhabited countries but also of the entire region. (Balochistan-e-Raji Zrombesh, 2004)

Lurs (or Lors) are another ethnic group speaking an Iranic language. Inhabiting the provinces of Lorestan, Bakhtiyari and Kohkiluyeh, the Lor community differs from the Kurds and Baluchs in two main areas. First, whereas Kurds and Baluchs have their strong coethnic communities in the neighboring countries surrounding Iran, the Lors have lived almost exclusively within the boundaries of Iran with no significant coethnics outside Iranian borders. Second, unlike Kurdish and Baluch communities, the majority of Lors adhere to the principles of Shia Islam. Despite their similarities with the Persian community, like other non-Fars ethnic groups and nationalities, the Lors have not been immune to the wrath of central governments in Iran. On the contrary, during the reign of Reza Shah they have suffered one of the greatest genocidal acts of militarism and forceful resettlement.

Gilaki-Mazandaranis constitute another ethnic group in Iran that speaks an Iranic language. The Gilaki and Mazandarani community comprises about 7 percent of Iran's population. While Bakhtiyaris are mainly concentrated in the province of Chaharmahal va Bakhtiyari, the Gilakis and Mazandaranis inhabit mainly the province of Gilan in northern Iran (see also Garthwaite, 1983). They practice the Shia branch of Islam and have held revolutionary uprisings against the central governments. Most well known of these uprisings was the Jangal Movement that took place in 1920 under the leadership of Mirza Kuchik Khan, demanding, among other things, national reforms and regional autonomy from the central government. Due to the closeness and affinity of their language to Farsi, on the one hand, and their adherence to Shi'ism, on the other, the community has been integrated successfully into the Fars-centered sphere and enjoys a comparatively high level of socioeconomic and cultural development.

Turkic-Speaking Groups

Azerbaijanis or Azeris are the largest Turkic-speaking ethnic group in Iran, inhabiting northwestern parts of the country. Their traditional homeland, Azerbaijan, is geopolitically divided into two parts: northern Azerbaijan, which became an independent republic after the fall of Soviet Union in 1991, and southern Azerbaijan, which is a part of Iran. The language of the people of Azerbaijan is Azeri (otherwise known as Azeri-Turkic) and the religion of the majority of them is Shia Islam. The population of Azeris in today's world is approximately 44 million, of which 20 to 30 million are believed to be living in Iran, over 8 million in the Republic of Azerbaijan, close to 2 million in Turkey, and the rest in countries such as Russia, Georgia, Iraq, and Ukraine.

Historically, Azerbaijan has been the center of various social movements such as the Constitutional Revolution (1905–1911), Sheikh Mohammed Khiabani's Azadistan Movement (1920), and Mir Ja'far Pishevari's Democratic Movement (1954–1946) that led to the creation of the Azerbaijan Democratic Republic from December 1945 to December 1946. In recent times, the demise of the Soviet Union and the independence of northern Azerbaijan have had an enormous impact on notions of identity, political activism, and the revival of national consciousness among the Azeris of Iran (see also B. Shaffer, 2002). Additionally, similar to the case with other Iranian ethnic groups, recent developments in the neighboring countries of Iraq, Afghanistan, and Turkey have continued to influence the views of Azeris about politics, culture, national homeland, and national identity.

Since the Islamic Revolution, a national movement has developed in Azerbaijan that is commonly referred to as Azerbaycan Milli Herekati (The National Movement of Azerbaijan) whose aim is the attainment of proportional representation, sociocultural rights, and the right for self-determination for Iranian Azeris. A glaring manifestation of this resurgent movement can be witnessed in powerful displays of strength, mobilization, and determination that have been taking place for the past decade in commemoration of the birthday of ancient Azeri hero, Babak Khorramdin. Every year in July, hundreds of thousands of people gather around the mountainous Fortress of Bez near the town of Kaleyber and voice their demands for the realization of their repressed national, social, and cultural rights. In their July 3–4, 2003 gathering, the participants issued a joint declaration, signed by over 250 Azeri intellectuals, academics, writers, and poets, which included politically significant demands such as the transformation of the current Iranian political system into a democratically representative federal republic, putting an end to the politics of monolingualism and monoculturalism in the country; and lifting the ban on the use of non-Farsi languages. As they put it in their June 28 manifesto,

> Due to the geographical vastness and ethnic plurality and historical backgrounds of our country, a transition to the federal system is inevitable. In the recent century the very existence of such well-known institutions as The Provincial Councils and The Islamic Councils in the charter of the Mashruteh (Constitutional) Revolution and that of the Islamic Republic indicate the inevitability of the federal system in Iran, which has been further enforced by the idea of dividing the country into 10 provincial sectors in the last 2 years. (*Azerbaycan Danishir*, June 28, 2003)

On May 12, 2006 *Iran Newspaper*, an official organ of the Islamic Republic of Iran, published a cartoon with an accompanying article where Azeris were identified as "cockroaches" who "did not know the language of humans" and therefore had to be "exterminated" (*Iran Newspaper*, May 12, 2006). Following this offensive publication, thousands of Azeris took to the streets for several days all over Azerbaijan, demanding equal treatment and justice. Hundred of demonstrators were arrested, and scores of them were killed in Naqadeh, Tabriz, Ormiyeh, Meshkin-shahr, and other areas. The demonstrators chanted slogans such as

> Hear me out
> I am Turk
> My mother tongue will not die
> My mother tongue will not be supplanted
> Down with Chauvinism
> Down with racism . . .

The Association of Azerbaijani Academicians summarized the main demands of the Azeri movement:

1. The Azeri-Turkic should become an official language throughout Iran, given the sheer size and number of its speakers.
2. The Azeri-Turkic should become the language of instruction and education throughout Azerbaijan as well as in other Turkic-populated areas.
3. The Iranian government should create television and radio stations, nationwide media outlets and newspapers in Azeri-Turkic (*Shams Tabriz News*, May 20, 2006). Following the unrest in Azerbaijani provinces, the Iranian President Mahmoud Ahmadinejad traveled to Tabriz on July 11, 2006. During his official four-day visit, he offered the east Azerbaijani province an impressive economic package, although there was no mention of cultural, linguistic, and ethnic rights.

Turkmens are another major Turkic-speaking group with their own distinct culture, language, history, and ethnic identity. They make up about 2 percent of Iran's total population and live in the region known as Turkmen-Sahra in eastern Golestan (Mazandaran) and northern Khorasan provinces in northeastern Iran, forming the frontier with the independent Republic of Turkmenistan in the north. Unlike the Azeris, the majority of Turkmens are Sunni Muslims, and this adds another dimension to their marginalized status in the country. Like many other non-Persian communities, the Turkmen community has been subjected to forceful resettlement and assimilatory policies in modern Iran. Immediately after the fall of the Pahlavi regime, the community became a hotbed of revolutionary uprisings, ethnic demands, and nationalistic activism centered on the revival of Turkmeni identity. Notwithstanding the influence of leftist groups in these movements, the Turkmen uprising during the early years of the revolution showed a deep sense of ethnic consciousness among the community members, particularly the youth. In issue number 209, *Kar* (Central Organ of the Organization of Iranian People's Fedaian) published an article titled "Dard-e mellat-e Turkmen" ["The Grievance of Turkmen Nation"] which cites various grievances that Iran's Turkmen community has been encountering ever since the Pahlavi era. Immediately after the fall of Pahlavi dictatorship, it was only natural that "all the eyes were on Kurdistan and Turkmen-Sahra," observes the article:

For these two regions had unique conditions that distinguished them from other regions in Iran. The Turkmen nation had been under severest and most systematic economic, social, and cultural pressures. By labelling the Turkmens as "barbaric Turkmens" and "uncivilized Turkmens" they tried to annihilate the national Turkmeni culture. They claimed that Turkmens did not know anything "other than gun, horse, pillage, plunder, rebellion and killing." . . . In administrative division of the country, they divided Turkmen-Sahra to pieces, so that the Turkmen could never assert a political existence. (Morad, 2003, pp. 5–6)

In addition to Azeris and Turkmens, Iran is home to a host of other Turkic-speaking groups and communities such as the Qashqayis, Afshars, and Khalajs who are scattered throughout the country (see, e.g., Beck, 1986). As far as the violations of their cultural and ethnic rights are concerned, these diverse communities are in no better shape than the Turkmens. If anything, the smaller size of their population has made it much easier for them to quickly and easily assimilate into the Farsi-speaking dominant group. With the current rate of advancement of the assimilation processes, it is expected that among various Turkic-speaking communities in Iran, only the major national groups such as the Azeris and Turkmens may survive through the twenty-first century.

Arabs

The Arab community makes up slightly over 3 percent of Iran's population. For the most part this community is concentrated in the southwestern part of the country, in the province of Khuzistan, along the Persian Gulf coast. While the majority of Khuzistani Arabs are Shia Muslims, a portion of the community residing along the coastal areas are Sunnis. The Iranian Arabs constitute a major ethnic group that, along with Turks, is considered in the dominant racist literature as *anirani* (un-Iranic). As such, it is a group that has been subject to the most vicious acts of racism and xenophobia in Iran. The racism against the Arab community is for the most part rooted in history, when the Arab Muslims conquered Iran in the seventh century and brought about the Islamization of the region. The racist mentality against the Arab minority reached a climax during the Pahlavi era, when Arabs were openly blamed for Iran's backwardness and for the demise of a supposedly "superior" pre-Islamic Persia (see also M. Ansari, 1974). The community has struggled against various racist, ultranationalist, and discriminatory policies during both the monarchic and the Islamic regimes.

In an open letter to the special representative of the Office of the United Nations High Commissioner for Human Rights, dated October 25, 2002, an Arab group under the name of the Ahwazi-Arabs for Freedom and Democracy in Iran notes,

> We, the Ahwazi Arabs of Iran, this oppressed and ill-treated national minority, are being denied our basic human rights. These rights include our ability to study our native language, our right to speak our native language, and our right to exercise our culture and our customs. We seek our cultural and linguistic rights in accordance with the United Nations' Universal Declaration of Human Rights. . . . Our demands and call for our basic human rights, including education in our mother tongue, have often been labeled as "nationalistic," "separatist," and "secessionist" by the Iranian regime. They see our calls for cultural rights as "disintegration tendencies" and as "threatening Iran's national security." The fact is that we seek peaceful coexistence with other national ethnic and religious groups in Iran. However, we demand more autonomy and self-rule for the Arabistani population of Iran. We are not seeking to secede from Iran or engage in a violent confrontation. (Al-Ahwazi Arabs, 2002, p. 6)

Other Ethnic and Religious Minorities

In addition to the above-mentioned major groups and communities, there are still other smaller groups such as the Armenians, Assyrians, and Jews who make up about 1 percent of Iran's total population. Likewise, aside from the practitioners of Sunni Islam who make up about 15 percent of Iran's population, there are other religious minorities such as Christians, Zorothustrians, Bahais, and followers of other faiths. Based on the government-sponsored national census of 1996, about 99.56 percent of the people of Iran subscribe to Islam, 0.13 percent to Christianity, 0.05 to Zoroastrianism, 0.04 percent to Judaism, and 0.22 percent to other faiths (Aghajanian, 1983; Abrahamian, 1970; Ramezanzadeh, 1996; Dei and Asgharzadeh, 2003). It is interesting to note that while the dominant discourse designates various minority groups such as the Armenians, Jews, and Bahais as religious minorities, many of these groups would define themselves as ethnic minorities.

CONCLUSION

On August 3, 2005, the more moderate and reformist President Mohammad Khatami was replaced by a conservative and somewhat fundamentalist Mahmoud Ahmadinejad. From the beginning of his term, the new president has pursued a provocative foreign policy vis-à-vis the United States, Israel, and other countries. These provocative policies coupled with a relentless promotion of Iran's nuclear program have brought the country under the international spotlight. Fearing that a situation similar to the invasions of Iraq and Afghanistan may happen to Iran, the Islamic regime has increasingly become nervous, particularly in its relationship with Iran's diverse ethnic communities. Increasingly, ethnic demands are viewed suspiciously and are forcefully suppressed under the pretext of maintaining Iran's national security and territorial integrity. Suppression of ethnic-based demands takes place under the pretext of fighting the foreign elements seeking to break up Iran while minority rights activists are seen as spies and agents of foreign governments. A clear example of this accusatory practice was manifested in the way the supreme leader Ayatollah Ali Khamenei referred to the Azeri unrest in the wake of events following the publication of racist cartoons in May 2006. In an address to Iran's parliament on May 28, 2006, he stated,

> These ethnic and religious instigations are the last arrow left in the quiver of the enemies of the Islamic Republic of Iran. . . . Their plans are based on a wrong assessment of the situation. And now they have decided to turn to Azerbaijan. Our enemies do not know Azerbaijan, for the Azerbaijani has always fiercely defended the Islamic Revolution and our country's territorial integrity and independence. (Khamenei, 2006)

The labeling of minority rights activists as foreign elements is an old notion that has been used by the dominant group for the past 80 years in Iran. Not only the officials and government authorities have consistently used this and similar labels, but many individuals, writers, and intellectuals outside the governing circles have also been using such labels to discredit the legitimate demands for racial, ethnic, linguistic, and religious equality in the country. The ruling group sees itself as representing a unified, "authentic," and "essentialized" Iranian nation whose fixed parameters are defined by Iran's geographical borders, Persian language, and Islamic faith (Shi'ism). The opposition's stance does not fundamentally differ from the official stance when it comes to defining Iran's national identity, except perhaps in defining the ruling ideology. Thus, while the current government cites the Islamic faith (Shi'ism) as a strong feature of Iranians' national identity, the opposition groups may replace religious ideology with a socialist or an ultranationalist (Aryan) one. At any rate, they both share a fixed, essentialist, and essentializing notion of identity based on Persian language and culture. It is this essentialist notion of identity and its parameters that are being challenged now more than ever before by Iran's diverse ethnic groups in Kurdistan, Azerbaijan, Khuzistan, Baluchistan, Turkmen-Sahra, and other regions of the country.

CHAPTER 2

The Journey between Theory and Practice: Text, Context, and Language

Conceptual and analytical frameworks for understanding and interpreting society must be grounded in individual and collective lived experiences. There also has to be a grounded understanding of how, as individuals and groups, we are differently and differentially implicated in ways of knowing and articulating social experiences. There is no need to mystify or reify social reality in order to understand individual and collected lived experiences. However, in order to understand and appreciate each other and our society we must listen to and hear each other.

(George J. Sefa Dei, 1996, pp. 18–19)

INTRODUCTION

This chapter sets the ground with a discussion of literature review, methodology, data collection, data analyses, and discursive frameworks, highlighting a variety of approaches, theories, and methods that have influenced the outcome of research in this study. The chapter also explores the importance of text, context, and language in current social sciences and humanities by bringing together the important aspects of critical discourse analysis as a suitable research method and discursive frameworks such as anti-colonial, antiracism, and postcolonial theories as they relate to issues of language, text, interpretation, representation, and expressions of identity.

The use of multiple theoretical and methodological frameworks is important in that the dominant literature on Iran has seldom, if ever, benefited from multidisciplinary and interdisciplinary scholarship. For instance, the dominant Iranian literature on race and ethnicity still defines race in the context of its now discredited biogenetic attributes. A familiarity with antiracism scholarship will clarify that race is no longer defined as a "biological truth" but as a social and political construct. Thus, it saves a lot of trouble when it is outlined from the outset on what the contemporary scholarship is on notions such as race, racism, colonialism, and antiracism.

The same applies to other methodological and theoretical approaches employed in this book. For instance, an understanding of critical discourse analysis reveals the central place of language not only in relations of power and domination but also in how social scientific research is conducted and presented. Just as language plays a central role in issues of inclusion, exclusion, racism, oppression, and power configurations in real social settings, so too does it influence the way social reality is researched, analyzed, interpreted, presented, and understood. For language is the main medium through which social reality is both presented and received. As such, it is imperative that attention is paid to the ways in which language is contextualized and put to use in systems of interpretation, writing, and presentation. Language has the power to obscure, marginalize, and exclude. This is as true in real life situations in societies as it is in research projects and discursive genres. Each theoretical approach used in this work adds new dimensions to doing critical research in contemporary times. Their inclusion in this chapter will give the reader an idea regarding various theoretical, methodological, and conceptual issues upon which this book is based.

RESEARCH ON THE SUBJECT

In an article titled "Linguistic Racism and Its Ramifications" (Asgharzadeh, 2002), I have explored some aspects of modern racism in Iranian society. As far as I know, this article is the only piece of literature that directly discusses the subject of racism in Iran. This article, for the first time, touches upon the connection between the Iranian version of Aryanism, the Indo-Europeanist project, and the manifestations of European racist agendas particularly against non-Aryan and non-Persian communities in Iran. More specifically, the article analyzes the linguicidal policies of Iran's dominant Persian group vis-à-vis the implications of those policies for non-Persian ethnic groups. Following this article, another essay, coauthored with Professor George Dei, appeared in *Language and Education: An International Journal* (Dei and Asgharzadeh, 2003) and explored issues of language-based discrimination, racism, and exclusion in a Ghanaian as well as an Iranian context. Through an examination of the dominant role of Farsi in Iran, the paper explored the role of language as an instrument of power, oppression, domination, and assimilation. It also showed the complicity of the education system in both maintenance and reproduction of hegemonic systems. To my knowledge, these two articles are among the rare publications that directly and concretely address issues of racism and hegemony in an Iranian context.

One could also mention three other works that indirectly relate to the subject matter: M. Vaziri's (1993) work titled *Iran as Imagined Nation*, B.J. Saad's (1996) *The Image of Arabs in Modern Persian Literature*, and F. Kashani-Sabet's (1999) *Frontier Fictions*. Although very important in their own specific areas, these works touch upon the subject of racism in Iran only marginally and indirectly. Modeled on Anderson's (1983) *Imagined*

Communities, Vaziri's work concentrates on the processes of (imaginary) nation building in Iran. In this important work, Vaziri discusses a variety of perceived, imagined, and biasedly constructed processes that led to the creation of what is termed as the Iranian nation in the dominant literature.

Vaziri's work is extremely important in that it is among a few pathbreaking works that for the first time in the history of Iranian scholarship casts doubt on the authenticity of such a thing called the Iranian nation. Important is also the way in which Vaziri implicates the Indo-Europeanist and Eurocentric projects in the construction of the Iranian nation. Essentially, in this book "the racial and national methodologies used by the European Orientalists to study Iran are challenged and disputed" (1993, p. 3). And in effect, this is as far as Vaziri goes. He effectively challenges the Orientalist accounts of Iranians' history and nationality, only to reach a conclusion that "the alleged racial and national consciousness of these remote communities—specially of the Iranians—is purely imaginary" (1993, p. 214).

Evidently, the author did not wish to discuss the impact of racism, in fact the subject of racism itself, in Iranian society and in an Iranian context. He touches upon race and racism only to "prove" the "imaginary" nature of "national identities." The fact that racism has real material, physical, psychological, socioeconomic, political, cultural, and educational ramifications does not seem to concern him. Hence, there is a need for a study to fill the gap by focusing on the real thing: racism and its numerous ramifications not only for the marginalized and minoritized communities but for the dominant group as well.

Saad's (1996) work, on the other hand, discusses some aspects of the negative and discriminatory "images" assigned to Arabs in Persian literature. This work is important in that it brings to light certain aspects of discriminatory and racist attitudes toward the Arabs and, by extension, Islam, in dominant Persian literature. The book is also important in challenging the conventional notions of "Iranian" and "Iranianness" (*Irani va Iraniyyat*), which stands in contrast to members of the dominant elite such as Shahrokh Meskoob (1992) and Manochehr Dorraj (1990) who propose a narrow version of Iranian nationalism to the question of what it means to be an Iranian? Saad replies within a context of pluralism and diversity, emphasizing that "within the borders of Iran there are many different people who may have little in common, in terms of language, culture, and way of life" (1996, p. 18).

Saad goes on to show how by defining "the Arab Other" the Persian nationalists sought to define themselves and their own nationality. In order to define the Persian/Iranian nationality as "superior" and "civilized," the Arab Other had to be defined as primitive, uncivilized, and inferior. Her work is thus extremely important in investigating the construction of modern Iranian nationalism. It is also significant in articulating the way the Arab Other was minoritized and inferiorized in the dominant Persian literature. However, in and of itself, the book is not sufficient to shed light on the subject of racism in Iranian society as a whole. In fact, the work is way too conservative in dealing with concepts and issues such as racism, nationalism, along with ethnic-, language-, and culture-based oppression that exist in Iran.

Similar to Saad's work, Kashani-Sabet's (1999) work titled *Frontier Fictions* greatly contributes to the debate on Iranian nationalism in many important ways. First and foremost, it shows the degree of fascination and infatuation that Persian intellectuals have with Iran's national borders, with the land and an imaginary place variously called Iranzamin and Iranshahr. This extreme infatuation, in turn, helps to mold and craft the image of an Iranian nation, which is rooted for the most part in imagination. The book also mentions—albeit extremely inadequately—the repression and suppression of ethnic, linguistic, and cultural diversity in the country particularly under the pretext of "territorial integrity" and "national security." In similar ways, Kashani-Sabet every now and then alludes to the fact that "competing identities . . . posed challenges to the larger Iranian identity" (1999, p. 6). Regardless of their inadequacy and insufficiency, these kinds of allusions are important in challenging the monolithic and singular interpretation of Iranian nationality.

By and large, the book does a good job in articulating the centrality of land in Iranian nation-building processes, albeit up to 1946. In fact, the emphasis on land and territory is so great in the book that the author claims, "Iran, like other nation-states, came into existence as a result of frontier f(r)ictions and fluctuations" (1999, p. 14). Notwithstanding its obvious vagueness, perhaps this sweeping statement clearly points to the limitations of Kashani-Sabet's analyses, limitations that are first and foremost due to her overemphasis on land and territory. Obviously in and of itself land is not and cannot be a determining cause of nationalism and nation-statism. It is rather the people inhabiting the land who exercise their power and authority over land and who seek, as in the Iranian case, to dominate other owners of the same land and territory.

Instead of interrogating what has been said about the borders of Iran, the present study seeks to interrogate what happens to peoples living within the borders of Iran. Acts of racism, oppression, and injustice are committed by individuals and groups, not by lands and territories per se. Of course it is important to situate the land within a context of colonization and oppression. But to explain everything as secondary to the land ignores the complex relations of power and domination that are constantly played out among and between various peoples occupying these lands and territories. For this study then, the central concern is to see what happens to the peoples occupying the lands, not vice versa. A critique of land is important within the context of how people articulate their own condition, how differences of ethnicity, culture, language, class, gender, religion, sexual orientation, disability, and so forth are played out within certain borders and on certain territories.

In addition to the above-mentioned works, a few edited volumes on Iran have been published in recent years that contain important articles regarding difference and diversity in Iranian society. One such edited volume is titled

Iran and the Surrounding World, edited by Nikki R. Keddie and Rudi Matthee (2002). It contains interesting articles that will certainly contribute, in the words of Keddie, "to a better understanding of many aspects of Iran's recent history" (2002, p. 10). The editors also hope that by way of this book's "modest contribution" to the field of knowledge "Western leaders will gain a greater acquaintance with this culture, as well as with the reasons for Iran's past reactions against the West, and especially the U.S." (2002, p. 10).

The book tackles a variety of contemporary and old issues regarding cultures, politics, geographies, religions, and histories of Iran and its diverse inhabitants. In terms of cultural and ethnic heterogeneity in the country, a most important contribution to the volume comes by way of Kashani-Sabet's essay titled "Cultures of Iranianness." In this essay, the author explores variegated manifestations of nationality and nationalism in Iran as they reach their highest expression through Persian nationalism during the Pahlavi era. The author rightly observes that "by tracing the articulations of Iranianness for over a century, one is struck by the difference in emphasis placed by various nationalities on the basis of nationhood" (2002, p. 178).

Similarly, in an examination of Iranian "post-revolutionary textbooks," Golnar Mehran establishes that the "national character presented in schoolbooks undermines ethnic and linguistic diversity . . . in the country" (2002, pp. 248–249). In an article exploring the changing relationships among the Turks, Persians, and Arabs, T.J. Barfield concludes that "the modern nation of Iran itself was the by-product of the struggles between successive dynasties and tribal confederations within and outside of Iran" (2002, p. 85). Barfield is quick to add that though "Iran may now have transcended these roots as it enters a new millennium, the roots are still clearly there" (2002, p. 85).

Notwithstanding that the mentioned articles allude to the pluralist nature of Iranian society, they barely scratch the surface and fail to tackle the real and concrete issues emerging from difference and diversity in Iran. What is missing from the discussions in these articles, and by extension in the whole volume, is a realization of the fact that Iran is, and has always been, a multiethnic, multicultural, and multilingual society. Missing also is the responsibility to interrogate the privileged place of Farsi and its speakers within the current Iran. None of the mentioned works offers a comprehensive account of the ongoing racism in Iranian society. As such, a considerable "lack" and "gap" continue to exist regarding the issue of racism in Iran, a gap that this study aims to fill.

RESEARCH METHODOLOGY

The material analyzed in this book covers the representative samples of works of literature, history, and religion from the classical period of Persian language and literature up to the present. The study focuses on certain texts and analyzes them as relevant documents attesting to the existence of racism, aggressive nationalism, chauvinism, as well as antiracist resistance. These texts are mainly chosen due to their degree of relevance to the subject matter, that is, racism, colonialism, inferiorization, exclusion, and resistance against them. Authors are surveyed in accordance with their language, ethnic background, and gender, when and if applicable. Among the classical texts, the study looks briefly into the processes that led to the creation and construction of the image of Other in the existing book of Avesta (the holy book of Zarathustrianism) and the *Shahnameh* (the Book of Kings) of Abulqasem Ferdowsi (AD 940–1020). These are the two most important classical texts of Persian language and literature. Then the study moves on to the literature produced during the Pahlavi era, followed by the contemporary Islamic Republic. For each period, a select number of works and documents have been chosen that best represent the viewpoints of both the minoritized and the dominant groups. As stressed earlier, the main criteria for selecting any text is the degree of that text's relevance to the subject matter.

In order to provide an overview of Iranian historiography, the study also makes reference to non-Persian sources such as the Old Testament, Herodotus's *Histories*, and the works of certain Muslim historians and travelers who have contributed in one way or another to the unearthing or the problematizing of some aspects of Iranian history. The Old Testament, for instance, has been extremely important in serving as a primary source from which the image of ancient Persia, the Achaemenid era, and historical figures such as Cyrus the Great are constructed. The relevance of such sources becomes evident particularly in the light of the fact that in recent years the authenticity of narratives constructed through these texts has increasingly been questioned by local and indigenous historians in Iran (Poorpirar, 2000, 2002, 2004; Zehtabi, 1999).

These texts have been used anachronistically by the dominant elite to construct an identity for both the dominant Persian group as well as the minoritized communities. That is to say, the nationalist/elite intellectuals have interpreted these texts in accordance with contemporary notions of race, nation, nationality, country, ethnic groups, and identity that were either completely nonexistent at the time of the inception of these classical texts or else had completely different meanings from those used in the present. It is therefore crucial to go back to these classical texts and explore their relevance to the present, so that one may be able to interrogate a plethora of anachronistically constructed notions such as nationalism, Iranian nation, Iranian identity, and homeland.

Moreover, the study looks into the works of a select number of Western authors and Orientalists who pioneered in introducing the Indo-Europanist agenda, "the Aryan myth," "the linkage between language and race," and the methodology of "anachronistic treatment of history" into the fabric of modern Iranian society in particular, and to the world in general. Among these Orientalists, the study briefly discusses the works of authors such as William Jones (1746–1794), Freidrich von Schlegel (1772–1829), Count Joseph-Arthur Gobineau (1816–1882), and

Friedrich Max Müller (1823–1900). A critical examination of the Orientalist literature is significant for this study in that it shows the processes through which notions such as Aria, Aryanism, Indo-Europeanism, white supremacy, nationalism, and nation-statism were reimagined and reconstructed particularly from the eighteenth century onward. In the case of Iran, this reconstruction was done by the Orientalists as well as the local intelligentsia and elite who stood to benefit from such reconstruction.

In addition to above genres, the book explores what I have called the dominant literature and the marginalized literature. The dominant literature covers samples of texts written by members of the dominant group, that is, first and foremost, those whose language is the national/official language of communication, instruction, education, and literary production in the country. Individuals in this category are identified by their ethnicity, their place of residence, and more significantly, their language. Farsi being the dominant and imposed language in Iran, it is important to see how the speakers of this language view the conditions, rights, and freedoms of non-Farsi-speaking individuals, groups, and communities vis-à-vis their own privileged position. An interrogation of the dominant literature also exposes the role of Farsi-speaking writers and intellectuals in the processes of nation building and the maintenance of unequal ethnic, racial, and linguistic relations in the country.

On the opposite side of the dominant literature is the marginalized literature, produced by minoritized bodies, groups, and communities. This literature covers the works of those individuals who do not speak Farsi as their mother tongue and who do not belong to the dominant Persian group. These individuals have written in their own mother tongue as well as in the dominant Farsi language. In the comparatively relaxed post-Pahlavi era, there has been an atmosphere of resurgence in non-Farsi literature production. Although non-Farsi languages have not been given complete autonomy and independence in the Islamic Republic, they have at least been left alone to fend for themselves, without visible official punishments or penalties to their practitioners and developers.

Allocation of a central space to the exploration of the marginalized literature is essential to this work. The conventional research on Iran normally and almost exclusively relies on the dominant literature. Provision for the marginalized literature is in essence a decolonizing methodology that challenges the validity and truthfulness of research that exclusively relies on dominant voices, texts, methods, and tools of investigation and exploration. Modern Internet technology in this regard is a useful space that freely grants access to hitherto forbidden languages, voices, and literatures. Free from the tyranny of "editor's censorship," hitherto forbidden narratives, stories, and texts are freely and fairly easily produced in numerous online journals, Web sites, and Internet discussion groups. In exploring samples of the marginalized literature, online "hypertexts" and cybertexts have become rich sources of reference throughout this work. In order to effectively interpret this information, the book uses critical discourse analysis as an appropriate research methodology in dealing with issues emerging from sociolinguistics, culture, text, and context.

Critical Discourse Analysis

Critical discourse analysis is a common method of research that is based on the analysis of texts, contexts, and languages. This particular methodology has to do with the rereading, deconstruction, investigation, and critiquing of texts for the purpose of uncovering new conclusions or building different cases (Wodak, 1989; Weiss and Wodak, 2003; Young and Harrison, 2004). It is also about understanding, challenging, and exposing the way relations of power and domination are concealed in language, speech, text, context, and discourse. It aims to analyze overt and covert relations of dominance, control, and power as manifested in language. In short, it is about relationships, inter-connectivities, and interdependencies between language and society (Wodak, 1997). As van Dijk points out,

> Critical Discourse Analysis is a type of discourse analytical research that primarily studies the way social power abuse, dominance and inequality are enacted, reproduced and resisted by text and talk in the social and political context. With such dissident research, critical discourse analysts take explicit position, and thus want to understand, expose and ultimately to resist social inequality. (van Dijk, 2001, p. 1)

The rapidly expanding field of critical discourse analysis initially was concerned with the study of the use of language for communication in specific contexts. Now this particular methodology has come to cover a broad range of disciplines such as sociology, anthropology, education, psychology, and linguistics, among others. Currently, critical discourse analysis is used to analyze a whole range of social problems, discursive power relations, sociocultural issues, ideological issues, issues of history and historical subjects, the link between text and society, and issues related to social action (Fairclough and Wodak, 1997).

Critical discourse analysis emerges from the need to bring together the study of structure with that of function, the role of agency with that of structure, the relationship between text and context, and the connection between discourse and communication. What is important in this particular methodology is the multidisciplinary and interdisciplinary nature of its functioning. It combines culture with politics, economics with literature, notions of spirituality and indigeneity with resistance against imposed values. It seeks to uncover relationships between speech and silence, language and dominance, text and authority, author and writer, having a voice and being silenced.

Text and context are the two key concepts in critical discourse analysis. The present study adopts a Bakhtinian definition of text and textuality.

According to Bakhtin, the text is

> the primary given of all these disciplines and of all thought in the human sciences and philosophy in general. . . . The text is the unmediated reality (reality of thought and experience), the only one from which these disciplines and this thought can emerge. Where there is no text, there is no object of study, and no object of thought either. (Bakhtin, 1986, p. 103)

Bakhtin (1981) says that language is irreversibly "heteroglottic." What this means is that many languages and languages of many different groups of people simultaneously exist together. We use different languages based on our ethnic background, race, class, gender, occupation, religion, and so on. This rich diversity and difference makes language a site for conflicts and contestations. Language is never a system of abstract traits, elements, terminologies, phonetics, and grammars. As a manifestation of language, the text is a hierarchical meaning-producing practice within which different schools of thought, different ideologies, worldviews, realities, in fact realities of different individuals/authors, and groups/communities are articulated. And as Frow has pointed out, this "articulation involves relations of dominance and subordination between registers, and this clash of languages is a clash of realities" (1988, p. 169).

Seen this way, text can be any kind of signification, any means of communication and expression. It can include written materials, pictoral materials, verbal and nonverbal components, movies, photographs, books, newspapers, magazines, advertisements, and commercials. If we bring together all these components of the text, we may get a chart already envisioned by Mikko Lehtonen (2000, p. 48):

	auditory	visual
verbal	speech	writing
non-verbal	music	picture

As the above chart shows, verbalism links writing and speech together; correspondingly, nonverbality links music and picture together. Writing is also a kind of visual text just as speech can be considered a verbal form of text. These auditory and visual forms of text can be comprehensible to us through our eyes and ears. Music, speech, pictures, body languages, facial expressions, forms of dress, and so forth are all mediums of expression and communication that ought to be contextualized in order to be effectively interpreted.

And this is where the notion of context comes in. If the text is characterized by relations of power and dominance, by the clash of languages, and by the realities of the subordinated and the superordinated, then surely an analysis of the text must go beyond the mere written words. In effect, the context factor enables us to carry the textual conflict beyond the text itself and onto the real society. Context serves as a primary factor in recognizing the necessity of looking beyond language and the text to understand the discourse of any given text.

> Context is defined as the (mentally represented) structure of those properties of the social situation that are relevant for the production or comprehension of discourse. . . . It consists of such categories as the overall definition of the situation, setting (time, place), ongoing actions (including discourses and discourse genres), participants in various communicative, social or institutional roles, as well as their mental representations: goals, knowledge, opinions, attitudes and ideologies. (van Dijk, 2001, p. 358)

Such a definition of context involves, first and foremost, the identity of the speaker, the author, and the writer. Context means the implication and explication of the owner of the voice in the production of the text, of knowing from which gender, what race, what nationality, what social class, and from what ethnic, religious, cultural, and linguistic background any particular "voice" is coming. Similarly, a clear understanding of the way texts are produced, financed, distributed, and consumed is central for an understanding of the critical discourse analysis and for making effective use of it. But most of all, critical discourse analysis is a methodology that is clearly oriented toward social justice and equality. It has a vision of society that is based on relations of power and domination, and it seeks to uncover these unjust relationships and to subvert them. As Kress has maintained,

> [C]ritical studies of language, Critical Linguistics (CL) and Critical Discourse Analysis (CDA) have from the beginning had a political project: that of altering inequitable distributions of economic, cultural and political goods in contemporary societies. (Kress, 1997, p. 15)

Simply put, critical discourse analysis is an action-oriented methodology— just like the anticolonial and antiracist discursive frameworks—that goes well with the overall research project of this study, that is, with its discursive/theoretical frameworks, its area of concentration, and the subjects of its analysis. As discussed earlier, this study engages in a content analysis of the literature produced in Iran since 1925 (and also prior to that) by both the dominant as well as the minoritized/marginalized groups. This literature includes the official documents produced by the government apparatuses and those in power since 1925, along with newspapers, magazines, and books published during both the monarchic and Islamic regimes in Iran.

In analyzing these genres, along with such discursive frameworks as antiracist and anticolonial stances, the study makes use of critical discourse analysis as a sociological methodology to interpret and make sense of the data. critical discourse analysis is extremely helpful particularly in dealing with issues of language, voice, inferiorization, and superiorization. More concretely, it provides the necessary tools to analyze the way the government uses its economic power to promote certain languages, the way it uses its military force to suppress other languages, the way it uses its publishing and textual organs to justify its actions, to marginalize other cultures and other ethnic groups, and so on. Critical discourse analysis is very helpful in uncovering power relations, notions of representation, privilege, identity, and the context within which the dominant texts are produced, maintained, and reproduced. A research methodology based on critical discourse analysis is most capable of throwing light on all the above issues. This study deals with texts and literature that are not produced under what may be called normal conditions. On the contrary, these texts are produced under extreme conditions of political repression, oppression, and censorship. Hence, the language used in these texts is overly coded, metaphorical, and allegoric. And critical discourse analysis provides important analytical and interpretive tools to deal with this kind of language.

DISCURSIVE FRAMEWORKS

This study deals with a number of complex issues such as race and racism; relations of power and domination at various local, national, and global levels; as well as literature, language, culture, history, and their interconnectivity and interdependence. Given the complex nature of the study, I use multiple theoretical/discursive frameworks that have proved helpful in dealing with the subject matter. In addition to facilitating an effective interrogation of complex, interconnected spheres and subjects, a use of multiple methods is also important in bringing different interpretations and insights to the discussion. This study is multidisciplinary and interdisciplinary in nature. As such, the use of multiple theories in it would be quite appropriate. The following pages offer a brief account of each theory and explain its importance for this work.

The Anticolonial Discursive Framework

Drawing on the works of Fanon (1961/1990 and 1967), Memmi (1969), Dei (1996, 1999), Foucault (1969, 1977, 1980, 1983), Said (1978, 1983, 1993), and others in dealing with issues of power, domination, racism, and injustice, this study makes use of anticolonial discursive framework (among other theories) from the initial stages of data collection to methods of research, data analysis, and interpretation. An anticolonial discursive framework is most capable of effectively enabling one to analyze, critique, and interrogate a combination of racist, hegemonic, and colonial relationships like the ones existing in current Iran. As Dei (1999) has argued, "colonial" in this context is conceptualized, not simply as "foreign" or "alien," but rather as "imposed" and "dominating":

> The anti-colonial framework is a theorization of issues emerging from colonial relations, an interrogation of the configuration of power, embedded in ideas,

cultures and histories of knowledge production. The anti-colonial approach recognizes the production of locally produced knowledge emanating from cultural history and social interactions/daily experiences. (Dei, 1999, p. 399; see also Dei and Asgharzadeh, 2001)

Obviously, race is a most effective entry point to this particular study. However, the use of an anticolonial prism compels one not to ignore issues of gender, class, sexuality, age, (dis)ability, and all other categories that serve as potential sites for oppression and exclusion. Along with casting our gaze on race and racialization processes, the anticolonial discourse encourages us to interrogate the interlocking and intersecting nature of systems of power and domination; of how dominance is produced, maintained, and reproduced; and how the disempowered are subjugated and kept under constant control.

While directly tackling racism and xenophobia, the anticolonial framework calls into question all other relations of domination emanating from classism, sexism, heterosexism, ageism, ableism, and all dominant forms of social relations. On the one hand, it allows us to interrogate notions of class exploitation, colonialism, dogmatic nationalism, imperialism, and the exploitative functioning of global capital. On the other, it calls into question all sorts of microlevel individual-based impositions and oppressions such as the ones taking place at home, the workplace, or other similar settings. The anticolonial framework realizes the need to go beyond the notion that race and racism are "relatively autonomous" social phenomena. Instead, it acknowledges the irreducibility of race and racism to class and economic relations. It views race as an autonomous category that stands independent of other categories such as class and gender. At the same time, it sees race as interconnected and interdependent with those other categories in forming a common zone to resist oppression, racism, and colonialism (Gabriel and Ben-Tovin, 1978; Dei and Asgharzadeh, 2001).

Colonialism and racism inflict lifelong psychological pains and spirit injuries on the oppressed—the colonized. Colonialists, through their methods of writing and teaching, as well as through production, validation, and dissemination of knowledge, compel the colonized subjects to view themselves, their cultures, their languages, their ancestors, their histories, and their identities negatively. They teach the colonized to internalize the conditions of servitude and bondage. In essence, they enslave the colonized body's imagination, mental faculties, and modes of thinking (Fanon, 1961/1990, 1967; Memmi, 1969). Frantz Fanon, for instance, offers an original insight into the internalization of conditions of coloniality by the colonized. In *Black Skin, White Masks* (1967), he examines the psychological effects of colonialism and hegemony on both the colonized and the colonizer. His work explores the processes and ramifications of identity formation particularly for the colonized subjects. Fanon comes to the realization that colonialism will not end with the end of political and economic domination; it will end through the eradication of psychological dominance and mental bondage. Benefiting from Fanon's psychoanalytic insights, an anticolonial discourse will assist researchers in sorting out various colonialist and dominating methods that are embedded in the texts particularly written under colonial conditions.

By way of an anticolonial discursive framework we learn that there is no such thing as self-professed impartiality, nonpartisanship, and indifference; that "discursive practices are never neutral or apolitical" (Dei, 1999, p. 403); and that historical accounts and narratives "are shaped and socially conditioned by particular interests, histories, desires and politics" (Dei, 1999, p. 403). The knowledge gained through this insight enables us to interrogate conventional notions of objectivity, impartiality, and positivist methodology:

> The anti-colonial thought realizes the interlocking nature of various systems of oppression and rejects the privileging of any one single site over and above the others. Such a realization comes from the acknowledgement that our social lives are profoundly affected by relations of power and domination, which are oppressive and colonial by nature and which are products of a multiplicity of forces, structures, actions, ideologies, and beliefs. (Dei and Asgharzadeh, 2001, p. 311)

An anticolonial discursive framework is extremely important to this study for several reasons. First, it asserts the rights of colonized bodies/communities to self-identification and self-definition. This goes against hegemonic forms of identification that essentially and exclusively define the colonized subjects on the colonizer's terms. Rather than being defined by the colonizer, an anticolonial stance encourages the colonized bodies and communities to define themselves and to articulate their condition through their own voice. This is very important in an Iranian context particularly in the light of contested definitions and designations that exist about various nationalities and ethnic groups. Iran's Azerbaijani nationality, for instance, is identified under various names and titles that not only contest one another but even at times run counter to each other and contradict one another. Depending on who is assigning the designation, this particular nationality is identified under such terms as Azeris, Turks, Azeri-Turks, Iranian Azeris, Iranian Turks, Azerbaijanis, Azerbaijani Turks, and other combinations. Each designation has its own definition, history, and meaning whose articulation changes considerably from language to language, depending on who is doing the act of articulation (see also Asgharzadeh, 2002). The same contestations exist for the Arab nationality, which is variously referred to as Khuzistani, Arab, al-Ahvazi, Iranian Arab, Khuzistani Arab, and so on. An acknowledgment of the right to self-expression and self-definition will empower the subordinated groups to self-identify and self-designate their own identity. That is why so much emphasis has been placed on the ability to use one's own language to articulate one's own condition. As Bakhtin has astutely observed,

> The word in language is half someone else's. It becomes "one's own" only when the speaker populates it with his own intention, his own accent, when he appropriates the word, adapting it to his own semantic and expressive

intention. Prior to this moment of appropriation, the word does not exist in a neutral and impersonal language (it is not, after all, out of a dictionary that the speaker gets his words!), but rather it exists in other people's mouths, in other people's contexts, serving other people's intentions: it is from there that one must take the word, and make it one's own. (Bakhtin, 1981, pp. 293–294)

Second, an anticolonial discursive framework offers some basic theoretical and discursive means that make solidarity possible in the face of various class, gender, racial, and cultural differences. It seeks to provide a common zone of resistance and struggle against oppression and hegemony of imposed orders. This notion is also extremely important in that various communities in Iran, just like anywhere else, are fragmented along class, gender, ethnicity, language, and religion lines. A comprehensive theoretical and conceptual framework capable of providing a common zone of struggle for all (without privileging any single site of difference) is central for solidarity to take place. An anticolonial prism is very effective in this regard, because by not privileging any site and category above and over others, it has the potential to bring together various individuals, groups, and communities based on a common sense of lived/experienced oppression and the need for resistance.

Third, the anticolonial discursive framework celebrates certain aspects of indigenous culture and indigeneity as a whole in defiance of colonial paradigms and as a means to resist oppression, assimilation, and annihilation by encouraging the use of alternative knowledge, oral histories, literatures, and cultural products as counterparts to hegemonic forms of knowledge. This kind of empowerment is vitally important in an Iranian context where one language is constantly glorified as superior while other languages are demonized and criminalized. By revoking their own indigenous languages, histories, and cultures, the oppressed communities are provided with effective means to resist symbols of imposed culture and its discursive justification.

Fourth, an anticolonial discourse offers the means through which to identify, challenge, and subvert new and unknown hegemonic orders in the form of neocolonialism, imperialism, global capitalism, and so on, by constantly exposing relations of power and domination. This aspect is also significant in that, much like the rest of the south, the Middle Eastern societies are constantly penetrated, influenced, dominated, and abused by colonial and imperial powers. The never-ending conflicts in Palestine, recent interferences in Afghanistan and in Iraq are clear examples of forceful imperial intrusions into these regions. Like other Middle Eastern countries, Iran is no stranger to Western penetrations and influences. In the face of the constant external intrusions, an awareness of a plethora of colonial intentions, interests, and schemes is pivotal to designing effective means and strategies to resist and upset them. The anticolonial thought calls for the obtainment of such an awareness as well as the subsequent struggle and resistance.

Thus, by using an anticolonial discursive framework, this study aims to unravel the power relations in Iran's multiethnic, multicultural, and multilingual society along the lines of race, ethnicity, class, gender, religion, and, more importantly, language. In Iranian society, for over 80 years, the imposed order has sought to establish its hegemony by constantly humiliating, belittling, and gradually annihilating the culture and language of minoritized communities. An anticolonial vision permits us to challenge and expose that hegemony by celebrating the repressed indigenous values, cultural forms, and vernacular languages. An anticolonial stance is the most suitable stance to take when studying the multiple and multifaceted relations of power and domination in Iran in that it allows us to locate and critique the influence of external colonialism and imperialism in the form of economic and politicocultural impositions. Simultaneously, it enables us to interrogate the functioning of hegemony and colonial relations within Iranian society itself, which may or may not exist independently of global imperialist orders.

Antiracism Theory and Praxis

Antiracism theory is another discursive framework that informs all aspects of this work. In order to make an effective use of this theory, it is imperative that one understands two key concepts: race and racism. In the course of the past three centuries, definitions of the concept race have shifted from fixed biogenetic attributes to cultural/linguistic attributes to a social/political construct with real consequences. In the age of Enlightenment, the Industrial Revolution, expansion of capitalism, and scramble of European powers over "colonies," race came to be defined in terms of essentially fixed genotypical and phenotypical characteristics (see, e.g., Montagu, 1965).

The emergence and persistence of such schools of thought as biological determinism, Eugenicism, social Darwinism, and sociobiology were clear examples of the powerful impact of earlier biogenetic racist projects. Basically, this kind of racism saw biology as detrimental in establishing who is, and who can be, "superior" and who is genetically and biologically conditioned to be "inferior." Individuals were seen as unchangeable entities whose abilities, mental capacities, intellectual powers, cultural productions, and degree of civilization were determined by unalterable physiological and genetic factors. The white European and Caucasian races were assumed to posses superior genes while others had inferior genes that destined them to produce inferior cultures, languages, and civilizations (Gobineau, 1915/1967; Gunther, 1927; Hitler, 1925/1943).

The first half of the twentieth century was characterized by the rise and fall of Nazism and fascism in Europe, with the breaking up of colonial empires, as well as with the decolonization of India, of various parts of Africa and Asia. It was also marked by the struggle of oppressed and marginalized peoples of Africa, Asia, and America for self-determination, independence, and autonomous nationhood. Paralleling these struggles, similar resistances took place in various towns and cities of the United States of America, through the Civil Rights Movement, African-American people's struggle, and struggles of other marginalized groups such as the indigenous communities, women, and workers for equal rights, justice, and democracy. Out of these and many other struggles grew the intellectual interrogation and challenge of a concept of race seen as an essentially fixed biological category. More and more, the meaning of race came to be articulated in political, social, and historical terms (see, e.g., Cox, 1948). Following the theoretical contribution of Cox (1948) and many others, the socially constructed nature of race came to gain a wider recognition "so much so that it is now often conservatives who argue that race is an illusion" (Omi and Winant, 1993, p. 3).

As Dei has argued, race is a social relational category that may be defined "by socially selected physical characteristics" (Dei, 1999, p. 396; see also Dei, 1996), whereas ethnicity is defined more in terms of socially selected cultural characteristics. Race has relational, physiological, internal, external, and interactive components. Each of these components may be regarded as a site for domination and oppression on the basis of their real, perceived, or imagined distinctions. Lopez (1995) has identified four important features through which race is socially constructed:

> First, humans rather than abstract social forces produce races. Second, as human constructs, races constitute an integral part of a whole social fabric that includes gender and class relations. Third, the meaning-systems surrounding race change quickly rather than slowly. Finally, races are constructed relationally, against one another, rather than in isolation. (Lopez, 1995, p. 196)

Similarly, racism may be defined as a negative, dehumanizing, and oppressive view, attitude, behavior, and action toward members of another group. It "refers to oppressive behaviors, policies and attitudes ranging from institutionalized murder to unwitting support of insensitive practices by the well-intentioned" (Card, 1999, p. 258). Just as the meaning and definitions of race have been constantly changing from generation to generation, era to era, and across time and space, so too there has emerged different kinds of sophisticated racisms. Ranging from a variety of social, scientific, biological, institutional, linguistic, and cultural kinds, contemporary racisms are to be understood in terms of class, religion, culture, national affiliation, citizenship and the intersections of these diverse markers. As Fanon has pointed out, in its contemporary, sophisticated form, the primitive biological racism "that aspires to be rational, individual, genotypically and phenotypically determined, becomes transformed into cultural racism" (1967, p. 42).

Racism may be defined as a situation in which individuals, groups, communities, or institutions exercise abusive power over other human beings, or in any way inferiorize, subordinate, exploit, or exclude them on the basis of the following:

1. physiological differences: for example, skin color, hair texture, facial features, and racial heritage;
2. cultural differences: for example, language, customs, behavior, clothing, mode of dress, and eating habits;

3. ideological differences: for example, religion, political affiliation, and belief; and
4. geographical differences or differences in the place of birth: for example, Thirdworldian, Asian, African, Palestinian, and Latino.

Thus, a definition of racism/racist in this study includes the following categories:

- The individuals or groups who think of themselves as superior to others on the basis of their racial, ethnic, ideological, geographical, and cultural backgrounds engage in racist activities and are racist.
- Any individual, group, organization, or institution that denies equal access and opportunity to others on the basis of their real or perceived racial, ethnic, ideological, geographical, cultural differences engage in racist activities and is racist.
- Any individual, group, or institution that suppresses the others' language, religion, history, and culture engages in racist activities and is racist.

On the other hand, antiracism may be defined as an action-oriented vision seeking to challenge and subvert the imperialist, colonialist, and racist approaches of governments, corporations, institutions, groups, and individuals (Fanon, 1961/1990, 1967; Dei, 1996; Card, 1999; Dei and Calliste, 2000). Such a vision involves the processes of identifying, challenging, and eventually eliminating the individualistic, systemic, organizational, or governmental barriers to equity, equal access, and full development of every community's linguistic, cultural, socioeconomic, and spiritual needs. It is such a vision of antiracist theory that makes it all the more central to studies such as this one.

Throughout most of Iran's recent history, the majority of Iranians have been victims of racism and xenophobia. The dominant group, through its monopoly over texts, language, and means of expression, has not allowed for any meaningful investigation of the dehumanizing impact of racism on Iranian society. It thus becomes all the more urgent that various dehumanizing and evil aspects of racism be exposed and combated in Iran. As such, an antiracist stance ought to be a main entry point to any kind of social, political, cultural, and particularly ethnic/national research on Iran and Iranian society. Iranians have always coexisted within a mosaic of different ethnic, racial, cultural, religious, and linguistic groups and communities. It is, therefore, imperative that our vision for the future is based upon principles and epistemologies of antiracism theory and praxis. To this end, we ought to have a clear idea as to what racism is and what an antiracist stance entails. The fact that antiracist research is an action-oriented methodology enables the researcher to actively introduce this vision to his/her community of research and thereby contribute to the field of race and ethnic relations in pluralistic contexts such as the Iranian case.

Postcolonialism

In addition to anticolonial and antiracism discourses, this work is also informed by postcolonial theory particularly in areas concerning the rereading and reinterpretation of literary, educational, and historical texts. In making use of postcolonial theory, I particularly draw on the works of Edward Said, Homi Bhabha, and Gayatri Spivak as important figures in the field of post-colonial narration. While Fanon's valuable insights on decolonization and marginalization as reflected in *The Wretched of the Earth* (1961/1990) and *Black Skin, White Masks* (1967) is extremely helpful in analyzing the conditions that lead to internalization of colonialism and mental bondage, Said's *The World, the Text, and the Critic* (1983), *Orientalism* (1979), and *Culture and Imperialism* (1993) are important in dealing with notions of secular criticism, necessity of interpretation, representation and identity, as well as the Eurocentric construction of the Empire and the Orient, which also includes the crafting of a history for Iran.

Said's contribution to the field of postcoloniality is immense. His greatest contribution to the field comes through his groundbreaking work, *Orientalism*, first published in 1978, followed by *Culture and Imperialism*, published in 1993. Through these seminal works, Said looks at the complex web of relations of power, domination, and (mis)representation that colonialism and imperialism create. Drawing on Foucault's (1980) views on the power/knowledge nexus, and Gramsci's (1971) articulations of hegemony, he explores issues of represen-tation, domination, as well as resistance in colonial and postcolonial conditions. He interrogates the implications of cultural and discursive products such as works of literature, history, religion, poetry, landscape description, travel writ-ing, as well as academic writings and official documents in colonizing our imag-ination and maintaining the empire. *Orientalism* and *Culture and Imperialism* deal with the relationship between Orient and Occident in both colonial and postcolonial contexts by positing, among other things, the notion that there was no objective, neutral scholarship either on the Orient or the Middle East.

In a narrative employing instruments of historical, humanistic, and cultural research, Said interrogates the ways through which Western scholarship and the West in general has for centuries misrepresented the East and the Orient, through its discursive, intellectual, literary, as well as economic and colonial power. His work helps us to better understand how colonial powers colonize human imagination and understanding by their misrepresentation of the Other through literature, media, press, and various discursive methods, in such a way that freedom from the material and physical conditions of bondage will not, in and of itself, lead us to desired emancipation. In order to obtain any kind of emancipation, one has to, first and foremost, free oneself from mental, ideational, and perceptual bondage.

Said also contributes a great deal to our understanding of the role of lan-guage in representations of history, culture, and society. He questions the methods and discourses that present history and historical events as unques-tionable and irrefutable "truth." Said effectively demonstrates that such representations take place within the domain of language, which itself is contextualized within a real world, characterized by relations of economic, political, and ideological power. As he puts it in *Culture and Imperialism,*

> [T]he persistent disparity in power between the West and non-West must be taken into account if we are accurately to understand cultural forms like that of the novel, of ethnographic and historical discourse, certain kinds of poetry and opera, where allusions to and structures based on this disparity abound. (Said, 1993, p. 230)

Culture and Imperialism also allocates greater space to the articulation and analysis of "resistant literature." If literature of the dominant group plays a significant role in the maintenance of empire, marginalized literature could also play a parallel function in the dismantling of the same empire. The power of knowledge and language do not exclusively reside with the dominant. The marginalized "subaltern" can also use such power to articulate her/his position through her/his own words, and in so doing, disrupt the hegemonic version of representation and dismantle the discursive formations of domination. It is with such understanding of the power/knowledge nexus, and with the functioning of power in general, that Said discusses works of such southern writers as Frantz Fanon, Ngugi Wa Thiong'o, Salman Rushdi, Rabindranath Tagore, Pablo Neruda, and Chinua Achebe, highlighting their function as counternarratives vis-à-vis the canonical literature of empire.

In his collection of essays titled *The World, the Text, and the Critic* (1983), Said introduces the central concepts of "secular criticism" and "the worldliness of texts." The book collects Said's various essays on literary theory and future of criticism where he emphasizes the role of "critical consciousness" vis-à-vis the received ideas, conventional structures, and established ideologies. While manifesting his unwavering commitment to secularism, these concepts are also very important in situating texts of all sorts and kinds within the sociopolitical context of the milieu in which they are produced. Secularism and worldliness of texts are significant as well, in challenging various ideological/religious fundamentalisms that regard certain texts above and beyond criticism, interpretation, and rereading. For Said, all texts are produced within a web of interconnected social, political, economic, and humane relations, which do not allow them to be studied, interpreted, and analyzed independently of and in isolation from such relations. This is as true of works of literature as of various religious and ideological texts. Said makes it clear that no text stands above criticism, interpretation, rereading, and reevaluation, just as no individual, or group and class of individuals, holds monopoly over interpretation of texts of religion, literature, history, culture, and so on.

Similar to Fanon's work, Said's work teaches us to see how dominant groups colonize our imaginations and influence the way we interpret our world, view ourselves, and identify our colonizers. As such, it is imperative that we free ourselves not only from the material and physical conditions of bondage, but more importantly from mental, ideational, and perceptive bondages. This insight, of course, leads us directly to the importance of texts, discourses, and linguistic formations in the creation and maintenance of systems of power and domination. Given the significance of language and text in this study, Said's work provides important insights into my method of reading and interpreting various texts.

Homi Bhabha's work is also useful in articulating issues of marginality, hybridity, mimicry, and subalternity. His main text/collection titled *Nation and Narration* (1990), of which he is an editor as well as a contributor, is insightful particularly in dealing with issues of identity, nationality, nation, nation-statism, and their correlations with culture, language, discourse, and narration. In his work on "mimicry," for instance, Bhabha discusses the possibility of reading colonial literature as continuously "ambivalent," "split," and "unstable." He also shows that the image or idea of "the nation" cannot be separated from the nation's narration.

Bhabha's influential essay titled "Dissemination" (1990) interrogates the conventional articulations and definitions of "nation" that ignore the rich heterogeneity, diversity, discontinuity, lacks, elapses, and splits within nations. Instead, he argues that nations and cultures must be understood in terms of "narrative constructions" that are largely a result of heterogeneous, contested, and conflicting discourses of different groups and communities within nation-states and nation-spaces. As he puts it in *The Location of Culture* (1994),

> It is in the emergence of the interstices—the overlap and displacement of domains of difference—that the intersubjective and collective experiences of nationness, community interest, or cultural value are negotiated. How are subjects formed "in-between," or in access of, the sum of the "parts" of difference (usually intoned as race/class/gender, etc.)? . . . Terms of cultural engagement, whether antagonistic or affiliative, are produced performatively. The representation of difference must not be hastily read as the reflection of pre-given ethnic or cultural traits set in the fixed tablet of tradition. The social articulation of difference, from the minority perspective, is a complex, on-going negotiation that seeks to authorize cultural hybridities that emerge in moments of historical transformation. (Bhabha, 1994, p. 2)

Irrespective of its overemphasis on hybridity and fluidity, this kind of articulation is useful in critiquing a variety of literary, social, cultural, and historical works whose aim has been to "glorify" and reconstruct the nation, based exclusively on the values of a single ethnic group. Bhabha's narrative is insightful in deconstructing overly essentialist notions of nationhood, nationalism, nation-state, and the sense of identity that they engender. However, care must be taken that such deconstruction does not fall within a broader notion of "pluralities" and "hybridities" where "everything goes." Another advantage of using multiple theories in this study is in their ability to balance out each other's shortcomings. For instance, the use of anticolonial and antiracist theories allows research to be critical of such postmodernist notions as sweeping rejection of any kind of ethnic, national, racial, class, gender, cultural, and linguistic rootedness.

While it is important to acknowledge the contested and contingent aspects of identity formation, it is equally important to realize that categories such as ethnicity and nationality are not and cannot be totally arbitrary. They may be unfixed and contested; however, there are certain qualities to them that cannot be explained in terms of mere constructionism, hybridity, imagination, or choice. Dei (1999), for instance, has rightly emphasized the "saliency of skin color" in the processes of race-based identity formation. What this means is that certain bodies, individuals, groups, and communities do not have the luxury to deconstruct, change, transform, or ignore their already existing ethnic/racial identity. While a white American may have a wide variety of choices in selecting an identity, an African-American's choices are not so generous and may even be limited to a single identity: black. One has to realize that compulsory ethnic, racial, and cultural categories are imposed on individuals and groups by other members of society in the face of which the minoritized body is left with all but little choice to adopt a preferably advantageous form of identity.

Spivak's theories are also significant in deconstructing various racist texts particularly in view of her feminist-Marxist-deconstructionist approaches. Her unique interpretation of Derrida is also helpful in bringing Derrida's insight into the discussion. Her main work *In Other Worlds* (1987) may be used as a major point of referral particularly when she discusses the "subaltern studies" and the way they deconstruct India's conventional elitist historiography. Through her effectively useful essay, "Can the Subaltern Speak?" (1988), and a number of other articles, Spivak explores, indeed questions, the possibility of recovering voices of marginalized subjects within colonial literature. She wants to see whether it is possible to make that recovery and, if so, whether those voices have the potential for subversion and disruption. This kind of critique is important for this study particularly in light of the fact that much of it deals with analyzing "subaltern voices" as reflected in marginalized literature.

The central focus of my study is on reading, rereading, and analyzing of texts. To this end, the postcolonial theory is extremely important at least in three ways:

1. reading texts produced under colonial conditions;
2. reading texts produced by members of the dominant group; and
3. reading texts produced by members of the minoritized groups.

A different way of reading and analyzing texts is essential for this study, due to the centrality of language and appropriation of voice in colonial conditions. Theories of colonial and postcolonial discourses alert us to the way language constructs notions of superiority and inferiority. The dominant language compels the colonized to view the world through the lens of the colonizer. A juxtaposition of postcolonial theory and anticolonial discursive framework enables research such as this one to overcome certain aspects of postcolonial narrativizing that may not be entirely applicable to the Iranian context and vice versa.

CONCLUSION

The methods of research, analyses, and discussions in this book revolve around the following concepts: race, racism, language, Indo-Europeanism, Aryanism, nationalism, and nation-statism in an Iranian context. As noted earlier, I have carried out this research using multiple theories and discursive frameworks. Obviously, every discursive framework, school of thought, methodology, and paradigm has its own way of defining concepts and interpreting terminologies. And concepts, words, or terms get their meanings from the way they are situated within a linguistic system or a language. In other words, how we define a term or a concept is very much related to how that term or concept is contextualized within a text.

It is the textual/linguistic nature or the textuality of our understanding of the world that is at the core of social scientific analyses. In essence, our means of gaining access to what has been going on in the social world is made possible through text and language. Language plays a central role in the production of knowledge. It plays an equally important role in the perception, selection, validation, and presentation of knowledge products. In addition to its philological and etymological attributes, language provides narrators with an enormous pool of resources in terms of vocabulary, syntax, myths, rituals, folklore, poetry, and their interaction with culture, environment, society, and economy. It is from an amalgamation of all these that the basis of what is considered to be a legitimate, true, pure, or authentic ethnicity, nationality, language, nation, state, and other powerful categories are consolidated. In turn, such categories are used as powerful sites of exclusion, oppression, othering—and also resistance.

It, therefore, is of the utmost importance to allocate to language a central place when it comes to our comprehension of any given social phenomena. More than this, in this particular area of study, language has played a direct role in various processes of superiorization, inferiorization, minoritization, exclusion, and othering. Thus, various linguistic systems, linguistic components, concepts/terminologies, along with the language itself occupy an essential place in this work. As such, an understanding of these linguistic products is very important in the way the data and information are gathered and analyzed. The study makes use of a variety of techniques and insights provided by such research methods as critical discourse analysis and theoretical/discursive frameworks such as anticolonial thought, antiracism theory, and postcolonial theory to interpret the texts, concepts, terminologies, and linguistic components that are produced under relations of power and dominance. The use of these methodologies and theoretical frameworks has been crucial in reading, rereading, reinterpreting, and deconstructing various textual/linguistic products, while enabling the researcher to better understand and analyze the social reality within an Iranian context.

CHAPTER 3

Planting the Seeds of Racism:
Diversity and the Problematic of
Orientalist Historiography

*Unlike the historiography of other places and peoples, in our country, Iran,
historiography has developed in a quite catastrophic and for the most part
dishonest manner. . . . Just as today's Iran is home to a variety of nations, so
too had the ancient Iran been home for diverse nations. It is for this reason
that the obliteration and misrepresentation of Iran's ancient history is
tantamount to concealment, suppression, and misrepresentation of the
history of Iran's contemporary nations.*

(Mohammad Taqi Zehtabi, 1999, pp. 5–6)

NATION AND ITS CONSTRUCTION

In his *History of the Persian Empire*, A.T. Olmstead (1948) casts some light,
albeit extremely feeble and obscured, on the existence of Iran's pre-
Achaemenid indigenous peoples and their civilization. Although faithfully
following the conventional Eurocentric and Orientalist tradition, he does
dare to venture into the annals of forgotten histories and pay some lip
service to the lives and civilizations of peoples who existed prior to the
migration of Aryan/Indo-European tribes to "the great plateau."
Considering the existing "conspiracy of silence" on the topic by both
Orientalist and the official nationalist/local historiographies, Olmstead's
fleeting allusion to Iran's indigenous peoples is in itself a sort of risk taking,
and hence admirable:

> Long before the great plateau was called Iran it was well populated. Obsidian
> flakes have been found under the alluvial deposits from the last glacial period,
> while men of the late Stone Age left their flint implements in the open. By the
> fifth pre-Christian millennium, numerous tiny hamlets sheltered a peaceful
> agricultural population, which satisfied its aesthetic instincts through fine
> wheel-made pots decorated with superb paintings; an elaborate though lively
> conventionalization of native flora and fauna betrayed more interest for all
> subsequent art on the plateau. (Olmstead, 1948, p. 16)

Olmstead's colorful depiction of indigenous life on the plateau begs the questions: What happened to the indigenous populations of that great plateau after the arrival of the nomadic groups who later on came to be identified as Aryans, or Indo-Europeans? What happened to the civilizations, cultures, languages, arts, and artifacts that preexisted the Aryan tribes in the region? A lively rainbow of cultures, languages, races, and communities coexisting side by side for millennia surely cannot disappear into thin air. Or can it? If it cannot, then how is it that there is no mention of its existence in Iran's Orientalist, official, national, conventional, and elite historiography? Strangely enough, being vanished and banished from the official history is exactly what has happened in the case of Iran's pre-Achaemenid indigenous populations. The Orientalist historiography on Iran and its offshoot, the Iranian official, national, conventional, and elite historiography, have been deafeningly silent about the existence of the plateau's indigenous peoples, their cultures, languages, and civilizations. For this dominant pseudo historiography, the history of Iran starts with the history of Achaemenid dynasty (559–330 BC), and particularly with the adventures of its founder "Cyrus the Great" (580–530 BC), presumably the first Aryan king in the region.

The denial of Iran's pre-Achaemenid past has excluded indigenous non-Aryan histories from the region. In turn, this exclusion has culminated in the denial of difference and diversity in the country both historically and at the present time. And that is why an overview of Iranian historiography within the context of diversity is very important for this work. In essence, the denial of difference and diversity in the country begins with the acknowledgment of the Achaemenid dynasty as the starting point of Iran's official/national history. The historical denial of existence of diverse groups and communities on the Iranian Plateau has translated into the denial of their contributions to the making of Iran and its civilization. In effect, their contributions have been appropriated by the dominant nationalist and Orientalist historiography that seeks to accord the ownership of the entire country to one group alone: the Persians. An interrogation of this historical denial points to the relevance of historical constructions for the present situation, that is, for what is happening currently in terms of denials, appropriations, racism, and exclusion. The process of denying the contribution of non-Aryan groups to Iran's history was a conscious project that started from the early twentieth century for the sole purpose of assigning the ownership of Iran to the so-called Aryan race. It is therefore imperative to see how and why such a project was created, how it was implemented, what sources and material it has used, and what goals it has accomplished.

It is for the purpose of addressing some of these questions and concerns that I start this chapter with a discussion of the construction of an image of Cyrus the Great in the Old Testament, an ancient and influential source for later reconstructions. I then move on to brief discussions of Greek sources and Islamic historiography on Iran in order to show the existence of difference and diversity in ancient Iran as illustrated in these sources. Given the central place of Orientalism in reconstructing Iran's ancient history, a large portion of the chapter is allocated to the interrogation of Orientalist historiography on Iran.

CONSTRUCTION OF CYRUS AND PERSIA IN THE OLD TESTAMENT

The pre-Islamic historiographies of what is today called Iran consisted of oral accounts such as stories, narratives, myths, legends, epics, poetry, parables, and other forms of saying that passed on from generation to generation. Given the rich multiethnic and multilingual character of Iranian society, the oral narratives varied based on geography, locality, ethnicity, and, more significantly, language. After the introduction of Islam and Islamic civilization to the region in the seventh century, a major improvement took place in existing primitive writing systems, and important texts of religion, history, and literature such as the Zarathustrian holy book of Avesta, Dede Qorqud Kitabi, Khoday-nameh, and Ferdowsi's *Shahnameh* emerged in the new reformed script that incorporated segments of the surviving pre-Islamic narratives in the region.

The written sources of Iranian pre-Islamic historiography consisted of various inscriptions and cuneiforms that were mainly unearthed and partly deciphered in the twentieth century. Among these are the Urarto inscriptions in Azerbaijan, inscriptions belonging to the Achaemenid kings, as well as thousands of clay tablets, artworks, and handicrafts that have been discovered in such places as Hassanlu, Amlash, Marlik, Jiroft, Tappeh Yahya, Shush, Lorestan region, and various other places. Among these artworks and handicrafts, those belonging to the Achaemenid era have been given considerable attention by Orientalists and Western scholars; those belonging to pre-Achaemenid indigenous peoples of Iran have received very little or no attention (see also Zehtabi, 1999; Poorpirar, 2004). The languages used in the cuneiforms vary from the agglutinative language system of the ancient Elamites to Assyrian, Aramaic, Phrygian, Greek, and to what is termed Old Persian.

The important point to highlight in these cuneiforms is the variety of languages used and diversity of peoples depicted. Noteworthy also is the fact that the unearthing, translation, and interpretation of these cuneiforms have from the beginning been an Orientalist enterprise. In the course of the past two decades, many local Iranian scholars have increasingly become suspicious of the effectiveness of these inscriptions as valid sources of historical inquiry and have questioned the biases in their selection as well as the authenticity of their interpretation (Zehtabi, 1999; Poorpirar, 2001a, 2002, 2004).

One of the most important sources discussing some aspects of ancient Persia is the Old Testament. Actually, rather than Persia, it is Cyrus the Great who the Old Testament discusses in a glorifying manner. Persia is mentioned almost exclusively in relation to Cyrus and his adventures. Cyrus is the founder of the Achaemenid dynasty, at the time of whose ascendancy to power, the Jews of Israel had been persecuted by the Babylonians and were scattered all over Mesopotamia, including Persia. It is against such a backdrop that the Old Testament prophecies occur about the coming of a great warrior named Cyrus, who would emerge from the North with his army and restore the Jews back to Israel, defeating the Babylonians and building "the house of the LORD God of Israel . . . in Jerusalem":

> Now in the first year of Cyrus king of Persia, that the word of the LORD by the mouth of Jeremiah might be fulfilled, the LORD stirred up the spirit of Cyrus king of Persia, that he made a proclamation throughout all his kingdom, and put it also in writing, saying,
>
> Thus saith Cyrus king of Persia, The LORD God of heaven hath given me all the kingdoms of the earth; and he hath charged me to build him an house at Jerusalem, which is in Judah. Who is there among you of all his people? his God be with him, and let him go up to Jerusalem, which is in Judah, and build the house of the LORD God of Israel, (he is the God,) which is in Jerusalem. And whosoever remaineth in any place where he sojourneth, let the men of his place help him with silver, and with gold, and with goods, and with beasts, beside the freewill offering for the house of God that is in Jerusalem. (Ezra 1:1–4)

Thus Cyrus was charged with the task of building a house for the God of Israel in Jerusalem. It is extremely important to note that in the above passage, Cyrus is identified as the king of Persia. The Iranian historian Naser Poorpirar (2003) argues that at the time of Cyrus the term Persia was not in use yet and it was used for the first time by Darius I (522–5486 BC). Cyrus talks not of Persia but of a place called Anshan. "Logically, then, the Book of Ezra must have entered into the Old Testament after Darius" (Poorpirar, 2000, p. 187). The God of Israel even identifies Cyrus as His shepherd and performer of all His wishes:

> That confirmeth the word of his servant, and performeth the counsel of his messengers; that saith to Jerusalem, Thou shalt be inhabited; and to the cities of Judah, Ye shall be built, and I will raise up the decayed places thereof: That saith to the deep, Be dry, and I will dry up thy rivers: That saith of Cyrus, He is my shepherd, and shall perform all my pleasure: even saying to Jerusalem, Thou shalt be built; and to the temple, Thy foundation shall be laid. (Isaiah 44: 26–28)

It is noteworthy that these prophecies were made long before the time of Cyrus. Isaiah is believed to have prophesied around 700 BC, whereas Cyrus had conquered the city of Babylon in 539 BC (see also Wells, 1920/1931). So Isaiah was making these prophecies roughly one and a half centuries prior to Cyrus's birth. Moreover, at the time of Isaiah's writing, the city of Jerusalem was fully built and the entire temple was standing. It was more than a century later, in 586 BC, that Jerusalem and the Temple were destroyed by King Nebuchadnezzar. As such, how would Isaiah possibly know that a man named Cyrus will say to Jerusalem that it shall be built and that the Temple's foundation shall be laid? This discrepancy has led some scholars to argue that these portions of the book could not have been written by Isaiah but have been authored by other writers around the sixth century BC. "Because the book of Isaiah includes prophecies concerning events during and after the Exile, critical scholars generally attribute portions of the book to one, two, or more prophets in addition to Isaiah" (Myers, 1987, p. 531).

Cyrus is also entrusted with the task of "subduing nations":

> Thus saith the LORD to his anointed, to Cyrus, whose right hand I have holden, to subdue nations before him; and I will loose the loins of kings, to open before him the two leaved gates; and the gates shall not be shut; I will go before thee, and make the crooked places straight: I will break in pieces the gates of brass, and cut in sunder the bars of iron: And I will give thee the treasures of darkness, and hidden riches of secret places, that thou mayest know that I, the LORD, which call thee by thy name, am the God of Israel. For Jacob my servant's sake, and Israel mine elect, I have even called thee by thy name: I have surnamed thee, though thou hast not known me. (Isaiah 45: 1–4)

The God of Israel empowers Cyrus to accomplish all the above tasks without Cyrus's knowledge of it. In other words, these prophecies were made long before Cyrus was even born. The accurate realization of these biblical prophecies has led to major arguments among historians. In general terms, those believing in divinity and the sacredness of religious texts regard these prophecies as signs of authenticity of the Old Testament, in that the prophecies have come true exactly the way they were earlier prophesied (Price, 1899, p. 234). On the other hand, there are those such as the Iranian historian Naser Poorpirar (2000, 2001a) who cite these narratives as an act of reconstruction of a figure for broader political and cultural projects. These critics argue that the Semites were conscious of historical process and they sought to manipulate it to their advantage in historical and religious texts.

Most surprisingly, the Old Testament even talks about the practical aspect of preparing Cyrus for the task ahead:

> Then rose up the chief of the fathers of Judah and Benjamin, and the priests, and the Levites, with all them whose spirit God had raised, to go up to build the house of the LORD which is in Jerusalem. And all they that were about them strengthened their hands with vessels of silver, with gold, with goods, and with beasts, and with precious things, beside all that was willingly offered. Also Cyrus the king brought forth the vessels of the house of the LORD, which Nebuchadnezzar had brought forth out of Jerusalem, and had put them in the house of his gods; Even those did Cyrus king of Persia bring forth by the hand of Mithredath the treasurer, and numbered them unto Sheshbazzar, the prince of Judah. And this is the number of them: thirty chargers of gold, a thousand chargers of silver, nine and twenty knives, Thirty basins of gold, silver basins of a second sort four hundred and ten, and other vessels a thousand. All the vessels of gold and of silver were five thousand and four hundred. All these did Sheshbazzar bring up with them of the captivity that were brought up from Babylon unto Jerusalem. (Ezra 1:5–11)

Obviously, restoration of the Jewish people to Babylonia and the subduing of nations could not possibly take place without sufficient funding. Thus the

Old Testament directs the exiled Jewish people to provide the financial means for the rise of Cyrus, and facilitate the attack of his army on Babylonia. In the Book of Jeremiah, it is clearly expressed that "out of the north" will Cyrus's army come and destroy Babylonia (Jeremiah 50: 1–3, 9–10, 41–42). It is noteworthy that the emphasis here is on "the north." There is no mention of Persia or of Cyrus being the king of Persia. The passage prophesies that some-one will come from the north, with cruel armies and ruthless fighters, and will destroy Babylon. This "north," according to Poorpirar (2000, 2001a), cannot be Persia. It must be somewhere in Central Asia and the Steppes of southern Russia from which this cruel force comes. According to this interpretation, the subjugation of Persia takes place after the subduing of Babylonia by Cyrus, not the other way around. The passages just quoted show the extent to which the Old Testament was instrumental in channeling the knowledge about Cyrus, the Achaemenid, and ultimately Persia to the Greeks, Christians, and, by extension, the entire world. As mentioned earlier, this knowledge has been approached with caution and its accuracy has often been questioned:

> The account which the Jewish Prophets give of the Persians of those times is, in general, a very favorable one; but we have to be on our guard not to accept as fact all that we read in their books respecting Persia and her people. The tolerance and kindness displayed by Cyrus the Great and certain of his successors towards the Jews make it the less surprising that they should have spoken well of the Persians and have remained faithful to them for so long. (Lockhart, 1953, p. 326)

Notwithstanding the positive image of Cyrus projected through the Old Testament, many historians and scholars continue to emphasize Cyrus's negative, "bloodthirsty," and antihumane character (Zehtabi, 1999; Poorpirar, 2000, 2001a, 2002–2005). Poorpirar argues that Cyrus was glorified by the Old Testament because he was, in effect, created and financed by the Jews to overthrow the rulers of Babylonia and return the Jews to Jerusalem. Poorpirar (2002–2005) vehemently rejects the idea that Cyrus was a Persian king, arguing instead that he was a warlord belonging to the Khazar and Islavic tribes of the north. The Greek historian Herodotus's account of Cyrus's death also serves to confirm the idea that Cyrus was not as friendly, humane, and passionate a figure as the dominant literature makes him out to be.

According to Herodotus, when Cyrus intends to capture the lands of Massagetai north of the Araz (Araxes) River, Tomyris, the queen of Massagetai advises him to reconsider such a decision and return back to his lands without any bloodshed. She also warns Cyrus that if he refuses her offer, "I swear by the sun, the sovereign lord of the Massagetai, bloodthirsty as you are, I will give you your fill of blood" (Herodotus, *Histories*, I.214). Cyrus pays no attention to Queen Tomyris's message. At this point,

> Tomyris, when she found that Cyrus paid no heed to her advice, collected all the forces of her kingdom, and gave him battle. . . . First, the two armies stood

apart and shot their arrows at each other; then, when their quivers were empty, they closed and fought hand-to-hand with lances and daggers; and thus they continued fighting for a length of time, neither choosing to give ground. At length the Massagetai prevailed. The greater part of the army of the Persians was destroyed and Cyrus himself fell, after reigning nine and twenty years. Search was made among the slain by order of the queen for the body of Cyrus, and when it was found she took a skin, and, filling it full of human blood, she dipped the head of Cyrus in the gore, saying, as she thus insulted the corpse, "I live and have conquered you in fight, and yet by you am I ruined, for you took my son with guile; but thus I make good my threat, and give you your fill of blood." (Herodotus, *Histories*, I.214)

Not surprisingly, the Persian sources glorifying Cyrus's life and achievements never mention the way he dies at the hand of Queen Tomyris. They cite Herodotus's narratives to validate various aspects of Cyrus's life, but when it comes to this important passage about his death, they all but forget to mention it, replacing Herodotus's account of Cyrus's death with various colorful narratives of their own imagination. Be as it may, two important questions to be posed are: Why so much emphasis on Cyrus and the Achaemenid? Out of Iran's over 6,000 years of history, why focus on this particular era?

The Semitic and Greek sources focused on Cyrus for their own reasons. The Old Testament glorified him because of the positive relationship that he had with the Jews. And the Greek sources focused on him mainly because it was during his reign that the Greeks came in contact with Iran and the Persian world. Because of his insatiable desire to subjugate other peoples and their lands, Cyrus occupied Lydia in 546 BC, followed by his capturing of the cities of the Ionian Confederacy in Asia Minor. This brought the Greeks in close contact and confrontation with Cyrus and his army for the first time, thus triggering a whole genre of narratives engendered around Persia.

Thus, such Greek writers as Herodotus, Thucydide, Xenophon, and Strabo tried to make sense of who the inhabitants of what is today known as Iran were, what languages they spoke, what kind of gods they worshipped, what kind of political systems they had, and how they viewed the world. Although the narratives of these writers are for the most part fictional and lack serious authentic observation or analysis, they have nonetheless been used and referenced by generations of writers and historians in crafting a history for Iran's inhabitants:

The Persian nation contains a number of tribes . . .: the Pasargadae, Maraphii, and Maspii, upon which all the other tribes are dependent. Of these, the Pasargadae are the most distinguished; they contain the clan of the Achaemenids from which spring the Perseid kings. Other tribes are the Panthialaei, Derusiaei, Germanii, all of which are attached to the soil, the remainder—the Dai, Mardi, Dropici, Sagarti, being nomadic. (Herodotus, *Histories*, I.125)

Noteworthy is also the Greek historian Xenophon's (c. 430–c. 355 BC) book titled *Cyropaedia*, which offers a romantic and for the most part imaginary account of the education of Cyrus the Great. In fact, the Cyrus character plays a central role in popularization of what became known as Persia. Almost all the information on Persia in Greek sources starts after the emergence of a Cyrus character, his establishment of the Achaemenid dynasty in the middle of the sixth century BC, and his numerous pillages and conquests in the region and beyond. Many local and international scholars have questioned, critiqued, and interrogated reconstruction of the image of Persia and Persian in many classical texts such as the narratives of Herodotus or the information found in the accounts of the Assyrian kings. For instance, in his important work entitled *The Decline of Iranshahr*, Peter Christensen (1993) reminds us that

> we must keep in mind the limitations of these sources. Often they have been accorded great authority, as if their every word was well thought out and every single detail carefully checked. In fact the authors were not especially well-informed and inflated their accounts with rumors and various stereotypes. . . . The authors' exaggeration and their Hellenocentric selection of data are not the only difficulties. The way in which the image of Persia was put together also raises methodological problems. (Christensen, 1993, pp. 23–24)

An important methodological problem for this kind of historiography is perhaps the way an image of a vast region of the globe with diverse populations, cultures, languages, and ways of life was portrayed as being represented by the image of a single ethnic group—Pars/Persian. (The province of Pars being the center of Achaemenian power, the Greeks named the entire geography under the Achaemenids as Persia and their inhabitants as Persians.) This was a major methodological and ethical error that later on proved to be devastating for non-Persian ethnic groups and nationalities particularly after the Orientalist reconstruction of Iran's history starting more vigorously from the early twentieth century.

CLASSIC PERSIAN SOURCES AND EARLY SIGNS OF ETHNOCENTRISM

Before we begin to look at the impact of European racist ideas on Iranian nationalists, it is worth noting that nationalistic and Fars-centric ideas have not been strange to Iran's history prior to the infiltration of racist ideas from Europe and elsewhere. We can see the tracks of ethnocentric Persian views in such historical texts as the holy book of Avesta and the *Shahnameh* of Ferdowsi. An examination of the Avesta and *Shahnameh* is extremely important not just for historical reasons but for the significance that they have for the present. The way they are read and interpreted in the present by the dominant group to otherize non-Persians represents a useful methodological example of an anachronistic reading of works of history and literature. That is to say, the dominant group interprets these classic texts based on contemporary notions of race, nationality, border, and nation-state; it then uses such interpretation to legitimize its privileged position.

Zarathustra and the Holy Book of Avesta

The Avesta is a written source believed to have survived from the pre-Islamic era. Notwithstanding the current debate about the authenticity of the existing version of Avesta (Zehtabi 1999; Poorpirar 2001a, 2001b, 2002–2005), this holy book contains many important passages that bear witness to the rich multiethnic, multilingual, and multicultural character of the pre-Islamic Iranian society. In fact, both the Avesta and *Shahnameh* depict vivid accounts of the diverse makeup of Iran's pre-Islamic inhabitants. Zarathustra (630–553, or 628–551, or 618–541 BC) is said to be an Iranian prophet who lived and died in northwestern Iran during the sixth- and seventh century BC (Jackson 1899; Zehtabi, 1999). As Jackson puts it, "Oriental tradition seems to be fairly correct in assigning, as his native land, the district of Atropatene or Adarbaijan, to the west of Media, or even more precisely the neighborhood about Lake Urumiah" (1899, p. 17). The Avesta contains two kinds of distinct teachings: the *Gaths* and the *Yashts*. The Gaths are believed to be what remains of Zarathustra's original doctrines, whereas the Yashts are understood to have been added to the Avesta long after Zarathustra's death (see also Gershevitch, 1967).

Some scholars have distinguished the authentic and inauthentic segments of the Avesta by identifying it as a book containing two distinct religious doctrines: Zarathustrianism and Zoroastrianism. By Zarathustrianism, they refer to the original religion of the indigenous peoples of Azerbaijan and Ekbatan, founded by Prophet Zarathustra, a man who was one of those indigenous people who spoke their language, and who lived among them (Zehtabi, 1999). By Zoroastrianism, they refer to doctrines developed by Indo-European-Persian races, who were not Zarathustrian themselves but who usurped and fabricated the original teachings of Zarathustra during the Sasanid dynasty. This process of usurpation and fabrication of original Zarathustrianism has been referred to as Zoroastrianization of Zarathustra (see also Gershevitch, 1967). At the time of Zarathustrianism's prominence in Azerbaijan, the Indo-European "Persians thought of themselves as Mazdah-worshippers, not as Zarathustrians" (Gershevitch, 1967, p. 16). Zarathustra's name appears nowhere in the records left behind by the most ancient Persian dynasty, the Achaemenians (550–330 BC). Conversely, in original Avesta texts, there is no sign indicative either of Achaemenians or their vast empire (see also Gershevitch, 1967; Yarshater, 1985).

Avesta's Antidemonic Law

In the Avesta there is a section titled "Videvdat" (Vendidad by some accounts) or the "Law against Demons." There can be little doubt that the Avesta had borrowed these segments from the rituals and traditions of indigenous peoples in the region. In ancient Azerbaijan's shamanist tradition, all natural disasters such as earthquakes, floods, and storms, were regarded as demonic forces that sought to destroy humans and their means of livelihood. Moreover, the inhabitants of northern parts of Iran were constantly threatened by other human enemies as well. According to Shamanist tradition, the threats and catastrophes could be prevented by rites and rituals of aversion (Zehtabi, 1999). It is some of these prayers that Videvdat has recorded:

> Perish, demon fiend! Perish, demon tribe! Perish, demon-created! Perish, demon-begotten! In the north shall you perish! (Videvdat 10:9, 19:43; see also Olmstead, 1998, p. 18)

There are also prayers against various illnesses:

> Thee, Sickness, I ban; thee, Fever, I ban; thee, Death, I ban; thee, Evil-Eye, I ban. (Videvdat 8:21, 20:7; see also Olmstead, 1998, p. 18)

Building upon the existing tradition and culture, in the original Avesta, *div*, or demon would mean whatever was against the welfare and happiness of human beings. As Zarathustrianism advances, at some stage in its history Div comes to be synonymous with whoever opposed the Truth, which also meant the doctrines of Zarathustrianism. In its original form, there were no implicit or explicit racial and cultural biases intended by Videvdat. Zarathustrianism claimed to be a universal religion that favored no one particular race and group over another. It never intended to demonize one race and glorify another.

However, after the addition of the section known as Yashts, the notions of impartiality and universalism all but vanished (see also Gershevitch, 1967). It is in these added sections that the Aryan/Indo-European races are depicted to be favored by Ahura-Mazda, the God of Goodness, Truth, and Light. All non-Aryan, non-Indo-European, non-Persian races are demonized, converted to divs and evils who fought alongside the Ahriman against Ahura-Mazda, whom the Aryans alone defended (see, e.g., Yashts 5:37, 13:61, 15:27, 19:56; Yasnas 9:10, 11:7). Yasht 9:18, for example, depicts the famous Turanian King Afrasiyab as a worthless thief who is slain by Kai Khosrau:

> Frangrasyan [Afrasiyab], from his cleft in the earth swam across Vouru-kasha in a vain attempt to steal the "farr" [the Magnificent Royal Glory] that bestowed permanent sovereignty. Captured and bound by a loyal vassal, he was brought to be slain by the Kavi Haostravah [Kai Khosrau]. (Yashts 9:18, 19:56; Yasna 11:7)

Like any other religious book, the Avesta contains stories, heroes, and villains. And like any other text, the heroes of the Avesta are drawn from the tales, legends, stories, and actual struggles that characterize all human societies. In the original text of Avesta, as well as in the section known as the Gaths, it appears that Zarathustra has carefully chosen his legends, heroes, and villains from the existing narratives among various races. From the Gaths we can see that the original text has not given preference to any particular race in terms of selecting their legends and heroes. Not only are the names of heroes equally selected from the legends of various races, but more importantly they have been molded into the story in a nonracial fashion; we can see a mixture of heroes from various races fighting side by side against a variety of villains from different races, including the race of heroes in the opposing camp. There are both heroes and villains from each and every one of the races on the side of both good and bad.

However, with the doctoring of the original Avesta and the introduction of Yashts into it, the impartial picture fundamentally changes to the advantage of Aryan/Indo-European elements, where members of non-Aryan races become divs, demons, villains, and supporters of darkness. The Aryans/ Indo-Europeans, on the other hand, become the custodians of light, goodness, and Ahura-Mazda (see, e.g., Yashts 5:29, 5:16, 5:37, 13:87, 5:21; see also Zehtabi, 1999, pp. 750–760). In the words of Jackson, the "inveterate foe and mortal enemy of Vishtaspa, however, is Arejat-aspa (Arjasp), or the infidel Turk, as later history would have styled him" (1899, p. 103). In later Persian texts, particularly in Ferdowsi's *Shahnameh*, the fight between Aryans and demons takes more vivid forms, as the Aryans openly kill and destroy the divs.

Ferdowsi and His Shahnameh

Ferdowsi's *Shahnameh* is the greatest epic poem of the Farsi language. It is a history of Persian kings, imaginary and real, in rhyme. Many Persian nationalists and even scholars have considered the epos as the document of Iranians' national identity (Meskoob, 1992). The word *Shahnameh* literarily means the Book of Kings. Its theme is an imaginary story of Fars/Persian race and its rulers, from the very beginning up to the Islamic-Arabic overthrow of the Sasanid dynasty in the seventh century. From a historical viewpoint, perhaps the most salient defect of the book is the absence of Median, Achaemenian, and Ashkanian kings (see also Yarshater, 1985). In effect, with the exception of some allusions to the Sasanid kings, particularly the last of them, Yazdgerd, the names and events depicted in the book bear no resemblance to peoples, histories, and stories of the Iranian Plateau. Despite this, it has played a most important role in the construction of a national identity for the Persians, an identity that has masqueraded as the national identity of all Iranians, regardless of their different ethnic, linguistic, and cultural backgrounds.

In composing the epic, Ferdowsi has been influenced by a group of "patrons" who have in effect sponsored the compilation of the *Shahnameh*. According to Ferdowsi, these patrons provided the stories for him and asked him to put the narratives in a rhyming, poetic format. In exchange for his labor, they promised to financially support him (Poorpirar, 2004, p. 7; see also Warner and Warner, 1905, pp. 108–112). Dismissing any claim for originality and authenticity, Ferdowsi asserts that the story was compiled by others and all he had to do was to put it together in a poetic style. Completed on February 25, AD 1010, it took 30 years for Ferdowsi to complete the *Shahnameh*. The result was the glorification and superiorization of his own Persian race, culture, and language at the expense of non-Persian and non-Aryan races. How much of such Fars-centric narrative was the creation of Ferdowsi's fertile imagination and how much the demand of his patrons remains a subject of debate and controversy (Poorpirar, 2000, 2004).

Ferdowsi's mythical history of the Persian race begins with the reign of Keyumers, the first king of imaginary "Pishdadiyan" dynasty. According to Ferdowsi, around the seventeenth century BC, Keyumers and his tribe lived on mountains. They were not familiar with the art of house building and dwelling on the ground. Nor did they know the art of dress making and clothing; they wore leopard skins:

> The lord was Keyumers, who dwelt upon a mountain
> There his throne and fortune rose
> He and all his troops wore leopard-skins
> Under him the learning began
> For food and dress were new to them
> (Ferdowsi, 1010/1960, p. 28;
> see also Warner and Warner, 1905, p. 118)

Thus, the founder of the first Indo-European-Persian civilization, who lived some 3,700 years ago upon a mountain, knew nothing of urban dwelling, clothing, agriculture, and so on (for a detailed account of this see Zehtabi, 1999, pp. 403–410).

From the remnants of pre-Achaemenid civilizations we know that seven millennia prior to arrival of the first Indo-European nomads to what is now known as Iran the indigenous peoples there knew the art of agriculture, animal husbandry, house building, dress making, and so on. It is important to note how Ferdowsi and his Orientalist/nationalist interpreters appropriate the existing knowledge to the advantage of Ferdowsi's imaginary race:

> In the whole world Keyumers had not an enemy
> Except the ill-mannered wicked Ahriman
> He had a son too, like a savage wolf
> Grown fearless, amongst great warriors
> (Ferdowsi, 1010/1960, p. 28;
> see also Warner, p. 119)

The Lord Keyumers had no enemy, says Ferdowsi, except for the indigenous people and their ruler who dwelt on the ground and to whom Ferdowsi refers as Ahrimasns, divs, and demons. According to Ferdowsi, the demon ruler of the indigenous people had a son, just like Keyumers. The Lord Keyumers's son Siyamak comes down with his troops to destroy the Div's son:

> He gathered troops, arrayed himself in leopard skin
> For he had no mail nor knew anything of the art of war

So here too we see that the son of "the Lord of World" had no clothing, no weaponry, and knew nothing of the art of war:

> When host met host the warrior challenged the div
> Siyamak came with neither uniform nor armors

And grappled with the son of the Demon
That horrible Black Div clutched at
Bent down that prince of lofty stature
And rent him open. Thus died Siyamak.
(Ferdowsi, 1010/1960p. 30;
see also Warner, p. 120)

Hearing the news of Siyamak's death at the hands of "the Black Div," the Lord of the World Tehmuras comes to avenge the young demon prince:

The illustrious world-lord Tehmuras
Advanced girt up for battle and revenge
There were the roar of flame and reek of divs
Here were the warriors of the lord of earth
(Ferdowsi, 1010/1960, p. 37;
see also Warner, p. 127)

Tehmuras defeats the demons and attempts to kill them. But the divs offer to teach Tehmuras new knowledge in exchange for their lives:

The captives bound and stricken begged their lives
"Kill us not," they said
"And we will teach thee a new fruitful art"
(Ferdowsi, 1010/1960, p. 38;
see also Warner, p. 127)

Tehmuras agrees:

He gave them quarter to learn their knowledge
When they were released they had to serve him
(Ferdowsi, 1010/1960, p. 38;
see also Warner, p. 127)

And the divs teach their knowledge, languages, ways of life, and culture to "the Aryan Lord" and his people:

They taught the Shah how to write
They enlightened his mind and heart with knowledge
They taught him to write not in one but in thirty languages
Such as the Roman, Persian, Arabic
Sughdi, Chini, Pahlavi and whatever language that was heard of
(Ferdowsi, 1010/1960, p. 38;
see also Warner, p. 127)

Thus, following the Indo-European tradition before him, Ferdowsi identifies the indigenous peoples of Iran as divs and demons. However, even in his capacity to demonize, he is still forced to admit that these so-called demons were far more knowledgeable and resourceful than his Aryan shahs and their armies. The divs know how to read and write. They speak not one or two but thirty languages—another testimonial to the multilingual character of the region—they know how to cultivate the land and domesticate the animal, whereas the supposedly superior Aryan race of Ferdowsi knows none of these and lives on mountaintops. Ferdowsi's account clearly indicates that the real or perceived Aryan tribes, at the time of their arrival to Mesopotamia, were indeed backward compared to the indigenous peoples living there.

Notwithstanding the demonization of non-Aryan/non-Indo-European peoples in the Avesta and *Shahnameh*, the fact remains that pre-Islamic Iran was a rich multiethnic, multicultural, and multilingual society. The Avesta and *Shahnameh* attest to such diversity even in their depiction of different ethnic groups as divs and demons. The diverse nature of pre-Islamic Iran is a fact that even some Western scholars are beginning to acknowledge:

> In the first place, Iranshahr lacked uniformity. The lands under Persian domination differed from each other in their ethnic composition, geographic features, and patterns of subsistence. In Mesopotamia the mass of population spoke Syriac as late as the 10th century. In Khuzistan the inhabitants retained their own language, *Khuzi*, though they usually spoke Arabic or Persian as well. On the plateau, where Arabic never achieved a serious foothold, people spoke different languages and dialects. Their conversion to Islam and to the use of standard Persian were prolonged processes; in fact the latter is not yet completed. Thus in pre-modern times the uniform and unifying "Persian-Muslim culture" was largely confined to a small elite. (Christensen, 1993, p. 17)

And regarding the pre-Achaemenid civilization of Elam, Walther Hinz concluded that

> [a]s far back into the past as the historian's gaze can penetrate, the constitution of Elam appears to have been federal. Only as a federation was it possible for an empire to hold together a territory which was made up of utterly different components, namely the plain of Susiana on the one hand, and the mountain ranges and high valleys of Anshan—the modern Bakhtyari district—on the other. However, it was not only in the interest of the ruler, but also of the people of Elam to live in an empire uniting the fruitful agricultural plains of the lowlands with the mountainous regions of the north and east, which were rich in timber, stone and metal. It was precisely in this union that Elam had the advantage over Mesopotamia. (Hinz, 1964–1973, pp. 3–4)

Following the introduction of Islamic civilization to the region in the seventh century, a new Islamic historiography emerged containing an enormous corpus of works of history, geography, ethnography, travel-writing, and other genres produced by such prominent scholars as al-Tabari, Ibn al-Faqih, Ibn Rusteh, Al-Mas'udi, Ibn Khaldun, al-Istakhri, Ibn Howqal, al-Muqaddasi, and Ibn Battuta. As far as the historians' observations and experience of various places that they visited are concerned, these Islamic writers produced sensible histories of the people and places they met. For instance, the tenth century Arab traveler al-Muqaddasi observed that "over 70 languages were spoken in Azerbaijan," which was considered to be a part of the Iranian Plateau (1906, p. 260). Ibn Howqal, another tenth-century Arab historian determined the number of languages spoken in Azerbaijan and Caucasia to be "360 spoken languages" (1966, p. 82). It is not surprising then to see a certain Caucasian mountain referred in Arabic sources as "Jabal al-Alsana" or "the Mountain of Languages" (see also Ibn Howqal, 1966). This goes to show that many languages were spoken in ancient Azerbaijan, and by extension in Persia or Iran.

Notwithstanding the rich linguistic and ethnic diversity, following the Greek tradition, the region was identified in the majority of Arab sources as "amlak al-Fars" (the lands of Fars/Persia/Persians). For instance, the tenth-century Arab historian, Al-Mas'udi, describes the Persians as follows:

> A people whose borders are the Mahat Mountains and Azerbaijan up to Armenia and Aran, and Bayleqan up to Darband, and Ray and Tabaristan and Masqat and Shabaran and Jorhan and Abarshahr, and that is Nishabur, and Herat and Marv and other places in the land of Khorasan, and Sistan and Kerman and Fars and Ahvaz. . . . All these lands were once one kingdom with one sovereign and one language. (Al-Mas'udi, 1967, pp. 191–192)

A problematic aspect about this kind of blanket generalization is that the borders and nationalities were at the time identified by the dynasties and kings who ruled over them, not by the masses who occupied the land and were ruled over. In other words, the identity of the ruling dynasty, clan, or family was given also to the populations under their rule, regardless of whether these peoples' identity actually coincided with that of the rulers or not. Thus, if the same Persian king was ruling over a territory in Azerbaijan, Georgia, or Armenia, that territory was often referred to as Persia and its inhabitants as Persians, regardless of their original ethnic and racial background. Many modern historians and writers have overlooked this simple fact as they try to offer an anachronistic reconstruction of Persian nationality and history. This kind of reconstruction made it much easier for the dominant group to consolidate its hegemony over non-Persian ethnic groups through adherence to claims of authenticity, originality, and historical ownership. By and large, Al-Mas'udi's above testimony clearly indicates the extent to which a large segment of the Islamic historiography of ancient Iran is unreal and superficial. For the most part, these historians relied on Greek and other sources whose authenticity was in question.

EUROPEAN CONNECTION AND THE ORIENTALIST HISTORIOGRAPHY

Added to the already existing rich and diverse literature on Iran is the Orientalist body of works that started to emerge in the eighteenth century, reached its peak around the mid-twentieth century, and still continues with its agenda and politics of misrepresentation. Included in this corpus of writing are works of many Western scholars, missionaries, statesmen, and travelers who have mainly concerned themselves with Iran's supposedly "superior" pre-Islamic past, with discursive construction of such absurd notions as "the Aryan race," and with the fashioning of a history for Iran and its inhabitants. Irrespective of the existence of some 7,000-year-old civilization on the Iranian Plateau, the dominant Indo-European/Orientalist historiography has discouraged any meaningful research on pre-Achaemenid histories and civilizations of Iran's diverse inhabitants. The remnants of written manuscripts and historical records from that era are largely ignored, allegedly because of "incomprehensibility of their language" (see also Sayce, 1885; Field, 1939). The only comprehensible reason behind such a disinterest must lie in the fact that Iran's indigenous peoples such as the Elamites spoke non-Indo-European, non-Aryan languages, and admission of this fact is in sharp contrast with the Aryanist project that for centuries has sought to claim that civilization in the world originated from the Aryans (see, e.g., Rendal, 1889; Childe, 1926). More than half a century ago, the prominent Orientalist scholar and historian A.T. Olmstead, on the construction of Iran's ancient history, and the Achaemenid Empire in particular, concluded,

> Through these years a new picture of the Achaemenid Empire has gradually emerged. As a result of recent excavations, the prehistoric cultures of the Iranian plateau are now known; one of the most important excavations, that near Persepolis itself, was the work of the Oriental Institute, and the final synthesis of the results of all these excavations was made here by my most recent candidate for the doctorate. Another candidate has brought together the written documents for the pre-Achaemenid history of Iran. Thus we now possess a fairly adequate background for the special period to which this book is to be devoted. (Olmstead, 1948, p. xii)

By "this book" Olmstead (1948) means his seminal work entitled *History of the Persian Empire*, which has been a major source of reference to many Iranian and non-Iranian historians. On the role of "the Oriental Institute" in crafting a history for Iran, Olmstead's testimony is self-explanatory enough, and in the light of this testimony, perhaps it is high time to pose the question: to what extent is Iranian history really Iranian? This is a very significant question that has been recently addressed by such visionary local historians of Iran as Naser Poorpirar. Evidently, there is more to the question than meets the eye. Implicit within it are notions of relevancy and irrelevancy of Orientalist methods used in Iranian historiography modeled on Western modes of research, analysis, interpretation, and representation. Explicit in such historiography is also the obvious exclusion of the non-Aryan, non-Persian elements along with the subaltern strata, that is, the oppressed masses, women, workers, peasants, and the historically silenced groups.

In a recent work titled *The Great American Plunder of Persia's Antiquities: 1925–1941*, Mohammad Gholi Majd (2003) chronicles in great detail the handling of Iran's archaeological heritage and art treasures by European and American institutions, scholars, missionaries, and Orientalists. He notes that with "the advent of the Pahlavi dynasty in 1925, Persia was rapidly opened up to foreign archaeologists" in such a way that Erich F. Schmidt of the University of Pennsylvania referred to the country in 1931 as "a virginal archaeological paradise" (Majd, 2003, p. 7). Meanwhile, the Oriental Institute of the University of Chicago expressed its satisfaction with the way "the plundering of Persia's antiquities" continued. In a letter to the Iranian government, dated July 20, 1934, the institute stated,

> The Oriental Institute would express herewith its pleasure in maintaining cordial cooperation with the Persian government in carrying out its great scientific responsibilities which are of deep interest to the whole world. At the same time attention must be called to the fact that the Oriental Institute has rendered the Persian government very notable services and made discoveries which have attracted universal attention to Persia throughout the civilized world. The most important journals of Western civilization have published full accounts of these great discoveries which have for the first time restored to the modern Persians the vanished glories of their ancestors. (Cited in Majd, 2003, p. 164)

It is interesting to note how the letter emphasizes the Oriental Institute's role in attracting the entire world's interest in Persia. By the entire world of course it is meant the Western "civilized world." And these findings were significant for the civilized world because the way they were deciphered and interpreted served to secure a prehistoric origin for the supposedly Aryan ancestors of the white Nordic race. The letter also highlights the fact that the most important journals of the Western world are offering coverage for the Orientalist interpretations of Iran's history and archaeology. Through these publications, Western journals sought to restore to the modern Persians "the vanished glories of their ancestors." This testimony alone suffices to show the degree to which the Oriental Institute was instrumental in crafting a history for Iran's diverse populations. Instead of emphasizing heterogeneity and diversity, however, they singled out a certain ethnic group as the sole founder of civilization on the plateau. We can only now have a clear understanding of the many ramifications that such a biased reconstruction has had for Iran's non-Persian communities. Before turning to these ramifications, it is important to briefly discuss the views and works of some influential Oriental scholars.

Sir William Jones and After

Although the existence of some kinds of similarities among various European languages were occasionally alluded to from time to time prior to the eighteenth century, it was the English judge Sir William Jones (1746–1794) who for the first time spelled out in 1786 the resemblance among Sanskrit, Persian, Latin, Greek, and certain other languages. Sir William Jones was born in 1746 in London. He was the scholar in the classical sense of the word: in addition to being a judge and a legal expert, he was also a poet, a polyhistor, a classicist, and an outstanding Oriental scholar who had mastered Arabic, Persian, and Hebrew. In 1783, he was appointed to a judgeship on the Bengal Supreme Court in India. On arrival in Calcutta, among other tasks and preoccupations, he vigorously took up the study of Sanskrit, the language of ancient Indian religious and literary texts. In January 1784, he founded the Asiatic Society of Bengal and was elected as its first president. As Said puts it, this society "was to be for India what the Royal Society was for England" (1979, p. 78):

> To rule and to learn, then to compare Orient with Occident: these were Jones's goals, which, with an irresistible impulse always to codify, to subdue the infinite variety of the Orient to a "complete digest" of laws, figures, customs, and works, he is believed to have achieved. (Said, 1979, p. 78)

In the year 1786, in his Third Anniversary Discourse to the Asiatic Society of Bengal, Jones presented his famous discourse on Indian culture. In the course of his lecture, he briefly mentioned an observation he had made on Sanskrit having strong linguistic, grammatical, and verbal connections with Greek and Latin:

> The Sanskrit language, whatever may be its antiquity, is of a wonderful structure; more perfect than the Greek, more copious than the Latin, and more exquisitely refined than either, yet bearing to both of them a stronger affinity, both in the roots of verbs and in the forms of grammar, than could possibly have been produced by accident; so strong indeed that no philologer could examine them three, without believing them to have sprung from some common source, which, perhaps no longer exists; there is a similar reason, though not quite so forcible for supposing that both the Gothic and the Celtic, though blended with a very different idiom, had the same origin with the Sanskrit; and the old Persian might be added to the same family, if this were the place for discussing any questions concerning the antiquities of Persia. (Jones, 1788, pp. 348–349)

With this brief remark, Jones brought a fresh insight to the questions concerning the ancestral language of peoples of Europe and their original homeland, sparking a debate that eventually culminated in the creation of Comparative Linguistics and the Aryanist/Indo-Europeanist enterprise. To what extent Jones's "discovery" was original and to what extent it borrowed from other works is not a major concern here, although allegations have been made that his research was an appropriation of the observations of local scholars and historians (see, e.g., Tavakoli-Targhi, 2001). In a recent work titled *Refashioning Iran*, M. Tavakoli-Targhi notes that European students of the Orient, including Sir William Jones, had heavily relied "on research findings of native scholars" (2001, p. 32):

> By rendering these works into English, the colonial officers in India fabricated scholarly credentials for themselves, and by publishing these works under their own names gained prominence as Oriental scholars back home. The process of translation and publication enabled the Europeans to obliterate the traces of the native producers of these works and thus divest them of authorality and originality, attributes which came to be recognized as the distinguishing marks of European "scholars" of the Orient. (Tavakoli-Targhi, 2001, p. 32)

As mentioned earlier, Jones was not the only one to allude to the existence of relationships among different languages. Scholars such as Joseph Scaliger

(1540–1609) had long before Jones pointed out the relation among various languages of Europe such as Italian, French, Spanish, Latin, English, Germanic, and Portuguese. The famous physician and antiquarian James Parsons had also published a book in 1767 titled *The Remains of Japheth: Being Historical Enquiries into the Affinity and Origins of the European Languages.* In this work, Parsons had looked into the close relation among such languages as Celtic, Greek, Italic, Germanic, Old English, Slavic, as well as Bengali and Persian, remarking that these languages had all originated from a common ancestor going as far back as the Prophet Noah's son Japheth.

Although the existence of resemblances between Latin and Sanskrit had been observed prior to Jones's discovery, it was Latin that was usually identified in prior observations as the common source of Europe's languages. It was Jones's strong defense of the status of Sanskrit that sparked a new discourse in the endeavor to locate "the common source" outside Europe. Perhaps the German philosopher George Wilhelm Friedrich Hegel (1770–1832) said it all when he compared Jones's linguistic discovery of Sanskrit affinities to the finding of a new continent. Regardless of its linguistic/scientific orientation, Jones's view was not entirely detached from the dominant religious visions of the time that sought to trace the origin of humanity to the Book of Genesis. According to biblical accounts, Prophet Noah had three sons: Shem, Ham, and Japheth. Shem and Ham were identified as the ancestors of the Semites (Jews and Arabs) and the Hamites (Africans, Egyptians, Cushites), respectively. It was the lot of Japheth to account for the remainder of humanity, that is, the Europeans and those not covered by Semites and Hamites. This third category was identified as Japhetics.

Following the well-established biblical line, Jones initially sought to locate the original homeland in Mesopotamia and the Middle East. Through his later lectures to the Asiatic Society of Bengal, he made it clear that his interest lay in the biblical version of "common origin." So the Book of Genesis was Jones's guiding framework that directed him to follow the trail of Noah's offspring to the Ark in the Middle East and locate the common source of humanity there. In the words of Mallory, "Jones was content to follow the trail again back to the Ark whence issued the three great branches of humanity whose sons 'proceeded from Iran where they migrated at first in great colonies' " (1989, p. 13).

Thus, Jones identified Iran as the place of common origin (see also Marshal, 1970, p. 15). This was a major attempt to refute the earlier arguments that acknowledged the influence of African and particularly Egyptian heritage in the creation of Greek and Roman civilizations. As a result of Jones's discovery, the attention shifted from Africa to Asia, and from Europe to places such as Iran and Indian subcontinent. While early scholarship had established the tremendous influence of Egypt on Judaism and Judaism on Christianity, now this view was being replaced with an Indo-European alternative, which sought to do away with both African as well as Semitic/biblical narratives of origination. As a result, the accomplishment of Egyptian civilization came to be viewed as the consequence of "labors of Indian missionaries" (see, e.g., Poliakov, 1974). And India became identified as "The Cradle of Aryans" (Rendal, 1889), which, in the words of Karl Marx, "has been the source of our languages, our religions, and who represent the type of the ancient German in the Jat and the type of the ancient Greek in the Brahmin" (August 8, 1853/1979, p. 221).

Jones's observations were soon taken up by other scholars such as Freidrich von Schlegel and Franz Bopp and were brought to new perfection. They were not only served up as the basis of modern linguistics, but more importantly they laid the foundation of what soon came to be known as Aryanism, Indo-Europeanism, and white supremacy. In the following quotation, F.W. Farrar (1831–1903) gives a glimpse of the way in which Sir William Jones's views developed and were put into use. Alluding to the branches of Indo-European language family set on a table in front of him, he remarks,

> When we look at the table which is before us . . . it is but a concise statement of the astonishing truth, that we Europeans, together with the Persians and the Hindoos, however wide may be the apparent and superficial differences between us, are, nevertheless, members of a close and common brotherhood in the great families of nations. First westward and northward, afterwards east-ward and southward, the Aryans extended; they forgot the rock from whence they were hewn, and the hole of the pit whence they were digged: they became wholly ignorant of their mutual relationship; and when, in their various emigrations, they met each other—like the lion-whelps of a common lair—they met each other no longer as brothers but as foes: yet brothers they were; and now, at least, the science of language has restored to them the knowledge of this unsuspected truth. (Farrar, 1878, pp. 306–307)

It was thus accepted as a "scientific truth" that the Persians, Hindus, and Europeans were "brothers" who came from the same biological, cultural, and linguistic ancestry. The then emerging "science of language" was used to locate one's line of blood where language itself became a primary factor in determining one's race and lineage. How scientific this emergent science of language was remained to be seen. Suffice it to say that, soon after the hallu-cinatory effects of this "major discovery" subsided, white Europeans began to reject the idea that sought to establish a direct link between race and language. In general, up until 1859 the biblical stories constituted the basis of all sorts of historical, mythological, anthropological, and intellectual pursuits in Europe. Building on the myths and narratives of the Book of Genesis, James Ussher (1581–1656), the archbishop of Armagh, primate of all Ireland, and vice chancellor of Trinity College in Dublin had reached a conclusion that maintained the year 4004 BC to be the year in which the world was created.

The classical European scholars more or less accepted the perimeters set by the archbishop and the sacred books. It was only after the publication in 1859 of Charles Darwin's *On the Origin of Species* that an evolutionary alternative view became possible. Among other things, Darwin's theory established that the earth was indeed very, very old and it had taken millions of years for the natural and animal world to evolve into the present form. Within the context of this evolving view of the world, the knowledge of Sanskrit and other Eastern languages provided the Europeans with the long-sought opportunity to distance themselves from Semitic races and their religious, mythological, and historical worldview. In fact, many scholars have argued that the main purpose behind the manufacturing of the Aryan race was to distance the Europeans from the Semites:

> The political purpose of the Aryan myth (which had arisen from linguistic studies that traced German and other Indo-European languages to ancient Sanskrit) was to distinguish Germans and other northern Europeans from Jews. Since ethnologies generally regarded Semites as a branch of the Caucasian race, mere "whiteness" would not do to designate the master race. (Fredrickson, 2002, p. 90)

In order to establish the existence of a proto-Aryan "mother race," signs and symptoms of such a race had to be constructed historically. However, there were no historical texts, artifacts, and cultural fragments to indicate the prehistoric existence of a superior white race in Europe. In essence, William Jones's discovery made it possible to find that missing link in places such as India and Iran and motivated the necessity of reinterpreting various textual remnants, cultural fragments, and linguistic forms in these regions for the purpose of reconstructing a proto-Aryan language and civilization. Thus, an era of creation of a series of "new Bibles" began. A series of books were produced that distinguished themselves from the Semitic Bible based on the race and geographical location of their authors. As Michelet put it,

> My book is born in the full light of the sun among our forefathers, the sons of light—Aryans, Indians, Persians and Greeks. . . . Now that our parent Bibles have come to light, it is more apparent to what extent the Jewish Bible belongs to another race. It is a great book, without doubt, and always will be—but how gloomy and full of gross equivocation—beautiful but full of doubt like death. (Cited in Poliakov, 1974, pp. 208–209)

Beginning with Jones's discovery, two fundamental questions came to dominate the intellectual activity of at least three generations of historians, archaeologists, and linguists: Who were the real ancestors of the contemporary white Europeans? Where was their original home? In search of answers to these questions, many Western scholars, Orientalists, and intellectuals set out to study geographies, histories, mythologies, and languages of numerous peoples in the Indian subcontinent, Iran, Anatolia, Steppes of Russia, Caucasia, Central Asia, and elsewhere. The result of their cumulative activity culminated in the creation of a project that was variously referred to as Aryanism and Indo-Europeanism.

Freidrich von Schlegel (1772–1829), a German statesman and novelist was among the first to realize the revolutionary potential of Jones's discovery.

Upon learning the new linguistic discoveries, he immediately proceeded to connect these views to various anthropological and racial issues. Having studied and learned Sanskrit in Paris in 1802–1803, Schlegel became convinced that "everything, absolutely everything, is of Indian origin" (cited in Poliakov, 1974, p. 191). In a book titled *Essay on the Language and Wisdom of the Indians* (1808/1849), Schlegel asserted that the Sanskrit-speaking Aryan race had brought civilization to India, Egypt, and Europe from their Himalaya homeland. In 1819, Schlegel used the term Aryan to identify this discursively emerging Indo-European race who had presumably brought culture and civilization to the world. The term Aryan had been derived from Herodotus's Arioi and Sanskrit's Ariya. He associated the root Ari with *Ehre*, the German word for honor and gave a new dimension to the rising importance of language by connecting it to racial and national issues:

> Every important and independent nation has the right, if I may say so, of possessing a literature peculiar to itself; and the meanest barbarism is that which could oppress the speech of a people and a country, or exclude it from all higher education; it is mere prejudice which leads us to consider languages that have been neglected, or that are known to ourselves as incapable of being brought to a higher perfection. (Cited in Hayes, 1928, p. 54)

Juxtaposed against the backdrop of a Latin-dominated Europe and Germany, Schlegel's views were enthusiastically received by many philosophers and scientists such as the German philosopher George Wilhelm Friedrich Hegel (1770–1832), the Norwegian Sanskritist Christian Lassen (1800–1876), the German lexicographer Jacob Grimm (1785–1863), and August Wilhelm von Schlegel (1767–1845), brother of Fredrick von Schlegel, followed by Count Joseph-Arthur Gobineau (1816–1882) and Joseph Ernest Renan (1823–1892) of France, and the Anglo-German Friedrich Max Müller (1823–1900), who nurtured and carried the Aryanist project from the latter half of the nineteenth century to the twentieth century.

The French writer and diplomat, Count Joseph-Arthur Gobineau, was among the first to point out the central importance of the Nordic (Aryan) race for the survival of humanity and civilization. Between 1853 and 1855, Joseph-Arthur De Gobineau wrote his influential *Essai sur l'inégalité des races humaines* (*Essay on the Inequality of Human Races*) in which he argued that the Aryan race was superior to all others. He maintained that race was the driving motor of history, determining the outcome of civilizations and holding the key to all sociohistorical problems. He divided humanity into black, yellow, and white races, and claimed that only the pure white, or Aryan, race was and could be truly noble.

Seeing racial crossbreeding as central to the decay of civilizations, Gobineau argued that civilizations mixing with peoples incapable of civilizing will be ruined eventually. In his view, "the blood" was the source of all human ability, power, intelligence, creativity, imagination, and resourcefulness. These qualities were passed on through blood from one individual to the next, and from one racial generation to another. If a race's blood was contaminated, then the entire race and its civilization would be contaminated. Gobineau insisted that different races were innately unequal in talent, worth, and ability, and only the "white Aryan races" were capable of creating culture and civilization. The non-Aryans and "darker races" could not produce higher forms of culture and civilization; they could only borrow from the white races:

> Recognizing that both strong and weak races exist, I preferred to examine the former, to analyze their qualities, and especially to follow them back to their origins. By this method I convinced myself at last that everything great, noble, and fruitful in the works of man on this earth, in science, art, and civilization, derives from a single starting-point, is the development of a single germ and the result of a single thought; it belongs to one family alone, the different branches of which have reigned in all the civilized countries of the universe. (Gobineau, 1915/1967, pp. xiv–xv)

Gobineau maintained that white Aryan races had migrated to Egypt and had built its civilization; that the center of human history had always been in the areas inhabited by Aryan races; that they alone had developed civilization, culture, and sophisticated languages; and only their spread to the corners of the globe expanded civilization everywhere. In Gobineau's view, history developed "only as a result of contact with the white race" (1915/1967, p. 79). As a result of their biological contact and blood infusion with the white race, the non-Aryans were able to be racially "uplifted," which happened only through the intermixing of "European blood" with their "inferior blood" (1915/1967, p. 76):

> The white race originally possessed the monopoly of beauty, intelligence, and strength. By its union with other varieties, hybrids were created, which were beautiful without strength, strong without intelligence, or if intelligent, both weak and ugly. Further, when the quality of white blood was increased to an indefinite amount by successive infusions, and not by a single admixture, it no longer carried with it its natural advantages, and often merely increased the confusion already existing in the racial elements. (Gobineau, 1915/1967, pp. 209–210)

The prevalent racism of the time led most white intellectuals to uncritically accept Gobineau's view. Among his devoted admirers were such figures as his student Houston Stewart Chamberlain and Adolph Hitler, among others. Chamberlain (1855–1927) was an English Orientalist who advanced Gobineau's racist views into a fully fledged doctrine of Aryan-Teutonic racial supremacy. In 1889, he published his *Foundations of the Nineteenth Century* where he refined the concept of Aryanism and "the Teutonic race" to its final supremacist and Nazist-Hitlerite conclusion, where the white European was identified as a superior being not only biologically but also spiritually, culturally, and intellectually. As Gunther put it,

> Judgment, truthfulness, and energy always distinguish the Nordic man. He feels a strong urge towards truth and justice. . . . Passion in the usual

meaning of the rousing of the senses or the heightening of the sexual life has little meaning for him. . . . He is never without a certain knightliness. (Gunther, 1927, pp. 51–52)

The German Orientalist and philologist Max Müller was another important contributor to the bourgeoning Aryanist enterprise. He extensively studied and tirelessly wrote on linguistics, mythologies, and religions of Eastern societies. After specializing in Sanskrit in Germany, he went to Oxford, where he lived for the remainder of his life. He studied the Zarathustrian religious book of Avesta, wrote works on Indian religions and philosophy, and edited the collection of "Sacred Books of the East" that amounted to some 51 volumes. But most of all, Müller played a major role in synthesizing biology and language, asserting as early as 1853 that the term Aryan denoted both a racial and linguistic entity. He too jumped on the bandwagon of Aryanist frenzy and argued that etymologically the word Arya was derived from *ar*, meaning plough, to cultivate. This insight led him to interpret Arya/Aria as cultivator or agriculturer, which in his interpretation meant a civilized sedentary, as opposed to nomads and hunter-gatherers (Müller, 1862, p. 213). He emphasized that "the first ancestors of the Indians, the Persians, the Greeks, the Romans, the Slavs, the Celts and the Germans were living together within the same enclosures, nay under the same roof" (1862, p. 213). However, in 1888, Müller refuted his earlier definition of Arya and Aryan, arguing,

> I have declared again and again that if I say Aryas, I mean neither blood nor bones, nor hair, nor skull; I mean simply those who speak an Aryan language. The same applies to Hindus, Greeks, Romans, Germans, Celts, and Slavs. When I speak of them, I commit myself to no anatomical characteristics. . . . To me an ethnologist who speaks of Aryan race, Aryan blood, Aryan eyes and hair, is as great a sinner as a linguist who speaks of a dolichocephalic dictionary or a brachycephalic grammar. (Müller, 1888, p. 120)

Thus, the same Max Müller who popularized the word Arya as a racial designation came to repudiate his earlier assertions, realizing that nowhere in the Sanskrit literature did the term Arya denote either a racial or a linguistic people. Although he rejected the racial connotation of the term, he hung on to the linguistic interpretations and their various implications. So he pronounced that Aryan only alluded to speakers of a language and never applied to a race. However, deny as he may, the notions of Aryan race and Aryan blood had already entered Europe's colonialist/racist lexicon and it could not be removed from that literature even by Max Müller's rejection of his own earlier conviction.

Vere Gordon Childe (1892–1957) was another important twentieth-century archaeologist who was most influential on the issue of Aryan origins. In 1926, he published his major work on the subject titled *The Aryans*. Through this and other works he wanted to shed light on the "original home" of the Aryans. He was of the opinion that the Middle East was the original place where the early inventions and developments in the realms of science, agriculture, animal husbandry, and metallurgy had taken place. According to Childe, it was the Aryans who appeared "everywhere as promoters of true progress," refining the "primitive" arts and sciences along with the "primitive races" to a higher perfection (1926, p. 211). The Aryans were able to do this, argued Childe, because the language they spoke was of a higher quality that manifested their higher mental development. Thus, instead of relying on blood and biology, Childe relied on language. Irrespective of this shift in emphasis, he too saw the Europeans as superior to Eastern races in terms of their mental capacity, energy, inventiveness, boldness, and daring:

> [T]he lasting gift bequeathed by the Aryans to the conquered peoples was neither a higher material culture nor a superior physique, but . . . a more excellent language and the mentality it generated. It is particularly signifi- cant that where, as in Mitanni, the Indo-European language was not retained, the effects of an infusion of Aryan blood did not come to fruition. (Childe, 1926, pp. 211–212)

The racist and nationalist groups in Germany, France, and other parts of Europe used the Aryan supremacist literature abundantly and brought it to its logical extreme in Adolph Hitler's Nazi Germany. In fact, it is not difficult to trace the racist mentality of Gobineau and his cohorts in Adolph Hitler's think- ing. For instance, let us take a look at how Hitler views cultures and civilizations:

> If we divide mankind into three categories—founders of culture, bearers of culture, and destroyers of culture—the Aryan alone can be considered as repre- senting the first category. It was he who laid the groundwork and erected the walls of every great structure in human culture. Only the shape and colour of such structures are to be attributed to the individual characteristics of the various nations. It is the Aryan who has furnished the great building-stones and plans for the edifices of all human progress; only the way in which these plans have been executed is to be attributed to the qualities of each individual race. (Hitler, 1925/1943, p. 290)

Hitler saw slavery and subjugation of other (in his view inferior) races not only as normal and natural but also necessary for the advancement of the Aryan race, and hence, in his view, the human civilization. From his perspective, if the Aryans had not conquered and enslaved others, they would not be able to create a higher form of civilization.

> Had it not been possible for them to employ members of the inferior race which they conquered, the Aryans would never have been in a position to take the first steps on the road which led them to a later type of culture; just as, without the help of certain suitable animals which they were able to tame, they would never have come to the invention of mechanical power which has subsequently enabled them to do without these beasts. . . . For the establishment of superior types of civilization the members of inferior races

formed one of the most essential pre-requisites. They alone could supply the lack of mechanical means without which no progress is possible. It is certain that the first stages of human civilization were not based so much on the use of tame animals as on the employment of human beings who were members of an inferior race. (Hitler, 1925/1943, p. 295)

Following Gobineau's theory on the decline and erosion of civilization as a result of the fusion of races and intermixing of their blood, Hitler believed that humanity was doomed to failure because the Aryan blood was polluted by the blood of inferior non-Aryan races. He saw the Jews as responsible for tainting the Aryan blood by both their own blood and that of other inferior races. In his view, the Jews were seeking to dominate the world, and the only way that they could do this was to "bastardize" the white race (1925, pp. 310–315):

> The adulteration of the blood and racial deterioration conditioned thereby are the only causes that account for the decline of ancient civilizations; for it is never by war that nations are ruined, but by the loss of their powers of resistance, which are exclusively a characteristic of pure racial blood. In this world everything that is not of sound racial stock is like chaff. Every historical event in the world is nothing more nor less than a manifestation of the instinct of racial self-preservation, whether for weal or woe. (Hitler, 1925/1943, p. 296)

Thus, a minor linguistic observation on the part of Sir William Jones evolved to become a most important intellectual preoccupation in Europe. This racial/intellectual preoccupation gave birth to what is now known as the Aryan myth, which has so far culminated in the most horrendous crimes of the twentieth century. In order to justify their racist agenda, the earlier Aryanists saw a clear connection between one's race and one's mother tongue. They shared this common view that languages, just as the humans who spoke them, had a polygenesis character. The opposite of monogenesis, polygenesis advocates the existence of multiple origins, in particular of humanity and languages. According to this view, human races have different points of origination, and based on such differences they speak different languages. From this perspective evolved the idea of classification of languages into different categories. Although the idea of a common ancestry of speakers of Aryan/Indo-European languages was accepted at first, racist elements in Europe more and more came to find the idea unpalatable. It was just unthinkable for them to accept that they were genetically related to Indians and shared same ancestors with the Persians.

Despite the attempts to trace back the ancestors of Europeans to places such as Iran and India, many European nations, and the British in particular, did not find the idea of having their forefathers in their current colonies particularly attractive. For the British, the Indian origin theory implied that the current Indians shared the same blood with their English masters, and this was not something that they could easily accept (see also Poliakov, 1974). At the end of the day, the Church of England affirmed that the origins of races were clearly established within the Judaic tradition. Similarly, Adolph Hitler and others also distinguished between speakers of a language and their racial/blood line:

> It is not however by the tie of language, but exclusively by the tie of blood that the members of a race are bound together. And the Jew himself knows this better than any other, seeing that he attaches so little importance to the preservation of his own language while at the same time he strives his utmost to maintain his blood free from intermixture with that of other races. A man may acquire and use a new language without much trouble; but it is only his old ideas that he expresses through the new language. His inner nature is not modified thereby. The best proof of this is furnished by the Jew himself. He may speak a thousand tongues and yet his Jewish nature will remain always one and the same. His distinguishing characteristics were the same when he spoke the Latin language at Ostia two thousand years ago as a merchant in grain, as they are to-day when he tries to sell adulterated flour with the aid of his German gibberish. He is always the same Jew. (Hitler, 1925/1943, p. 312)

In the above assertions, Hitler clearly illustrates the deviation that Aryanists had to make from earlier assumptions that regarded language as an inseparable component of race. This was a major blow, particularly to the overexcited Aryanist elements in places such as Iran and India who were preparing their own versions of Nazism, based on the presupposition that they were biologically related to the same "superior race" as Hitler's Aryan race. The chauvinistic and ultranationalist elements in Iran and elsewhere were using the earlier racist assumptions of European scholars to establish their own "superior" Aryan heritage—hence domination—over ethnic groups and communities deemed to be non-Aryan. Notwithstanding that the racist idea equating language with race was now being rejected by Europeans, the local "Aryanists" continued to reap the fruits of European-constructed racist/Aryanist ideology.

Meanwhile, interpretations and definitions around language evolved from being directly related to race and biology to being treated as a cultural entity that existed independently of race and biology. Despite all the paradigm shifts around the concept of language, it still continued to occupy a central place in the formations of ethnic, racial, cultural, and national identities. As a most important component of each individual's, group's and community's identity, language continued to manifest a close connection with race, nationality, sociopolitical power, and domination.

LANGUAGE, NATIONALISM, AND POWER

From a historical viewpoint, perhaps a modern approach to the elevated status of language could safely be traced back to the seventeenth century, and particularly the declining status of Latin as a major imperial language. Around the late seventeenth century, a variety of economic, social, and cultural forces that brought about the decline and eventual fall of the Roman

Empire were calling into question the status of Latin as a holy and sacred language. Latin, the language of ancient Rome and the neighboring territory of Latium, had become the dominant tongue of western Europe, thanks to the power and hegemony of the Roman Empire. Closely related to the extinct Italian languages of Oscan, Umbrian, and Venetic, Latin belongs to a linguistic category referred to as the Italic Family (see also Jasanoff and Nussbaum, 1996, p. 179).

The fifteenth and sixteenth centuries witnessed the emergence of a refined "New Latin," otherwise known as Modern Latin. Almost all the literary, scientific, and philosophical works of Renaissance thinkers such as Desiderius Erasmus, Francis Bacon, and Isaac Newton, to name a few, were produced in Latin. Latin was the language of European diplomacy, inter-/intragovernmental correspondence, and religious communications until the beginning of the eighteenth century (see also Anderson, 1983). The decline around the late seventeenth century of Latin was concomitant with the rise of vernacular languages all over Europe. Thanks to the revolutionary advances in print technology, language in Europe came to be valued as the main symbol of national identity, a source of pride, and a vehicle for progress and development. Language was seen as a primordial backbone of nationalism and nationhood that reflected intellectual as well as spiritual growth of nations and distinguished different races and groups of people from one another. It also became a marker of racism, narrow-minded nationalism, and egoistic patriotism. As Anderson put it, "What the eye is to the lover . . . language is to the patriot" (1983, p. 140).

The central role of language in Europe's nation-building process came to find its mirror image, via colonialism and imperialism, in the lives of non-European peoples living far away from this continent. Colonization of hitherto unknown distant lands and subjugation of their peoples provided the Europeans and their scientists with new opportunities to "study" the non-European peoples. Europeans came to evaluate themselves vis-à-vis the colonized peoples of Africa, Asia, America, and Australia. Subjugation and enslavement of other peoples gave the Europeans a sense of superiority.

By the mid-seventeenth century, large segments of the colonization of Africa and America had been completed. Domination by European powers of Africa, Asia, and America was followed by the interest of the colonizers to study their subjects of colonization—the colonized. When it was revealed that the supposedly inferior races of Africa and Mesopotamia had produced civilizations far more sophisticated and magnificent compared to those of Europe, the biological inferiority thesis could hold no longer. It had to be fundamentally reexamined. The colonizers were faced with a fundamental question: how to explain the magnificent civilizations of Africa, Sumeria, Mesopotamia, and so forth? In their rush to "prove" superiority of the white Aryan race, European scholars and social scientists had to shift their attention from biology to language, in order to prove that Africa's, Asia's, and more specifically Egypt's ancient civilizations were products of none other than Aryan races who had migrated to those places in prehistoric periods. This migration they came to prove through remnants of Indo-European linguistic fragments that they "discovered" throughout Africa, the Indian subcontinent, and the Middle East (Poliakov, 1974; Childe, 1926).

Beginning from the late eighteenth century, a number of theories and hypotheses appeared in European intellectual and academic circles that stressed the existence of a close kinship among the major European languages, on one hand, and certain languages spoken in India and Iran, on the other. These languages were classified as Indo-European language family and were believed to have originated from a prehistoric Proto or Mother Language that was spoken some 6, 000 years ago. The people who presumably spoke this prehistoric language were called the Proto-Indo-Europeans or the Proto-Aryans who were assumed to be the linguistic (and by some accounts the racial) ancestors of the current Indo-European, Aryan, racial, linguistic, and ethnic groups. The Indo-European language group was said to include the Baltic, Germanic, Greek (and former Greek), Albanian, Slavonic, Romance/Italic, Armenian, Celtic (and former Celtic), Indo-Iranian, Tocharian, and Hittite languages. The non-Indo-European languages of Europe included the Basque, Hungarian, Estonian, Caucasian, and Finno-Ugrian languages.

The term Indo-European was coined in 1813 by the English physician and Egyptologist Thomas Young (1783–1829). Before him, in 1810 the term Indo-Germanic family was used by the Danish-French geographer Conrad Malte-Brun (1775–1826). Likewise, the German Orientalist Julius von Klaproth (1783–1835) had come up with the alternative designation Indo-Germans in 1823, which was somewhat popularized by the Sanskritist and comparative philologist Franz Bopp in 1833–1835. Nevertheless, none of the alternative designations was able to satisfy the majority of European scholars in replacing Arya/Aryan. As V.G. Childe put it,

> Of course, I know that only the Indians and Iranians actually designated themselves by this name [i.e., Aryan]. But what expression is to be used conventionally to denote the linguistic ancestors of the Celts, Teutons, Romans, Hellenes, and Hindus if Aryan is to be restricted to the Indo-Iranians? The word Indo-European is clumsy and cannot even claim to be scientific now that Indian Sanskrit is no longer the most easterly member of the linguistic family known. Dr. Giles' term, Wiros, is certainly accurate, but, as thus written, it is so ugly that the reviewers have laughed it out of literature. Aryan on the other hand has the advantage of brevity and familiarity. I therefore propose to retain it, quite conventionally, in the traditional sense. (Childe, 1926, p. xi)

Up until the emergence of Hitler's National Socialism, the term Aryan enjoyed an almost universal popularity in European literature. Academic disciplines such as anthropology, linguistics, history, and antiquity were brought into service of the Aryan race, to determine, as it were, its origins, its homeland, and its numerous linguistic/racial branches. The Aryan race was believed to speak an Indo-European language that was divided into different sublanguages. Indo-European languages were said to include Albanian, Baltic, Celtic, Germanic, Greek, Indo-Iranian, Italic, and Slavic subfamilies. In the words of Martin Bernal, the Indo-European language family includes the following:

> all European languages—except for Basque, Finnish and Hungarian—the Iranian and North Indian languages and **Tokharian**. Although **Phrygian** and **Armenian** were situated in **Anatolia**, they are Indo-European languages not **Anatolian** ones. (Bernal, 1991, pp. 641–642; emphasis is in the original)

By the nineteenth century, the existence of a close kinship between Sanskrit, Latin, and ancient Greek had been discovered. In 1808, Freidrich von Schlegel proved in his *Essay on the Language and Wisdom of Indians* the kinship between Sanskrit, Persian, Greek, and German. In 1908, the extinct Tocharian tongue, spoken in medieval eastern Turkistan, was identified as Indo-European. In 1915 the extinct Hittite language, spoken in parts of ancient Azerbaijan and central Anatolia, was also discovered to be an Indo-European tongue. All these "discoveries" added new dimensions to the development of a "Parent Indo-European tongue," also called Proto Indo-European. And finally,

> In 1933 the White Russian Indologist N.D. Mironov tried to reinforce the Aryan hypotheses for both the Kassites and the Hyksos not only by finding Indian etymologies for names that had not been explained in terms of Semitic or Hurrian but also by even challenging some of those given in these languages. (Bernal, 1991, p. 341)

From all these discoveries a conclusion was reached to the effect that the original Indo-European tongue must have been unified around six millennia ago (see, e.g., Jasanoff and Nussbaum, 1996, p. 179). And from this, it was extrapolated that the prehistoric Aryan race, solely and exclusively, must have been the primordial source from which all civilizations had sprung. Numerous scientific theories and hypotheses were offered to establish a plausible explanation for the supposedly prehistoric migratory or otherwise movements of the Aryan race from Europe throughout the globe (Rajaram and Frawley, 1994; Renfrew, 1987; J. Shaffer, 1984).

Through their linguistic speculation, proponents of the Indo-European project came to reconstruct a proto or an original language based on the existing language fragments. The idea was to imagine or perceive cultures and communities in accordance with certain common or similar words that more or less exist in all languages. The history of deviation or evolution of these similar words were somehow determined, by means of speculation or otherwise, which was in turn used as a basis upon which the imaginary parent community or protoculture and language was constructed. In the case of Persian language and Iran, for instance, a few words from Avestan language, a few words from Median language, 400 words from Old Persian, and words from Middle Persian, Soghdian, and Parthian languages were "discovered" to support the existence of an Aryan culture in prehistoric Iran, on the one hand, and the kinship between this Aryan culture and the Aryan culture of Europe, on the other (see also Vaziri, 1993, p. 61).

Needless to say, if such linguistic speculations are presumed to be bases for "scientific discoveries," then "linguistic evidence" may prove an original home for the Aryan race everywhere from India to Iran to Turkey to Western China to Egypt and Africa. The proponents of the Indo-Europeanist agenda tend to ignore the basic fact that linguistic and racial boundaries do not necessarily coincide. For instance, the Greeks are not considered Indo-Europeans, but they speak an Indo-European language (Jasanoff and Nussbaum, 1996, p. 180). Languages are socially produced and learned cultural phenomena. And like any other cultural phenomenon, they can easily be transmitted, evolved, adopted, and learned. To speak a certain language does not necessarily mean that the speakers of that language are genetically and racially related as well.

After the horrors of Hitler's National Socialism and World War II, the term Aryan fell out of favor and the designation Indo-European replaced it. However, the fascination and infatuation with Aryan and Aryanism were never completely abandoned. Although an overly racist and genocidal usage of Aryanism was abandoned in Europe, such abandonment had no effect in places such as Iran, where ultranationalist elements continued to feed on the Orientalist/racist construction of Arya, Aryan, Aryanism, and Aryan race. Beginning from 1925, the Aryanist discourse became a dominant narrative in Iran, providing the ideological basis for an aggressive, chauvinistic Farsism and a narrow-minded, reactionary nationalism. Aryanism served as a tool for refashioning Iran's exclusionary history, for asserting the absurd superiority of the Persian/Aryan element, and for marginalizing the majority of the populace deemed to be non-Aryan. In a word, Aryanism became the basis of Persian identity and the Iranian nation-statism in the twentieth century.

The Iranian Connection and Formation of a Racist System

So far we have seen the way terms such as Aryan, Indo-European, Aryanism, and Indo-Europeanism were constructed and reconstructed by European scholars in order to craft an identity, an origin, as well as a homeland for Europe's white race. This was of course one side of the story. The other side was to construct an identity for certain ethnic groups in places such as Iran and India in which the absurd Aryan myth was to be grounded. Understandably, when certain ethnic groups in Eastern societies came to realize in the wake of Oriental constructions that they were Aryans, and hence, supposedly superior, they tried to take advantage of this newfound identity in numerous ways. One salient way was to forge a nationalist project to the exclusion of all the other races and ethnic groups deemed to be carriers of non-Aryan blood. It is therefore extremely important to see how these

European constructs were received, taken up, and used by various ethnic groups in places such as Iran and India. In Iran, it was the Persian ethnic group that sought to cash in from the glamorous identity that the Europeans had constructed for the Persians. To see a glimpse of this Oriental construction, once again let us turn to Gobineau as he describes the Aryan origins of the Persian race:

> In very remote times the white race began to settle into its first home in the heights of Asia. It slowly spread into the west and south-west of the continent. One by one, its growing tribes separated. Some of them, having penetrated into Europe, were to become the Celts, the Thracians, the Latins, the Hellenes and the Slavs. At the same time, other no less important branches of the original stock, moving southwards, took with them a flourishing population, of which one group long remained connected with their motherland: the Scythians. Another, having separated from them, turned eastwards and became the progenitors of the Hindus: then a third, splitting off much later from the Scythians and the future votaries of Brahma, and putting behind them the springs of the Indus, reached the lands of Central Asia, to give birth to the people whom the Greeks and Romans called the Persians, but who still use the name Iranian for themselves. (Gobineau, 1971, p. 6)

So, the same Gobineau who divided humanity into superior and inferior races and who elevated the "Aryan race" to a Godlike status, irrefutably and overconfidently identifies Iranians as Aryans. The fact that "Iranians" were not, are not, and have never been, a homogenous people does not seem to bother Gobineau. After all, his racist ideology does not allow for any kind of humane and dignified recognition of non-Aryan peoples. However, it should not be difficult to imagine the extent of power and authority this kind of pseudo-construction would give to any ethnic group claiming to inherit the Aryan genes, particularly in a multiethnic setting such as Iran. Much like other Orientalist discourses, the Indo-Europeanist project was hardly an innocently objective and purely scholarly enterprise. On the contrary, from the very beginning it was loaded with overtly and covertly racist, expansionist, and colonialist tendencies.

The assigning of the status of a superior race to Iran's Persian minority assumed a very normal and innocent-looking intellectual/academic preoccupation on the surface. Prominent Western scholars of Iran and the Middle East recycled the Aryanist reconstructions of the likes of Gobineau and reproduced them as purely academic and scholarly knowledge. This knowledge was then taken up by local elitist/dominant historians, writers, and intellectuals who put them to use for the purpose of excluding the non-Persian, non-Aryan communities from the sources of power and privilege in the country. Below is a sample of an "innocent-looking" academic description of the Persians, Aryans, and Iran, offered by another Western scholar, Richard N. Frye:

> Persia, of course, is a designation we obtained from the Greeks, who knew perfectly well that Persia meant the province of the Achaemenian empire where the Persians

lived in the land of the Aryans. Aryan, with an approximate derived meaning "noble, lord," seems to have been the general designation of those people, speaking eastern Indo-European tongues or dialects, who migrated into the lands between the Ganges and Euphrates rivers at the end of the second and the beginning of the first millennium BC. Ancient authors knew that the Persians and Medes were Aryans, and the sources do use the term "Aryan" for both. With the expansion of the Parthians it would seem that the term Arya, or Ariane in Greek sources, expanded as well so that it finally becomes "greater Arya,"the equivalent to "realm of the Aryans," which is the term the Sassanians used for the extended homeland of their empire, Iranshahr. The use of the word Iran for the modern country is thus a continuation of the ancient term. (Frye, 1963, p. 2)

There are of course hundreds of similar assertions in Orientalist texts just like the ones quoted above from Gobineau and Frye. These assertions explicitly and implicitly seek to establish such notions as "superiority of the Aryan race" and "Iran's superior Aryan heritage" that are taken up and recycled time and again by the dominant Iranian scholars. For instance, below is a modern recycling of the European-constructed meaning of Iran and Arya by a contemporary Iranian scholar:

The term "Iran" means "the land of Aryans." Politically, however, this term refers to the country situated in south-west Asia. . . . Geographically, the term covers an area much greater than the state of Iran. It includes the entire Iranian Plateau. Culturally, the term includes all peoples speaking Iranian languages— a subdivision of Indo-European family of languages. . . . The early Iranians themselves were thought to have been nomadic groups of Indo-European origin, who, moving southward from east and west of the Caspian Sea, gradually overwhelmed and absorbed previous inhabitants. (Mojtahed-Zadeh, 1995, pp. 14–15)

It is not difficult to detect signs of overt and covert attempts in the above quote to conceal and deny the multiethnic and multicultural character of Iranian society both prior to the arrival of Aryan tribes and at the present. This kind of academic-looking denial, which is reconstructed and based on Eurocentric, Orientalist scholarship is increasingly becoming suspect in Iran, by being relentlessly challenged and interrogated through an emergent local/indigenous scholarship. The contemporary indigenous historiography pioneered by such scholars as Mohammad Taqi Zehtabi (1999) and Naser Poorpirar (2000, 2001a, 2001b) acknowledges that Orientalist methods of knowing and research are deeply imbedded in Iranian historiography, that such imbeddedness calls into question the authenticity and autonomy of Iranian historiography, and that articulations and explorations of Iranian history through indigenous-oriented local ways and methods of research are essential for the emergence of a more realistic and sensible Iranian historiography. It is through this realistic local historiography that terms such as Arya, Aryan, Iran, Fars, and Persia are now being reinterpreted and re-presented.

What Arya meant was a form of reference and address that conveyed by some accounts gentleness and modesty and by others aggressiveness and wickedness (Poorpirar, 2000). As far as the Persian texts are concerned, we come across the word Arya for the first time in Achaemenid inscriptions and, more specifically, in the inscriptions written in the era of Darius and Xerxes. In the Behistoon Inscription of Darius, "Arya" appears three times as "Arik," two times as "Arika," and one time as "Ariya." In the Darius inscription of *Naqsh-e Rostam* it appears once as "Aryi"; in Darius inscription of Shush it appears once again as "Aryi"; it appears one more time in Xerxes Inscription of Takht-e Jamshid as "Aryi." So it is interesting to note that "Arya" appears only in inscriptions accounting for 50 years of Darius and Xerxes rule within the Achaemenid era (Poorpirar, 2000). The question is: why does this term appear only in the beginning of the Achaemenid era and why is not repeated in subsequent years of the Achaemenid dynasty?

The Iranian historian Naser Poorpirar argues that the Western Orientalists have intentionally misinterpreted the term Arya only to serve their own utopic/colonial agendas. He convincingly demonstrates that in the above-mentioned inscriptions the word Ariya meant nothing other than such derogatory notions as revolt (*shouresh*), and thug, rouge, gangster (*sharir*) and their derivatives (Poorpirar, 2000, pp. 217–219). Poorpirar maintains that nowhere in the inscriptions does the word Ariya have a racial or a linguistic connotation. The same observation has been confirmed by a number of other Iranian scholars, including Mostafa Vaziri. In his valuable work *Iran as Imagined Nation*, Vaziri explores the genealogy of words such as Iran, Iranzamin, and Iranshahr and concludes that none of these terms has anywhere denoted a racial or a linguistic meaning, and none of the existing sources on ancient Iran (with the exception of Ferdowsi) "refers to the name of the land and to the identity of its inhabitants synonymously" (1993, p. 89).

The Pahlavi monarchism in Iran was founded on a racist model of superiority of "the Aryan race," a race whose point of origin according to the Pahlavis was supposedly nowhere other than Iran and whose unques-tionable offspring were none other than Persians. During the Pahlavi era in Iran there was no shortage of linguistic, racial, archaeological, and philological "theories" seeking to establish the absolute superiority of the Aryan race in general and the Persians in particular. However, nearly three decades after the demise of Pahlavi dynasty, only recently have some independent Iranian scholars been able to critically examine the ideological, cultural, intellectual, and discursive legacy of the racist Pahlavi regime. It is this emerging indigenous historiography that challenges the Orientalist construction of Iran's history and seeks to redefine and rearticulate concepts such as Iran, Persia, and Arya. According to historian Poorpirar, the indige-nous peoples of Iran in the pre-Achaemenid era at some historical juncture were forced to face a ruthless and ferocious tribe, bent on annihilating their entire existence. They identified this ruthless adversary as "Parseh" or Persian:

It is here that for the first time the Iranian people named this unnamed, unknown and blood-spelling tribe "Parseh," a title which in both ancient and contemporary Iran, as well as in Median and Elamite culture has been interpreted as "beggar, astray, and intruder." From this title the derivative "wandering around" (Parseh zadan) has been conceived; and even by comparison, the Iranians have named the angry barking of dog as "pars." (Poorpirar, 2000, p. 218)

On the legacy of Persian empire he concludes,

Thus, the emperors of Parseh . . . with the plundered wealth and forced labor of conquered Iranian and non-Iranian artisans built the palaces of Pasargad and Shush and Takht-e Jamshid, whereas in reality never ever before that time their own tribe had put so much as a brick on a brick. These achievements, now, after our familiarity with the true history of the Achaemenids find greater value and indeed become sacred. For they all testify to the great extent of art among the conquered Iranian and non-Iranian peoples, [samples of] which are now collected in Takht-e Jamshid Museum. (Poorpirar, 2000, p. 220)

It is noteworthy that up to 20 years ago, no one could even dare to question the Aryanist/racist history of Iran modeled on supremacy of Persian race and its language. The current acts of interrogation, suspicion, and reexamination are the initial steps necessary to disrupt and dismantle Iran's colonial, racist, and exclusionary institutions. The emerging decolonizing historiography acknowledges the significance of history as a legitimating instrument. It, therefore, seeks to deconstruct, disrupt, and dismantle this instrument by posing new questions, offering alternative interpretations, revisions, critiques, and interrogations.

CONCLUSION

The emergent indigenous historiography in Iran is a decolonizing scholarship that has already started in Africa and the Indian subcontinent, with the obvious aim of disturbing and disrupting the dominant Orientalist historiography and its local/chauvinistic extension. More than four decades ago, a great African historian T.O. Ranger spoke of an urgent need

to examine whether African history was sufficiently African; whether it had developed the methods and models appropriate to its own needs or had depended upon making use of methods and models developed elsewhere; whether its main themes of discourse had arisen out of the dynamics of African development or had been imposed because of their over-riding significance in the historiography of other continents. (Ranger, 1968, p. x)

Beginning in the early 1980s, a new genre of subaltern studies has similarly appeared in India with the aim of promoting "a systematic and informed discussion of subaltern themes in the field of South Asian studies" and rectifying "the elitist bias characteristic of much research and academic work in this particular area" (Guha, 1988, p. 35). In Edward Said's view, these subaltern studies of South Asia represent "a crossing of boundaries, a smuggling of ideas across lines, a stirring up of intellectual and, as always, political complacence" (1988, p. x). Derived from Antonio Gramsci's (1971) usage in *The Prison Notebooks*, subaltern is defined in this genre "as a name for the general attributes of subordination in South Asian society, whether this is expressed in terms of class, caste, age, gender and office or in any other way" (Guha, 1988, p. 35).

The concerns of both Ranger and subaltern studies about elitist/nationalist historiography are applicable with the same force and clarity to countries such as Iran whose ancient history, in effect, has been written by Europeans. Not only is the Iranian historiography a faithful replica of Orientalist/ Western historiography, more importantly for the most part, the history of Iran has been constructed and produced by the institution of Orientalism. Paradoxically, outstanding scholars such as Martin Bernal, Samir Amin, and Edward Said, in their groundbreaking works to dismantle Aryanism, Eurocentrism, and Orientalism, have uncritically accepted the official data on the history of the Iranian Plateau and its peoples. As a result, terms and concepts such as Indo-Iranian language, Aryans of Iran, and Indo-Iranian elements, abound in their texts, which are directly taken from Orientalist texts without critiquing and interrogating their degree of authenticity and applicability.

Even today, after 80 years of state-sponsored racism, chauvinism, and forced assimilation, the Persians comprise no more than 37 percent of Iran's population (Dei and Asgharzadeh, 2003). And yet, many critical progressive thinkers and antiracist pedagogues use the terms Persian and Iranian interchangeably, unknowingly and unconsciously serving the racist Indo-Europeanist project. Bernal, for instance, agrees that "by 1700 BC the language of the Steppe was not proto-Indo-European but distinctively Iranian" (1991, p. 399). He does not, however, see a need to further elaborate on what is meant by "Iranian language" and who the speakers of such "a language" were (Asgharzadeh, 2002).

It is important to note that there was no cohesive "Aryanist" ideology serving as a uniform blueprint for a variety of different Aryanist groups. The Indo-Europeanist project did not follow a well-focused universal logic either inside Europe or outside its borders. In *Black Athena* (1991), Bernal talks about the three different models of "Aryan," "Ancient" and "Revised Ancient" to illustrate the degree of disagreement among the founding fathers of the Aryanist project. Their disagreement centered around issues such as "migration or invasion," "the nature and timing of Afro-Egyptian influence," and "the status of Greek as an Indo-European tongue."

Although the founding fathers of the Aryanist project aimed to provide a uniformly universal theory, the project worked differently in different settings when put into practice. Its function fundamentally differed from country to country, and from region to region, depending on the power configurations and the population makeup in various cultural, linguistic, and geographical zones. The Indo-Europeanist ideology was articulated completely differently, for instance, in India as opposed to Iran, Pakistan, and even in Turkey. Whereas some original hypotheses considered the Turks as remnants of the ancient "Turanians" (another manufactured term) and therefore as Aryans, the Persian Aryanists in Iran viewed the Turks as a savage, non-Indo-European inferior race (Meskoob, 1992). And this was at a time when the Turks saw themselves even "whiter" than the Aryans. As early as 1923, the famous Turkish scholar Zia Gökalp wrote, "To classify Turks who are fairer and more handsome than Aryans with the 'yellow race' has no scientific foundation, as the supposition of a linguistic unity among the ethnic groups, usually called the 'Altai race,' is far from being proven" (1923/1975, p. 271).

And whereas the bulk of Europe-based Aryanist scholarship viewed the Persians as migrants to the Iranian Plateau from India, the elitist Persians of Iran looked down on their Indo-Parsi cousins, considering them as an inferior and backward race! The late shah of Iran on various occasions asserted that "Iranians looked more like the French rather than the Indians or the Pakistanis" (see also Shawcross, 1988). Pakistanis, on the other hand, emphasize the common culture that they share with "the Iranians." For instance, in its May 13, 1973 issue, the Pakistani paper *Dawn* wrote,

> We the Pakistanis and our brethren living in Iran are the two Asiatic branches of the Aryan tree who originally lived in a common country, spoke the same language, followed the same religion, worshipped the same gods and observed the same rites. . . . Culturally we were and are a single people. (Cited in F. Ahmed, 1976, p. 18)

In India itself, the British divided the population along racial lines, seeking to create a northern Aryan zone and a southern Dravidian culture inherently opposed to each other (J. Shaffer, 1984). And whereas the Kurds were by all accounts believed to be speakers of an Indo-European language, this particular quality did not prevent them from becoming subject to various genocidal acts of racism throughout the Middle East, including the Persian-dominated Indo-Europeanist Iran (Hassanpour, 1992a). All this discursive/ideological confusion, disharmony, and Aryanist mumbo jumbo means that notions such as the Aryan myth, the superior Aryan race, pure blood, and superior civilization were nothing more than powerful ideological/discursive tools to facilitate the desire and aspirations of certain groups for power and domination.

These concepts were employed as effective instruments in the war of power and domination over colonies, communities, and individuals. While from the latter half of the twentieth century, efforts have begun (and succeeded for the most part) to deconstruct these concepts, such efforts in places such as Iran are just beginning. The initiators of such efforts are scholars and intellectuals mainly from minoritized communities and subaltern strata of society. At this infantile stage of the struggle, the minoritized scholars are extremely powerless in terms of resources, facilities, and means of publishing and distribution. Conversely, the adherents to and maintainers of the Aryan myth are still quite powerful, with most of them in positions of influence and authority even within the Islamic Republic. Aryanism and the power imbalances that it creates are still very much alive in Iran and certain other neighboring countries. It is therefore imperative that this racist and discredited ideology is opened up to full interrogation throughout the world.

CHAPTER 4

The Flourishing of Racist Ideology: From Pahlavi Monarchism to the Islamic Republic

Lur after Lur was beheaded. Again and again the plate was heated red hot and slapped on the stub of a neck. Once the colonel was slow with the plate, and the blood shot five feet in the air. The colonel started betting on how far these headless men could run. He and the soldiers would shout and yell, encouraging each victim to do his best. . . . The colonel won most of the bets. He won a thousand rials . . . on the headless Lur who ran fifteen paces after he was beheaded. . . . The colonel became a general and later Minister of War in Reza Shah government. He was the Butcher of Luristan, Amir Ahmadi.

(Excerpts from narratives of a Luristani man, cited in Douglas, 1951, pp. 107–108)

INTRODUCTION

World War I (1914–1918) significantly altered the geopolitical landscape in the Middle East. The Ottoman Empire disintegrated into a number of states under British and French rules, with the Turkish Republic emerging as an independent entity. Meanwhile, the triumph of the Bolshevik Revolution in Russia created a new atmosphere for the flourishing of the idea of struggle for a variety of social, political, economic, and cultural rights in the region. Throughout Iran, various anticolonial and antioppression movements started to form. For instance, a liberation movement took place in southern Azerbaijan in 1919–1920, led by Sheikh Mohammed Khiabani, a progressive Azeri nationalist. Khiabani's "Democratic Party of Azerbaijan" put out a newspaper called *Tajaddud* [Progress] and began spreading revolutionary and democratic ideas in Azerbaijan. Invoking the memory of the 1906 Constitutional Revolution, Khiabani came to symbolize Sattar Khan, the legendary leader of Iran's Constitutional Movement. Within a short period, the Khiabani movement was able to gain the support of the Azerbaijani people, disarm the central government's forces, and declare Azerbaijan an autonomous republic called Azadistan or "the Land of Freedom" (Azeri, 1955).

In the province of Arabistan (now Khuzistan), Sheikh Khaz'al continued to challenge the dictatorial rule of Reza Khan in the country. The sheikh enjoyed the backing and support of the local population and considered himself to be the legitimate ruler of Arabistan. Like other autonomous and semi-independent regions in the country, the Arabistan region during the rule of both Safavids and Qajars enjoyed a considerable degree of autonomy and even entered into various relations with Britain, and other countries in the region (M. Ansari, 1974; Strunk, 1977).

Influenced by democratic and socialist movements in the region and within Iran, in the Kurdish city of Sanandaj a group of workers and peasants came together and formed a party called Social Dimukrat (the Social Democratic Party). Enjoying tremendous popular support, the organization took control of the Sanandaj municipality and began redistributing grain from the warehouses of big landlords among the needy population (see also Ghods, 1989, p. 48). The socialist nature of the movement and its obvious goals to eliminate poverty ran counter to the interests of the upper-class elite, landlords, members of the religious establishment, and bazaar-based merchants. They mobilized their forces and awaited the opportunity to crush the spontaneous movement of workers, peasants, and the subaltern strata.

In 1915, Mirza Kuchik Khan launched the Jangal Movement that eventually culminated in the formation of the Socialist Republic of Gilan in Rasht on June 4, 1920 (Ghods, 1989, p. 65). An experienced activist in the Constitutional Revolution, Mirza Kuchik Khan launched the movement in the forests of his native Gilan, demanding, among other things, autonomous status for the province of Gilan, an end to corruption in the central government, as well as an end to foreign involvement in the affairs of the local people (Abrahamian, 1982, p. 112). The movement had strong popular bases, enjoying the support of grassroots population, the peasantry, workers, and lower strata of populace (Abrahamian, 1982; Ghods, 1989). There were similar movements, disturbances, and discontents all over the country, including the regions of Khorasan, Luristan, and Baluchistan. In such an environment the big landlords, merchants, and the elite segment of Iran's population craved a strong central authority to put an end to various regional movements and bring about the security and stability that they needed in order to continue their privileged existence. At the same time, the antiestablishment and antioppression nature of these movements worried some outside forces, and the British government in particular, who were extremely nervous in the wake of the Bolshevik Revolution in neighboring Russia.

THE RISE OF REZA KHAN AND A RACIST VISION OF GOVERNANCE

Reza Khan was the figure who took advantage of the uncertain situation in the country, and by destroying various movements one after another, he marked his way in Iranian politics. Introduced to the British by an MI6 (the British Secret Intelligence) agent named Sir Ardeshir J. Reporter, Reza Khan was brought to power by the British through the 1921 coup d'état, and worked his way through to become prime minister in 1923, and finally the shah of Iran in 1925 (Shahbazi, 1990). Having enjoyed the unconditional support of the British, Reza Khan was able to suppress numerous socialist, nationalist, and ethnic movements all over Iran. As early as 1925, he was able to replace the ruling Qajar dynasty with his own Pahlavi dynasty. Soon after, he centralized power and authority in Tehran, terminated the semiautonomous status of major regions such as Azerbaijan, Arabistan (Khuzistan), Luristan, and Kurdistan. Simultaneously, he banned the usage of all non-Persian languages in any written form, and set out to enforce his ultranationalist ideology throughout the country. Having centralized the government, he introduced Farsi as the only legitimate Iranian language and placed a ban on the languages of other nationalities. The other languages were repressed either as an imperfect dialect of Farsi, such as Kurdish, Luri, or as alien, non-Indo-European languages, such as Turkish and Arabic. The non-Persian communities were thus forced to witness the eradication of their native culture, language, history, and heritage on a daily basis (Asgharzadeh, 2002; Dei and Asgharzadeh, 2003).

Under Reza Khan's rule, the officially sanctified Iranian history rapidly replaced the existing oral and written histories of various ethnic groups and nationalities. Based on the dominant racist ideology, all peoples living in Iran were to have the common "Aryan ancestry." The non-Persian nationalities were written new histories in line with an Aryanist racist ideology. They were not encouraged to be proud of who they were, because according to the dominant ideology, their heritage and culture were nothing of which to be proud. They were required to be assimilated to "the superior Aryan/Persian race and culture," and if they did not acknowledge the "superiority of Aryan/Persian race," they would then become subjected to humiliation, marginalization, and exclusion.

The presumably Aryan roots of Iran's Persian minority—already recognized in Orientalist literature—were "discovered" in Iran only after the usurpation of political power in 1925 by Reza Khan. Reza Khan adopted Pahlavi—the name of the Middle Persian language—as his last name, and renamed the country Iran, which presumably meant "the birthplace of the Aryan race." Fueled by racist flames spurting up from Nazi Germany, Reza Khan's Pahlavi regime indoctrinated the idea of a superior monolithic racial/ethnic group, the Persian minority in this case, bent on destroying all non-Aryan cultures. Despicable acts of linguicide and deculturation were committed in order to achieve the chauvinistic agenda of ethnic and linguistic purity for the Persian race in Iran.

Reza Khan's racism echoed the racist ideology of European fascism and Nazism, as he came to identify the Persian minority as the sole founder of civilization on the Iranian Plateau and called on non-Persian ethnic groups to abandon their culture and language for the supposedly superior Aryan/Persian culture and language. The Persian tongue was elevated to the status of Iran's national language, replacing all other tongues. To read and write in non-Farsi languages became prohibited, and those other languages were officially identified as "criminalized" tongues. Much like Foucault's (1969) depiction of subjugated peoples, from this point on the economics, histories, social practices, languages, mythologies, and even stories of non-Persian peoples of Iran began to be governed, shaped, and articulated by forces beyond their own control (Baraheni, 1977; Saad, 1996):

> He [Reza Shah] outlawed the traditional dress; appointed a committee to purge Persian of Arabic words; eliminated the provinces of Kurdistan and Arabistan; divided Azerbaijan into two provinces, with one section incorporating a large community of Kurds; began building the Trans-Iranian railway; channeled all foreign trade through the capital; created a centralized bureaucracy; closed all the non-Persian publishing houses; and, most important of all, destroyed minority language schools, building in their place a state educational system with Farsi as the only official language of instruction. (Abrahamian, 1970, p. 296)

Concomitant to Reza Khan's takeover of power in the political sphere, a fierce battle began in cultural and linguistic spheres. Numerous Persian scholars, academicians, writers, and poets began subscribing to the principles of a racist ideology hitherto unknown in Iran. The new regime's racist project was warmly received by both the Persian elite in Iran and their Indo-European-Aryan "blood brothers" abroad (see also Wilber, 1975). The racist project was built around the notion of one country, one nation, one language and Reza Khan vigorously set out to implement it. A major step to achieving this goal was to eliminate signs and symbols of difference and diversity that were manifested mainly in the lifestyles and living conditions of various non-Persian communities, who were largely identified in the dominant discourse as tribes and tribal groups:

> [Reza Khan] felt that most of the tribesmen were of an alien culture. . . . [He] did not think that tribes belonged to 20th century [Iran]. . . . Besides he was hypersensitive to any criticism in the foreign press and was haunted by the fear that Persia might be regarded as a backward country. . . . To him, tribes constituted a shameful anachronism and the very sight of camels, tents and tribal attire [so picturesque to Western eyes] was repugnant. (Oberling, 1974, pp. 149–150; see also Ghani, 1998, p. 333)

Of course, there is more to the above observation than meets the eye. For instance, tribes are said to have "an alien culture." This begs the question, what does alien culture really mean? Evidently, for Reza Khan and his cohorts it meant more than "tents and tribal attire." First and foremost it meant different languages that these supposedly "tribal" communities spoke, which were not the same as the language that Reza Khan spoke—Farsi. However, the nomadic, transitory lifestyle of these communities served to effectively resist, among other things, the attempted amputation of their language, culture, and history. And this posed a major challenge to Reza Khan's

Persianization politics. So, he became determined to annihilate this unique lifestyle by all means possible. Parts of his genocidal acts toward "tribal" communities were revealed immediately after his removal from power in September 1941. For example, a member of parliament from the town of Behbehan, Sultan-Ali Sultani, testified shortly after the dictator's departure:

> The Qashqa'i, Bakhtiyari, Kuhgiluya and other nomads, . . . not only have their property been looted, but group after group of these tribes have been executed without trial. Only in one case they killed several groups of [Kuhgiliya nomads] whom they failed to find guilty in military courts, claiming that they were trying to escape. . . . They killed 97 of the Bahrami tribe . . . in one day, including a thirteen year old boy, and they gaoled four hundred of them in Ahvaz, of whom three hundred lost their lives. They brought khans of the Boyr Ahmad to Tehran with pledge of immunity, and then killed them saying they were rebels. . . . The way they settled the tribes was the way of execution and annihilation, not education and reform. And it is precisely this approach that has sapped the strength of the Iranian society and weakened the hope of national unity. (Katouzian, 2003, p. 28)

The killing of people in the name of modernism and progress is the most barbaric act that shows the savagery of those who consider themselves "modern" and "civilized." Certainly a modern, progressive, and civilized way of dealing with difference and diversity should not culminate in executions, eradications, and annihilations. But this was how the "superior" Aryan mentality functioned and continues to function in Iran. Their perceived sense of "superiority" allowed them to kill and destroy whoever and whatever they considered "backward," "uncivilized," and "inferior."

The Role of the British

The literature exploring the role of the British in Reza Khan's coup d'état is rich and growing (Shahbazi, 1990; Amuzegar, 1991; Ghani, 1998; A.M. Ansari, 2003; Majd, 2003). A recent work in this regard is Mohammad Gholi Majd's (2001) *Great Britain and Reza Shah*. In this book Majd explores the impact of the Russian Revolution of 1917 and the defeat of the Ottomans in 1918 on the sociopolitical situation in Iran. According to him, these developments resulted in Iran being surrounded by the British forces from the east, south, and west. Eventually, British forces invaded the entire country (with the exception of Azerbaijan province) in April 1918. In Majd's view,

> The British military invasion and occupation of 1918 is a cardinal event in the history of Iran. For the next sixty years, Iran effectively lost its independence. For nearly twenty-five years (1918–42), Iran was completely controlled by Britain, and thereafter, and until the Islamic revolution of 1979, Iran fell under the domination of the United States. (Majd, 2001, p. 1)

Although this kind of British hegemony differed from a fully fledged colonization, it nonetheless provided them with sufficient means to effectively control Iranian politics. During the early years of invasion, the British tried to exert their control through their approved and appointed civil governments, puppet members of the parliament, ministers, and even the prime minister. It was to that end that Vossough-od Dovleh was appointed as prime minister in August 1918. Simultaneous with this appointment, the British pushed for the ratification of what was termed the Anglo-Persian Convention of August 1919, which sought to grant major concessions to Great Britain regarding Iran's natural and economic resources, particularly the booming oil industry. However, the proposed agreement was viewed by the general public as an extortionary move levied against their government by an outside force. They vehemently resented the agreement, and the British-backed government of Vossough-od Dovleh was not able to implement it. Many analysts have seen this failure as the failure of civil governments to safeguard British interests in Iran (Majd, 2001; A.M. Ansari, 2003). As a result, it was only logical that the British would turn their attention from a civil government to a military dictatorship. Hence, the invention of Reza Khan Mirpanj.

In recent years, the Iranian historian Abdollah Shahbazi has shed new light on the whole enterprise of Reza Khan and his Pahlavi dynasty. Shahbazi has done so by focusing attention on the role of two otherwise obscure British secret agents in Iran: Sir Ardeshir J. Reporter and his son Sir Shapoor J. Reporter. According to Shahbazi (1990), these two were from the Parsis of India who successively served as MI6 agents in Iran and played crucial roles throughout the Pahlavi era. The Persians or Parsis of India are a small Farsi-speaking community in the western Indian subcontinent who consider themselves to be seventh-century migrants to India, when the presumably Parsi regime of Sasanid collapsed as a result of the Arab-Islamic invasion. This small group has profound attachment to the Farsi language, the Aryan/Persian race, and Iran as a whole (see also Shahbazi, 1990). Shahbazi's research reveals that it was Ardeshir J. Reporter who in effect had "discovered" Reza Khan and presented him to British authorities as a suitable military alternative for a civilian government (Shahbazi, 1990, 1998).

Under the close supervision of the British, as the commander of the Cossack Brigade stationed in Qazvin, Reza Khan entered the capital city on the night of February 21, 1921. He immediately put a number of prominent politicians under arrest, and demanded from the shah of Qajar that a pro-British journalist named Seyyid Ziya Tabatabayi be appointed as the prime minister. The increasingly powerless shah was compelled to concede. By May 1921, Reza Khan acquired the position of minister of war, and by 1923 became the prime minister, replacing Seyyid Ziya Tabatabayi. In 1925, he persuaded the Majlis to officially depose the then powerless Qajar dynasty and establish the new Pahlavi dynasty, headed by Reza Shah Pahlavi as the new king of Iran. Commenting on the occasion, the American minister Joseph S. Kornfeld, reported,

Reza Khan's influence in Persian affairs is most sinister. He must be either curbed or crushed. Unfortunately he is receiving the secret support of the British who feel that they can accomplish their own ends far more easily through him than through the constitutional government. . . . My own observations have forced on me the conclusion that, notwithstanding their protestations to the contrary, at heart the British are opposed to the Open Door in Persia. Finding it impossible to close the door, they seek to bring into the house such chaos and confusion as will deter others from entering. Reza Khan is an admirable tool in their hands. (Kornfeld, August 21, 1923, cited in Majd, 2001, pp. 75–76)

There may still exist a few diehard monarchists insisting that Reza Khan took power through his own merit. However, in the light of overwhelming evidence, such assertions amount to nothing more than wishful thinking. The origin, nature, and character of contemporary racism, oppression, and exclusion cannot be adequately analyzed without looking at the role that outside powers such as Britain, Russia, and America have played in the creation of such injustices. The point is not to just establish that the British played a central role in bringing to power a hated dictator. More importantly, the point is to highlight the responsibility that they still have for the ongoing racism and oppression that are a legacy of the 1921 coup d'é tat. Reza Khan's vision of a chauvinistic regime grounded in a reactionary nationalism, racism, monolingualism, and monoculturalism still functions in Iranian society. As such, it is only logical to remind those who brought him to power of their complicity and responsibility throughout this history of oppression, beginning from the coup of 1921 and continuing into the present.

The Impact of Nazi Germany

The year 1933 witnessed in Germany the rise to power of the National Socialist Party. Taking note of the successful commercial ties with Iran, and realizing Reza Shah's fascistic tendencies, the Nazi leadership sought to increase German influence in all political, social, and economic spheres in Iran. As early as 1933, the Nazis began to publish a racist journal titled *Iran-e Bastan* [The Ancient Iran]. The journal was financed by Siemens-Schuk-kert, and Major von Viban of the Political Department of the NADFA in Berlin handled the editorial issues. A pro-Nazi Iranian intellectual named Sheikh Abdul-Rahman Seif worked as coeditor of the journal (Blucher, 1949, p. 137).

Iran-e Bastan played a very important role in advocating Persian racism among the Iranian elite and intellectuals. It provided a starting point for Persian nationalists to launch their chauvinistic attack on whoever they did not see as Aryan. Following the Nazi journal, all kinds of chauvinistic magazines, journals, and newspapers such as *Iranshahr, Mehr-e Iran* [The Love of Iran], *Partow-e Iran* [The Light of Iran], *Anahita, Takht-e Jamshid* [The Seat of Jamshid, Imaginary Ancient Persian King] dominated the Persian literary scene. All these publications highlighted the past and the pre-Islamic glories of the Persian nation and blamed the supposedly "savage Arabs and Turks" for the backwardness of Iran.

In 1936, Dr. Hjalmar Schacht, the German finance minister and president of the Reichbank paid a visit to Reza Shah. A year after, Hasan Esfandiari, the speaker of Iranian Majlis, visited Berlin and was cordially received by Hitler, Goring, Schacht, and other Nazi Party members (Lenczowski, 1949, p. 161). Toward the end of 1937, Reza Shah was visited by Baldur von Schirach, the head of the Nazi Youth Organization. Through him, Hitler sent an invitation to Reza Shah to visit Germany. Reza Shah declined, fearing that such a visit may upset the Russians and the British (Yazdi, 1945, p. 39). In the same year (1937) Reza Shah granted to German Lufthansa a concession to fly passengers, freight, and mail across Iran's northern sector to link Berlin with Tehran and Kabul. Reza Shah even went so far as granting Lufthansa the permission to land in an important military airport in Mashhad (Rezun, 1982, p. 25).

The Nazis found a favorable climate amongst the Iranian elite to spread fascistic and racist propaganda. The Nazi propaganda machine advocated the (supposedly) common Aryan ancestry of "the two Nations." In order to further cultivate racist tendencies, in 1936, the Reich Cabinet issued a special decree exempting Iranians from the restrictions of the Nuremberg Racial Laws on the grounds that they were "pure-blooded Aryans" (Lenczowski, 1944, p. 160). In 1939, the Nazis provided Persians with what they called a German Scientific Library. The library contained over 7,500 books carefully selected "to convince Iranian readers . . . of the kinship between the National Socialist Reich and the 'Aryan culture' of Iran" (Lenczowski, 1944, p. 161). In various pro-Nazi publications, lectures, speeches, and ceremonies, parallels were drawn among Reza Shah, Hitler, and Mussolini to emphasize the charismatic resemblances among these leaders (Rezun, 1982, p. 29).

The Reza Shah regime began to sponsor conferences in which Nazi lecturers were invited to deliver speeches on race, ethnicity, culture, and history. Among Iranian intellectuals, those who demonstrated pro-Nazi tendencies were awarded titles and honorary degrees. Reza Khan's regime went so far as accepting the emblem of the swastika as a permanent decoration of art in Iran (see also Rezun, 1982, p. 29).

It was around this time that pro-Nazi and profascist propaganda reached their peak in the dominant Iranian discourse, and Hitler became a national hero of Iranians and all so-called oppressed Aryan peoples. For instance, a journal titled *Nameh-ye Iran-e Bastan* [The Journal of Ancient Iran] identified Hitler as "one of the greatest men in the world":

Adolph Hitler, this great scholarly man of the Aryan race, has destroyed a 200-year old plan of the Jews against nationality in the world [against] nationalism, and particularly the Aryan races on earth . . . and has created a new day for the new world. (*Nameh-ye Iran-e Bastan*, August 1933, issue 28, p. 1; see also JAMI, 1983, p. 74)

Regarding the Nazi symbol of the swastika, the journal wrote in issue 28, August 1933:

It is truly rejoicing to see that the symbol of Iran from 2000 years before Christ has today become a symbol of pride for the Germans, who are of one race and ethnicity with us. (*Nameh-ye Iran-e Basta*, August 1933, issue 28, p. 1; see also JAMI, 1983, pp. 74–75)

Again, in issue 35, September 1933, in an article titled "Why We Are Superior?" the following was written in the journal:

[T]he sign of Aryan triumph (swastika) is everywhere Aryan and respectable, be it on ceramics of Isfahan's Masjid-e Shah or on the column of Darvazeh Dovlat in Tehran; or be it placed on the flag of Germany or embellish the arm of "Hitler." From ancient times the Black dress has been an exclusive property of the Iranic race. If other nations have also made it their official dress or for instance the Fascists of Italy have made it their specific symbol, one must know that based on the absolute rule of history this has been an idea of the Iranians who are the father of all civilized Aryan nations. (*Nameh-ye Iran-e Bastan*, September 1933, issue 35, pp. 1–2; see also JAMI, 1983, p. 75)

It is important to note that infatuation with Nazism and Aryanism was not limited to official circles. The ideology of Aryan racial superiority was nurtured and advocated by a vast majority of Persian elites and intellectuals. Even some members of non-Persian minority groups were eager to identify themselves with the Nazis and the superior Aryan race. In the following passage a member of the Turkic-speaking Qashqayi community remembers how he and his friend used to dream about the coming of their "superior Aryan saviors":

Germany was our age-old and natural ally. Love of Germany was synonymous with love for Iran. . . . The sound of German officers' footsteps was heard on the shores of the Nile. Swastika flags were flying from the outskirts of Moscow to the peaks of the Caucasus Mts. Iranian patriots eagerly awaited the arrival of their old allies. . . . My friend and I would spin tales about the grandeur of the superior race. We considered Germany the chosen representative of this race in Europe, and Iran [its representative] in Asia. The right to life and rule was ours. Others had no choice but submission and slavery. We discarded the old maps and remade Iran into a country larger than what it was in Achaemenian times. (Beygi, 1989, cited in Sprachman, 2002, pp. 203–204)

In the above passage, Beygi talks about the way he and his young friend considered Iran to be the representative of "the superior race" in Asia, just as Germany was supposed to be in Europe. The writer is looking, retrospectively, at the prevailing ideas during World War II when he was a young man in Iran. His depiction of Nazi mentality, of the superior Aryan race and their connection to Iran is a reflection of how the majority of Iranian intellectuals viewed the world at the time. This pro-Nazi mentality was, no doubt, fueled by the racist agenda and mission of the Reza Shah government, which now preferred the overt racism of Hitler's regime to his own initial custodians, the British. The bourgeoning racist mentality was never limited to the government apparatuses alone. It was shared and commonly nurtured by a great majority of poets, writers, artists, and intellectuals who mainly came from the privileged ethnic and linguistic background. It was for this reason that when the allies deposed Reza Khan in August 1941 due to his pro-Nazi activities, racism and Aryanism did not disappear with the removal of the dictator. On the contrary, they continued to grow and flourish under the rule of Reza Khan's son, Mohammad Reza Pahlavi.

WORLD WAR II AND THE RISE OF MOHAMMAD REZA SHAH

Since the beginning of the war in 1939, Reza Khan had supported pro-German and pro-Nazi activities in the country. Fearing the Soviets and the British he declared Iran's neutrality, but he made no serious attempt to restrict the activities of pro-German forces. In June 1941, German forces began their offensive against the USSR. Soon after the offensive, the Soviet and British diplomatic missions in Tehran demanded the expulsion of a large number of Germans, accusing the Iranian government of sheltering a German fifth column (Lenczowski, 1949, p. 168). On August 25, 1941, Soviets from the north and the British from the south invaded Iran. On September 16, 1941, the allied forces deposed Reza Shah and put his young son Mohammad Reza in power. On the following morning, September 17, British and Soviet forces entered Tehran. Reza Shah's brutal army, which was so "fierce and brave" in killing dissenting Iranians and plundering non-Persian communities, humiliatingly capitulated in the face of the occupying forces. More surprisingly, there was no public protest against the dethroning of Reza Khan, a fact that testified to the extreme shallowness and unpopularity of the Pahlavi regime.

Reza Khan fled the country, seeking exile first on the island of Mauritius and then in Johannesburg, South Africa, where he died on July 26, 1944. After digesting the hallucinatory impact of his father's fall from grace, the young Mohammad Reza cautiously followed the orders of his new masters, first the British, and later on the Americans. He faithfully continued to improve his father's dream of a Fars-centered, aggressive nationalism, a powerful centralized state, and a superficially emulative westernization of the country. The first serious challenge to his rule came through the demands of various nationalities and ethnic groups for equal treatment, cultural rights, and the right for self-determination. Among various ethnic movements, those of the Azeri and Kurdish nationalities posed the most important challenge to the new shah's rule. Their struggle eventually culminated in the formation of the democratic republics of Azerbaijan and Kurdistan in 1945. The movements of these two major nationalities were the most salient examples that redefined notions of nationalism, ethnicities, homeland, national identity, and parameters of national/geographic boundaries in Iran.

The Challenge of Two Autonomous Republics

It is an undisputable fact of Iranian politics that, whenever there has been a weakening in the authority of the central government, various regional and ethnic movements have erupted throughout the country. This was the case immediately before the takeover of Reza Khan, when the Qajar dynasty was at its weakest. It was the case during World War I, and most certainly during World War II. Similar to previous cases, the breakout of World War II brought about the conditions for various national, ethnic, and antiracist sentiments to explode. On August 25, 1941, the Red Army invaded northern parts of Iran, pushing the Pahlavi regime's military out of Azerbaijani territory. Following these changes, an ethnic organization called the Azerbaijan Society was formed and started publishing a journal titled *Azerbaijan*. The journal was written in Azeri and Farsi languages and aimed to expose the racist nature of the Pahlavi dictatorship.

In October 1943, Mir Ja'far Pishevari, a seasoned journalist and political activist, was nominated from Azerbaijan to the Fourteenth Majlis of Iran. He was a 50-year-old native of Azerbaijan who had spent most of his life in Baku and had returned to Iran after the 1917 Bolshevik Revolution. Due to his antigovernment activities, he had been imprisoned by Reza Shah's regime for 12 years. After Reza Shah's fall, Pishevari, along with other political prisoners, had been set free. After his release, he went to Tehran and started a newspaper called *Azhir* [The Siren]. The people of Tabriz had voted for him unanimously. Despite his victory in Azerbaijan, the Iranian Majlis had rejected his candidacy on the grounds that he was a communist, a traitor, and disloyal to Iran's territorial integrity. Khoyi, another Azerbaijani deputy from the city of Tabriz, had met the same fate as Pishevari.

The Azeris viewed the parliament's rejection of their elected candidates as a direct insult to their integrity and their nationality (JAMI, 1983). Following his rejection by the parliament, Pishevari entrusted the editorship of Azhir to friends and returned to Azerbaijan in August 1945 to form the Azerbaijan Democratic Party (Azerbaycan Demokrat Firqesi, ADF). On November 23, the Central Committee of the Azerbaijan Democratic Party issued a proclamation defining its aim as the obtainment of complete autonomy for Azerbaijan. The party made it clear that autonomy for Azerbaijan did not mean secession from Iran. The people of Tabriz warmly welcomed the formation of the Azerbaijan Democratic Party. Following the ADF's proclamation, a regional Congress of Azerbaijan that was composed of party supporters, designated a 39-membered commission to organize elections to a national assembly.

On December 12, the provincial National Assembly was formally inaugurated in Tabriz. The assembly was composed of 101 deputies, all democrats and Azeri nationalists from various backgrounds such as workers and laborers, who were determined to demand autonomy for Azerbaijan (see also Atabaki, 1993, p. 129). As its first important task on the day of inauguration, the National Assembly proclaimed the autonomous Republic of Azerbaijan and designated a government under the premiership of Mir Ja'far Pishevari, the founder of the Azerbaijan Democratic Party (ADF). The newly formed government of Azerbaijan announced that the autonomous state would be run on "democratic principles." It issued a program that granted women the right to vote; it announced that private property would be respected but that the government would distribute to landless farmers state-owned lands as well as the lands of reactionary landlords who had run away from Azerbaijan, as a result of the ongoing movement. Further, the government assured the Azerbaijani people that "traitors and reactionaries" would be purged from the gendarmerie, that a "people's army" would be formed from local militia groups, and that Azeri-Turkic would be the official language of the state.

Simultaneously with the Azerbaijani movement, a Kurdish movement took place in the province of Kurdistan, west of Azerbaijan. On December 15, 1945, the Democratic Party of Kurdistan proclaimed a Kurdish People's Republic. On January 21, 1946, Qazi Mohammad was elected to the presidency of the Kurdish Republic. The Kurdish Republic set out to follow the democratic reforms and events taking place in the neighboring Azerbaijan. While sending observers to the Azerbaijan parliament, the Kurds maintained their distinct identity and insisted on the independence of the Kurdish Republic. Following the negotiations between the two republics, a treaty was signed on April 23, 1946 between the Kurdistan and Azerbaijan governments. While emphasizing the mutual respect, cooperation, and fraternity between the two oppressed nations, the treaty provided for military alliance, exchange of diplomatic missions, fair treatment of minorities, and common diplomatic action toward the Pahlavi regime in Tehran (see also A. Roosevelt, 1947).

The Azerbaijan democratic government quickly proceeded to carry out its plans. As a major step in eliminating feudal oppression, it started a land distribution program all over the Republic of Azerbaijan. On February 16, 1946, the National Assembly of Azerbaijan passed two important bills regarding the land reform. Based on these bills, lands belonging to reactionary feudals who had opposed the national government, or who had left Azerbaijan due to the democratic movement, were to be distributed among landless farmers. Considering the fact that the majority of Azerbaijani feudal lords had already run away from Azerbaijan in the process of the democratic movement, this distribution amounted to a significant portion of agrarian land (see also Atabaki, 1993). Moreover, the bills asked for the redistribution of all state-owned lands, along with the water rights, rivers, springs, and qanats, among the peasants who lived on those lands and who cultivated them. The reform resulted in the distribution of over 380,000 hectares of land amongst more than 1 million landless peasants (Atabaki, 1993).

Following the two above-mentioned bills, another bill was passed that dealt with the system of sharecropping. Traditionally there was no viable agreement between the peasant and the landlord regarding the peasant's share of the crop. Normally it was left to the benevolence of the landlord to decide what to give to each peasant in exchange for his cultivation of the land. The new bill guaranteed to each farmer a minimum share of the crop that he produced on a landlord's land. Now the farmer's share rose from about 20 percent in the old system to more than 43 percent (see also Atabaki, 1993, p. 150). Considering the fact that about 75 percent of the people in Azerbaijan were farmers at the time (Kazemi, 1980, p. 14), the land reform testified to the profoundly popular nature of the Azerbaijani democratic movement.

In the course of less than one year, the democratic government was able to lay the foundation of a modern educational system in Azerbaijan. In terms of education and pedagogy, the national government completely revolutionized Azerbaijani society. The first provincial university in Iran was built in Tabriz. Thousands of schools were built in small towns and villages all over Azerbaijan, accompanied by the introduction of compulsory primary education for all kids beginning at the age of six. For the first time, Azeri-Turkic became the official language in Azerbaijan and was taught in Tabriz University (the only university in Azerbaijan), schools, and adult education centers, replacing Farsi.

For the first time in the history of Iran, universal suffrage was introduced. Women gained the right to elect as well as be elected. The ADF encouraged women to take active parts in the sociopolitical life of the republic. As a result, women participated in various positions from administration to teaching to working in the hospitals and even to serving in the national army of Azerbaijan (JAMI, 1983, pp. 289–295). Important measures were taken to secure the rights of the workers and emphasize the obligations of the employers, landlords, and owners/operators of small workshops. A labor code was introduced that limited the work to eight hours a day, introduced minimum wages, forbade child labor, acknowledged trade unions, recognized May 1 as a national holiday, and established the right of the workers to social benefits (ADF, 1946).

Under the democratic government, a big texture company named Zafar was established in Tabriz. An orphanage was created to take care of needy children. The National Theatre Center was opened in Tabriz. A radio station was established. Numerous publishing houses were opened and countless newspapers, journals, magazines, and books were published in the Azeri language (Berengian, 1988, pp. 186–210). Promotion of Azerbaijan's culture, history, language, and music was greatly emphasized. All the banks in Tabriz were nationalized, holding more than 3 million tomans at the time (Lenczowski, 1949, p. 289). Furthermore, a commission formed from representatives of ministries of Trade, Economics, and Finance was called upon to establish trade connections with foreign governments. William Douglas, an American jurist who was traveling in Azerbaijan shortly after the democratic movement, notes, "I learned from my travels in Azerbaijan in 1950 that Pishevari was an astute politician who forged a program for Azerbaijan that is still enormously popular" (1951, p. 43):

> Pishevari's program was so popular—especially land reform, severe punishment of public officials who took bribes, and price control—that if there had been a free election in Azerbaijan during the summer of 1950, Pishevari would have been restored to power by the vote of 90 per cent of the people. And yet, not a thousand people in Azerbaijan out of three million are communists. (Douglas, 1951, p. 50)

And finally, in the words of Swietochowski (1995), under the democratic government, "Azerbaijan had achieved more in one year than it had during the twenty years of the Pahlavi regime" (p. 149). Although the rate and pace of changes were faster in Azerbaijan than they were in the neighboring Kurdish Republic, Kurdistan was embracing many cultural, political, and socioeconomic transformations hitherto unknown in the region. Similar to the Azerbaijani situation, the Democratic Party of Kurdistan, led by Qazi Mohammad, was at the forefront of these transformations. On November 8, 1945, the party publicly announced its program and long-term policies:

1. The Kurds to be free and independent in the management of their local affairs and to receive Kurdish independence within the borders of Iran.
2. Be allowed to study Kurdish and to administer their affairs in the Kurdish language.
3. Government officials definitely be appointed from among the local population.
4. Members of the Kurdish Provincial Council to be elected immediately in accordance with the constitutional laws, to supervise all public and government works.
5. By the passing of a general law, the grievances existing between the farmer and the landowner to be amended and their future positions defined.
6. The Democratic Party of Kurdistan will make special efforts to create complete unity and brotherhood between the Azerbaijan nation and the people who live in Azerbaijan (Assyrian, Armenians, etc.).
7. The Democratic Party of Kurdistan will fight to take advantage of the boundless natural wealth of Kurdistan and to improve the agriculture, commerce, education and health of Kurdistan, in order to secure economic and moral welfare for the Kurds.
8. We wish the nations who live in Iran to be able to work for their freedom and for the welfare and progress of their country. (DPK, 1945; see also Koohi-Kamali, 2003, p. 106)

In addition to various economic, political, and cultural developments, the Kurdish Republic signed an important agreement of Friendship and Cooperation with its Azerbaijani counterpart. This agreement further highlighted the common goal of the struggle of two oppressed peoples and their common desire for autonomy and self-determination. Based on this mutually signed treaty,

1. Representatives will be exchanged between the two National Governments in such places as may be considered necessary.
2. In specified parts of Azerbaijan which are inhabited by Kurds, Kurds will take part in the administrative work of government and in specified parts of Kurdistan which are inhabited by Azerbaijanis, Azerbaijanis will take part in the administrative work of government.
3. In order to solve the common economic problems of the two nations a mixed Economic Commission will be formed and the heads of the two national governments will endeavor to put into practice the decisions of this Commission.
4. Cooperation between the military forces of the Azerbaijan national government will be organized and in time of need the military forces of each government will mutually render each other all necessary assistance.

5. If any negotiating with the Tehran Government becomes necessary it shall be undertaken after agreement between the views of both the Azerbaijan and Kurdistan National Governments.
6. The Azerbaijan National Government will as far as possible create the necessary condition for the development of the national language and culture of the Kurds living in Azerbaijan and the National Government of Kurdistan will likewise as far as possible create the necessary conditions for the development of the national language and culture of Azerbaijanis living in Kurdistan.
7. The two contracting parties will take joint steps to punish any person who attempts to destroy or smirch the historic friendship and national, democratic brotherhood of the Azerbaijan and Kurdish peoples. (Cited in Koohi-Kamali, 2003, pp. 114–115)

This joint treaty of friendship and cooperation was a major blow to the dominant Aryanist/racist ideology that considered the Kurds an Aryan people and looked upon the Azeris as a non-Aryan, non-Indo-European, Turkic people. This experience once again showed that being subjected to a common oppression is capable of creating a common zone of resistance against racism and colonialism. It also showed that divisions such as Aryan and non-Aryan were artificial constructs created to secure the privileged position of the dominant group particularly by dividing the oppressed communities and turning them against each other. When it came to destroying the marginalized communities' autonomous nationhood, civic rights and democratic freedoms, the Indo-European-speaking Kurdish community was as much a target as the Turkic-speaking Azeri community. It was and is only through cooperation, sharing, and the common struggle of these oppressed communities that the racist and colonialist system in Iran can be defeated.

The Triumph of Racist Order and the Collapse of the Republics
The elections for the Fifteenth Majlis of Iran were to begin on December 7, 1946. At this time, Soviet forces had already left Azerbaijan and the Soviet Consulate in Tabriz was pushing the ADF for negotiation and peaceful settlement of the issues with the Iranian government. Qavam-us-Saltaneh, the Iranian prime minister, after promising a major oil concession to the USSR, had returned to Tehran from his Moscow trip. The oil concession had been granted to the Soviets on the condition that it be ratified by the future Majlis.

The oil concession did not only mean establishing of a strong economic relationship between the two countries, but, more importantly, it meant the security of Soviet borders in Iranian northern zone, particularly in the rivalry with the British and the newly arrived Americans. The Soviets were very concerned about the security of their borders with Iran and a beneficial oil concession meant that their active presence in northern and northwestern parts of Iran would be guaranteed. After extorting the oil concession, now the Russians needed its ratification. And this called for a speedy election processes to the new Majlis. Qavam had made it clear that the elections would not be held unless the government was in a position to supervise them all over the country, including Azerbaijan and Kurdistan. The existence of autonomous Azeri and Kurdish republics had thus become an obstacle for the ratification of the Russian oil concession. Without considering any ethical, ideological, or political consequences of their actions, the Soviet authorities decided to side with the Pahlavi regime, pressing the republics to surrender.

In a famous letter written to Pishevari on May 8, 1946, the Soviet dictator Joseph Stalin threatened the Azerbaijani leader over the latter's diversion from what Stalin called the Lenin's path. He advised the Azeri leader that the advantage of Azerbaijan's working class, as well as the working peoples of Iran and the whole world, would only be maintained through ADF's cooperation with Prime Minister Qavam-us-Saltaneh (Stalin, 1946). In the meantime, the British, now working hand in hand with Qavam, had engineered another scenario in the south. In September 1946, a puppet Qashqayi chief in the south led his Qashqayi tribes to capture a number of towns and villages. They then issued a list of demands asking for autonomy similar to that of Azerbaijan and Kurdistan. They made it clear that if the government did not destroy the autonomous republics, the Qashqayis would capture more towns and would constitute their own autonomous republic. The ADF considered the Qashqayi rebellion a scenario orchestrated by the central government in order to crush the autonomous republics (JAMI, 1983, pp. 374–397).

Through the Qashqayi rebellion, the British manifested their strength to the Iranian ruling elite and, thereby, further emboldened Qavam-us-Saltaneh in his determination to destroy the autonomous republics (see also Lenczowski, 1949, p. 307; Hassanpour, 1994). Around mid-October 1946, Qavam formed a new cabinet and reached an agreement with Qashqayi chiefs in the south, promising them that he would use all his power to protect Iran's territorial integrity and to return Azerbaijan and Kurdistan back to the motherland. Meanwhile, George V. Allen, the newly appointed American ambassador to Iran, made it clear that his government was supportive of Prime Minister Qavam's "democratic decisions" and would do whatever it could to implement them (Lenczowski, 1949, p. 308).

On the pretext of supervising parliamentary elections, on November 24, 1946, Qavam ordered the troops to march into Azerbaijan. On December 3, Pishevari assured the Azerbaijnis that the national army of Azerbaijan was ready to defend the republic. He made it clear that there would be "death but no return" to colonial conditions (Pishevari, December 3, 1946). On December 10, Qavam's army reached Azerbaijani territory. The first confrontation took place in the outskirts of Mianeh. The Azerbaijani army pushed the invading forces back and advanced toward Zanjan (JAMI, 1983, p. 415). Nevertheless, two days later, the ADF, under heavy pressure from the Soviets, decided to give up resistance and allow the Iranian army to enter into Azerbaijan.

The premier of Azerbaijan, Ja'far Pishevari, rejected the Soviet demand to surrender and argued in favor of resistance (JAMI, 1983, pp. 416–417).

The other Central Committee members of ADF followed the Soviet line. Pishevari resigned from the government and left for Baku. On December 12, 1946, the remaining ADF leaders called on all Azerbaijanis to abandon resistance and allow the Iranian army a peaceful entry into Tabriz. The army, on the other hand, was anything but peaceful. Conscious and assured of nonresistance on the part of Azerbaijanis, the army, accompanied by gangs and thugs hired and armed by local landlords, entered Azerbaijan and savagely massacred its unarmed people:

> When the Persian Army returned to Azerbaijan, it came with a roar. Soldiers ran riot, looting and plundering, taking what they wanted. The Russian Army had been on its best behavior. The Persian Army—the army of emancipation—was a savage army of occupation. It left a brutal mark on the people. The beards of peasants were burned, their wives and daughters raped. Houses were plundered; livestock was stolen. The Army was out of control. Its mission had been liberation, but it preyed on the civilians, leaving death and destruction behind. (Douglas, 1951, p. 45)

After the invasion of Azerbaijan, the shah's army marched into the neighboring Republic of Kurdistan. The leader of the Kurdistan Democratic Party, Qazi Mohammad, was hanged in Mhabad, along with his supporters. Mass executions of participants, sympathizers, and those suspected of supporting the national movements were performed in public, followed by the burning of books, magazines, and pamphlets published in ethnic languages. Shortly after the fall of national governments, the "book-burning ceremonies" became a source of celebration and entertainment for the members of the dominant group and their invading army. The racist ruling elite made it clear that the book-burning rituals were conducted for the purpose of sealing the destiny of Azeri-Turkic in Iran once for all (see also Heyat, 1983, 1990; Berengian, 1988; Haqqi, 1993; Farzaneh, 1998).

As a boy growing up in Tabriz at the time, Professor Reza Baraheni recalls some painful memories regarding the book-burning ceremonies in his hometown:

> They forced us to take the books which were written in our mother tongue to the Shahrdari Square, and made us set the books on fire. The rising flames were reaching the feet of the men hanging from the gallows over our heads. After the fall of the Democratic Party, they would drag the Fadayis—those who guarded Tabriz on days and asphalted its streets at night—out of the houses, and right in front of us kids of that period, they would order them to walk. . . . And then, right before our eyes, they would shoot them from behind and leave their bodies in the gutter. (Baraheni, June 9, 2006)

The world renowned north Azerbaijani poet Samad Vurghun recited a poem at the 1952 World Peace Congress held in Paris, by way of protesting the massacre of Azerbaijani people. The poem was titled "Yandirilan

Kitablar" ["Books That Burned"] and was addressed to the shah of Iran who was referred to as "the butcher." Below I have rendered parts of Vurghun's poem into English:

> Hey Butcher!
> Don't you know
> The pile upon pile of books you're burning
> Are symbols of a thousand creativities?
> And desires of a thousand hearts?
>
> Hey Butcher!
> They're in my language
> Those proverbs, those poems
> In each of them
> Hearts of a thousand mothers are beating
> In each of them
> Thousands of children are laughing
> Tell me butcher
> Do you understand this?
>
> Hey Butcher!
> What are those gallows?
> Who are those upon them?
> It's no game, Butcher!
> The blood that you're drinking like a wolf
> Is my people's blood
> Those hanging from your gallows
> Are my flesh and blood, my people
> Do you understand this, Butcher?
>
> (Vurgun, 1952, cited in Heyat, 1990, pp. 133–135)

The invading army remained in Azeri and Kurdish areas and continued the persecution of supporters of the national movements. After a few years, the shah declared a national amnesty and military rule was lifted. The Persian chauvinistic propaganda, along with a relentless campaign against the democratic movements, continued. December 12, 1946, the day of occupation, was commemorated as a national holiday and was celebrated in all government offices, schools, and streets. The young Mohammad Reza Shah was praised as the mighty hero of "Azerbaijan Crisis" and "the Bringer of Azerbaijan to the Bosom of the Mother Land." Eyewitnesses and unofficial Azerbaijani sources have estimated the number of people killed in Azerbaijan and Kurdistan during the occupation to be over 50, 000 (see also Hassanpour, 1994). Although the movements were brutally suppressed, they made a lasting impact in the history of the struggle of Azeri and Kurdish peoples for self-determination. The democratic parties that led the two movements remain active and pursue the aims and goals of the fallen republics. The knowledge gained from the two republics has been a valuable experience in self-governance and nation building. In the words of

Professor Amir Hassanpour,

> The two nationalist movements were powerful engines of social change in the multinational country of Iran. They were an inseparable link in the successive struggles for democracy, freedom, and independence—the Babi movement (1848–53); the tobacco movement (1890–92); the Constitutional Revolution (1905–11); the revolutionary struggles of Azerbaijan, Gilan, and Khurasan (1918–21); the oil nationalization movement of 1951–53; the 1967–68 uprising of Kurdistan; the 1978–79 revolution; and the autonomy movement of Kurdistan (since 1979). The two movements were distinguished from their predecessors by their distinctively nationalist character. (Hassanpour, 1994, p. 98)

Prime Minister Mosaddeq and the Coup of 1953

Dr. Mohammad Mosaddeq (1882–1967) was an old politician who in 1951 became Iran's prime minister. He was a Western-educated lawyer well known for his nationalistic and somewhat anti-British views. Prior to his appointment to the post of prime minister, he was an eloquent spokesperson for the nationalization of Iran's oil industry, which was then under British control, functioning by way of the Anglo-Iranian Oil Company (see also Abrahamian, 1982; Diba, 1986; Torkman, 1996). On April 28, 1951, with the help of like-minded deputies in the parliament, Mosaddeq managed to have an important bill ratified by the Majlis pertaining to the nationalization of the oil industry. The law was approved by the Senate the following day and signed by the shah shortly after (see also Zabih, 1986; Katouzian, 1999; A.M. Ansari, 2003). This was a major achievement that for the first time showed an Iranian political body acting from a position of strength vis-à-vis the interests of British colonial power. As expected, the nationalization of the oil industry did not sit well with the British. Irrespective of this, Dr. Mosaddeq was hailed as a popular national leader in Iran; he was also looked upon as an anticolonial figure of great importance in the Middle East and various Southern countries (Katouzian, 1999; A.M. Ansari, 2003).

Nationalization of the oil industry was by no means the only achievement of the Mosaddeq government. He also exacted considerable blows to the shah's absolute power, creating various legal and administrative obstacles in the way of the Pahlavi family's misuse of public funds and national resources:

> Mosaddeq followed up his victory with a rapid succession of blows struck not only at the shah and the military but also at the landed aristocracy and the two Houses of Parliament. He excluded royalists from the cabinet and named himself acting minister of war. . . . He transferred Reza Shah's lands back to the state; cut the palace budget, and allocated the savings to the Health Ministry; placed the royal charities under government supervision; . . . forbade the shah to communicate directly with foreign diplomats; forced Princess Asharaf, the politically active twin sister of the shah, to leave the country. . . . By May 1953,

the shah had been stripped of all the powers he had fought for and recovered since August 1941. (Abrahamian, 1982, pp. 272–273)

Mosaddeq's democratization of the state apparatuses appealed not only to the general public but also to a vast majority of leftist activists and socialist groups such as the pro-Soviet Tudeh Party of Iran. His increasing popularity with leftist groups served to further alienate the already disillusioned Islamist/religious faction headed by Ayatollah Abol-Qasem Kashani. The British, on the other hand, used the pretext of "leftist influence" to appeal to the American government on the grounds that Mosaddeq was getting too close to the Soviets. The slogan of "spread of communism" emboldened the British and the Americans to take action against the Mosaddeq government, a joint action that came to be known as the first CIA-orchestrated (the U.S. Central Intelligence Agency) coup d'état against an independent government (K. Roosevelt, 1979).

The initial joint attempts of the Pahlavi family and their foreign backers to replace Mosaddeq miserably failed on August 16, 1953, forcing the shah to flee to Baghdad and later to Italy. Three days later, on August 19, the British Intelligence Service (MI6) and CIA staged a more organized attack, accompanied by tanks, army personnel, and forces from the gendarmerie under the command of General Fazlollah Zahedi. The plotters also managed to organize a large number of bribed thugs and hooligans led by "Shaban the Brainless" (Shaban Bimokh), who filled the streets of the capital city and demonstrated against the Mosaddeq government. After nine hours of battle around Mosaddeq's residence, he was captured and his government was over-thrown. The coup d'état prime minister, General Fazlollah Zahedi, took charge of the government, and the shah was restored to power as an American puppet. Shortly after his return, in a meeting with Kermit Roosevelt, the CIA agent who along with Shapoor J. Reporter and others had organized the coup, the shah thanked Roosevelt, and the U.S. government:

> The United States and Great Britain lent "successful" support [to the Shah's restoration to power]. At the end of this true account, in the late summer of 1953, the Shah said to me truthfully, "I owe my throne to God, my people, my army—and to you!" By "you" he meant me and the two countries—Great Britain and the United States—I was representing. We were all heroes. (K. Roosevelt, 1979, p. ix)

Much has been said about the details of this coup d'état and its overall impact. For our purpose here, suffice it to mention the open admission of the coup against Mosaddeq by the Clinton administration's Secretary of State Madeline K. Albright, who stated the following on March 17, 2000:

> In 1953, the United States played a significant role in orchestrating the overthrow of Iran's popular prime minister, Mohammed Mossadegh . . . the coup was clearly a set back for Iran's political development and it is easy to see why so many Iranians continue to resent this intervention by America in their internal affairs. (Albright, March 17, 2000)

With full American backing, the shah was now confident of the security of his throne (see also Alexander and Nanes, 1980). He set out to exercise his absolute power, without any regard for human rights and democracy. Like his father before him, he continued to build a totalitarian, centralized state, based on the absolute power of the king in the political sphere, and modeled on the Persian identity in discursive and sociocultural realms.

The Father and Son's Racist Legacy

The two Pahlavi monarchs ruled Iran for over half a century. Throughout their reign, they managed to establish a number of fallacies in state and nation building that continued to flourish well past their era, defining in a very narrow sense the perimeters of Iranianness, the status of national/official language, and the notion of Iranian identity. If one could sum up the legacy that they left behind particularly in terms of governance and nation building, it should be the legacy of "one nation, one language, one country" slogan, a racist doctrine that still continues to haunt Iran and Iranians.

One Country, One Nation, One Language
At the same time that the British were preparing Reza Khan for the infamous coup d'état, a chauvinistic organization named Anjoman-e Iran-e Javan (The Young Iran's Association) was in the process of formation. This organization officially began its activities in 1921, the year of Reza Khan's coup d'état against the Qajar king. Mahmoud Afshar, a well-known pan-Aryanist, was selected as the chairman of the organization. The group published a journal titled *Ayandeh* [The Future], as its official organ. In the inaugural issue of *Ayandeh*, published in June 1925, the group put forth its manifesto, expressing the urgent need for "national unity" in Iran:

> [A]chieving national unity means that the Persian language must be dominant throughout the whole country, that regional differences in clothing, customs and so on must disappear, and that political autonomy of different regions must be eliminated. . . . Unless we achieve national unity in realms of language, behavior, clothing, etc., we will be in constant danger of losing our sovereignty and territorial integrity. . . . Certain Persian speaking tribes should be sent amongst groups who speak a foreign language, while the tribes of that region which speak a foreign language should be transferred and settled in Persian speaking areas. . . . Geographical names in foreign languages . . . should be replaced by Persian names. The country should be subjected to new administrative divisions if national unity is to be maintained. (M. Afshar, 1925, pp. 5–6)

After studying the organization's manifesto, Reza Khan summoned the group members and listened to their views. Then he proclaimed,

> These things that you have written are very important. . . . Go and propagate your ideology among the people, open their eyes and ears to these ideas. You put forth the idea and I will implement it. I assure and promise you that I will

enforce all your wishes, which are mine too, from the beginning to the end. (Cited in Sadr, 1997, p. 40)

As the absolute ruler of the country, Reza Khan embarked on a racist mission to "purify" not only Iran's various racial/ethnic groups but also their languages, cultures, histories, and identities. The country's economic resources were lavishly used to finance these acts of cultural/linguistic liquidation, which were mainly done through schools, universities, publication houses, newspapers, and the media; meanwhile, the government's military power was brought to oversee the implementation of various racist and assimilationist policies. The politics of "purification" were not limited to non-Persian ethnic groups; the Persian language, history, identity, and culture too underwent extreme forms of "purifying" in order to be brought closer to the "mythical Aryan race" manufactured by Orientalists. Reza Shah's son, Mohammad Reza, faithfully continued the process of turning Iran into a unified country with a single "national" language, national identity, history, and culture. In all of the books bearing his name such as *Mission for My Country* (1961), *Enqelab-e sefid* [The White Revolution] (1967), *Answer to History* (1980a), and *The Shah's Story* (1980b), Mohammad Reza Pahlavi time and again emphasizes his important role in reviving Iran's past glories, revitalizing the spirit of the "Iranian nation," and forging a unified national identity for Iranians. His understanding of Iran's history did not go beyond a linear chronology of glories of ancient Persian kings starting from the Achaemenids and culminating in, of course, the Pahlavis. This is the same official history that is taught in schools and universities throughout the country, a history that excludes the contributions of non-Persian ethnic groups in Iran's historical development, reduces over 6,000 years of history to the history of the arrival of Indo-European tribes to the Iranian Plateau, and seeks to replace non-Farsi languages in the country with the language of the Persian minority.

In his later publications in exile—*Answer to History* and *The Shah's Story*—Mohammad Reza tried to justify the rule of the Pahlavi dynasty to both international and Iranian readers. The language used in these works was no longer that of a brutal tyrant but a broken man who scrambled to defend his discredited regime from the discomfort of exile. The exiled shah presented a colorful account of Iran's progress in terms of education, militarism, maintenance of territorial integrity, independence, and the march towards the great civilization. In spite of a glamorous account of progress and modernism, he still emphasized that his main preoccupation was and had always been the maintenance and revival of Iran's national identity, which to him was the identity of the Persian ethnic group to which he belonged. In both *Answer to History* and *The Shah's Story* he maintained that

[n]othing causes me more pain than the realization of this terrible threat which hangs over the national identity and the cultural and spiritual heritage of Iran.

For these are our greatest advantages, the essential foundations from which everything else could eventually be won back, but without which all is lost. (M.R. Sh. Pahlavi, 1980b, p. 210)

Thirteen years earlier, in the apex of his power, the shah had asserted similar feelings in *Enqelab-e sefid* [The White Revolution]:

I felt my mission was to enrich and pass on to the next generation the precious and ancient heritage of Iran, its sovereignty, independence, and national honour, all of which had been vested in me as a sacred trust. (M.R. Sh. Pahlavi, 1967, p. 8)

In order to pass on "the precious and ancient heritage of Iran," the shah had to annihilate signs and symbols of ethnic, linguistic, and cultural plurality in the country. By forcing everybody to speak Farsi and be assimilated into the Persian minority, he believed that he was moving all and everyone toward modernity, progress, and the great civilization. Little did he know (or cared to know) that modernism, civilization, and progress ought to emerge and evolve from one's own culture, language, and ways of living, which in a multicultural and multiethnic society such as Iran, first and foremost meant protecting the indigenous languages of each and every ethnic group, not just the language of the shah's Persian minority. Nor did he realize that to be civilized meant to accept others as they were, to respect difference and diversity, to provide conditions for the development of all cultures, languages, identities, and histories, as opposed to annihilating them. He mistook his father's and his own barbarism for civilization and progress. By forcing the majority of Iranians to abandon their own language for the imposed Persian language, the shah in effect deprived the majority of Iranians of their most basic means of psychological, spiritual, and sociocultural developments on both individualistic and collective levels. His project of one nation, one language, one country looked nothing like civilization, modernity, or progress. Barbarism and savagery are indeed most appropriate terms to describe his notion of great civilization.

THE ISLAMIC REPUBLIC AND THE CHALLENGE OF DIVERSITY

During the Pahlavi monarchy, the multiethnic, multinational, and multicultural character of Iranian society was vigorously denied and brutally suppressed. With the demise of the absolute monarchism, various nationalities and ethnic groups were expecting the restoration of their social, political, cultural, and national rights. Among various groups, two major Azerbaijani and Kurdish nationalities posed the greatest challenge to the new regime. The Azerbaijanis, as the largest nationality in Iran, comprised over 35 percent of the entire population at the time and were mobilized around the reformist Grand Ayatollah Shariatmadari and his Muslim Peoples' Party (Hezb-e Khalq-e Mosalman). Among other things, the party worked toward acknowledging Iran's multicultural, multiethnic, and multilingual character, emphasizing linguistic equality, lifting of discriminatory policies, and creation of a civil society (see also Razmi, 2000; Asgharzadeh, 2004a).

Unlike the Azerbaijani movement, the Kurdish struggle took a more radical turn, significantly mobilizing Iran's millions of Kurdish people around notions of autonomous nationhood, self-determination, and even secession from Iran if need be (see also Hassanpour, 1992a). In order to subdue these and other similar movements in Khuzistan, Baluchistan, Turkmen-Sahra, and Gilan, the Islamic rulers began preaching and praising the universalistic, non-preferential values of Islam. In a message to the people of Kurdistan on November 17, 1978, Ayatollah Khomeini wrote,

> The great Islam has condemned all sorts of discriminations and hasn't allocated special rights for any group in particular. Piety and devotion to Islam are the only markers of man's dignity. . . . In the bosom of Islam and Islamic Republic of Iran all nationalities have the right for determination of their own cultural, economic, and political destinies . . . in their own localities. (Cited in Khomeini, 1999, p. 7; see also McDowall, 1996, p. 271)

Immediately after the end of the Pahlavi days, under pressure from various ethnic and national groups, the new Islamic regime came to acknowledge the multiethnic character of the country and even attempted to present a more equitable language policy. According to Article 15 of the Constitution of the Islamic Republic, for instance,

> The official and common language and script of the people of Iran is Farsi. All official documents, correspondence and publications, as well as textbooks, must be in this language and script. However, the use of regional and national languages in the press and mass media, as well as for teaching in schools the literatures written in them, is permitted in addition to Farsi. (Article 15; see also Algar, 1980)

Also, based on Article 19 of the Constitution of the Islamic Republic,

> All people of Iran enjoy equal rights, whatever their ethnic group or tribe, and factors such as color, race and language do not bestow any privilege. (Article 19; see also Algar, 1980)

As can be seen from these constitutional articles, the new Islamic government has acknowledged the multicultural, multilingual, and multiethnic character of Iranian society. However, this recognition has remained only on paper. Although the government has permitted publication of a few bilingual newspapers in various localities, the teaching and learning of non-Farsi mother tongues still remain an ideal for millions of Iranians. Furthermore, aside from the actual endorsement of Farsi as the only "official" language, Article 15 singles out "Persian script" as the only legitimate script to be used by all

Iranians. It is noteworthy that in practical terms, the current Perso-Arabic script has a very divisive function in severing the linguistic/literary connections among a number of ethnic groups in Iran (e.g., Kurds, Azeris, and Turkmens) and their coethnics in the neighboring countries. Millions of ethnic Azeris, Kurds, and Turkmens are living in the neighboring republics of Azerbaijan, Turkmenistan, and Turkey (with a sizable number of Kurdish citizenry) who use a Roman script. The exclusive use of the Perso-Arabic script in Iran serves to keep the important literary/linguistic developments in the neighboring countries inaccessible to the non-Persian ethnic groups of Iran, and vice versa. They cannot read each other's literature, nor can they write to one another due to an alphabet barrier. This is a phenomenon to which the late Azerbaijani president Ebulfez Elchibey referred as the Alphabet Despotism (Elchibey, 1997; see also Dei and Asgharzadeh, 2003).

After the consolidation of Islamic rule, the highly romanticized rhetoric regarding racial and ethnic equality all but disappeared into thin air. Following the previous regime's racist doctrines, Farsi, the mother tongue of Iran's Persian minority, was accorded the status of "national language" of all Iranians. Further, Farsi was elevated to the status of "the second language of Islam," following Arabic. This way, not only all non-Persian Iranians had to learn Farsi but even non-Iranian Muslims were encouraged to learn and speak it (see also Meskoob, 1992). As a result, the language and culture of non-Persian nationalities such as Azeris, Kurds, Baluchs, Arabs, and Turkmens were subjected to eradication and annihilation.

In legal terms, Article 115 of the Constitution of the Islamic Republic clearly stated that the president of the country should be a male Shia Muslim. This was a blatant discrimination against over 20 percent of the population who were either Sunni Muslims or non-Muslims—not to mention the over 50 percent female population along with a sizable number of seculars. Other Articles in Penal and Civil Codes demonstrated sharp inequalities between Muslims and non-Muslims in areas of criminality, inheritance, citizenship, divorce, schooling, employment, and so on (see, e.g., Articles 12, 88, 121, 147, 207, and 494 of the Penal Code in 1992). Among the non-Shia religious communities, members of the Baha'í faith became subject to the severest forms of discrimination. Their Baha'í identity became criminalized; they became subject to open assault and persecution on all fronts; their assemblies even in the privacy of their homes were prohibited; the observance of their religious rites and rituals was banned (see also Cooper, 1985; Asgharzadeh, 2004a). In a word, under the Islamic rule, racism and xenophobia continued to flourish in Iran, just as they had been under the previous Pahlavi regime.

The Gender Dimension

Shortly after the establishment of an Islamic government in Iran, the new rulers dismantled the Family Protection Act, made veiling compulsory, reduced the minimum age for marriage from 18 to 13, and, while maintaining polygamy, took away the automatic right for divorce of a wife on the grounds of her husband's remarriage. "The law of the four wives is a very progressive law," asserted Ayatollah Khomeini,

> and was written for the good of women, since there are more women than men. More women are born than men and more men are killed in war than women. A woman needs a man, so what can we do, since there are more women than men in the world? Would you rather prefer that the excess number of women became whores, or that they married a man with other wives? (Cited in Sanasarian, 1983, p. 134)

Based on the information published by Statistical Center of Iran (1986), there were at the time of publication about 990,000 employed women in the Islamic Republic of Iran. This figure comprised 6 percent of the female population aged 10 and over and 9 percent of the total (male and female) employed population. About 332,000 women were classified as unemployed and seeking employment, 4.8 million as students, and over 11 million as homemakers. The female work/activity rate was 8 percent, compared to 45 percent for males. The overall participation of women in the labor force was only 9 percent, compared to 91 percent for men. Shahabi (1993, pp. 10–11) has documented that during the early 15 years of the Islamic rule, there had been an annual decrease of 2 percent in the number of employed women, reducing the number from 1,200,000 to 975,000; the rate of unemployment among women had increased from 16.3 percent to 25.6 percent; and maternity leave had been reduced from 90 days to 75 days with no job security existing after childbirth.

Based on the Islamic Law of *Qisas* or the Bill of Retribution, the *dieh* or "blood-money" to be paid for a female victim of murder is only half of that paid for a male victim. Under this bill, women's testimony in court is only half the value of men's testimony. Since Islamic law requires two women to testify for every one man, a woman can, therefore, not participate in the legal profession. Since a woman's right to form judgment is not fully recognized, it is rarely possible for her to become a lawyer or a judge. Since a woman's testimony alone does not carry any legal weight, proof of any kind of abuse, mistreatment, and crime against her is almost impossible (see, e.g., Articles 5, 6, 33, 46, 91, and 92 in the Islamic Republic of Iran's Penal Code, 1992).

"The prisons of the Islamic regime," an Iranian writer has observed,

> are full of women who have been subjected to the most degrading and inhumane forms of torture. Rape is one of the commonest, yet horrific, forms of torture. The rape of virgin women before their execution is performed as a religious ritual in all Iranian jails, carried out in the belief that these women are not worthy of the divine place allocated to virgins by Islam and the prophet. (Hendessi, 1990, p. 16)

"From the religious point of view," says one of the grand Ayatollahs, "it is not decent for a virgin girl to be executed; therefore, on the eve of their execution, the guards marry them to remove their virginity" (Ayatollah Montazeri, cited in Mojahedin-e Khalq of Iran, 1982, p. 121). Brutal and inhumane forms of punishment and execution abound under the Islamic rule. For instance, here is the observation of an eyewitness to a stoning scene, reported by the Amnesty International (1987, 1990):

> The lorry deposited a large number of stones and pebbles beside the waste ground, and then two women were led to the spot wearing white and with sacks over their heads. . . . They were enveloped in a shower of stones and transformed into two red sacks. . . . The wounded women fell to the ground and revolutionary guards smashed their heads in with a shovel to make sure that they were dead. (Amnesty International, 1987, p. 3)

Thus, since the establishment of Islamic rule in Iran, women in that country have been witnessing the absolute deterioration of their human, legal, economic, and sociopolitical rights. The politics of sexual apartheid and forceful segregation have been vigorously implemented in all imaginable public places such as universities, schools, factories, beaches, restaurants, and even buses and trains. Those who have dared to challenge the rigid funda-mentalist regulations have been subjected to torture chambers, secret dun-geons, fire squads, hangings, and stonings. Around the mid-1990s, particularly after the election of Mohammad Khatami to the presidency in 1997, overall repressive conditions were somewhat relaxed throughout the country. However, Khatami's reformist government failed to bring about major improvements in women's status as far as equal rights and freedoms were concerned.

Mohammad Khatami and the Reform Movement

In the course of the revolution of 1978–1979 and immediately after the fall of absolute monarchism, a discourse developed in Iran around notions of civil society, democratic rights, dialogue, and nonviolent methods of governance. This discourse and the resultant experimentations reached a climax with the election of Mohammad Khatami to the presidency of Iran on May 23, 1997. Having established a reputation for moderation, tolerance, and the rule of law, Khatami spoke of Iran belonging to all Iranians, which was to say not just the Iranians of various ethnic, religious, and cultural backgrounds but also to such excluded groups as women, youths, as well as individuals with different politi-cal views and persuasions. Khatami's message of toleration, dialogue, and inclu-sion manifested a new image from the totalitarian Islamic state, a state that was epitomized by rigidness, intolerance, fundamentalism, and complete disregard for the individual and collective rights of the citizenry.

In similar ways, his message of peace and hope found an enthusiastic audience in the international community, which came to regard him as a messenger of reform, understanding, and international cooperation. He con-stantly talked of establishing dialogue and good will among world's nations and even went so far as proposing the year 2001 as the "Year of Dialogue among Civilizations." In his speech before the 53rd Session of the UN General Assembly on September 21, 1998, he stated,

> I would like to propose, in the name of the Islamic Republic of Iran, that the United Nations, as a first step, designate the year 2001 as the "Year of Dialogue Among Civilizations," with the earnest hope that through such a dialogue, the realization of universal justice and liberty may be initiated. . . . Among the worthiest achievements of this century is the acceptance of the necessity and significance of dialogue and rejection of force, promotion of understanding in cultural, economic and political fields, and strengthening of the foundations of liberty, justice and human rights. Establishment and enhancement of civility, whether at national or international level, is contingent upon dialogue among societies and civilizations representing various views, inclinations and approaches. If humanity at the threshold of the new century and millennium devotes all efforts to institutionalize dialogue, replacing hostility and confrontation with discourse and understanding, it would leave an invaluable legacy for the benefit of the future generations. (Khatami, 1998, p. 4)

Just as in Iran, Khatami was hailed abroad as a man of peace, reason, and dialogue. Enthusiastically the United Nations accepted his proposal and in 1998, the UN General Assembly unanimously declared the year 2001 as the United Nations Year of Dialogue among Civilizations. However, notwithstanding the initial uproar and enthusiasm, with the passage of time Khatami's colorful messages paled and eventually faded away in the face of his inability to act on the many promises that he made. His notion of dialogue and diversity—which was mainly designed for external consumption—came under heavy criticism on the part of Iran's various ethnic and religious groups from the very beginning. A significant letter-writing campaign followed the introduction of his concept of dialogue and demanded that such a dialogue must be established first and foremost at home and within Iran's diverse ethnic, cultural, linguistic, and religious communities. For instance, a letter sent by National Spiritual Assembly of the Bahá'ís of the United States to Mohammad Khatami on January 1998, among other things, stated,

> We are particularly encouraged by your assertion "that religion and liberty are consistent and compatible." As you said, "Human experience has taught us that prosperous life should hinge on three pillars: religiosity, liberty and justice." These, you concluded, "are the assets and aspirations of the Islamic Revolution as it enters the twenty-first century." Are the Bahá'ís of Iran, your nation's largest religious minority, included in these aspirations? Your explicitly stated determination to fulfill the provisions of the Iranian Constitution and to establish the rule of law gives us hope that the freedom of the Bahá'í community in Iran openly to practice its religion will be guaranteed. May we not expect, in the light of your commitment to human dignity and freedom, that the United Nations General Assembly Resolution *(A/RES/52/142)*, which calls for the emancipation of the Bahá'í community of Iran, will now be implemented? (Henderson, 1998, p. 1)

Evidently, not only were there no significant changes in the treatment of members of the Baha'í faith, but there was also no sign of the promised dialogue and respect for law within the country, which was presumably to take place among and between various political groups, ethnic/national communities, women's groups, students, youth, workers, and so on. In terms of ethnicities and nationalities, for instance, the implementation of Articles 15 and 19 of the Constitution of the Islamic Republic of Iran, which granted the learning and teaching of non-Persian languages in schools and universities, continued to remain an ideal. And in spite of various campaigns demanding the enforcement of these constitutional articles, the Khatami government refused to even discuss the content of these articles. And all this took place in an environment where the so-called reformist government of Khatami had declared itself as the custodian of the constitution and the guarantor of its implementation. Over time, Khatami's colorful messages lost their appeal and more and more people came to realize that his speeches on dialogue and inclusion were nothing more than wishful thinking. Such a realization has found its manifestation in various students' demonstrations, ethnic discontents, and antigovernmental activities that continue to challenge the very existence of the Islamic Republic.

Developments in the Region: Afghanistan and Iraq

In recent years, significant changes have been taking place in the neighboring countries of Afghanistan and Iraq that have real ramifications in the formation and future development of an emerging political discourse in Iran. First and foremost, this discourse seeks to redefine the parameters of nationalism, ethnicities, pluralism, and the nation-state in a multicultural, multilingual, and multiethnic context. Regardless of the nature of conflicts in these societies, the resultant political changes in these countries have led to the establishment of completely new political systems and the adoption of new constitutions that influence the democratization processes in Iran and throughout the region, particularly pertaining to issues of difference and diversity. The new Constitution of Afghanistan, adopted by Grand Council on January 4, 2004, clearly stipulates the following:

(1) National sovereignty in Afghanistan belongs to the nation that exercises it directly or through its representatives.
(2) The nation of Afghanistan consists of all individuals who are the citizen of Afghanistan.
(3) The nation of Afghanistan is comprised of the following ethnic groups: Pashtun, Tajik, Hazara, Uzbak, Turkmen, Baluch, Pashai, Nuristani, Aymaq, Arab, Qirghiz, Qizilbash, Gujur, Brahwui and others.
(4) The word Afghan applies to every citizen of Afghanistan.
(5) No member of the nation can be deprived of his citizenship of Afghanistan.
(6) Affairs related to the citizenship and asylum are regulated by law. (Chapter 1, Article 4)

As can be seen from this article, the nation of Afghanistan is clearly defined in terms of citizenship. This is a democratic definition in that it removes the absurd notions that seek to define nationality in terms of such attributes as race, history, geography, and religion. The undemocratic aspect of relying on these attributes becomes evident when any one of them is given priority in terms of such notions as authenticity, origin, and precedence. The constitution also clearly identifies the major ethnic groups in the country. Similarly, Article 16 (Chapter 1) of the constitution clearly identifies the official languages in the country, and sets clear policies for the development of all languages in Afghanistan:

> From among the languages of Pashto, Dari, Uzbeki, Turkmeni, Baluchi, Pashai, Nuristani, Pamiri, Arab and other languages spoken in the country, Pashto and Dari are the official languages of the state. The Turkic languages (Uzbaki and Turkmen), Baluchi, Pashai, Nuristani and Pamiri are—in addition to Pashto and Dari—the third official language in areas where the majority speaks them. The practical modalities for implementation of this provision shall be specified by law. The state adopts and implements effective plans for strengthening and developing all languages of Afghanistan. Publications and radio and television broadcasting are allowed in all languages spoken in the country. (Chapter 1, Article 16)

This kind of acknowledgment of diversity, coupled with transparency and clarity in defining the multiethnic, multicultural, and multilingual character of the neighboring Afghan society, stands in direct opposition to general politics of avoidance and denial in the Islamic Republic of Iran. Iranian politics of denial of difference and lack of transparency about the existence of ethnic, cultural, and linguistic plurality have managed to avoid any direct mention of the existence of diverse ethnicities and nationalities in the country. Instead, the Islamic Republic, like the Pahlavi regime before it, has sought to equate Fars/Persian with Iranian. In the Constitution of the Islamic Republic, there is no mention of either the specific names or the languages of major nationalities and ethnic groups in the country. Instead of directly naming the major groups and nationalities constituting "the Iranians," it has become a habit for Iran's ruling elite and privileged citizens/groups to assert the absurd phrase "everyone is equal in this country." This ridiculous phrase has become a perfect decoy to cover any sense of responsibility in acknowledging the existence of diverse communities, languages, cultures, and histories. They use this politics of denial to channel the resources of the country toward the development of only one language, one culture, one history, and one identity: Fars/Persian.

Added to the undeniable impact of Afghanistan's constitution is the newly adopted Iraqi constitution that would seem to have far-reaching and concrete consequences for the Iranian situation. On March 8, 2004, the Iraqi Governing Council (2004) signed a temporary constitution that spelt out the nature of a new political system, the status of official languages, and the acknowledgment of ethnic and cultural pluralism in the country. According to Article 4 of the Iraqi constitution:

> The system of government in Iraq shall be republican, federal, democratic, and pluralistic, and powers shall be shared between the federal government and the regional governments, governorates, municipalities, and local administrations. The federal system shall be based upon geographic and historical realities and the separation of powers, and not upon origin, race, ethnicity, nationality, or confession. (Iraqi Governing Council, 2004, Chapter 1, Article 4)

Also, based on Article 9,

> The Arabic language and the Kurdish language are the two official languages of Iraq. The right of Iraqis to educate their children in their mother tongue, such as Turcoman, Syriac, or Armenian, in government educational institutions in accordance with educational guidelines, or in any other language in private educational institutions, shall be guaranteed. The scope of the term "official language" and the means of applying the provisions of this Article shall be defined by law and shall include:
>
> (1) Publication of the official gazette, in the two languages;
> (2) Speech and expression in official settings, such as the National Assembly, the Council of Ministers, courts, and official conferences, in either of the two languages;
> (3) Recognition and publication of official documents and correspondence in the two languages;
> (4) Opening schools that teach in the two languages, in accordance with educational guidelines;
> (5) Use of both languages in any other settings enjoined by the principle of equality (such as bank notes, passports, and stamps);
> (6) Use of both languages in the federal institutions and agencies in the Kurdistan region. (Iraqi Governing Council, 2004, Chapter 1, Article 4)

While Article 4 clearly identifies the political system of Iraq as republican, federal, democratic, and pluralist, Article 9 spells out issues emerging from linguistic pluralism and the parameters of a democratic way of dealing with them. Thus, Arabic and Kurdish are acknowledged as the two official languages of Iraq. For the first time in modern history of the region, Kurdish is elevated into the status of official/national language of a country. It goes without saying that such a status will have significant consequences in all countries bordering Iraq, particularly Turkey and Iran. As a matter of fact, immediately after the adoption of new Iraqi constitution on March 8, 2004, all major towns and cities in Iranian Kurdistan immersed themselves in joy and jubilation on an unprecedented scale.

In the days and weeks following the event, Iranian and Kurdish media reported demonstrations and massive arrests in Kurdish areas. In a joint statement signed by such major parties and organizations as Ettehad-e Enqelabiyyun-e Kordestan (The Unity of Kurdistan Revolutionaries), Sazeman e

Ettehad-e Fadaiyan-e Khalq-e Iran (The Organization of United Devotees of Iranian People), Hezb-e Demokrat-e Kordestan-e Iran (The Democratic Party of Iranian Kurdistan), Komite-ye Markazi-ye Sazeman-e Kargaran-e Enqelabi-ye Iran (The Central Committee of Iran's Revolutionary Workers), and Komoleh: Sazeman-e Enqelabi-ye Zahmatkeshan-e Kordestan (Komoleh: The Revolutionary Organization of Kurdistan's Toilers), the Kurds were congratulated for their great achievement in Iraq, while the Iranian government was condemned for the arrest of Kurdish demonstrators. In their joint statement signed on March 25, 2004, the above-mentioned groups and organizations wrote,

> Based on received reports, in the wake of the adoption of a new constitution for Iraq . . . which acknowledges the rights of Iraqi Kurdish people within the boundaries of Iraq, the Kurds of our country sought to express their joy and happiness for this occurrence. They staged meetings in cities of Sanandaj, Baneh, Saqqez, Marivan, and Piranshahr to show their support for the new constitution. However, these meetings were confronted . . . with the reaction and intervention of the Islamic Republic's military and police forces, which resulted in their attacking the residents. . . . As always, we repeat that the only solution for national question in Kurdistan and in Iran is through political means and only through the acceptance of democratic rights of the Kurds and other nationalities in Iran. It is the right of the Kurdish people of Iran to show their solidarity with the Kurds in Iraq and Turkey. More than that, they have the right to see their national and democratic demands realized in a free and democratic Iran. . . . We call upon all freedom loving peoples and individuals to support the rightful demands of the Kurdish people. (Cited in *Iran-e Emrooz*, March 15, 2004)

As mentioned earlier, due to rich ethnic/cultural affiliations within and between the boundaries of all major countries in the region, any development in the status of any given ethnic/national group in any of the countries is bound to have significant political and sociocultural ramifications in other countries. How long the Islamic Republic of Iran can continue with its politics of monolingualism and monoculturalism in an extremely volatile and rapidly transforming region remains a question.

CONCLUSION

Repression of ethnic and linguistic diversity is the official policy of Iran's ruling elite, implanted in the fabric of Iranian nation-state since 1925. Ever since the rule of Reza Khan, the governing system in the country has been functioning based on a racist ideology whose aim has been to turn the multinational Iran into a single nation with a single language and single identity. According to this ideology, any acknowledgment of difference and diversity in the country is and ought to be tantamount to the breaking up of Iran, its "nation," boundaries, and territories. This racist/chauvinistic mentality has been a camouflage for the supremacy of one ethnic group, Fars/Persian, and one language, Farsi. The Iranian racist ideology has empowered the dominant group with the authority to identify, whenever it desired to, the marginalized Other as traitor, separatist, foreign agent, and so forth.

It is only the dominant who has the luxury of labeling the minoritized Others; who has the power to render them as foreigners, traitors, and elements disloyal to the country's "territorial integrity." Notwithstanding the fact that the two shining representatives of this dominant group (the shah and his father) were in effect put in power by foreign governments and were working hand in glove with them, it is always the minoritized who gets accused of being traitor and foreign agent. The reason why the dominant can accuse Others is because, due to the normalcy of racism in Iran, they consider themselves the unquestionable, undeniable, authentic owners of the country. As such, it is only this group that believes it has the legitimacy to castigate Others as foreigners and foreign agents.

While the politics of repression, annihilation, and assimilation have been successful to some extent, the racist machinery has not been able to completely wipe out the signs and vestiges of ethnic and linguistic diversity in the country. In the dawn of the twenty-first century, Iran's oppressed and marginalized nationalities are more and more becoming conscious of their inalienable rights, freedoms, as well as their powerful status as the numerical majority in the country. Equally importantly, they are becoming aware of the barbaric politics of a racist order that seeks to annihilate their languages, histories, and identities. There are signs of resistance, discontent, and antiracist struggle among the oppressed communities in the country. At this stage, the important question to be posed is: how well prepared is the dominant group, either currently in power or in opposition, to respond to the challenge of diversity in Iran? The answer to this question will determine the trend of sociopolitical transformations in Iran and, by extension, in the wider Middle East.

CHAPTER 5

Reinforcing Racism:
The Dominant Discourse and Praxis

Linguicide, the deliberate killing of language, has been the official policy of three states that divide Kurdish speakers—Turkey since 1925, Iran especially in 1925–1941, and Syria especially since the 1960s. . . . I have experienced linguicide as a native speaker of Kurdish. Born into a Kurdish family in a Kurdish town, I had to get my education in Persian, the only official language in Iran, a multilingual country where Persian was the native tongue of only half the population. Fearing prison and torture of her children, my mother burnt, four times during my life, the few Kurdish books and records we had acquired clandestinely. . . . Silence about the linguicide of Kurdish or other language is, I contend, a political position which cannot be justified by claims to the neutrality or autonomy of linguistics.

(Amir Hassanpour, 2000, pp. 33–39)

INTRODUCTION

In the introduction that Jean Paul Sartre wrote to Frantz Fanon's *The Wretched of the Earth* (1961/1990), he implicated himself and other Europeans in the colonizing of Africa and other regions of the south. "With us, to be a man is to be an accomplice of colonialism, since all of us without exception have profited by colonial exploitation" (1961/1990, p. 21), wrote Sartre. He was one of the first European intellectuals and thinkers to acknowledge the privileged position into which being a European had placed him and his fellow Europeans vis-à-vis the Southern peoples. Against the backdrop of a brutal colonialism, he effectively questioned the discourse and praxis of those of his contemporaries who sought to justify colonialism under the guise of such useless phrases as "European human-ism," "civilized Europe," and "Western democracy." Sartre clearly saw the racism embedded in the fabric of colonialist Europe's economy, politics, and even notions of democracy and humanism, bravely admitting that "with us there is nothing more consistent than a racist humanism since the European has only been able to become a man through creating slaves and monsters" (196/1990, p. 22).

The acknowledgment of his privileged position was a positive step that distinguished Sartre from those of his contemporaries who failed to make such an acknowledgment. Sartre's statement was made within the context of France's colonization of Algeria, and the national independence war that the Algerians were waging against French colonialism. As a Frenchman, Sartre ventured to question his country's racist, colonialist, and imperialistic intentions in Africa. With his brave stance against the colonialism of his own people, Sartre showed that it was possible for a member of the dominant group to challenge that group's ideology of oppression, exploitation, and exclusion. And this is what makes Sartre a rare species amongst his kind; for one can hardly, if ever, come across a colonial situation where those benefiting from colonialism and oppression are courageous enough to question their own privileged place within that colonial system.

Before one begins to talk about human rights, democracy, fraternity, and equality, it is vitally important that one is aware of one's privileged positions and acknowledges them accordingly. This chapter explores the ways in which dominant Persian writers, scholars, poets, and journalists deal with issues of ethnic diversity, monolingualism, and the banning of non-Farsi languages from their own privileged positions. It examines a plethora of narratives, writings, statements, poems, and sayings from the members of the dominant Farsi-speaking group that not only do not acknowledge their privileged linguistic, cultural, and national positions, but more importantly help to maintain the status quo, which entails among other things the subordination of minority groups, and the superordination of the dominant one. In this act of colonialism we will see how the state apparatuses come together with seemingly innocent writers, journalists, intellectuals, poets, and narrators to foster the dominance of one ethnic group and the subordination of others. The chapter shows how acts of dominance are carried out through the education system, literature, and the intellectual discourse in the country.

As well, the chapter looks into samples of literature produced by members of the minoritized groups who, as a result of colonialism, have not only become completely alienated from their own culture, language, and community, but have also, in effect, turned against the very community from which they have come. Thus the chapter covers a whole range of narrations, views, and ideas that are extremely functional within a racist and colonial setting. These ideas are created and enforced by the dominant racist order in society; in turn, they function as effective means to nurture racism in society through schools, universities, as well as various texts of literature, history, culture, and so on. It is from these narrations that the system obtains its legitimacy, particularly in schools, universities, and within the intellectual segment of the populace. And it is through such narratives that the marginalized Other is forced into silence—and submission.

Racist literature instills a false consciousness in the minds of members of both the dominant group and the dominated ones from the early childhood. It gives the dominant an erroneous understanding that his/her ethnic group, language, nationality, culture, and way of life are superior to those of other individuals coming from different backgrounds. Equally importantly, it forces the idea on the colonized bodies that their history, culture, language, ethnicity, and nationality are inferior to those of the dominant group; that they have not contributed to the building of the society and functioning of the country in which they live; and that they should be constantly grateful to the dominant group for allowing them to live in "its country" and to enjoy the gift of life. To ask for anything more than a fully fledged Persianization would be an act of ingratitude on the part of the non-Persian "foreigners" and "intruders" who may seem to have overstayed their welcome in a land that belongs to one ethnic group alone.

This chapter explores how a racist system uses its power to maintain the status quo in Iran by Persianizing essentially everything in the country, from the indigenous names of territories to cultures, languages, educational system, and eventually the identities of non-Persian communities, groups, and individuals.

Persianization of the Land: Colonizing the Territory

There is a strong connection between one's sense of identity and the names that one uses to refer to oneself, one's ethnic group, and various features of the environment in which one lives, features such as land, territory, historical monuments, landmarks, rivers, and mountains. These names denote a profound connection between one's language/culture and one's surrounding environment. It is from the interconnectivity and interrelations between language/culture and culture/environment that one develops an authentic sense of self, self-perception, and self-expression. It is not an accident that the eradication and replacement of indigenous names and words have been a major preoccupation of all colonial powers. Supplanting of names, words, and concepts gradually give way to the replacing of a language in its entirety. And when a language is banned, discredited, and destroyed, with it is destroyed a part of consciousness that connects one to one's people, history, land, and culture into which one is born. In such cases, one cannot find "the right words" to tell his/her story, because such words no longer exist for him/her. One's indigenous language is the only direct means through which one transmits his/her people's oral knowledge, literature, myths, narratives, histories, and stories. Deprived of his/her means of communication and expression, the colonized person becomes a faceless, tongueless individual with no past, no history, and no place to call his/her own. It is at this point that the dominant group becomes emboldened to lay claim on lands and territories that belong to the colonized and excluded Other.

In an article titled "History, Representation, Globalization and Indigenous Cultures," Julie Gough (2000) notes,

When George Augusts Robinson endeavored to "civilize" and remove the aboriginal population of Tasmania to Bass Strait, he included renaming the people and places he "discovered" as a vital part of his appointment. Our people usually held three to five names, specially given at certain ages according to natural phenomenon best suited to that individual—which could include place, plant and animal terms. Robinson doggedly replaced the names, and thus integral identifying symbols, of the people he "collected." . . . This act of renaming was the European means of deliberately (linguistically then actually) displacing the original tenants in order to claim ownership and control. The land and the people had therefore no past, (re)emerging with names at the same time that the settlers had titled their new properties and districts in Tasmania. (Gough, 2000, pp. 96–97)

Ngugi Wa Thiong'o refers to "names and languages" as "the two immediate symbols of the means of self-definition" (1993, p. 79). In order to decapacitate the means that make such a definition possible, colonizing forces come to distort the colonized subjects' indigenous names and languages. It may not be so easy to claim ownership over a land bearing the indigenous names assigned to them by peoples and communities who have occupied those lands for generations. So the first thing a colonial power does is to rename territories, lands, mountains, rivers, and so on. This makes it easier to erase the indigenous histories, marks, and signs of identification with territories. The colonizing act of renaming indigenous peoples and territories is not limited to European colonial powers but is generally practiced in various colonial and imperialist encounters when the interaction between different groups is marked by relations of power and domination. Post-Qajar (1925–present) Iran presents a glaring example of this sort.

In Iran's modern history, there is no indication of any attempt to suppress or eliminate the country's diverse languages, cultures, and ethnic groups prior to the beginning of the Pahlavi dynasty in 1925. Up to this point, ever since the demise of Sasanid dynasty in the seventh century, almost all of the major ruling courts were of non-Persian ethnic and linguistic backgrounds. In spite of this, non-Persian dynasties never introduced their own language as the official language of the country. They never attempted to supplant the original names of peoples, territories, lands, and so on. Difference and diversity were accepted as a defining characteristic of Iran's identity and were reflected even in the name of the country that was widely used during the Qajar period: The Protected Countries of Iran (Mamalek-e Mahruseh-ye Iran) (see also Vaziri, 1993; Kashani-Sabet, 1999). It was only during the Pahlavi era that a policy of one nation, one language, one country became the official doctrine of the ruling elite in the country—hence the birth of an overall Persianization process.

Having become the shah of Iran in 1925, Reza Khan immediately changed his family name from Mirpanj to "Pahlavi," a name that according to the dominant view represented the name of "the Middle Persian language." This of course made perfect sense for a king who was determined to Persianize all aspects of life in Iran. Thus, the name-change started from the name of the king and continued to involve the name of the country, the cities, towns, villages, historical monuments, streets, as well as ethnic groups, communities, and personal names of the individuals. The renaming processes continued throughout the Pahlavi era, affecting every nook and cranny in the country. Similar politics are faithfully pursued in the Islamic Republic (see, e.g., Azizi-Banitorof, 2002). The colonial agenda behind such politics has been to replace all non-Farsi names of territories, geographical locations, landscapes, towns, cities, and villages with Persian names and words as a part of a major attempt to Persianize the entire country.

Up until 1934, the designation Persia was commonly used by the outsiders to refer to what later came to be known as Iran. The name Persia was itself an invention of the Greeks, popularized through Herodotus, and later on adopted by Orientalists and Western scholars. The name Persia had currency only in foreign languages and meant nothing to either ordinary Iranians or the dynasties that ruled them. At the time of initial contacts between the Greeks and Iranians, the province of Pars had been the seat of the ruling Achaemenid dynasty. And taking the part for the whole, the Greeks had referred to the entire country as Persia and to its inhabitants as Persians. Thus, even the names Persia and Persian were not self-designations but were designed by outsiders.

In 1934, the Reza Shah government issued a directive demanding the renaming (in foreign usage) of the country from Persia to Iran. As a major justification for this name-change, the directive cited the strong connection between the name Iran and the Aryan race. "Because Iran was the birthplace and origin of Aryans," it argued,

> it is natural that we should want to take advantage of this name, particularly since these days in the great nations of the world noise has gotten out regarding the Aryan race which indicates the greatness of the race and civilization of ancient Iran. (Prime Ministry Files, May 1934; see also Kashani-Sabet, 1999, p. 218)

Reza Shah's government officially changed the name of the country from Persia to Iran and prohibited outsiders from using the name Persia at least in their official correspondence with the Iranian government. Among the measures taken to enforce such prohibition was an order to Iranian post offices not to deliver foreign mail bearing the name Persia. The main justification for this major name-change was the dominant interpretation of "Iran" that equated it with "the birthplace of the Aryan race." The influence of Aryanist racism and Nazi mentality was so evident in the name-change that the French newspaper *Echo de Paris* claimed the whole idea to be initiated by Hitler himself. "Hitler, this is another one of your games," wrote the paper sarcastically in its February 10, 1935 issue (cited in Kashani-Sabet, 1999, p. 219).

Reza Shah's son, Mohammad Reza, went a step further than his father and identified himself as *Shahanshah Aryamehr*, which means the King of Kings, the Light of the Aryans. The adoption of Aryanist/racist personal names clearly reflects the degree to which the Pahlavi shahs were obsessed and infatuated by the West and its constructs such as Aryan and Aryanism. These obsessions were, from the beginning, a racist enterprise that affected all official institutions such as the education system, cultural organs, publishing industries, census centers, and so forth. Non-Persian ethnic groups were forbidden to name their children with indigenous ethnic names. In the meantime, indigenous, non-Persian names were being removed from indigenous territories. Thus, in the southern part of the country, the province of Arabistan was renamed as Khuzistan; the cities of Mohammareh, Al-Ahwaz, Khafajiyyeh, Howeizeh, Ma'shur, and Fallahieh were renamed as Khorramshahr, Ahwaz, Sousangerd, Azadegan, Mahshahr, and Shadgan, respectively (see also Azizi-Banitorof, 2002).

Yousof Azizi-Banitorof, a well-known scholar of Iranian Arabs, has observed that despite the official replacement of the original names of Arab towns and cities in Khuzistan, Arab inhabitants of the region still refer to these places in their original names when they talk or write among themselves. As he puts it,

> Now the majority of Khuzistani cities have two names, which is to say, in Farsi and in official correspondence their Persianized names are used, and in conversations among the local peoples their historical Arabic-Iranian names are used. For instance, if you ask a Khuzistani Arab on his way to Khorramshahr, "where are you going?" he will tell you that "I am going to Mohammareh"; he will not tell you, "I am going to Khorramshahr." This shows that [the Arab] people's historical-cultural consciousness still retains indigenous and Arabic names, despite over fifty years [of assimilatory policies]. This duality in naming— official versus indigenous-public—exists in most spheres of cultural life [in Khuzistan]. (Azizi-Banitorof, 2002, p. 7)

Other non-Persian areas are in no better shape than Khuzistan. In the region of Azerbaijan, the ancient city of Urmi/Urumiyya was renamed as Rezaiyyeh—people restored Urumiyyeh (Ormiyeh) after the Islamic Revolution; Qoshachay became Miyandoab; the famous Mount Savalan became Sabalan; the villages of Axmaqaya, Perküsh, and Esfistan became Ahmaqiyyeh, Khargush, and Asbestan, respectively, all of which had derogatory, humiliating, and negative meanings in Farsi. In the province of Gorgan, Gonbad-e Ghabus was changed to Gonbad-e Kavus; in Kurdistan, Abu'l-mu'min was supplanted by Parsa (see also Kashani-Sabet, 1999, p. 219). These colonialist policies against indigenous languages, names, and words have continued to date.

In addition to the supplanting of names of territories, towns, and landmarks, attempts have been made to replace and/or redefine the names of whole ethnicities and nationalities. To this end, a glaring case in point has been Ahmad Kasravi's (1890–1946) attempt to redefine the Turkic people of Azerbaijan in terms of the designation "Azari," a term that in Kasravi's definition referred to an Aryan people. In an essay titled "Azari ya zaban-e bastani-ye Azerbaigan" ["Azeri or the Ancient Language of Azerbaijan"] (1925), Kasravi claimed to have discovered a dozen words and poetic fragments in several Azerbaijani villages that supposedly proved that Azerbaijan, the homeland of Azeri-Turks, was originally populated by Farsi-speaking Aryans who had later become Turkified thanks to the Mongol invasion of Iran in the thirteenth century. According to Kasravi, Arab and Persian scholars were at fault in defining "Azeri" as a Turkic language. The original Azari had nothing to do with the Turkic peoples and their language; it originally was an Aryan tongue. Why and how? Due to Kasravi's "discovery" of a couple of unidentifiable linguistic and poetic fragments "here and there":

> If we had access to the same amount of poetry in "Azari" as we have in Kurdish or in Tabari, we could easily determine the complete identity of that language. However, with all the work and research that we have undertaken to find signs from that language [i.e., the imaginary Indo-European Azari], we have not been able to find anything more than a couple of sentences here and there, plus eleven couplets from Sheikh Safi ad-Din of Ardabil, and a couple of miscellaneous couplets that we can only guess they may belong to Azari. (Kasravi, 1925, p. 28)

Kasravi's assumptions about the Azeri language lacked serious historical, linguistic, or scientific credibility. He publicized such views because he believed they were going to be "good for Iran" (Kasravi, 1925; Zeka, 1955). After Kasravi's invention of a supposedly Indo-European Azari language, a chauvinistic literature developed around the term Azeri that aggressively advocated the following:

1. The old "Azari" language was a variant of Farsi; it fundamentally differed from the current "Azeri-Turkic."
2. The ancient Azaris living in Azerbaijan were not a Turkic people; they were an "Aryan" people just like the Persians and the rest of "the true Iranians."
3. The current Turkic-speaking Azeris have been Turkified due to the intrusions to Iran by the "Saljuqs" and "Mongols" that took place in the eleventh and thirteenth centuries, respectively.
4. The historical name of "the Caucasian Azerbaijan" (current northern Republic of Azerbaijan) was not originally Azerbaijan; it was "Arran" (also written as Aran, Eran). The designation Azerbaijan was given to that Caucasian region by the Ottoman/Turkish elements that was later endorsed by Joseph Stalin of Russia, for the purpose of laying claims on "the Iranian Azerbaijan" and annexing it in the future (see, e.g., M. Afshar, 1925; I. Afshar 1990a, 1990b; Shoar, 1967; Nateq, 1979; Katebi, 1986; Rezazadeh-Malek, 1973; Mortazavi, 1981; Reza 1981).

The terms Azerbaijan and Azeri thus became highly politicized after the publication of Kasravi's article titled "Azeri ya zaban-e bastani-ye Azerbaijan" ["Azari or the Ancient Language of Azerbaigan"] in the 1920s. It is important to note the various acts of mimicry and emulation of

Western/Orientalist methodology and ideology in the works produced by Kasravi and his cohorts. In essence, by constructing an imaginary Aryan language and by equating it with an Aryan race, they are emulating their Aryanist masters whose work is heavily based on positivist methodology, Eurocentrism, and blatant racism. In light of all the evidence contrary to Kasravi's assertions (Mohammedzadeh Sadiq, 2004), one would expect that his work and his name (as far as Azeri is concerned) should have been forgotten by now—at least in academic circles. On the contrary, his views are becoming fashionable nowadays more than ever before. For instance, the dominant group continues to insist that the name Azerbaijan is not the authentic name of the current Republic of Azerbaijan but was so designated by Stalin. According to this view, the historical name of those lands was not Azerbaijan but was Arran. It was a political decision on the part of Russian administrators to replace Arran with Azerbaijan, so that one day they could easily annex the Iranian Azerbaijan to the Russian territory (Kasravi, 1925; Zeka, 1955; I. Afshar, 1990a, 1990b; Matini, 1992).

Anyone familiar with the region's history and geography knows that the name Arran is mentioned in the writings of various Arab travelers and historians to indicate the name of a small town within Azerbaijan. Perhaps a most telling account of this is given by Al-Mas'udi, a tenth-century Moslem historian, who explicitly states, "al-Arran min biladi Azerbaijan," which literally means "Arran is but a town in Azerbaijan" (Al-Mas'udi, 1967, p. 78; see also Heyat, 1993, p. 6). Apparently, by rejecting the historical name of the northern Azerbaijan, Iranian extremists are trying to further isolate and marginalize the Azerbaijani community in Iran.

Following in the footsteps of the previous regime, the current Islamic Republic has introduced many similar changes in an attempt to erase concepts, signifiers, symbols, and marks bearing indigenous non-Persian names and words. For instance, in 1993, the government removed the name of Azerbaijan from a major segment of the Azeri lands and officially renamed these lands as the province of Ardabil. The government did this after a consensus had been reached in the Majlis to rename the new province as the Eastern Azerbaijan with the city of Ardabil being the provincial capital, followed by Tabriz and Ormiyeh as the capitals of central and western provinces of Azerbaijan, respectively (see also Chehabi, 1997). This act showed that the current rulers of Iran have now aimed to destroy non-Persian people's geographical and territorial identity. The Azer/Azeri/Azerbaijani identity is the identity that ties the Azerbaijanis most directly to their geography and territory. By removing the indigenous name of Azerbaijan from a large portion of these territories, the government seeks to destroy the connection of this ethnic group to their traditional lands, and to the identity that emerges from such a connection. Not surprisingly, there have been strong protests on the part of Azerbaijanis to this act of deterritorialization (see, e.g., B. Shaffer, 2002). In May 2004, the government divided the Farsi-speaking region of Khorasan into three provinces as well: Khorasan-e Shomlai, Khorasan-e Razavi, and Khorasan-e Janubi (North Khorasan, South

Khorasan, and Razavi Khorasan). Ironically, in this case the original name Khorasan was retained.

Here also it becomes clear how the governing apparatuses and the nationalist strata of the intellectuals have similar approaches to the denial and eradication of ethnic pluralism in the country, no matter how these group-ings may differ in their politics and ideological tendencies (see also Al-e Ahmad, 1978a). The policy that was set up during the absolute Pahlavi monarchism is being implemented by the Islamic government. Interestingly enough, it is the same policy that the current antigovernment ultranational-ists want to implement if and when they come to power. Paralleling the gov-ernment's assimilatory policies, the nationalist segment of Persian elite and intellectuals continue to champion similar racist, colonialist, and exclusionary policies and methods in their literature. For instance, the editor of *Majalle-ye Iran-shenasi* (Journal of Iranology), a journal specializing in Persian literature, language, history, and civilization, in one of its editorials states,

> In the currently vague and chaotic state of the world . . . our Iran continues to grapple with its previous problems in addition to new problems that have emerged from the [1978] revolution and the long war with Iraq: pan-Arabism and pan-Turkism are distorting the facts about [the province of] Khuzistan and the Persian Gulf and Azerbaijan. And our eastern neighbor [Afghanistan] is not without intentions towards Khorasan. Some of our so-called political parties in Iran and abroad are talking about "the multinational Iran" instead of a united Iran; [they also talk of] northern and southern Azerbaijan and of self-governance for the Kurds and Baluchs and Turks and Turkmens and Arabs. (Matini, 1992, p. 234)

Matini continues the article by talking about the evils of separatism, panism, the ill intentions of world powers toward Iran, and how these powers cannot wait to see Iran destroyed and divided. In fact, notions of pan-Turkism, pan-Arabism, and separatism are reoccurring themes in much of the dominant literature dealing with pluralism in the country. Instead of acknowledging the diverse nature of Iranian society and trying to address it in a democratic manner, the privileged dominant group tries to silence the non-Farsi voices by accusing them of being pan-Turkists, pan-Arabists, Pan-Baluchists, and pan-Kurdists. No one can deny the existence of individuals with racist and chauvinistic views within various marginalized communities. However, these individuals are, and have always been, in the minority within their own communities. By making such sweeping, blanket statements that regard entire communities as pan-Turkist or pan-Arabist, the dominant group aims to dismiss the legitimate demands of these communities for political, cultural, and linguistic fairness and equality in the country.

In essence, the dominant group's characterization of minority activists as pan-Arabists and pan-Turkists serves to strengthen the position of a handful of individuals within these communities who really do champion racist and panist notions. With its generalizing blanket statements, the dominant group gives a legitimacy of sorts to various undemocratic stances that would otherwise be dismissed and isolated within the minority communities themselves. On the one hand, this kind of statement coming from the dominant group helps the racist elements to recruit from the community, specially amongst the youth and students. On the other hand, it helps to marginalize the democratic segment of the activists who work within a framework of human rights, justice, and equality for all. Evidently, this kind of response on the part of the dominant is a conscious strategy to both weaken and discredit the resistance movements in their entirety, without considering their legitimate demands for social, political, and cultural rights.

In a later issue of *Majalle-ye Iran-shenasi*, Jalal Matini clearly states that his only concern is to obscure, problematize, and eventually deny the existence of difference and diversity in Iran. He writes that it made him very nervous when for the first time he read in a newspaper that "Iran is a multinational and multiethnic country" ("Iran keshvari-st kasir-ol melleh va morakkab az aqvam-e mokhtalef") (Matini, 1998, p. 229). He enlightens his colleagues that the concepts of multinational and multiethnic were infiltrated into Iran for the first time by Soviet communists, reflecting the unfriendly intentions that they had toward Iran. Matini warns his colleagues to take note that these concepts have not died out with the demise of the Soviet Union. On the contrary, the concepts have found more currency in recent years. What is to be done, then? "From now on, we should refrain from using such terms as 'Iran is a multinational country' or 'Iran is a country composed of different ethnic groups'" (Matini, 1998, p. 233). Matini's solution is typical of the dominant approach to issues of difference and diversity in Iran. This approach stubbornly insists that the existence of difference and diversity in Iran is not a real social fact but is an illusion created by construction of a couple of terms and concepts. If these terms and concepts are not used, difference and diversity will cease to exist. Below are excerpts from his manifesto that neatly summarize his racist view of Iran, its cultures, peoples, and languages:

–Iran is not a multinational country and it is not composed of different ethnic groups;
–In European languages Azerbaijan should be spelled as Azarbaijan, not Azerbaijan;
–We should call the ex-Soviet Republic of Azerbaijan "Arran," or the "Caucasian Arran";
–We should refrain from using the names "North Azerbaijan" and "South Azerbaijan";
–Our countrymen inhabiting Azerbaijan are "Azerbaijani" not "Azeri";
–We should definitely refrain from using the word "Turk" to refer to our fellow Azerbaijanis; they are "Iranians" like the other inhabitants of Iran;
–We should absolutely refrain from using "Azerbaijani" to refer to the inhabitants of the ex-soviet Republic of Azerbaijan. (Matini, 1998, p. 237)

It is interesting to see how the issue of human rights and freedoms of marginalized communities become a matter of terminologies, concepts, and grammar. The dominant group does not want to accept that more than half of Iran's population is non-Persian, people who have every right to govern their own affairs, have their political parties, study in their own language, write their own history, and represent themselves through their own voices and on their own terms. By forcing them to abandon their indigenous names, they will not become different from who they already are. They will still be the same Turks, Arabs, Baluchs, Turkmens, and Kurds, with the same languages, cultures, rights, and freedoms. Real progress would be to acknowledge their diversity and address it by way of democratic means in line with universal principles of human rights, justice, and equality for all. Denying the existence of non-Persian ethnicities, eradicating their identities, supplanting their languages, changing their names, and assimilating them have nothing to do with modernization and progress. On the contrary, these inhumane acts have everything to do with barbarism, racism, and fascism.

PERSIANIZATION OF CULTURE AND LANGUAGE: COLONIZING THE IDENTITY

The colonized groups' oral histories, traditions, myths, stories, and cultures are powerful sources that serve to validate their various territorial, political, and cultural rights in the face of their subjugation by colonialist forces. A major area in which the colonizer and the colonized come face to face is the realm of culture and language. Throughout history, dominant groups have used their own language to (mis)represent the dominated Other's culture, language, history, and entire existence. A most effective instrument in this regard has been the idea of discrediting, devaluing, and eventually annihilating the Other's means of communication and representation, where the dominant language and culture are represented as superior, modern, and progressive; while those of the colonized peoples are treated as primitive, backward, and reactionary. In his much celebrated work, *Decolonising the Mind*, Ngugi Wa Thiong'o (1986) highlights the dialectical relationships between the two related subjects of language and culture. He sees culture as constantly being created by language and communication; he also sees language simultaneously and constantly using culture as a source from which to extract meanings, relationships, signifiers, and the very concepts and words that constitute the essence of language. Since there exists such a dialectical interconnection between culture and language, it becomes possible for the colonizing powers to dominate the colonized subjects' language, and thereby, their culture, history, and means of self-definition:

> Language carries culture, and culture carries, particularly through orature and literature, the entire body of values by which we come to perceive ourselves and our place in the world. How people perceive themselves affects how they look at their culture, at their politics and at the social production of wealth, at their entire relationship to nature and to other beings. . . . Economic and political control can never be complete or effective without mental control. To control a people's culture is to control their tools of self-definition in relationship to

others. . . . The domination of a people's language by the languages of the colonizing nations was crucial to the domination of the mental universe of the colonized. (Wa Thiong'o, 1986, p. 16)

Language is a most powerful source of creating culture; it can also be a formidable cause of destroying culture and emptying it. By changing words and names in a certain language, the organic connection that the language has with the environment, nature, and culture gradually is disrupted. Through such disruption, the culture itself becomes empty as its originality is lost. The exercise of one's language and voice is a necessary requirement in resisting domination and colonial imposition. Language in this sense represents an authentic voice that empowers its owner with the ability to tell, express, explain, narrate, and understand one's own histories and lived experiences within a familiar space and environment. Linguistic powers and cultural values play extremely important roles in the development of individuals, communities, and societies. Meaningful growth and development can be achieved only in a harmonic and organic relationship with languages, cultures, beliefs, values, traditions, and knowledge systems that govern a people's ways of living in the world, just as a clear and transparent definition of democracy cannot be realized in the absence of a people's freedom to self-expression, self-rule, and self-governance.

Despotic governments use violent and militaristic methods to suppress the demands of various nationalities and ethnic groups within their borders, whose understanding of human rights, democracy, and self-determination necessarily does not conform to definitions and interpretations of those rights offered by the ruling dominant group(s). Dominant groups everywhere seek to assimilate minoritized communities, first and foremost, through the annihilation of their languages, cultures, and belief systems. Thus, the choice of language as medium of instruction, or as national/official tongue in a multiethnic, multilingual society, has a central bearing on the processes by which any nation-state functions. In pluralistic societies, language is more than a cultural symbol or a simple means of communication. It is an instrument of power, of unequal representation, uneven development, exclusion, and inclusion. As Nash has observed,

> Language seems straightforwardly a piece of culture. But on reflection it is clear that language is often a political fact, at least as much as it is a cultural one. It has been said that "language is a dialect with an army and navy." And what official or recognised languages are in any given instance is often the result of politics and power interplays. (Nash, 1989, p. 6)

Obviously, no ethnic group would willingly abandon its language and use the language of someone else. Whenever and wherever this happens, there is always the presence of dominance and subordination. As Bourdieu has noted, the choice of an official language is never an impartial and neutral act:

> To speak of the language, without further specification, as linguists do, is tacitly to accept the *official* definition of the *official* language of a political unit.

> This language is the one which, within the territorial limits of that unit, imposes itself on the whole population as the only legitimate language. . . . The official language is bound up with the state, both in its genesis and its social uses. (Bourdieu, 1991, p. 45; emphasis is in the original)

Phillipson, Rannut, and Skutnabb-Kangas (1994) have argued that in "many nation states the uneven distribution of power and resources is partly along linguistic and ethnic lines, with majority groups taking a larger share than their number would justify" (1994, p. 4). A clear manifestation of such a fact continues to be exercised in Iran, where a fully fledged coup d'état was staged against non-Persian languages and their speakers during the Pahlavi era. Just as the Persian culture has become the monoculture of the country, so too has the Persian language become the monolingua of the officially founded "Iranian nation." In terms of culture, it is the Persian culture that is singled out as the national culture of Iran. In terms of language, it is the Persian language—Farsi—that is officially selected as the national tongue of all Iranians. In terms of history, it is the history of the Persian race that has become the official history of the country. The previous shah's regime went so far as changing the chronological date in the country from the Islamic calendar to the pre-Islamic date of the establishment of the (supposedly) first Persian kingdom in Iran in the sixth century BC, a date that became the starting point of the national history of the peoples of Iran.

The Persian minority regards its race, culture, and language as most superior. The subjugated groups are encouraged to discard their own identity and culture in order to assimilate into the supposedly superior Persian racial and cultural group. The minoritized groups are forced to believe that their history and culture are not the great sources of pride and dignity that their ancestors have said they were. They are forced to be ashamed of their culture and identity, of their ancestry, and of where they come from. The processes of deculturation seem to be orchestrated to continue until such time as the subordinate groups are fully assimilated into the dominant culture. According to one dominant view,

> In some remote parts of Azerbaijan, Khuzistan and other frontier areas, the peasants and tribal people speak a Persian dialect mixed with Turkish or Arabic. The Baluchis have their own dialect too. But one is not conscious of these different tongues because the overwhelming majority, i.e., about 95% of the population of Iran, speak one language—the present-day Persian tongue—and write one script—the present-day Persian writing. (Hekmat, 1957, cited in Saad, 1996, p. 6)

The above comment was made about half a century ago. Since then, the assimilatory policies of Iran's successive governments have continued. Yet, reputable international organizations estimate the number of those speaking Farsi as their mother tongue not to exceed 37 percent of the total population (see, e.g., Dei and Asgharzadeh, 2003; www.etnologue.com, 2004). In multiethnic societies dominated by a single ethnic group, shrinking the number of marginalized groups is a colonizing act that takes place for very obvious reasons. The dominant group does not want to let the international community know that the Persians in Iran constitute a numerical minority and that the minoritized non-Persian groups are indeed, numerically, in the majority. Thus, one way of undermining the existence of minority groups is to misrepresent their real number in both internal as well as external sources. That is why they never allow for a general population census to take place that reflects the exact number of various groups based on ethnicity and language. They know very well that a real census would expose their lies— and hence their oppression—to the outside world. So they present a distorted picture of the numbers and figures indicative of a much, much smaller number of the non-Persian groups, thinking perhaps that a smaller number can easily be dismissed and disregarded.

Alongside the eradication of numbers and figures in official statistics, acts of eradication and annihilation take place in seemingly unofficial literature produced by the dominant group. Perhaps the linguistic and cultural geno- cide of Iran's non-Persian groups with the beginning of the Pahlavi era was best expressed through the following poem, composed by Aref Qazvini in October 1923:

> The Turkic tongue must be torn out by the roots
> The legs it stands on should be cut off in this land
> Sweep across the Araxes speakers of the Turkic language
> O, breeze of dawn arise! Tell the inhabitants of Tabriz:
> The sanctuary of Zarathustra is no place for the language of Genghis!
> Your women, silent and mournful from the tragedy of Siyavoush
> You must not forget these if you are of his race.
> (Qazvini, 1923, p. 103)

In the above poem, a member of the dominant group uses his poetic talent to issue a decree against the Turkic-speaking peoples of Iran. He cleverly associates the Turkic language of the people of Tabriz, provincial capital of eastern Azerbaijan, with the language of Genghis Khan, the thirteenth-century Mongolian conqueror of Central Asia and Iran. He finds it easy to make such an association, partly because like the Turkic languages, the Mongolian language belongs to a linguistic family known as Altaic. Thus, by calling the Azeri language of the people of Azerbaijan the language of Genghis Khan, the poet attempts to demonize both the Azeri language and its speakers.

Correspondingly, he calls Tabriz the sanctuary of Zarathustra, or in its Persianized form called Zoroaster. Zarathustra was (apparently) an Azerbaijani/Iranian prophet who lived and died in Azerbaijan in the seventh century BC. Currently there is much debate and controversy surrounding the ethnicity and language of Zarathustra (see, e.g., Zehtabi, 1999). However, by juxtaposing Zarathustra with Genghis Khan, the poet reinforces the dominant perspective that sees Zarathustra as a Persian and identifies his language as Farsi; at the same time, he views the Azeri-Turkic as a criminal tongue infiltrated into Iran by way of the Mongolian conquest in the thirtheenth century.

At the end of the poem, Qazvini makes reference to Siyavoush, an imaginary character from the *Shahnameh* of Ferdowsi. In Ferdowsi's epic poem, Siyavoush, runs away from his father Kaykawus, the king of Persia, and is given asylum by the Turanian Prince Afrasiab. Afrasiab marries Siyavoush to his daughter and grants him royal status. Later on, due to some provocation, Afrasiab kills Siyavoush, and this starts fresh hostilities between the Iranians and Turanians, or—as it has come to be interpreted in modern usage—the Turks and Persians. Qazvini invokes the memory of this fable to remind the Azeris of this ancient imaginary hostility between the two races. He warns the people of Azerbaijan that if they truly are from the race of Siyavoush—that is, Persian—then they should remain faithful to that race. Explicit and implicit in his threatening tone is a racist interpretation of an imaginary tale.

This kind of invocation is a clear example of how the nationalist Iranian writers and poets use racism in literature to maintain the subordinate status of non-Persian communities. Qazvini exploits an imaginary character from a book of poetry that was produced almost 1,000 years ago. He anachronistically interprets it in terms of the racism of his own time and society and uses it to delegitimize the language and ethnicity of an entire people. In essence, Qazvini's poem shows the degree to which the language of millions of Turkic-speaking peoples of Iran, in fact their entire identity, was (and still is) vilified, foreignized, and demonized. Such acts of foreignization have been practiced in a manner that denies an indigenous identity and authenticity to millions of minoritized citizens.

Similarly, humiliation and demonization of Iran's Arab citizens, along with foreignization of their culture and language, have become a daily preoccupation for Persian writers, poets, and intellectuals. The act of foreignization serves to take away the sense of indigeneity of Turkic and Arab nationalities, so that they would be deprived of an effective tool for resistance, which comes with one's longtime occupancy of a place, and with a sense of connectedness to the ancestral land. Otherization and foreignization of indigenous ethnic groups are conducted with the aim of loosening their attachment to their land, by reinforcing the belief that non-Persian ethnic groups are rootless vagabond intruders, now in the home of the dominant group and at its mercy.

The following are some examples of representation of Arabs in Persian literature and language:

A barefooted Arab with a black face, glaring eyes, and a thin beard, beat the mule's bleeding thigh with a thick iron chain. . . . A fearsome mob had formed—ragged Arabs, with stupid faces under fezzes, sly expressions under turbans, henna-dyed beards and nails, and shaved heads, counting rosaries, walking up and down in their sandals and cloaks and pajama trousers. They spoke Persian, babbled Turkish, or Arabic issued from the depth of their throats and from inside their bowels and resounded in the air. [There were] Arab women with tattooed faces, inflamed eyes, and rings through their noses. One of them had pushed half her black breast into the mouth of the dirty baby in her arms. . . . In front of a coffeehouse sat an Arab, picking his nose. With his other hand, he rubbed the dirt out from between his toes. His face was covered with flies, and lice crawled all over his head. (Hedayet, 1962, cited in Saad, 1996, pp. 34–35)

The passages just quoted come from Sadeq Hedayat, a prominent Persian writer whose work constitutes the core of "avant-garde" literature in Iran. During the Pahlavi regime, this literature was taught in Iranian schools and universities and in a country with millions of Arab citizens. Imagine the condition and feelings of an Arab student sitting in an Iranian school and reading this so-called avant-garde literature. In fact, during the Pahlavi era, this kind of literature was intentionally offered in schools particularly where the non-Persian communities lived. The government's aim was to accelerate the assimilation processes of non-Persian communities. By demonizing and devaluing non-Persian bodies and their culture, the idea was to alienate them from their culture, their heritage, and their ancestors. The function of such a literature was to make the students look down on their own backgrounds and feel ashamed of who they were and where they had come from.

And here is the prominent Persian intellectual and writer, Jalal Al-e Ahmad's view of Arabs and their language:

> Oh, how these Arabic terms, these Arabic names with their difficult letters to pronounce brought out the worst in me. How much 'ayn and qaf from the back of throat. How many tayns and zayns from the middle of the tongue! But how quickly we reached the station! It was a long way. I didn't notice how far we had come, but the sharp, bad-smelling cigarette of a headdressed Arab sitting next to me was finished. (Al-e Ahmad, 1970, cited in Saad, 1996, p. 96)

Linguistic chauvinism is promoted based on the assumption that Farsi was an Indo-European—and hence a superior—language, while other tongues are nothing more than minor "dialects" and incomprehensible gibberish infiltrated into Iran by savage Arabs and Turks. A "true Iranian" is believed to be the one who speaks the Persian language without an accent—Tehrani Farsi being the standard accent—and who constantly mocks, ridicules, and looks down on speakers of such foreign dialects as Azeri, Arabic, Baluchi, Kurdish, and Turkmeni. This literature of hate and mockery reached its peak on May 12, 2006, when a government newspaper identified the Turkish-speaking Azeris as cockroaches "eighty percent of" whom did not know even their own language "and prefer to talk in other languages" (*Iran Newspaper*, May 12, 2006). The Fars-centric ideology is so pervasive and deep-rooted that Changiz Pahlavan, a Persian intellectual and writer, makes any kind of political debate and dialogue conditional to the acceptance of Farsi as the only national language of all Iranians:

> In my view, two things must constitute the bases of our national discourse: First, an agreement on the maintenance of Iran's territorial integrity; and second, the acceptance of Farsi as the national tongue of all Iranians. Only after

reaching an agreement on these two essential bases, can we engage in discussions or even arguments on other issues. (Pahlavan, 1989, p. 522)

Pahlavan's foreignization of Iran's non-Fars communities goes to the extent that he compares these communities to migrant communities in Europe. "Do the Indian or Pakistani residents of England or the Algerian residents of France speak of self-ruling themselves within those countries?" asks Pahlavan (1989, p. 510). Why should our minorities demand special treatment? Pahlavan forgets that it is his Persian community that constitutes a numerical minority in Iran and that has come to that land at least 3,000 years after the other communities have been there. Speaking from his privileged ethnic and linguistic position, he allows himself the authority to lay out the condition based on which the minoritized groups and bodies should express their views. Where does he get this power to determine who should talk and who should not? What gives him the authority to single-handedly determine the terms and conditions of freedom of expression in Iran? Is it not his privileged ethnicity and language that make Pahlavan view himself as the true owner of Iran while looking upon others as tenants in their own homeland? It is only in a racist system that a single individual can so forcefully and shamelessly dictate to others the terms and conditions of their living. The same racism that has the power to ban certain tongues has also the power to give certain individuals such as Professor Changiz Pahlavan the authority to treat others as his personal chattels and slaves.

A distinguished Azeri scholar Mohammad-Ali Farzaneh has published excerpts from the text of his interrogation conducted in a prison run by SAVAK, the late shah's censor and torture organization:

The Interrogator: You write Farsi [the Persian language] very eloquently and elegantly; and yet you use a local dialect whose reading and writing the government has prohibited. Why? M.A. Farzaneh: . . . As my ethnic and mother tongue, I have a profound attachment to Azerbaijani language . . . which is a natural and legitimate tendency. I think that if I can express my feelings and thoughts in Farsi, why shouldn't I express them in my own mother tongue? (Farzaneh, 1998, p. 19)

According to a Hawaiian saying, "*i ka olalo ke ola; i ka olalo ka*: in language is life, in language is death" (Trask, 1993, p. 187). The disempowered and marginalized have long known that language is more than a medium of communication, more than an integral part of human cognition and understanding. It is more than the essential part of our poetry, stories, songs, and creative expressions. To the disempowered and minoritized, language is, first and foremost, an instrument of power, of oppression, marginalization, and exclusion. It has the power to colonize, to subjugate, and to criminalize. It is also a tool for resistance, for liberation, and for the restoration of human dignity.

[I]f you want to really hurt me, talk badly about my language. Ethnic identity is twin skin to linguistic identity—I am my language. Until I can take pride in my language, I cannot take pride in myself. (Anzaldua, 1987, p. 207)

We are all aware of the criminalization of black skin color in Euro-American racist settings. Black skins and bodies are often portrayed in Western media as symbols of criminality. If a crime has occurred in your neighborhood, and if you happen to be a black person, chances are that fingers of accusation will be pointed toward you. This is how the media has portrayed blacks. And this is a clear manifestation of "skin color racism." Those who have suffered "linguistic racism" will probably know that there are strange similarities between skin color racism and the racism based on language. Iran's non-Persian citizens have all experienced this kind of linguistic racism in which one's language replaces the color of one's skin in skin color racism. The speakers of the dominant language orchestrate a scenario in which the subordinate languages become criminalized. Through these criminalization processes, any attempt to learn, speak, read, and write the marginalized mother tongue becomes synonymous with crime and is treated accordingly.

Speaking your mother tongue means that you are disloyal to the territorial integrity of your so-called country, which in essence is the country of the dominant group. Your mother tongue becomes an antithesis to the "tongue of the nation," the so-called national language that is none other than the language of the dominant group. You become a danger to the sovereignty of the state, a separatist, a spy, a traitor, an agent of foreign powers—a criminal. True, skin color is more visible, more salient. One does not have the luxury to hide, conceal, and change the color of one's skin. But one can sometimes refuse to talk and in so doing hide one's language. One can sometimes fully master the language of the dominant group, particularly from second and later generations up on the ladder of assimilation. One can sometimes keep silent and not talk. But how and for how long?

> Your mother tongue becomes a criminal conspiracy against the great official culture of state. If you write anything in your own language, you automatically become a separatist and a traitor to the sovereignty of that state. So even in your childhood and youth in your own city you begin to live in exile, and you are told to hate your mother tongue. What happens to your own language? You simply swallow it. (Baraheni, 1998, p. 22)

As a direct result of "linguistic domination," the dominant language is usually seen as superior, with extremely high status and a "civilizing mission." Such language is often described as rational, logical, scientific, modern, and progressive, whereas the indigenous/dominated languages are viewed as irrational, incomprehensible, undeveloped, and backward "dialects," "idioms," "vernaculars," and "patois." In May 2000, the Iranian government had arranged a festival of art and culture for the country's university students. The authorities in Iranian Kurdistan had selected a group of 30 medical science Kurdish students to take part in festivities. They were supposed to exhibit their traditional clothing, songs, dances, and Kurdish poetry. After braving the tedious long journey through the mountainous roads they had reached their destination, only to be returned back in the middle of the night. They would only be allowed to participate in the program if they avoided speaking their mother tongue, wearing their national clothing, singing Kurdish songs, and performing Kurdish dances. The Tehran-based daily *Hamshahri* in its May 27 issue has published a letter from one of these students:

> After months of rehearsing, months of waiting and miles of long journey, we finally reached *Semnan*, the city hosting the Students Festival. . . . With an incredible desire and zest we slipped into our [Kurdish] clothing and impatiently waited for our turn to come. . . . We'd come from such a long journey to introduce our land, our language, our culture . . . to our fellow countrymen. . . . After interrogating our group leader for some disquieting time, we were told by the authorities: "Pack and leave if you like your lives!" . . . They thought that our Kurdish language, Kurdish clothing, songs and dances were bound to create disturbances. . . . We were turned back to Kurdistan in the dead of the night. (*Hamshahri*, May 27, 2000)

The dominant group's suppression of difference and diversity in this manner begs the question: For how long can it continue to exclude, marginalize, and vilify the non-Persian communities in the country? For how long can it use excuses such as separatism, national unity, and territorial integrity to deny the human rights of the majority of people in Iran who necessarily do not share the same language, religion, and culture as those of the dominant Persian group? Experiences of various countries show that, in diverse and multilingual societies, it is not so easy to discard, discredit, and annihilate ethnic languages, cultures, and ways of life.

However, acceptance of difference and diversity, coupled with respect for the Other's language, culture, religion, and way of life have the potential to bring various groups and communities together as equal citizens of the same society. If one learns anything at all from the unfortunate Yugoslavian experience, it is this bitter fact that suppression of ethnic groups and repression of their languages will not guarantee so-called national unity and territorial integrity. The prevalent myth that continues to view marginalized cultures and languages as obstacles to national homogenization, unity, and integration cannot be substantiated in light of various sociocultural, educational, and developmental concerns. Monolingual and monocultural policies shaped on Euro-American models and projects more and more are proving to be formidable obstacles blocking the path to inclusion, development, and progress (see also Dei and Asgharzadeh, 2003).

Not surprisingly, the racist literature produced inside Iran has been extended abroad as well, into the Iranian Diaspora. This diaspora came into existence after the Islamic Revolution of 1978, as a result of which millions of Iranians left the country for Europe, North America, and elsewhere. These émigrés who left in mass migratory movements particularly during the eight years of the Iran-Iraq war (1980–1988), number somewhere between 4 and 6 million, who have produced a remarkable literature that safely can be called Iranian diasporic literature (Asgharzadeh, 2005). A distinctive feature of this diasporic literature is in the way it both rearticulates and challenges traditional Persian narratives of identity, nationality, nation-state, and homeland. An example of this literature is a collection of stories in a volume titled *Another Sea, Another Shore*. The book is an admirable attempt to bring together in a single volume representative samples of the Iranian diasporic literature, rooted in at least 25 years of exilic experiences (see also Asgharzadeh, 2005).

Among the collected stories in the volume, Mehri Yalfani's "Without Roots" perhaps best captures the essence of what one may call an Iranian diasporic experience. In this powerful piece, Yalfani demonstrates a complex web of relationships, conflicts, and interactions that migration creates, like the ones between home and host cultures, old and young generations, males and females, as well as those emerging from class issues, racism, resocialization, and identity formation processes. The old generation of Iranian exiles, for instance, is represented in the figure of "the father," an ex-colonel in the Iranian army of the shah era, who now drives a cab in Toronto and "talks about women as if they are sheep" (Yalfani, 2004, p. 93).

The ex-colonel's generation is a product of a culture that has never come to terms with its own racist character. Many members of this generation come from a privileged ethnic, linguistic, and cultural background who in host societies for the first time find themselves at the receiving end of racism and exclusion. Unable to fully grasp this condition, they hold on to their homegrown racist mentality and resort to superiority complexes as a therapeutical mechanism to cope with their disadvantaged status in new societies. It is no wonder that when the ex-colonel's teenage daughter brings her friend "Salima" home, he and his wife make fun of Salima, asking their daughter, "Why do you make friends with colored children?" (Yalfani, 2004, p. 96).

Similar signs of racial prejudice are evidenced in other stories. In "The Road to Arizona," for instance, Nasim Khaksar, a seasoned writer, finds it necessary to comment on "the black fellow's" deep voice, "with that heavy black accent that never fades away even if they stay somewhere else for thirty years" (2004, p. 85). Likewise, in "The Wolf Lady," Goli Taraghi talks about the Iranian pride "rooted in 2,500 years of history . . . and a belief that we, descendants of Cyrus and Darius, even in our defeat, misery, and wretchedness, are superior to others" (2004, p. 130). This superiority complex is an inseparable component of modern Persian literature and is ingrained in worldviews of the majority of Persian intellectuals, writers, and poets. A flip side of this superiority complex has been to inferiorize non-Persian Others in the country by denying them spaces necessary for the development of their languages, literatures, cultures, and histories. This is a fact that is well illustrated in Ali Erfan's piece titled "Anonymous," in which a member of the dominant Farsi-speaking group describes his encounters with Iran's Baluchi community:

> You know that over there everyone has tanned, dark skin, and my white, fair skin stood out. Then and there I felt I was outside; outside Iran. They were speaking in a local language, Baluchi. A foreign language, like here. I did not

understand anything. . . . I could not accept that this place was part of Iran. (Erfan, 2004, p. 224)

Vilification and foreignization of marginalized communities have become normalized to the extent that even when the Baluchi community takes great risks to help a member of the dominant group to escape the country, this individual still demonizes that community, openly devaluing and belittling their acts of sacrifice and altruism. The dominant body foreignizes fellow citizens of his country just because they have "dark skins" and do not speak his language—the dominant Farsi language. Modern Persian literature has played a very central role in perpetuating this kind of linguistic racism. This literature has always sought to (mis)represent itself as Iran's only and exclusively authentic literature, just as it has sought to establish Farsi as the only legitimate language in the country. Racist and ethnocentric readings of social reality are not limited to works of literature and fiction. Quite to the contrary; such readings are more pronounced in social scientific and politic-ocultural studies. It is in these works that almost always "Iranian" and "Persian" are used interchangeably, just as the dominant group's language, history, and identity are taken to exclusively represent Iran's diverse histories, cultures, languages, and identities.

PERSIANIZATION OF EDUCATION: COLONIZING THE MIND

Education plays a major role in the creation, maintenance, and perpetuation of both dominance and subordination. As a major socializing agent, the educational system determines whose language will be taught in schools; whose culture transmitted; whose stories and histories learned; and whose stories and histories excluded, marginalized and criminalized.

> The key to the future of any society lies in the transmission of its culture and worldview to succeeding generations. The socialization of children, through education, shapes all aspects of identity, instilling knowledge of the group's language, history, traditions, behavior, and spiritual beliefs. It is for this reason that aboriginal peoples have placed such a high priority on regaining control over the education of their children. (Barman, Hébert, and McCaskill, 1986, p. 150)

Until the Constitutional Revolution of 1906, schooling in Iran was mainly privately organized. Better known as *maktabs*, these schools were opened by whoever could open them and teach. But it was the religious clergy who were in charge of the *maktabs* for the most part, where the pupils were taught the Quranic education, which mainly meant the reading and writing of the Quran and, by extension, the Arabic language. Alongside the Arabic, local languages were also taught. In effect, local languages were the languages of instruction throughout the learning cycle. Since education was not centralized, it was left to the local teachers and scholars to educate pupils in their own locality, which meant the use of the local language as the medium of instruction. Having advanced in their initial education, the students proceeded to study Islam, Islamic jurisprudence, mathematics, history, and literature.

In 1887, Mirza Hassan Roshdiyyeh of Tabriz built the first modern school in Azerbaijan and wrote the first modern textbooks in Iran. Roshdiyyeh's books were titled *Vatan Dili* [The Language of Homeland] (1905a), *Ana Dili* [The Mother Tongue] (1905b), and *Amsal-e Loqman* [The Sayings of Loqman] (Roshdiyyeh, 2001; see also Heyat, 1990). The books were written in Azeri-Turkic and were the first books of their kind that were designed to teach the art of reading, writing, spelling, composition, and grammar without relying on the Quranic methods of learning. In addition to using modern textbooks, Roshdiyyeh used for the first time blackboards and maps in his school in Tabriz (see also Behzadi, 1990).

Not surprisingly, the established teachers of old *maktabs* felt threatened by Roshdiyyeh's modern style of teaching. They figured that sooner or later his modern school was bound to undermine their long-held influence and authority. They constantly harassed Roshdiyyeh by calling him an infidel; by inciting thugs and hooligans to attack students attending his school; and by damaging school property, destroying supplies, and eventually setting the school on fire. At the end, the traditional clergy succeeded in forcing Roshdiyyeh out of Tabriz. He left for Tehran and opened a school there in 1898, adopting the same modern method of teaching. It was this school that gradually became a model for Iran's nontraditional, nonreligious, modern education system.

It was during the Constitutional period (1905–1925) that the importance of modern universal education was greatly emphasized by the ruling bodies. In 1906, schooling was made compulsory up to grade six for both girls and boys. In 1910, a Ministry of Education (Vizarat-e 'Ulum va Ma'aref) was established. In 1911, the Majlis approved an educational package called Fundamental Law of Education that limited the number of private schools and made their establishment conditional on the approval of educational authorities. It was in this period that public schools began to grow at an unprecedented scale.

At the time of Reza Khan's ascendancy to power, Iran's education system was on its way to becoming a fully government-sponsored modern schooling system. The number of public schools were on the rise and, naturally, so were the number of pupils. Reza Khan's regime was quick to realize the importance of a centralized education system in the project of nationalization, centralization of government, and to what was commonly referred as "modernization." Similar activities were already taking place in the neighboring country of Turkey, albeit on a much more comprehensive scale. A centralized education system meant that the same textbooks, curriculum, student uniforms, and schooling procedures would be designed, enforced, and implemented throughout the country. Most importantly, a centralized Iranian version of an education system implied that Farsi would be the sole language of education and instruction. In this sense, the education system was a godsend gift to Reza Khan's regime. So the regime gave unprecedented importance to building a centralized education system.

In the passage below, the late Mohammad Reza Shah explains this particular period and the prioritization of education by the Pahlavi regime:

> After my father's coup d'etat, which took place on February 22nd, 1921, a new era in our country's education and culture was innovated. Uniform syllabuses and systems were introduced for all state schools, private schools became subject to state control, and regulations were laid down for foreign schools. . . . Standard text-books were prepared and published by the Ministry of Education, and in 1933 a law was passed making tuition in all government secondary schools free. On February 4th, 1934, the corner-stone of the first university of Iran was laid. From 1935 onwards, co-educational primary schools for children up to ten years of age were established, and in the same year girls were admitted to the teacher's training college for the first time. (M.R. Sh. Pahlavi, 1967, pp. 107–108)

In short, the shah admits that "one of the greatest gifts that our revolution [the so-called White Revolution] could give the vast masses of Iran was undoubtedly that of education" (Pahlavi, 1967, p. 109). There is no denying that there is some truth in what he says. However, what he fails to say is that in this same period much more progressive educational developments were taking place in Iran's neighboring countries such as Turkey, Iraq, and the Soviet Union. It was the government's duty to use the country's resources and build a modern education system, whose importance by then had been acknowledged by all governments in the world. What his government was doing was the same thing that the Iraqi, Turkish, and Soviet governments were doing in their own countries. Why should the Iranians feel indebted to the Pahlavi regime for doing something that the regime was supposed to be doing as the ruling body in the country?

Likewise, he fails to mention that his regime in fact used the educational system to promote the racist doctrine of one nation, one language, one country in Iran. It fostered the idea that the Persian race was the superior race in the country and had therefore the exclusive right to rule over all other communities. It promoted the language of this particular race as a sacred, pure, and superior tongue, and it gave to this language the exclusive right to be taught and learned in schools as the national language of all Iranians. His father set out to build a modern centralized education system in which one of the primary tasks was to propagate Persian supremacy for the purpose of assimilating students of non-Persian origin. It was his father's racist educational policies that turned the classroom into the motor of assimilation in Iran. This assimilationist project has gone so far that some "educated" individuals end up turning against their own culture and language, and even call their own race and ethnic group a disgrace to humanity (see also Asgharzadeh, 2001).

Education was used to inculcate in non-Persian students the idea that their race, culture, and language were inferior to those of the dominant Persians and should therefore be discarded. The result of such an education for non-Persian students was a dreadful lack of self-esteem, self-worth, and self-reliance. On the one hand, education served to instill in Persian children a sense of superiority, dominance, and aggression. On the other hand, it served to maintain and perpetuate the subordinated status of non-Persian groups. At any rate, the modern education system in Iran was and has always been used for the purpose of subordination rather than liberation.

After absolute monarchism had ended, gender-based and religion-based discriminations were added to the already existing ethnic and linguistic racism in the Iranian education system. The Islamic Republic's education system has been one of the most visible sites for exhibition of gender inequality. Ever since the Islamic Revolution, the new rulers have reorganized the entire education system in Iran, which includes universities, schools, curricula, textbooks, school environment, extracurricular activities along with professors, teachers, and administrative personnel. By arguing that devotion to Islam is more important than specialty or professionalism, the Islamic regime dismissed all professors, lecturers, and teachers who were deemed to be "nondevoted" and "noncommitted" Muslims. Concurrent with the establishment of Islamic rule, the university curriculum, schooling policies, and all textbooks were rewritten in accordance with what is called the Islamic criteria.

According to an Iranian writer, by 1986 the Islamic regime had changed 700 topics from 636 textbooks at the elementary and secondary school level. These changes were made to inculcate in school children "the appropriate attitudes, values, and beliefs needed to maintain the status quo" (Mehran, 1989, p. 37). The policy of same-sex education was enforced at all levels, followed by the designation of separate curriculum for boys and girls. For boys the emphasis was placed on a variety of perceived masculinist notions such as leadership, hunting, war, and hard science. For girls the emphasis was placed on subjects that would prepare them to be model wives and mothers, or on those that train them for careers perceived to be suitable for women—for example, nursing, handicrafts and teaching of female students (see also Hendessi, 1990). In terms of religious discriminations, Shia Islam became the only official religious faith in all schools and universities. While Shia-centrism restricted religious activities of Sunni students to a considerable degree, it banned altogether any expression of faith-based identity for non-Muslim students such as Jews, Christians, Zoroastrians, and particularly the Baha'ís in Iran's public schools and universities. As "recognized religious minorities," the Jewish, Christian, and Zoroastrian communities were allowed to establish their own community centers and faith-based schools. However, even these limited rights were denied to the Baha'í community (see also Cooper, 1985; Yann, 1989; HRW, 2001; UNHCR, 2002).

In terms of linguistic exclusion and language-based oppression, it was in 1926 that for the first time the speaking of Azeri-Turkic became prohibited in Iranian and Azerbaijani schools. Reza Khan's handpicked chair of Cultural Office of Azerbaijan, a fellow named Dr. Mohseni, is well known for issuing the order: "Put donkey reins on whoever dares to speak Turkish in the classroom and throw them in the stable amongst the donkeys" (JAMI, 1983, p. 263). Ever since then, the banning of the mother tongue in schools has become the subject of numerous poems, short stories, and other creative expressions. In the passage below, the assimilatory role of Iranian education system is depicted through a short story:

"Why aren't there any penalty boxes in your classrooms? Hasn't His Majesty the Shah personally ordered penalty boxes installed in all classrooms in all schools in Azerbaijan, so that those who fail to speak the Persian language be penalized?" Shouted the gendarmerie lieutenant, pointing his finger at Hamid Agha the schoolteacher.

"The idea of penalizing students sounds very neat and easy on paper, but it's not so easy to implement in the real classroom," Hamid Agha said with an apologetic tone.

"How do you mean?" asked the lieutenant, obviously intrigued by Hamid Agha's frankness.

"I mean it's not practical. These kids don't know how to speak the Persian language yet. It'll take time and they need more time. For now they'll have to express themselves in their own language. But when they've learned more, I assure you they'll be singing Persian like a canary!"

"That's enough!" Lieutenant Tehrani yelled at Hamid Agha, the veins in the back of his neck swelling with anger.

"Are you stupid Turkish donkey saying that His Majesty was wrong in ordering the penalty boxes for each and every classroom in Azerbaijan? Haah? Is that what you're saying, boy?" . . .

Hamid Agha felt death in the morrow of his bones. "Obviously I haven't been able to explain myself well, Sir. I expressed myself poorly. I'm sorry. You've misunderstood me, Sir, it's not at all what I meant. . . ."

"What do you mean then, you stupid mangy dog?" (Asgharzadeh, 2002, pp. 17–18)

One may think that penalizing students for speaking their mother tongue was a thing of the past, and is not practiced anymore in the Islamic Republic. Far from it; the current government implements the same policies wherever and whenever it can. Although the government and the ruling elite have now understood that the racist policies of the previous regime do not work, they still insist on enforcing them in every opportunity they get. The same doctrines pertaining to aggressive Persian nationalism, assimilation of non-Persian communities, and the banning of their languages are enforced in the Islamic Republic. On December 27, 2002, the online Iranian newspaper *Gooya News* published a report titled "Reza-Khani Chauvinism Is Still Alive." The report was based on the observation of an eyewitness from two all-girls schools in the remote village of Mineq, in eastern Azerbaijan, and indicated that the students were being penalized for speaking their mother tongue:

If you enter either Sharaf elementary school or Parvin E'tesami Junior High, in each of these schools you'll find a big box, like the suggestion boxes in Tehran's schools, installed in the hallway. . . . On the orders of the principals of both schools, the students are required to place bills of 20, 50, or 100 tooman . . . in the penalty box if they are caught speaking their mother tongue in classrooms, schoolyards, and anywhere within the vicinity of the schools. This policy has caused the students to refrain from participating in class discussions. . . . As a result, they can't learn properly. . . . At home, they look down on their parents because they are Turks and cannot speak Farsi. . . . They look down on their own mother tongue. (*Gooya News*, December 27, 2002)

The racist policies and politics of the banning of students' mother tongues in schools are practiced in all non-Farsi-speaking towns, cities, and villages of the country. Mustafa Hijri, the secretary general of Democratic Party of Iranian Kurdistan (introduced earlier), explains the current schooling system in Kurdish-populated areas of Iran:

I have to say that the situation of education and the educative environment is dreadful across the country. It is even more dire in Kurdistan. The first issue is that parents are asked to pay under a whole range of guises. Although the regime insists that primary and secondary education is free, in practice the money asked is so large that it is beyond the means of the majority. Because of this many families only send two or three of their 4–5 kids to school. The next issue is the actual tutoring. As you know the culture, language, and religion of the majority of Kurds is different than the other Iranian nationalities. Yet most of the teachers sent into Kurdistan are foreign to all of these. . . . Teachers have been brought in because they are Hezbollah, believe in the Islamic Republic, or belong to the family of a martyr with some or other university degree. (Hijri, 2001, p. 5)

Thus, on the one hand, the cost of schooling is unbearable to the majority of families in Kurdistan, as it is for most families living in poverty in other parts of the country. This is a rejection of the government's claims that education in Iran is free to all students of school age. On the other hand, there is the problem of the intentional refusal to hire local teachers and administrative personnel from the Kurdish areas. When the students do not see their ethnicity, language, religion, and culture reflected in the curriculum and represented among the teaching staff, this leads to feelings of insecurity, lack of trust for the system, and humiliation on the part of the students. They may come to believe that their community is not competent enough to produce teachers and administrative personnel. And when they do not have local teachers as role models, they may feel that they may not be able to overcome the barriers and succeed in society:

This is why there are a large number of students in Kurdistan who abandon their education at various stages. They cannot continue both because of financial reasons and because they hate school and do not trust their teachers. Instead of being a place of fun, and healthy environment for learning and education, school and university is a place where they find themselves being humiliated, pressured and oppressed. A place where the student cannot express their views, yet there are non-native teachers that continuously try to indoctrinate things to them which are not only boring but hateful. When a student feels that their nationality, language, religion and even clothes are ridiculed and they cannot talk to their teacher as they want then clearly they will become resentful. In Iran, sadly, little attention is paid to a healthy relationship between pupil and teacher, especially in Kurd-populated areas which have always been regarded by suspicion by the Islamic Republic. (Hijri, 2001, p. 6)

A recent report in a local Iranian newspaper indicated that the Iranian educational authorities had decided to decentralize the design and publication of textbooks in the country (*Roozname-ye Iran*, January 29, 2004, p.1) The report stated that local scholars in various communities were to be given authority to design textbooks "based on their personal creativity and taste, as well as on social, cultural, and regional conditions of their particular area." According to the report, the final goal of such a plan was to enable each teacher "to teach in his/her class the textbook whose content is most appropriate to that particular classroom"(*Roozname-ye Iran*, January 29, 2004, p.1).Upon publication of this report, various nationalist groups and individuals bombarded Iranian media outlets, online publications, and Internet discussion groups with their criticism of the government's "irresponsibility" (as they called it) in this regard. Among the staunch critics of the plan was a political organization known as Iran's National Front (Jebhe-ye Melli-ye Iran). In an open letter addressed to Iran's president, Mohammad Khatami, and the minister of education, Morteza Haji, the leadership of Iran's National Front warned the authorities that such a decision "can be interpreted as an attack on Iran's territorial integrity and on the roots of the existence of the great Iranian nation" (*Heyat-e Rahbari-ye Jebhe-ye Melli-ye Iran*, February 9, 2004).

> The recent directive issued by the Ministry of Education to its offices in provinces . . . has permitted the provinces to design the textbooks for elementary and junior high schools in accordance with their customs, and regional, cultural, and social conditions. This directive will not only educate the future generation of the country with a locally-oriented culture instead of the national culture, but will also alienate them with the national culture, official language, and sub-cultures of the country. . . . Is not this act a cultural backwardness and a step towards disintegration of the country and separation and alienation of our people from one another? . . . We consider this decision, if implemented, a great betrayal on the part of the Ministry of Education in Iran's contemporary history and a dangerous preamble in line with the outsiders' plan to disintegrate the country. (*Heyat-e Rahbari-ye Jebhe-ye Melli-ye Iran*, February 9, 2004)

The above statement shows that the majority of ultranationalist groups and individuals opposed to the current Islamic government are in fact more chauvinistic and undemocratic than the current Iranian government when it comes to issues of diversity and ethnic/linguistic equality in the country. Within Iran, an interest has developed in recent years among some scholars to study various aspects of the education system, issues of bilingualism, multiculturalism, and the place of the mother tongue in education. One of the interesting works in this regard is Solmaz Modarres's (1993) study titled "Amuzesh-e kudakan-e do-zabaneh dar Azerbayjan-e sharqi" ["Exploring Educational Problems of Bilingual Children in Eastern Azerbaijan."] In conducting this research, Modarres has chosen 12 elementary schools from the Farsi-speaking greater Tehran area and 12 schools from Azeri-speaking Tabriz and its suburbs. She has done interesting studies on students, including classroom observations, interviews, and conducting of tests such as in dictation, arithmetic, and science. She then reaches some important conclusions:

1. In dictation, the Azeri speaking students had 7 mistakes on average; whereas the Farsi speaking students had only 1/5 mistakes on average.
2. Azeri-speaking students had their highest marks on mathematics; whereas the highest mark of Farsi-speaking students were on the subject of reading Farsi.
3. In rural areas the average mark of Farsi-speaking students with illiterate parents was 14; the average mark of Azeri-speaking students with educated parents was 10.
4. The overall average mark for the tests conducted was 15 for Farsi-speaking students and 8/5 for Azeri-speaking students.
5. The researcher posed science questions to a group of Azeri-speaking students in Persian and to another group in Azeri (their mother tongue). For the first group replying in Farsi the average mark was 9; for the second group responding to questions in Azeri the average mark was 16 (Modarres, 1993; see also Sarrafi, 2003, p. 4).

It is not surprising that *Statistics Yearbook* 1996 (Statistical Center of Iran, 1996) shows the Farsi-speaking provinces of Tehran, Esfahan, Semnan, and Yazd to have the highest rate of literacy, while non-Farsi-speaking provinces of west and east Azerbaijan, Kurdistan, and Baluchistan have the highest rate of illiteracy, respectively. Notwithstanding this fact, the intellectuals and writers from the dominant group still insist on continuation of the assimilatory processes. In essence, any time the government is busy with an important issue, for example an external war, and seems to be not directly suppressing the minoritized communities, it is the privileged intellectuals and writers who remind the government to keep an open eye on the minoritized communities. For instance, during the Iran-Iraq war (1980–1988), obviously the war was the main preoccupation of the Iranian government. At that time, many dominant thinkers were concerned that the war had diverted attention away from internal contradictions and differences among various communities that, from a dominant viewpoint, were equally essential for the government to suppress. It is in this period that an academic and writer named Javad Sheikhol-islami reminds the governing authorities of "too much growth of Turkish in Azerbaijan" and "illogical development of Arabic in Khuzistan" (*tovse'e-ye na-ma'qul-e arabi*) which in his view constitute "the two essential dangers that must never be underestimated" (1989, p. 442).

According to Sheikhol-islami, under no condition should the government refrain from supplanting the languages of non-Persian communities by Farsi.

He cautions that this important task must be completed with patience within a long-term planning process, at least within a 50-year period. He suggests some concrete measures through which the Islamic Republic can achieve the goal of complete assimilation of minoritized bodies:

> The means to be employed in this regard are establishment of free kindergartens, and the teaching of Farsi (as the first language) to the children in urban and rural areas of provinces of Azerbaijan and Zanjan and Khuzistan. For, a language which becomes dominant from the childhood in the mind of children, such language will not succumb to local languages. We can also accept as guests the younger Azerbaijani and Zanjani and Khuzistani boys and girls for a couple of years in honorable Farsi-speaking families, like a system of exchange that they have in Europe. This way we can help to advertise and strengthen the Persian language among this particular age group (12 to 16 years). (Sheikhol-islami, 1989, p. 445)

Sheikhol-islami considers the Iran-Iraq war as a positive occurrence in this regard. According to him, the war has provided Persians with ample opportunity to take in homeless Arabic-speaking Khuzistani children and teach them "proper Farsi." As he puts it,

> The current Iran-Iraq war has coincidentally created the condition to practically enforce the plan [of Persianization]. It is indispensable that the well-meaning inhabitants of important Farsi-speaking cities in Iran (Tehran, Mashhad, Isfahan, Yazd, Shiraz, Kerman) if possible, take some of the homeless children from these regions . . . within their warm families or educational settings . . . and with this good deed hit two goals with one shot: Help their homeless countrymen on the one hand; and teach the national language of the country to these deprived and homeless children, on the other. (Sheikhol-islami, 1989, pp. 445–446)

Sheikhol-islami's Persianization plan of the young Arab victims of the war is like stealing candy from a helpless kid. Under the pretext of helping homeless children, he wants Persian families to offer shelter to these children, and in so doing rob them of their mother tongue. This shows the degree to which the nationalist Persian and Persianized intellectual is determined to accomplish the doctrine of one language, one nation, and one country, without any regard to ethical, moral, and humane considerations of such a colonizing act. As if coping with homelessness, loss of community, separation from parents, friends, and schoolmates were not enough for these innocent victims of the war, Mr. Sheikhol-islami wants to annihilate their means of communication as well.

There can be no doubt that there is irreparable psychological and emotional damage that this kind of racism inflicts on its victims. The criminalization of one's mother tongue brings in its wake all sorts of humiliations, resentments, and injuries. One has to either identify with the dominant group—if such a thing is indeed possible—or else suffer the consequences of belonging to a criminalized ethnicity, language, and culture. This is suffering that starts with birth, follows us through our childhood, adolescence, adulthood, and even death. The following is a Persian proverb that best captures the humiliation, stigmatization, and torturous state of belonging to a criminalized language and identity:

> A Turkish family had just moved from Tabriz to Tehran. One day the child of this family runs home to his mother from the street, where he was playing with other children, and while crying his eyes out, says: "Mother, the Persian kids in the street call me *Turk-e khar* [Turk donkey]!"
> "This is nothing to be upset about, my dear," says the mother. "You go out there and this time you call them *Fars-e khar* [Persian donkeys]!" Excited and determined, the kid goes back to the street. Halfway through, he runs back to his mother again, shouting: "But mother! Don't you know that the Persians are no donkeys?!" (See also Asgharzadeh, 2002, p. 18)

This racist joke is an example of many racial insults, slurs, epithets, name-callings, and hate literature directed against Azerbaijani Turks in Iran. Victims of this kind of abuse know very well that it is not just a joke. It is not an invention of some sickly creative mind. It is a violent act committed against real persons, with real feelings, emotions, identity, dignity, self-perception, and self-worth. It is a depiction of actual racist practice behind which there is a real history and countless painful stories. In this "saying" we witness a racist act wherein both the victim and victimizers are children. It is evident from his behavior that the victim has already internalized—and hence accepted—the inferior status assigned to him (and to his people) by a racist society. He believes it to be okay for the Persian kids to call him a donkey—that is, a subhuman in this case. But he cannot imagine himself or his mother and anybody else for that matter calling the Persians "donkeys." For in his eyes, they are not subhuman, but he is! He already believes that they are superior and he is inferior. He has already internalized his position as a victim, as inferior, stupid, incompetent, savage, subhuman—donkey.

The imagery of "donkey" is a powerful epithet that is used to refer to Iran's Turkic-speaking communities (see also B. Shaffer, 2002). The sole purpose of this racist act is to deny a minoritized community its humanity. As Memmi has noted, "Making use of the difference is an essential step in the racist process" through which "the racist aims to intensify or cause the exclusion, the separation by which the victim is placed outside the community or even outside humanity" (1969, p. 185). For according to Memmi, racism is "the generalized and final assigning of value to real or imaginary difference, to the accuser's benefit and at his victim's expense, in order to justify the former's privileges or aggression" (1969, p. 185). Evidently, relegating the victim to the status of a donkey superbly satisfies the racist's need for aggression, superiority, and mastery. Here is Professor Reza Baraheni's account of how he, as an Azerbaijani, became subjected to this subhuman status:

> I learned Persian at great cost to my identity as an Azerbaijani Turk, and only after I had mastered this language and was on the point of becoming

thoroughly Persianized was I reminded of my roots by those who were directing polemics against me in the Persian press. Whenever I wrote something good about an originally Persian author, I was hailed as a man who had finally left behind his subhuman Turkish background and should be considered as great as the Persians; whenever I said something derogatory about a writer's work, the response was always that I was an Azerbaijani, and, given that according to Persian proverb all Azerbaijanis are *Turk-e-khar* [Turk donkeys], whatever I had written could be of no significance at all; since what of value could a Turkish donkey have to say in regard to Persian gods? When I succeeded in establishing myself in their literary *who's who*, in their own language and on their own terms, they came up with the sorry notion that there was not even a single drop of Azerbaijani blood in my veins. (Baraheni, 1977, p. 111, emphasis is in the original)

Assigning of a subhuman status plays out in practice when Baraheni is arrested, thrown in prison, and interrogated/tortured by SAVAK, the shah's secret and torture organ. The following is an account of his encounter with his interrogator:

Until now he [the interrogator/torturer] has found no opportunity to make a racist attack on me. He shifts rather uncomfortably in the sofa and all of a sudden blurts out: "You really are a *Turk-e-Khar* [Turk donkey]!" He rings the bell; the guard comes in. I am taken out, blindfolded and handcuffed to the guard, and we go back to the prison and into my cell. (Baraheni, 1997, p. 139)

It is indeed a matter of curiosity to understand why, of all the animals, the racist mentality has chosen donkey to dehumanize the minoritized Other. Compared to a variety of other animals, donkey seems to be rather smarter. However, it appears that in some cultures this particular animal denotes stubbornness, dullness, and plain stupidity. Ngugi Wa Thiong'o has recorded similar accounts of dehumanizing punishments when the Gikuyu-speaking students in Kenya were forced to carry a sign saying "I am a donkey," whenever they were caught speaking their mother tongue:

Thus one of the most humiliating experiences was to be caught speaking Gikuyu in the vicinity of the school. The culprit was given corporal punishment—three to five strokes of the cane on bare buttocks—or was made to carry a metal plate around the neck with inscriptions such as I AM STUPID or I AM A DONKEY. (Wa Thiong'o, 1994, p. 11)

Obviously, this kind of humiliation is done for the purpose of breaking the spirit, the sense of dignity, self-respect, and the belief of the victim in his/her humanity. As a result of this kind of psychological abuse, the victim begins to doubt his/her own worth. S/he comes to believe the accusations of the dominant group that s/he is stupid, ignorant, dirty, abnormal; that his/her language, culture, and heritage are embarrassing and shameful; that her/his race is backward, incompetent, inferior, and subhuman. All these stigmatizations leave the victim with one inhumane and destructive choice: either to hate his/her own self or to have no self at all, to be nothing, an alienated and selfless entity:

> Because they constantly hear racist messages, minority children, not surprisingly, come to question their competence, intelligence, and worth. Much of the blame for the formation of these attitudes lies squarely on value-laden words, epithets, and racial names. . . . If the majority "defines them and their parents as no good, inadequate, dirty, incompetent, and stupid," the child will find it difficult not to accept those judgments. (Delgado, 1995, p. 163)

The psychological response to "spirit injuries" inflicted on victims of Persian racism has taken many forms, ranging from self-hatred to self-denial to identification with the oppressor. The Azeri journals and magazines published both inside Iran and abroad abound with articles and letters discussing various defeatist symptoms on the part of Azerbaijani victims of Persian racism. A letter sent to the journal *Varliq*, for instance, discusses the punishment of a little girl by her Turk father for talking Turkish with her friend. The observer was a guest in the family's home:

> [T]he father got up and smacked his little girl on the head, shouting [in Persian]: "You daughter of a burnt father! Haven't I told you not to talk Turkish? When do you want to become a human-being? Such a rude girl!"
> The father's behavior agitated me. I protested, demanding an explanation. He said: "You don't understand! If a kid speaks Turkish, she becomes rude, ignorant, without a personality and devoid of character!" (*Varliq: Turkce-Farsca ferhengi dergi*, 1993, pp. 102–103)

Feelings of helplessness and worthlessness have also come to manifest themselves through strong attachments to "big brothers" of one kind or another. Some Azeris, after becoming disillusioned with the dominant Persian group, are now seeking to safeguard themselves under the umbrella of Turkey's dominant Turkish group, replacing one "big brother" with another (see also Asgharzadeh, 2002). For these Azeris, Turkey has become the center of the universe, a symbol of power, worth, and dignity. They try very hard to replace their own Azeri-Turkic with the Turkish spoken in contemporary Turkey. Some of them refer to their own Azeri-Turkic as a "dialect" compared to Turkey's official language known as the Turkish. They look down upon those Azeris who refuse to write in Anatolian (Istanbuli) Turkic instead of writing in Azeri-Turkic (see also Asgharzadeh, 2000, 2002). Aside from the "big brother syndrome," other responses include such symptoms as "inferiority complex"; "denial of self," particularly by uttering such statements as "my father used to be a Turk but I am a Persian now!"; identification with the dominant group; voluntarily speaking and teaching the language of the dominant group to children even in Europe and North America (see also Asgharzadeh, 2002; Ardebili, 1999).

The glorification of the Persian race and language at the expense of other cultures and languages was not limited to the members of the dominant Persian group. There were many non-Persian writers and intellectuals such as Ahmad

Kasravi, Taqi Arani, Rezazadeh Shafaq, Naseh Nateq, and Khalil Maleki who served as forerunners in the project of Persianization. The assimilated and Persianized intelligentsia lost no opportunity to demonize and vilify the non-Farsi-speaking ethnic groups. For instance, an Azeri intellectual named Taqi Arani found it necessary to come to the aid of the "Aryan" race and proclaim all Iranians to be of common "Aryan ancestry," vehemently denouncing and vilifying his own Turkic origins. He praised Reza Shah's banning of non-Persian languages and demanded that all Iranian children be forced to learn Farsi:

> It is a disgrace for an Azerbaijani to be taken for a Turk. . . . To deprive an Azerbaijani of the honor of being Persian is a flagrant injustice. . . . Well-meaning individuals must strive to eradicate Turkic from Azerbaijan and replace it by Farsi. . . . The Ministry of Education must post Farsi speaking teachers in that region in great numbers and publish free or less-expensive [Persian] books, articles and magazines for their use. (Arani, 1924, p. 251)

Similarly, Rezazadeh Shafaq Tabrizi, another Azerbaijani Turk, asserted the absurdity of calling Azerbaijanis "Turk" and zealously set out to prove their Persian origins. Included in his prescription for Persianization was the notion that Iran had to maintain Azerbaijan both physically and spiritually (*jesmani va ruhani*). By "physically" he meant military invasion and annihilation; by "spiritually" he meant cultural and linguistic annihilation:

> Iran has to protect Azerbaijan like a heart or an eye which is the target of the enemy's bullet. The method of protecting Azerbaijan must be both physical and spiritual. . . . To the same extent that it is necessary for cannonballs and enemy-smashing soldiers to line up around the borders of Azerbaijan and await their orders; it is also necessary that the education of thought and soul and the Iranian language be revived throughout this land; and through [the construction of] sufficient modern schools, the youth of this region must be prepared, and . . . competent teachers from Farsi-speaking regions must be brought and stationed there. (Rezazadeh Shafaq Tabrizi, 1924, p. 251)

In addition to open denunciation and humiliation of their racial/ethnic backgrounds, Persianized members of minoritized groups find various other excuses, from psychological to economic to pseudo-emancipatory, to justify the use of the dominant Persian language. Professor Sakina Berengian has observed an interesting example of this category of the Persianized intelligentsia:

> A young Azerbaijani poet who received his education in Tehran and who, furthermore, sought recognition throughout Iran would consciously or otherwise refrain from writing in Turkic. What is more, he would justify his preference for Persian by stating that Azeri was not fit for literary expression. The present writer had occasion to ask a famous contemporary poet, who wrote only in Persian, whether he had ever written anything in Turkic. Disposing of the centuries-long heritage of Azeri literature . . . he said: "Should one have at his disposal a machinegun and a kitchen knife, which do you suppose he would use for self-defence?" (Berengian, 1988, pp. 112–113)

It is interesting to see how the poet likens his own mother tongue to a kitchen knife, whereas he sees the Persian language as machinegun. In order to justify this analogy, he uses the term self-defence, implying that he is using Farsi for the purpose of defending himself, and implicitly, his people. The use of this kind of terminology begs the question: what self-defence? By promoting a dominant language, and through it himself, this particular poet expects others to believe that he is engaged in an act of defending himself and his community. Just like the majority of his type, this Persianized poet is under the illusion that, by writing Persian poetry, he is doing a service to his community, and hence, his community owes something to him.

Signs and symptoms of self-denial and self-hatred in the form of questioning one's own ancestors, culture, language, community, and race have long been identified in victims of skin color racism:

> When asked to describe dolls which had the physical characteristics of black people, young children chose adjectives such as "rough, funny, stupid, silly, smelly, stinky, dirty." Three-fourths of a group of four-year-old black children favored white clay companions; over half felt themselves inferior to whites. Some engaged in denial or falsification. (Delgado, 1995, p. 162)

The use of the dominant Persian language entails a great deal of privilege and prestige along with excellent employment opportunities and considerable material/political gains. So, the Persianized intelligentsia often uses all sorts of historical, psychological, and coercive methods to justify the perceived superiority of the dominant group and its language. Just like other assimilationist projects, the assimilated members of the non-Persian communities are often employed by the dominant group to demonize, foreignize, and humiliate their own indigenous culture, language, and tradition. Taqi Arani, Rezazadeh Shafaq, Ahmed Kasravi, and many others are glaring examples of Persianized intelligentsia faithfully serving the assimilationist project of the Pahlavi regime (see also Berengian, 1988; Morshedizad, 2001).

It is important to note that individuals who turn against their own community are able to participate in the cultural and linguistic annihilation of their communities only under the umbrella of the dominant group, under the protection of its political/militaristic power, in its language, and through its publishing and distributing facilities. Their acts of falsification and denial are committed freely, while members of the minoritized communities are not allowed to tell their own stories and to defend themselves. Although the minoritized resist various acts of annihilation, falsification, and denial in their own ways and at great risks, their voices are not allowed to reach larger audiences that the dominant group has the luxury of reaching.

CONCLUSION

Reza Khan's ascendancy to power marked the emergence of an aggressive Fars-centeric nationalism in Iran that sought to construct a sense of nationhood in opposition to such non-Persian groups, communities, and nationalities as the Turks, Arabs, Kurds, Baluchs, and Turkmens who together constituted the numerical majority in the country. In particular, the Turks and Arabs were singled out as the two major *anirani* (un-Iranic) nationalities for whom there was no place within a Fars-centered Iranian nation. The *anirani* Turkic and Arab nationalities were left with two clear choices: first, abandon their language and identity and become fully Persianized; second, be annihilated and/or swept across the Araxes, as Qazvini (1923, p. 103) suggested in his famous poem.

Based on the dominant racist discourse, Iran's progress depended on re-Aryanization. However, the degenerating effects of non-Aryan communities were major hindrances to the project of re-Aryanization. What was to be done, then? A very simple solution seemed to provide the remedy: one nation, one language, one country. Of course, what this remedy meant was an aggressive denial of the existence of ethnic and linguistic diversity in the country. Immediately after the consolidation of Reza Khan's power, the Persianization processes started to be implemented with the help of at least three major forces.

The first major force behind Persianization and assimilation was the use of government power. This included the power and authority of all governmental institutions such as the military, educational system, schools, universities, registration/census centers, courts, and all the official/authoritative bodies with power to implement the policies and politics of Persianization. These institutions were empowered to prohibit the use of non-Farsi languages, non-Farsi words, names, signs, and symbols in all the official spaces, and particularly in schools, universities, and learning centers where non-Persian students were punished and penalized for speaking their mother tongues. The government activated an Academy of Farsi Language (Farhangestan-e zaban-e Farsi) with the task of "cleansing" the Persian language from Arabic and Turkic elements, while coining new Farsi terms and names to replace the non-Farsi traits. Lists of these new terminologies were sent to all the official organs and institutions to be implemented whenever and wherever relevant, with the education system taking the lead in overly using them through textbooks, school curriculum, as well as in the classroom by teachers, professors, and lecturers.

The second force for Persianization came through the creation of a dominant discourse by the privileged scholars, writers, poets, and intellectuals who necessarily were not a part of the ruling establishment but who nonetheless pursued the same racist politics as the official establishment. These individuals worked tirelessly to develop a chauvinistic discourse complementary to the establishment's racist order. They produced works of history, literature, language, and culture that not only excluded the non-Persian communities but also aggressively denigrated, vilified, inferiorized, and foreignized them. For instance, alongside the creation of an official Academy of Farsi Language, a nonofficial institution named National Academy (Farhangestan-e Melli) was founded by Dr. Mahmood Afshar (I. Afshar, 1985). This National Academy was created to utilize the knowledge of nonofficial intellectuals and scholars for the purpose of complementing the shortcomings of the establishment's Academy of Farsi Language (I. Afshar, 1985).

It was the extension of this nonofficial National Academy that culminated in Foundations of Dr Mahmood Afshar (Movqufaat) whose primary task has been "to spread the Persian language and complement the national solidarity and create the National Academy of Persian Language and Literature" (Saleh, 1985, p. 31). In effect, whatever the successive regimes and governments have not been able to do vis-à-vis the marginalized communities through their coercive force, Mahmood Afshar's Foundations has managed to do culturally and linguistically. The activities of this foundation in publishing racist material, conducting racist conferences, and financing racist research are only matched by the similar activities of the ruling elite and the government apparatuses.

The third force for assimilation and Persianization came through the Persianized members of the minoritized communities. The assimilated members of the minoritized communities have proved to be extremely useful instruments in facilitating the assimilation of their coethnics into the dominant group. This group has also been most effective in foreignizing and demonizing the respective communities from which they come. The lasting impact of individuals such as Ahmad Kasravi and Taqi Arani is a clear manifestation of the effectiveness of using collaborators to carry out politics of assimilation. The work that these collaborators do cannot be done as effectively by the dominant group's military force. These collaborators simply claim that the current language and identity of their ethnic group are not "authentic"; that their community used to speak Farsi and their ancestors used to be Persian/Aryan in ancient times; and that it is because of the intrusions centuries ago of aggressive tribes such as the Arabs, Mongols, and Turks that the language and identity of their ethnic group are currently Arabic or Turkic, as the case may be (see, e.g., Arani, 1924; Kasravi, 1925).

Having made such essentialist assertions, they go on and vilify the current language, tradition, history, and identity of their community. Because of the enormous advantages that this category of collaborators has for the dominant group, the dominant group takes them under its wing and showers them with media, press, and publishing outlets; financial rewards; prestigious positions; and glamorous titles such as scientist, scholar, linguist, historian, intellectual, writer, and poet. Suffice it to say that the role played by the Persianized intelligentsia is so significant that in the absence of an analysis of their role, any discussion of racism, internal colonialism, and assimilation in Iran would be meaningless.

Thus, a racist body of knowledge has been produced in Iran through the collaboration and cooperation of such individuals, groups, institutions, and forces as the ruling elite, the privileged intellectuals, the Persianized intelligentsia, the educational system, the media, and the literary community. It is this body of knowledge that sustains, nourishes, and reproduces the racist order in current Iran. The seeds of this racist discourse were sown in the mid-1920s and its fruits are reaped today by the privileged dominant group. While the dominant group enjoys the benefits of its linguistic and cultural hegemony in the country, the marginalized and excluded continue to struggle for the survival of their languages, cultures, and identities. After the fall of the Pahlavi regime in 1978, the marginalized groups "gained" a very limited freedom to publish and disseminate their views in their own literature. No matter how limited and scarce this literature was, it has been effective enough to expose the dominant group's lies, falsifications, and appropriations. The next chapter explores samples of this marginalized discourse of resistance.

CHAPTER 6

Resisting Racism: The Counterhegemonic Discourse and Praxis

Little is more traumatic than the suppression of one's mother tongue. The suppression does not result in a total amnesia. You use it one way or another. Racial or ethnic suppression of the mother tongue can never be total, because you use it with your family, and friends. But the dominant language and its culture (in my case Persian) are imposed on you, supplanting your mother tongue and culture (mine is Azeri, a Turkic language), labeling it the language and culture of traitors.

(Reza Baraheni, 1998, p. 22)

NARRATIVES OF RESISTANCE

Narratives reflect relationships among individuals, groups, communities, and peoples. Since colonial conditions are characterized by relations of power, domination, and resistance against them, the produced narratives are also narratives of dominance, subordination, as well as resistance. According to Foucault, "[T]here is no power relation without the correlative constitution of a field of knowledge, nor any knowledge that does not presuppose and constitute at the same time power relations" (1977, p. 27). If applied to a colonial relationship, as Said (1979) does in Orientalism, Foucault's articulation of the knowledge-power nexus can be manifested in discourse that carries with it the very means of misrepresenting, reifying, vilifying, and controlling the dominated Other.

This kind of Foucauldian analysis, while highlighting the importance of discourse in the maintenance of dominance, leaves little space for resisting the dominant discourse by other discursive means. Yet one can hardly find a decolonizing movement without having a discourse of its own, a counternarrative vis-à-vis the dominant narrative of power. Although there are hierarchies of power, status, and authority within the discourse of the colonized, the fact remains that this discourse stands in direct opposition to the discourse of the colonizer, and as such it has the potential to disrupt and challenge the dominant discourse. By its very existence, this discourse confesses the inauthenticity and fictionality of the dominant narrative about the dominated Other (see also Agger, 1992).

A clear example of the effectiveness of this kind of counterdiscourse can be found in the narratives produced by various marginalized individuals and communities in Iran. In the face of their subjection to the dominant group's assimilationist project, Iran's minoritized communities and ethnic/national groups have fought tooth and nail to safeguard their indigenous identity, culture, and language. Apart from their numerous grassroots movements, regional upheavals, and mass resistances against the centralized authority (Foran, 1994; Atabaki, 1993; Fawcett, 1992; W. Eagleton, 1963; Azeri, 1955), Iran's minoritized groups have vigorously defended their ethnic, cultural, and particularly linguistic rights in their songs, stories, narratives, and discursive activities. In spite of obvious restrictions and limitations, they have produced an enormous body of knowledge that speaks volumes about their attachment to their ethnic identity and their resistance against assimilation and annihilation. The production of this marginalized literature has acquired new dimensions particularly after the overthrow of Pahlavi regime in the 1978–1979 popular uprising.

In addition to a limited number of outlets available to them to publish in the form of books, periodicals, bilingual magazines, journals, and newspapers, the advancement in Internet technology has also provided them with ample opportunity to express themselves in hypertext and in cyberspace away from the interference of a variety of official and nonofficial censor organs. In recent years, numerous Web pages and online journals have been established that explore the condition of Iran's nationalities and ethnic groups exclusively from the vantage point of these minoritized groups themselves. This enormous body of work clearly challenges the legitimacy of the dominant group's (mis)representation of minoritized communities. In what follows, I explore a number of common themes running through this body of marginalized, yet highly resistant, literature. These common themes include various acts of resistance and decolonization in areas such as identity, language, literature, culture, history, education system, and other discursive and practical activism that the marginalized communities are engaged in for the purpose of challenging the legitimacy of the dominant group's bases of oppression.

DECOLONIZING THE IDENTITY, CULTURE, AND LANGUAGE

As discussed earlier, following in the footsteps of Orientalist/Aryanist historiography after the establishment of Pahlavi dynasty, the dominant Persian group in Iran has been attempting to construct a single identity for all the nationalities and ethnic groups in the country. The ultranationalist history that they have constructed presents a picture of ancient Iran populated by a single race speaking a single language. This race is of course Aryan and the language is Farsi. The speakers of such variants of Indo-European languages as Baluchi, Luri, Kurdish, Taleshi, Gilaki, and Mazandarani are easily classified under the racial designation Aryan. The dominant historiography maintains that all these groups are carriers of "pure Aryan blood" who speak only slightly different accents of the same Persian/Aryan language. Again, language comes to serve as a formidable link that connects race/ blood with speech/tongue. The Kurds, Baluchs, Lurs, Gilakis, and Mazandaranis are seen as belonging to the same biological race just because they speak different variants of the Indo-European language family. According to such categorization, Iran belongs to these Aryan groups because they speak an Aryan language and carry the pure Aryan blood in their veins. As such, they are "the true and authentic owners of Iran" (see, e.g., Varjavand, 2004).

Having thus taken care of the Kurdish, Baluchi, Luri, Taleshi, Gilaki, and Mazandarani communities, the challenge has been to come to terms with the speakers of such non-Aryan languages as the Turks, Arabs, and Jews. Among these supposedly non-Aryan groups, the Jews are numerically very insignificant, posing no serious threat to the politics of monolingualism and monoculturalism. So they were and currently are mostly left alone, as far as race and language are concerned. However, in terms of regional geopolitical issues and issues relating to Israel, the Jewish minority is under tight surveillance and pressure. The Turks and Arabs, on the other hand, have significant numbers who inhabit strategic regions in the southern, northern, and central parts of the country. The Arabs are concentrated in the southern oil-rich region of Arabistan (the current province of Khuzistan) and are seen as a serious threat to the politics of assimilation, centralization, and homogenization. Likewise, the Turkic-speaking groups constitute a numerical majority in the country, inhabiting the vast provinces of east and west Azerbaijan, Zanjan, the region of Turkmen-Sahra, and various other areas in Khorasan and central parts of Iran. The Turkic-speaking groups have ruled the country for over 1,000 years. This is a group that has had the potential to destabilize the Pahlavi rule, and it poses the greatest challenge to the new government's Persianization project.

In order to completely neutralize the challenge posed by the non-Aryan Turkic- and Arabic-speaking groups, the Pahlavi regime orchestrated a process of dehumanization that aimed to vilify the race, nationality, culture, and language of these two groups. It has been in reaction to this dehumanization and vilification that the marginalized communities have sought to defend themselves not only through their collective mass movements but also through their discourse, songs, dances, poems, and narratives, which are juxtaposed as counternarratives to the dominant discourse.

A shining example of this counternarrative is offered in Bulut Qarachorlu (Sehend's) writings and poems. A prominent Azeri poet, Qarachorlu vividly captures the predicament of Iran's non-Persian ethnic groups in his widely disseminated famous poem titled "Yasaq" [Forbidden]:

Look at my misfortune!	Tale'ime sen bax!
My thoughts Forbidden	Düşüncelerim yasaq
My feelings Forbidden	duyğularim yasaq
Remembering of my past Forbidden	Geçmişimden söz açmağim yasaq
Dreaming about my future Forbidden	Geleceyimden danişmağim yasaq
Mentioning of my ancestors Forbidden	Ata-babamin adini çekmeyim yasaq
Talking about my mother Forbidden	Anamdan ad aparmağim yasaq
Do you know?	Bilirsen?
The time when I was born	Anadan doğulanda bele
Without my own knowledge	özüm bilmeye bilmeye
The language into which I was born	Dil açib danişdiğim dilde
was Forbidden?	Danişmağim yasaq imish
Yes, Forbidden!	Yasaq!

(Qarachorlu, 1965, cited in Akpinar, 1994, p. 130)

Although depicting the situation of Azerbaijani nationality, Qarachorlu's testimony can be applied to the situation of other minoritized groups with the same force and veracity. For in his poem, he talks of forbidden mother tongues, forbidden histories, and vilified ancestors. With his poem, he attests to the existence of racism, race-based repression, and language-based oppression in the country. His testimony is a brave act of resistance that seeks to expose a dehumanizing system and its antihumane character. Through this and many other poems, Qarachorlu articulates the condition of his people in Iran as that of an oppressed, dehumanized, and colonized people. In so doing, he delegitimizes the dominant group's representation of his community, his language, and his people. By his very act of articulation, Qarachorlu renders useless and shallow all the attempts of the dominant scholars and writers along with the governing officials who seek to deny the existence of race-based and language-based oppression in Iran. Qarachorlu's statement is as true for the Azeris as it is for the Kurds, Arabs, Turkmens, Baluchs, and others. An echo of Qarachorlu's poetic testimony can be seen in the following statement, in which Professor Amir Hassanpour testifies to this sort of racism practiced in Iran against the Kurdish minority and Kurdish language:

[A]s a primary school student, I began to feel the sting of linguistic repression in Iran. Kurdish dress and language were proscribed in schools. In my high-school years, I was able to acquire a few Kurdish books and phonograph records through the underground network. However, fearing house searches, arrest and jail, my parents destroyed them, no less than four times during the 1960s and 1970s. In Tehran University classes, symbolic violence against Kurdish and other non-Persian languages was commonplace. In rare occasions when Kurdish was mentioned, it was regularly identified as a "dialect" of Persian; calling it a language was considered "secessionism" or "treason." (Hassanpour, 1992a, p. xxvii)

Qarachorlu and Hassanpour come from two different Azeri and Kurdish communities. One speaks Azeri (a Turkic language); the other speaks Kurdish (an Indo-European language). Yet they both suffer under the same repressive and dehumanizing conditions. Similar to Qarachorlu's case, Hassanpour's testimony stands to repudiate the dominant view that considers the Kurds to be "real Aryans" and hence "the true owners of Iran." The fact that the dominant Persian group cannot tolerate the practice of the Kurdish language and identity shows that all the ongoing mumbo jumbo about the Kurds being of the Aryan race is just a ploy to silence the Kurdish community and prevent their solidarity with other marginalized groups.

"Esir Ellerin Shairi" [The Poet of Captive Peoples] is the title of a poem in which Habib Sahir (1903–1985), an Azerbaijani poet, identifies himself as the poet of enslaved peoples and captive communities.

Under this limitless sky	Binehayet bu göyün altında
There is not even a blue shelter for us	Bize bir qübbe-yi firuze de yox!
Thousands of lamps are alight in the sky	Yanar eflakde minlerce çıraq,
There is not even a candle burning for us	Bize bir şem', bir avize de yox!
Amongst all these stars in seven skies	Bu qeder ulduz arasında bize
There is not a single star for us	Yeddi göylerde bir ulduz yoxumuş!
Have they divided the birds in the world	Böldüler quşları alemde meger,
And the mourning owl was our portion?!	Bize de çatdı o ağlar bayquş?!
Everyday I am followed by sorrow	Qovalarken meni her gün mehnet
Every night despair knocks on my door	Qapımı döymededir her gece qem
All free peoples have their poets	Hamı azade elin şairi var
I am a poet of-ah! the enslaved peoples.	Men esir ellerin ah! şairiyem.

(Sahir, 1973, cited in Akpinar, 1994, p. 141)

In the last stanza, Sahir conveys a very powerful message: articulation of the condition of his people as an enslaved people for whom he is a poet and a spokesperson. By his very act of confessing the condition of his people as enslaved, the poet rebels against the very conditions that sustain states of subjugation and slavery. By announcing himself as the poet of a captive people, Sahir assigns himself the very task of a spokesperson for that people. He seizes the language, the narrative, and poetry to resist against the dominant racist order. A people can become enslaved when it loses the power to determine its destiny as a free people. A community becomes enslaved when it is not allowed to read and write in its own language, to educate its children in their mother tongue, and when it is denied the right to promote its history, culture, and way of life.

When a people is not allowed to talk of its contributions, to be proud of its ancestors, its ethnicity, and nationality, that people becomes an enslaved people. It is this kind of enslavement that Sahir talks of in the above poem. A poet's language is his/her window to the soul of his/her people. Perhaps there is not a crime more horrendous than cutting off a poet's mother tongue. And this is exactly what happens to the writers and poets whose mother tongue is forbidden and, in effect, is cut off. It is not surprising to see the high importance that Sahir allocates to the role and place of the mother tongue in one's life:

Mother is like a flower that will pale one day	Ana güldür, bir gün solar
The mother tongue is always sweet	Ana dili şirin olar
Our Turkic is a sweet language	Bizim Türkü şirin dildir
It is a well-tuned rich language	Xoş sedalı, zengin dildir
Language is like sun, spilling out light	Dil güneşdir, ışıq saçar
It opens the door to freedom	Azadlığa qapı açar
	(Sahir, 1961/2004, p. 7)

One's mother tongue is the gateway to freedom, a freedom that comes with the ability to self-express, to articulate one's condition in one's own voice and words. In order to break away from mental and spiritual bondage, it is the mother tongue that first and foremost ought to be freed from the bonds of oppression and enslavement. All mother tongues are sweet, and one's own, of course, sweetest. This statement is a protest on the part of Sahir against the dominant view that considers marginalized languages as incomprehensive gibberish. In continuing his poem, Sahir goes on to talk about the evils of an imposed language, of how it destroys a people's self-esteem and self-reliance, and of the shame that it brings upon the bodies and the communities that are compelled to abandon their languages. Sahir talks of the way in which an imposed language robs one of one's dignity, sense of self, and independent personhood.

Perhaps that is why Sahir prefers to remain a poet of enslaved peoples and banned languages in spite of the dangers and risks that such a stance entails. In a racist environment, being a poet of enslaved peoples means that the poet's voice will become silenced, that s/he will not be published and will not be given an opportunity to express her/himself. The poet will remain marginalized and isolated for the rest of his/her life. In the end, the poet will die an unknown figure—impoverished and destitute. And this is how Sahir lived and died: isolated, marginalized, and unknown. It was a price that he was willing to pay for being a poet of enslaved peoples. But even in his silence, even in his isolation and infamy, he challenged the oppressive conditions that had denied him his freedom.

On August 23, 2004, the online newspaper *Shams Tabriz* published some of Sahir's unpublished poems. In these poems, Sahir is even more transparent about the ongoing racism, chauvinism, and ethnic oppression in Iran:

The old bloody enemy of lands of fire	Odlar diyarinin ezeli qanli duşmani
Is treacherously Persianizing the Azeri people	farslaşdirir siyaset ile Azer ellerin
It doesn't know that our culture flows like flood	O anlamaz ki kültürümüz sel kimi axar

and the powerful floods can never be stopped	hergiz önü alinmaz olur güclü sellerin
A dignified person cannot be enslaved	Insan qul olmayib düşuner öz vüqarini
Nor will a free person lose his/her dignity	Qul olmayan itirmez olur qeder-o qimetin
Despair not, this dawn will bear a red sun	ğem etme bu seher doğacaq qirmizi güneş
my mother tongue's breeze will blow cool	Ana dilimin yeli esecek serin-serin

(Sahir, 1961/2004, pp. 1–8)

Notwithstanding the unbearable repression of non-Persian cultures and languages, the minoritized groups continue to resist the policy of decculturation and linguicide. Anytime that history and society offer them a chance, they vigorously defend their inalienable linguistic and cultural rights. For instance, due to somewhat relaxed conditions in the period 1945–1946, numerous journals and newspapers were published in ethnic languages particularly in Azerbaijan and Kurdistan. In the very first issue of the daily paper *Azerbaycan*, an editorial titled *Ruznamemiz in Dili* [The Language of Our Newspaper] defended the Azeri language against the imposed Persian language. "It is high time," wrote the editor, Ja'far Pishevari, "that Persian intellectuals realized there was such a language called Azeri" (*Azerbaycan*, September 25, 1945):

> We have absorbed our mother tongue with our mother's milk and have taken it with the exhilarating air of our land. Those who are insulting it and endeavor to show it as an imposed and artificial language are our true enemies. Many perfidious foreign elements have tried for centuries to prevent the flourishing of this beautiful language. In spite of this, our language has survived in a strong and persistent manner. Azeri is not a baseless [deymi] language. It has a strong, solid base, the people. It boasts not only of tales, proverbs, and poems which depend on the people at large for authorship, but also of the works of poets and writers of distinction in the course of its history. (Pishevari, September 5, 1945; see also Berengian, 1988, p. 146)

Ja'far Pishevari was a minoritized writer and leader who passionately defended his mother tongue in defiance of those who constantly insulted it, undermined it, and sought to deny its legitimacy and authenticity. It is a fact of living under colonial conditions that you always have to defend the legitimacy and authenticity of your culture, your language, your history, and your identity. For the first thing that colonialism does is to devalue your history, delegitimize your culture, vilify your language, and demonize your ancestors. Perhaps this is why the minoritized groups find it so necessary to place greater emphasis on their sense of indigeneity, on their indigenous knowledge, cultures, languages, and values. More than half a century later after Ja'far Pishevari's above statement, non-Persian nationalities are still repeating the same arguments about their languages, cultures, and histories. They are still trying to prove that their languages exist and that their languages are not dialects, foreign, incomprehensible, disgusting, worthless, secessionist, and criminal.

Professor Reza Baraheni's personal experience in the burial ground of the city of Qom reveals that the use of non-Farsi languages has been prohibited even on graves and tombstones belonging to the members of marginalized communities. His powerful narration of the experience is a permanent testimonial against the racist Pahlavi regime and its unofficial apologizers:

> We buried father in the religious city of Qom, on the northern shoulder of the desert that covers almost one-fourth of the entire country. . . . As we left the graveyard, my brother said that maybe we should order a tombstone for father. I walked up to the man who was cutting the stones and engraving names, prayers and versus on them. . . . He handed me a piece of paper: "Write and tell me what I should put on it."
>
> There was a poem that father loved to recite when he was in Tehran and not yet incapacitated by cancer. . . .
>
>> When I came here sometime ago
>> The pomegranate trees were blooming
>> My life rotted in exile
>
> I handed the poem to the man. He looked at it, bedazzled by the strength of the poem in his own mother tongue. When he raised his head, there was a look of nostalgia in his eyes. He handed the poem back to me:
>
>> "I cannot put this on the stone!"
>> "Why? What's wrong?" I asked.
>> "Government orders," he said. "We've been ordered not to use Turkish on the graves."
>
> Thus there is only a small number on the grave. Father is now a number on the sandy shoulders of the desert. His identity is buried deep down in the bowels of the earth. Cancer was in the roots of his tongue when he was born. Cancer has been in the roots of all the subject Iranian nationalities at birth. By the decree of the Shah's father, and the execution of the same decree by the son, we were christened to become Aryans. (Baraheni, 1977, pp. 88–89)

The forced Aryanization of various ethnic groups in the country has come to find its expression in the humiliation and marginalization of Iran's non-Persian peoples. Non-Indo-European-speaking nationalities and ethnic groups in Iran have been constantly attacked in the Persian literature for being subhuman savages, donkeys, barefooted lizard eaters (this latter title was given to Arabs paralleling a poem in Ferdowsi's *Shahnameh* with the same theme) and so forth. The glorification of the Aryan race at the expense of all other peoples has been manifested through unofficial literature produced by Persian poets, journalists, and writers. Echoing the governing apparatuses, the majority of Persian intellectuals along with the Persianized intelligentsia have advocated the notion that the Persian Aryan race is the superior race in Iran and has therefore the exclusive right to rule over all other nationalities and ethnic groups. Aryanism and Persian racism have continued to be the dominant ideology in Iran despite the revolution of 1978 and the resultant overthrow of the rule of the Pahlavi dynasty in the country.

In January 1999, more than 65 Azeri parliamentarians, writers, and poets wrote an open letter to President Khatami of Iran, demanding that, among other things, the use of Azeri language in media as well as its teaching in schools and universities be permitted. In the letter, they passionately voiced their demands and concerns regarding their cultural, ethnic, and linguistic rights:

> [A]ll segments of our people's social life has been cut off from their mother tongue. Our radios, our televisions, our press, our wedding cards and obituaries, even our tombstones are talking in a language other than our mother tongue. . . . [I]t is a bitter fact that Iran is the only country in the world where the language of millions of people are absolutely discarded. (*Qurtulush*, 1999, p. 56)

Ever since this important collective letter, numerous similar letters continue to be written to various figures and organs of the Islamic Republic, bearing signatures of hundreds and thousands of individuals. In spite of these requests and demands, there has not been a single positive step taken on the part of government to address these legitimate concerns that are perfectly in line with the Islamic Republic's constitution. The demands made by the marginalized communities illustrate the high importance that non-Persian groups attach to the use of their language in every walk of life.

DECOLONIZING THE EDUCATION SYSTEM

With Reza Khan's coming to power in 1925, the education system in Iran was turned into a fully fledged engine of Persianization. Reza Khan's son, Mohammad Reza, significantly increased the power and speed of this engine throughout the country. And contrary to the initial expectations of minoritized communities, not only did the engine of assimilation not stop with the fall of Pahlavi regime, but it got even stronger and acquired new dimensions within the Islamic Republic. Through this system of assimilation, Farsi has been elevated to the status of the only legitimate language of instruction, of literature, science, technology, business, correspondence, governance—in a word, literacy. The education system promotes the history of the Persian ethnic group as the only legitimate history of all peoples living in Iran. Consequently, those graduating from this schooling system come to believe that the Persians are the true owners of Iran with exclusive right to use the country's resources and promote the Persian culture, history, music, arts, language, and literature. In effect, the education system fosters an environment of apartheid where one ethnic group is singled out to enjoy all the economic and educational resources in the country whereas the others are brushed aside as deviants, foreigners, and aliens.

In the face of this politics of apartheid in the schooling system, the marginalized communities have started to offer their own versions of how the education system ought to be governed in a multicultural, multiethnic, and multilingual society such as Iran. We will now explore some of the innovative methods through which the marginalized bodies resist the politics of apartheid in education while offering solutions to reform it in such a way that it would be inclusive of all ethnicities, languages, religions, regions, and cultures in the country.

Samad Behrangi and His Pedagogy of Resistance

Samad Behrangi (1939–1968) was an Azerbaijani schoolteacher who left behind a rich legacy of exemplary teaching, curricular innovations, and a corpus of critical/literary work that emerged from years of pedagogical activities in Iranian society. Born in 1939 in the impoverished Cherendab district of Tabriz, from the very beginning Behrangi came to know the horrible face of poverty and deprivation. "I was not born like a mushroom, with no father and no mother," he wrote later on. "But I grew up like a mushroom, with no one feeding me, no one taking care of me. . . . I grew up nonetheless and became a teacher in Azerbaijani villages" (A. Behrangi, 1999, p. 1). This is how his brother Asad Behrangi remembers Samad's early childhood:

> [T]he passerby vendors in the morning would see a little boy running fast, with his shoes under his arms. They would ask each other: who is this kid? Why is he always running? Why does he take his shoes in his hands? The passerby vendors remained surprised until they found out that this kid was son of a laborer named Ezzat who had recently rented a room in the neighborhood. He ran because his school was far away and he was afraid that he might not reach it on time and he took his shoes under his arm because they were tattered and he could not run with them and this boy's name was "Samad." (A. Behrangi, 1999, p. 319)

The boy named Samad finished high school and entered Teachers' Training College in his hometown of Tabriz. At the age of 18 he became a teacher and set out to educate the impoverished Azeri children in rural areas. For the following 11 years, he traveled from village to village, town to town, and region to region. This constant travel and experience of life in various localities nourished his creative imagination and became a rich source for his literary creations, which were considerable by any account. During this period of intense teaching and writing, Behrangi also continued with his formal education and managed to earn a BA in English from Tabriz University.

His firsthand experience with poverty transformed Behrangi into a teacher deeply familiar with class inequality and the negative impact of poverty on the students' personal development, educational performance, aspirations, achievements, and overall life chances. He entered the Iranian education system with a clear understanding of class stratification, class consciousness, and the economics of schooling, to which was later added an understanding of gender, culture, ethnicity, and particularly language-based oppression. His profound awareness of social, economic, cultural, and linguistic differences in the country made Behrangi an exemplary pedagogue not only by Iranian standards but also from an international viewpoint. He was the first educator in Iran who realized the importance that class, language, ethnicity, and place of birth played in the equitable delivery of education and throughout the learning processes of students.

Behrangi realized the power of knowledge in freeing the individual from both mental and societal bondages. Aside from being a teacher and writer, he functioned as a mobile librarian in rural Azerbaijan. One cannot but wonder at imagining his agile figure in his mid-twenties, wrapped up in a wornout black coat, wearing a pair of dusty circular glasses, with half a sack of books over his shoulders wandering around from village to village. His passion for the written word was matched only by his love for knowledge, both of which he pursued keenly. Out of a meager salary that he received from the Ministry of Education, he bought books and distributed them amongst needy students from rural areas. He also borrowed books from libraries in the city and lent them to students for whom a library was inaccessible.

Behrangi was a determined young man who had set himself the challenging task of educating the poverty-stricken Azerbaijani village children. His daily encounter with Azerbaijani village life placed him at the center of an exposure to Azeri culture and language hitherto unknown to him. It was from such a rich exposure that he derived the primary material as well as the insight and vision for his future literary work. Just like his pedagogical endeavors, his literary activities for the large part focused on educating the children and youth in Iran. As he wrote in the preface to one of his short stories "Kechal-e kaftarbaaz" [The Bald Pigeon Keeper]:

> Children, the future is in your hands and its good and ill belong to you. Whether you want to or not, you are growing up as time passes. You come after your fathers and elders and will take their places and inherit everything. You will be master of society. Poverty, oppression, power, justice, joy and sorrow, loneliness, punishment, work and idleness, prison and freedom, sickness and hunger and need, and a hundred strengths and weaknesses of society will belong to you. . . . Poverty, oppression, lies, stealing, and war are illnesses seen only in an unhealthy society. (S. Behrangi, 1969c, p. 143)

Only a person familiar with class inequality and class-based oppression in society could make such a powerful connection among poverty, hunger, injustice, and other societal pathologies. Behrangi saw problems such as stealing, lying, dishonesty, illness, and poverty as symptoms of an unhealthy society. In his view, it was not the individual who should be responsible for such pathologies; it was the social system that created and perpetuated the environment in which such illnesses, unhealthy symptoms, and pathologies flourished. He wanted children to be aware of this and take active roles in transforming their society. He turned his attention to children because he strongly believed in the power of education to transform the individuals and, through them, societies. He did not find it as easy to educate adults because in order for the adults to learn pedagogies of resistance first they had to be able to unlearn the dominant knowledge that they had acquired from the viewpoint of the dominant. This was an extremely difficult task for which Behrangi had no time. By the same token, children in rural areas were less exposed to the ways and ideologies of the dominant group. Hence, they constituted for Behrangi the most suitable category of individuals for whom a pedagogy of resistance, transformation, and hope could be developed.

Elsewhere, Behrangi clearly spelled out the aims, goals, and future prospects of "children's literature" in a country such as Iran. Here too his strong pedagogical aims in educating the children and youth of the country were evident:

> That time is past when we limited children's literature to passive propaganda and indoctrination. . . . Why should we suffocate the child in a useless cocoon of hope and happiness and joy while his elder brother is craving for one free breath, one breath of fresh air? The child should be made disappointed with baseless and unrealistic expectations and in their stead be given another type of hope based on knowledge of the realities of life and society. . . . Should we not tell our children that there are children in your country who have not seen the color of meat or even cheese on monthly and yearly basis? . . . Should we not tell our children that more than half of the world's population is hungry; and why they are kept hungry; and in what ways we can fight to alleviate their hunger? (S. Behrangi, 1969a, p. 120)

Behrangi sought to educate the students, kids, and youth through his pedagogical endeavors. At the same time, he tirelessly worked on his corpus of fiction, as well as on sociocultural and critical essays. By way of these essays and narratives, he boldly criticized the sources and causes of various social, class, ethnic, and linguistic inequalities in Iran. Excerpts of his refreshing interrogation of the Iranian educational system appeared in the collection titled *Kand-o-kav dar Mesa'el-e Tarbiyeti-ye Iran* [Investigations into the Educational System of Iran] (1965). By way of this work, Behrangi brought into the open the assimilationist function of the Iranian education system. He clearly illustrated the uselessness of the ruling elite's exhibitionist attempts to educate the impoverished Azerbaijani children through description of postcards, mailboxes, color televisions, fancy dining tables, and luxurious automobiles. He firmly maintained that this sort of Westernized education was not only alien to life experiences of a majority of students in Iran; they were also most inappropriate in a society where most of the pupils went to bed on hungry stomachs, and where their own mother tongue was banned, and their own culture was crucified.

> The problem is the kid from rural areas has not seen or heard about such things as cinema, theatre, newspaper, magazine, traffic officer, postal card, mailbox, autobus and taxi, eating food with spoon and fork and knife, sausage, baseball, picnic. . . . When s/he comes across them in textbooks

s/he does not understand anything and keeps watching the teacher perplexedly. (S. Behrangi, 1969a, p. 9)

The degree to which Behrangi regarded class issues as central to an equitable education system is again evident from the above quote. At the time the opulent ruling class in society, over which resided the Pahlavi family, attempted to present a healthy, happy, and prosperous image of life in Iran. Through his pedagogical and literary activities, Behrangi rebelled against such falsification and tried to expose it to the general public and particularly to children. In his view, children ought to be given a realistic picture about the ongoing struggles, hardships, and inequalities in society. Through his narratives and short stories, Behrangi worked tirelessly to instill such a realistic image in the minds of the Iranian children and youth. Thus, class distinctions and class-based oppression occupied a central place in his vision for educational and social reform in Iran.

The emphasis on class inequality did not mean that Behrangi was unaware of other sites and categories of difference such as language, gender, ethnicity, culture, place of birth, and so on. He intensely interrogated all aspects of Iran's education system from the methods employed in Teachers Training Colleges to textbooks, methods of teaching, language of instruction, and the school environment. At the time it was fashionable for educational authorities to translate works of Western and particularly the American pedagogues and present them for use in an Iranian context. Behrangi was the first educator who boldly refuted and ridiculed this mimicry, arguing that the educational texts produced in America were written for a fundamentally different school environment and were generally useless in an Iranian context. He reminded the educational authorities about the crucial issue of providing the most basic needs of students such as "pen and paper," as opposed to talking about fancy blackboards and sufficient levels of oxygen in the classroom, which was absolutely ridiculous in an Iranian setting:

All you have to do is provide the students from the rural areas with sufficient paper and pencil and a pair of shoes and socks for the cold and snow of winter. Do not worry about the summer, in summer they can get around barefooted. They are used to it. Just be kind and don't grant them "the honor of roasting sandwiches" and "preparation of Italian macaroni which is eaten by spoon and fork in the right manner." You may keep these to yourselves! (S. Behrangi, 1969a, pp. 17–18)

The privileged ruling class and educational authorities were absolutely ignorant about the living condition of the majority of people who lived in rural areas, shanty towns, and impoverished southern segments of major cities. Nor did they have any sensible awareness of issues of difference and diversity among the student populations in terms of language, culture, place of birth, and so on. Despite this, they were the ones in charge of designing the text-books and a centralized "national curriculum" for the entire student popula-tion throughout the country. Obviously, the curriculum and textbooks designed under their supervision had no relevance to the living conditions, languages, and cultures of students from various regions of the country. Not surprisingly, Behrangi criticized the centralized designing of textbooks and curricula for being insensitive to the needs of non-Farsi-speaking students, students in rural areas, and those living in different regions of the country. In his view, the curriculum and textbooks had to be designed by local scholars familiar with the conditions of the environment in which they lived.

> Unless we have seen an environment closely, have lived in it, have mingled with its people, have heard their voices and demands, it is useless for us to feel sympathy for that environment and its people, let alone writing stories for them. . . . I also address those who live in the comfort of the capital city, eat to their heart's content, laze in comfortable sofas and chairs, use coolers in summer, use electronic heater . . . in winter, have maids and servants and the rest at their service, have excellent salaries and permanent jobs, and with the help of a few American texts on psychology and education, turn around and write book[s] for the kid of Chahbahar and design curriculum for the child of Gavgan, ordering that schools be opened from the beginning of Mehr and teachers be ready from the beginning of the month of Shahrivar and the school year be finished at the end of month of Khordad. They don't know that the Gavganis have not yet picked their grapes till the end of Mehr and can't be present in the class and when it is Khordad, they are still needed in garden and in farm. And in the month of Shahrivar they are so busy that they often forget the day of their examination. (S. Behrangi, 1969a, pp. 51–52)

The related topics of language in education and linguistic inequality in the country were two thorny issues that preoccupied Behrangi throughout his teaching and writing career. Like any normal human being, Behrangi loved his mother tongue, the Azeri-Turkic. With the help of his friend and comrade Behrooz Dehqani, he collected Azerbaijani folklore, folksongs, folktales, mythologies, and sayings. He published them in the original language whenever he could. Whenever the shah's censor organ refused their publication in Azeri language, he translated them to Farsi and published them in "the national tongue of the nation-state." Whenever there was a book published about Azerbaijan, the Azeri language, Azerbaijani poetry, history, culture, and society, Behrangi was the first to review that work, uncompromisingly pointing out its shortcomings-and strengths. In his spare time, he translated samples of Nima Yushij and Ahmad Shamlu's poetry from Farsi into Azeri. He never kept a secret his love of Azeri language. As the famous playwright Gholam-Hoseyn Saidi has pointed out, Behrangi "loved his mother tongue more than one could imagine and was extremely skillful in reading and writing it" (1976, p. xxiv).

> He would start a class in a stable, school, village square or graveyard. And he took part in village life. Harvest, mourning ceremonies, Koran readings, mosques, weddings, he went everywhere. . . . He knew hunger, he knew poverty, he knew disease and oppression. . . . He firmly believed in the power of every language. . . . He was only surprised that he didn't have the right to publish in his mother tongue. (Saidi, 1976, pp. xxiii–xxiv)

In all the above-mentioned activities the medium of expression was not the imposed Farsi but the Azeri language. Behrangi wholeheartedly participated in these activities and learned his mother tongue, his culture, and his heritage through them. The language transmitted the culture, the tradition, ways of life, and worldviews. The mother tongue was the gateway to the learning and psychological/cognitive development. Behrangi was aware of this. In the classroom, he would watch the pain and agony of Azeri students as they labored to pronounce symbols and elements of an alien language. To them, learning had been reduced to understanding of the Persian language; literacy was made to be synonymous with the knowing of Farsi. And this language, this foreign and alien language they had to learn by a "parrot method." That is to say, the pupils were to imitate the pronunciation of their teacher. They were asked to read aloud after the teacher and to memorize the text regardless of whether they understood its meaning. Many Azerbaijani teachers tried to convey the meaning of Persian words by showing the pictures or the objects that these words represented. This method was helpful in regard to certain available solid objects and elements such as water, bread, apple, and shoe. However, it was completely useless when it came to explaining the abstract concepts. As a result, the joy of learning had all but vanished from Azerbaijani schools and the idea of education itself had become a horrible nightmare for many students.

Rebellious spirit that he was, Behrangi could not tolerate such an unbearable injustice. To him, the banning of students' mother tongue just went against the grain of everything that learning and education stood for. He was a teacher in an education system that virtually worked as the engine of assimilation. It seemed, as a teacher in an Azerbaijani school, he had actually become an operator in the assimilationist educational machinery of the Pahlavi regime. The realization of this bitter fact appalled and disgusted him. There in Azerbaijan, the language of people was different than the language of "the Nation." There, the real language of the people was banned and the artificial language of "the Nation" was an alien language. Having found himself extremely helpless in fighting the oppressive regime, and being unable to liberate the mother tongue, Behrangi endeavored to reform the Iranian education system.

How can you teach a dominant language to a minoritized student whose own mother tongue is banned? More significantly, how can you tell a child that s/he is forbidden to talk in his/her own mother tongue and s/he must learn somebody else's language? How you tell a kid that the language of your "nation" wants to supplant the language of your "people"? That it is the aim of the language of "your nation" to replace your mother tongue and to kill it in the name of literacy, knowledge, and education? The educational authorities and the ruling elite realized the hard way that the killing of a people's language was not so easy, just as it was not so easy to impose a new language on millions of students overnight. Behrangi knew that this imposition was impossible:

> The Azerbaijani kid, after years of study and regardless of all those small and big instructions demanding s/he must speak Farsi, is still unable to speak two words

of Farsi and even properly say "hello and how are you" in Persian. . . . This inability to speak Farsi has become a major psychological/spiritual injury for the kids, especially when they encounter a Farsi-speaking kid or become classmates with him/her. Don't you think this injury will maintain its effect for years to come? (S. Behrangi, 1969a, pp. 57–58)

Behrangi realized that there were important linguistic differences between Azeri and Farsi languages. In essence, they were two completely different languages. However, there were certain common elements, traits, and terminologies that both languages shared. If one were to teach Farsi to an Azerbaijani kid in such a way that the emphasis was placed on common elements shared by the two languages, one might have eliminated some of the difficulties faced by the Azeri pupils. It was to this end that he designed his own Alphabet Book, and with the help and direction of his friend Al-e Ahmad he offered it to the educational authorities.

Through this work, Behrangi outlined the necessity of teaching the dominant Farsi language to non-Persian children by way of different methods than the ones used for teaching Farsi-speaking children. Time and again he had emphasized the necessity and importance of designing textbooks based on local conditions, indigenous languages, cultures, ways of life, and worldviews of the people to whom these texts were being designed. He had clearly laid out the methodological differences to be considered when teaching Farsi to Azeri students and made a detailed proposal in this regard to be followed by educationalists and education systems throughout the country (see also Hanson, 1983).

The prominent Iranian writer Jalal Al-e Ahmad had convinced the educational authorities in Tehran that Behrangi's Alphabet Book was an innovative work of exceptional value that would immensely alleviate the insurmountable difficulty of teaching Farsi to non-Persian learners, particularly to the Turkic-speaking population who constituted the numerical majority in the country. An agreement had been reached for the book to be published under the auspices of an organization named the National Committee of International Fight against Illiteracy ("Komite-ye Melli-ye Peykar-e Jahani ba Bisavadi"). So Behrangi was invited to the capital city and given an office on the committee property to complete the work. The high-ranking members of the committee had seized the opportunity to publicize Behrangi's book as a major undertaking on their own behalf and had sent word to the authorities above them that the committee was in the process of producing a major text as a part of its mission to eliminate illiteracy in the country.

When the work was finally completed, in line with the custom the authorities wanted to place pictures of the shah, his wife, and their son in the first three pages of the text respectively. During the Pahlavi regime, having pictures of the shah, the first lady, and the crown prince was a common feature of all textbooks in the country. Behrangi, however, could not swallow the idea of having pictures of a hated dictator and his family within his book.

The whole idea horrified Behrangi and almost drove him to the shores of insanity. Without uttering a single word to the authorities in Tehran, he tucked the book under his arm and left the capital city. Here is how the famous playwright, Golam-Hossein Saidi sums up the whole event:

> Al-e Ahmad pulled some strings and Samad came to Tehran for a few months, in order to publish his book, with the hope that this work would be an official textbook in all villages and towns of Azerbaijan. However, before long, experts of shahanshahi culture put their finger in a sensitive place: What about the name of "Shahanshah" and "Shahbanoo" and "Valiahd" and "the imperial dynastic family" that was necessary to be at the beginning of the book? . . . In the noon of the same day that this warning was made, Samad was like a wounded lion in Nil Publishings, pacing to and fro and turning around himself and cursing the regime. . . . The next day he tucked his book under his arm and hopped on the bus and returned to the same beloved remote villages of his. (A. Behrangi, 1999, p. 292)

Samad's brother Asad says that when Samad returned to Tabriz, he encouraged Samad to get on with the book project, saying that the money from the project would help the Behrangi family with their dire economic situation, that they could fix the house that was about to cave in, pay their debts, and so on. Upon hearing this, Samad turns pale and gets very angry, bellowing,

> It has nothing to do with these things. I could not put my name on a book that fed the same nonsense to the people like the other books do. I have never taught the word "shah" in my life and have always skipped the pages containing the first lady and the crown prince. How could I allocate the first page of my book to their pictures? What do you want me to do, lose the truth and my honor over this book? And what will I say to my students and to the kids? (A. Behrangi, 1999, p. 326)

Discrediting and dismissing the ruling family in such a bold manner was a major risk for which Behrangi was going to pay dearly sooner or later. Turned out it was sooner. He could easily have said yes to the ruling dictatorship and enjoyed all the privileges that such a "yes" entailed. But he chose to be on the side of truth, honesty, decency, and dignity. He spoke truth to power and was ready to suffer the consequences. As of that moment of refusal, the authorities did not leave him alone. They even offered to publish the book under multiple authorship, without mentioning Behrangi's name. But Behrangi would not budge.

Behrangi's bold defiance of the authorities begs the question: Was it all about the pictures, or was there more to the story? In an interview with the Azeri Radio, Odlar Yurdu, on September 7, 2002, the Azerbaijani scholar M.A. Farzaneh revealed how Behrangi had come to see him prior to the publication of his *Alifba* book. After reading the manuscript, Farzaneh had convinced Behrangi that this work would considerably accelerate the assimilation of Azeri students in Iran. "What about the phonetics and sound system in our language? I asked him. Don't you think your work will force our kids to speak their mother tongue in a different accent? Have you thought of the responsibility for maintaining our own language?" (Farzaneh, September 7, 2002). According to Asad Behrangi, in one of his encounters with the authorities a retired army colonel threatened Behrangi, humorously saying, "Do not play Turk-khar [Turk-donkey] with us and turn over the book. We will not let you off the hook so easily" (A. Behrangi, 1999, p. 239). It was shortly after this event that they found Behrangi's dead body in the Araz River.

In his most famous book *The Little Black Fish* Behrangi told the story of a little fish who in search of knowledge and freedom set out to find the end of the stream. These constituted the themes of *The Little Black Fish*: the anxiety of search, the thirst to know, to find out, the insatiable curiosity, and the spirit to go ahead, to break the norms and regulations, to break the taboos and commonsense, to rebel against the conservatism of parents and elders, to swim against the flow, to defy the accepted rules of your environment, to run, to struggle, fight and be defiant of that which limits your freedom, to live and die in the open seas, in the ocean. The story of the black fish, no doubt, bore a striking resemblance to the story of the life and death of the writer himself, so much so that by way of a comparison, one almost becomes convinced that in *The Little Black Fish*, Behrangi was writing his own story. Just like the black fish, throughout his short life, Behrangi too fought deceitful and despotic enemies. The little black fish struggled against the tyranny of old values, against the despotism of the pelican, swordfish, and heron. Behrangi fought against injustice and rebelled against the unbearable social, class, and ethnic inequality in Iran. He called into question the legitimacy of the ruling family, ruling class, ruling race, and ruling language. He challenged the politics of monolingualism and monoculturalism in a multicultural, multiethnic, and multilingual society.

On September 8, 1968, Behrangi was drowned in the Araz River of Azerbaijan. He was only 29 years old. The circumstances of his death were no doubt mysterious and suspicious. Regardless of whether he was truly murdered by the Pahlavi regime or not, all fingers of blame pointed toward SAVAK, the shah's torture and censor organization, as the real orchestrator of his death. "Araz Araz Ay Araz" is the title of an Azeri folksong dedicated to Samad Behrangi. It is through memorabilia like these that his heroic life and death are immortalized in the collective consciousness of his people:

Araz Araz ay Araz	Araz Araz ay Araz
Sultan Araz, Khan Araz	Sultan Araz, Xan Araz
I wish you'd burn up	Görum seni yanasan
Understand my pain, Araz	Bir derdimi qan Araz
Upon the Araz, upon the ice	Araz üste buz üste
Upon the embers burn kebabs	Kabab yanar köz üste
Let them come and kill me	Qoy meni öldürsunler
Because of what I say	Danişdigim söz üste
They divided the Araz	Arazi ayirdilar
And filled it with sand	Qumulan doyurdular

I would never separate from you	Men senden ayrilmazdim
They forced us into separation	Zulmile ayirdilar
Samad's coming, smiling	Semed gelir güle güle
Look at the roses on his chest	Bax döşunde qizil güle
Holding four books in each hand	Her elinde dörd kitab
He translated into our language	Dönderib bizim dile
Who did cross over you, Araz?	Araz senden kim gechdi?
Who drowned and who crossed over?	Kim ğerq oldu kim gechdi?
Let the world come and prove to me	Felek gel sabit eyle
Which of my days was joyous?	Hansi günüm xoş gechdi?

The Continuous Struggle for an Inclusive Education

Samad Behrangi died in 1968; however, the idea of creating an inclusive education in Iran was not buried with him. The struggle to reform the Iranian education system and to make it inclusive of all experiences, languages, and cultures still continues. Non-Persian communities in Iran are still trying to convey the message to the dominant group that literacy is not synonymous with Persianization, that to be educated does not mean to understand and speak the Persian language, that to receive an education should not be equated with the learning of Farsi. Zohreh Vafayi, an Azerbaijani writer and activist, has put this message succinctly to the members of the dominant group and the ruling Islamic government:

> The designers of the educational system, if they really have the intention of educating, certainly must realize this fact that knowledge-acquisition is not equal to Farsi-learning. The world is full of scholars and scientists who do not know even a single Persian word! The publication of statistics regarding illiteracy in our region, which always occupies the first place amongst provinces, not only is not a sign of uneducated individuals in this region, but is an indicative of their strong belief in a soil in which they are born and a culture from which they have obtained the lessons of life. (Vefayi, 2003, p. 1)

In August 2004, a collective letter signed by over 100 Turkic-speaking students of the city of Maragheh was sent to the office of Ayatollah Ali Khamenei, Iran's supreme spiritual leader. By way of this letter, the students complained that despite the passing of 25 years since the Islamic Revolution, they still are not allowed to read and write in their mother tongue. They said that the future looked even bleaker as far as their right to education in their language was concerned, and asked for an explanation for such an unbearable discrimination:

> The Esteemed Order of Jurisprudence and Leadership,
>   As a group of Azerbaijani-Turkic students from the city of Maragheh, we would like to respectfully bring to your attention that we have sincere belief in and practical obligation to the Islamic Republic and the rule of Jurisprudence.

Given that the current year has been identified on your part as the year of answerability of the authorities [to the public], and the past year was identified as the year of struggle against poverty, corruption, and discrimination, we demand answers from you and other authorities regarding the existing linguistic discrimination in Iran. . . . We would like to know why articles 21 and 22 and 26 of the Universal Human Rights Manifesto [to which Iran is a signatory] and articles 15 and 19 of the Constitution of the Islamic Republic, which is a result of our martyrs' blood and the national covenant in relation to the right to education in the mother tongue . . . are not implemented? (Gruhi az danesh-amuzan-e Marageh, August 2004)

This letter was followed by similar letters from all over the country, on the occasion of the beginning of a new school year in Mehr (September). Collective letters were written and signed by hundreds of students from such non-Farsi-speaking areas as Tabriz, Ormiyeh, Zanjan, Hamadan, and even the capital city Tehran. In each and every one of these letters, the students demanded answers as to why Articles 15 and 19 of the constitution of the country, which allow for the use of non-Farsi languages in various regions, were not implemented by the educational and governing authorities. They regarded the enforcement of an unofficial ban on their mother tongue as discriminatory and asked for the recognition of their right to education in their own languages. "From the standpoint of the signatories of this announcement," read a letter sent to the minister of education by a group of Azerbaijani students in District Three Tehran Schools, "any continuous intention or mistake in the implementation of the Constitution, particularly the Article regarding the study of ethnic languages . . . implies the abandonment of their legal duties" on the part of the authorities. "Without a doubt," continued the letter, "all those committing these kinds of mistakes, or God forbid intentional acts, must be held responsible before God, the honourable nation of Iran, and the judicial branch of the government" (Gruhi az danesh-amuzan-e Azerbaijani, August 26, 2004).

Thus, a flame that Behrangi had kindled in the 1960s is kept alive well into the twenty-first century. His vision on equitable educational delivery, educational reform, decentralization of curriculum, consideration of regional conditions and particularities, centrality of local indigenous languages, the detrimental role of poverty on school performance, closer attention to economics of schooling, and elimination of unbearable regional and class differences are as fresh today as they were in the 1960s. The dominant group seeks to brush aside his urgently relevant pedagogical views by limiting his role to a teller of children stories. Irrespective of their useless attempts, Behrangi is remembered today more than ever as an educator par excellence, a visionary pedagogue, and an exceptional teacher. His lasting pedagogical legacy is a testimonial on the part of Iran's marginalized communities to continuously decolonize Iran's racist education system, to challenge the politics of "killing of mother tongues," to obtain an inclusive schooling system where everyone feels comfortable to be a part of learning process, where no language, no culture, and no ethnicity is excluded from the school environment.

DECOLONIZING INDIGENOUS HISTORIES

While the dominant order in Iran has sought to colonize the identities, languages, cultures, and histories of marginalized non-Persian communities, these communities have resisted in various ways. Amongst different sites that the dominant group has used to maintain the status quo, along with language, literature, and education system, history and historiography have emerged as privileged spaces from where acts of dominance and racism are legitimated. Similarly, the marginalized have used these same sites to challenge various acts of domination and colonization carried out by the dominant. The decolonizing of Iran's Fars-centered Orientalist/Aryanist historiography has been one of the most effective acts of resistance against the dominant order. This act of decolonization has taken place in many forms, particularly after the fall of the Pahlavi regime.

In recent years, the emergence of what may be called local historiography has fundamentally challenged the official/national historiography of diverse regions and communities in the country. This particular historiography has been developed from within various marginalized communities such as the Azerbaijanis, Arabs, Kurds, Baluchs, and Turkmens. Using indigenous/local knowledge as its points of reference, this historiography questions the official history for ignoring local realities and indigenous conditionalities. Produced mainly in marginalized nonofficial languages, this historiography seeks its audience first and foremost from the local communities, as opposed to seeking them amongst the conventional Farsi-reading audiences. For instance, a well-respected Azeri scholar Mohammed Taqi Zehtabi has published a two-volume history book that traces the indigenous history of Iranian Turks well over 6, 000 years back, challenging thus the legitimacy of the dominant group's denial of indigenous history for the Turks in Iran (Zehtabi, 1999). Himself an outstanding professor of Persian language and literature, Zehtabi has produced his work in Azeri-Turkic, as opposed to being in the dominant Farsi, emphasizing thus the importance of communicating with one's own community in the process of decolonization and emancipation. By writing in a marginalized language, he has also shown the significance of revitalization, recovery, and reclamation of indigenous languages in subverting colonialist and racist agendas.

In a similar way, the Iranian Arab scholar Yousof Azizi-Banitorof has used a combination of indigenous Arab-Khuzistani knowledge, narratives, stories, and histories to challenge and subvert the dominant racist discourse that seeks to deny a historical rootedness and legitimacy to the oppressed Arab community in Iran (Azizi-Banitorof, 1979, 1993, 1996, 2003). In an interview with the newspaper *E'temad* (November 28, 2002), Azizi-Banitorof explains the nature of his scholarship:

> I have been seeing from the past that there was very little work done regarding ethnic groups in Iran, and particularly the Arab people of Khuzistan. Consequently, from those years I was interested in collecting the folklore and oral literature of the Arab peoples of Khuzistan. During those years that I was

in Khuzistan, time and again I went to villages and shared the life stories of the villagers. I listened to them and talked with them and whatever they had in their memory, I recorded and wrote down. In fact, my work has two central sources: one is the ordinary people, scholars, intellectuals, and elders of the Arabs; and the other is books and writings which exist in Arabic and English about this people. (Azizi-Banitorof, November 28, 2002)

Added to this growing list of resistant historiography are the works of historians such as Naser Poorpirar (2000, 2001a, 2001b, 2002–2005) and Abdollah Shahbazi (1990, 1998) who have been relentlessly challenging the Orientalist foundation of Iran's official/national historiography on both national and international levels. Naser Poorpirar, in particular, has in effect dropped a bombshell on Iran's Aryanist/Orientalist historiography by way of his seminal multivolume *Reflections on the Foundation of Iran's History* (2000–2004). As he puts it in one of his books,

I consider it an honour that in this environment filled with animosity, I have been deconstructing historical illusions from the minds of this region's children, and have been faced, as a result, with those whose understanding of cultural issues in this country is so little and limited. . . . My pride is in exposing those masked ones who have used the history and historical thought of Iranians as a veneer on their open and concealed dishonest intentions. (Poorpirar, 2001b, p. 262)

An obvious manifestation of this act of resistance and decolonization has been the direct challenge of the elite national/official historiography by going back to history itself, exploring and unearthing archival materials, archaeological finds, and other sources that repudiate the fabricated and falsified version of history writing during the Pahlavi era (see, e.g., Rayisnia, 1975, 1990; Vaziri, 1993; Shahbazi, 1990, 1998; Poorpirar, 2000, 2001a, 2001b; Zehtabi, 1999). This emergent historiography is challenging the national/official historiography whose task has been to marginalize and exclude histories of the non-Persian communities from the mainstream works of history, anthropology, sociology, and social sciences in general.

Festival of Babek: A Powerful Act of Resistance against Historical Appropriations

In conjunction with the writing of their indigenous/local histories, marginalized communities have developed a distinct method of resisting the national/official historiography that boldly challenges the representation of their historical events, heroes, and figures by the dominant group. This creative act of decolonization takes place not by way of actual writing of the history but through the establishment of festivals, gatherings, and rituals whose aim is to validate various historical events, heroes, and figures that have often been appropriated by the dominant group. A shining example of this kind of decolonization is an event known as the Festival of Babek in which tens of thousands of Azeris come together every year in July to pay homage to a historical hero named Babek Khorramdin.

As an act of engaging in an action-oriented research methodology, I followed closely the events of Festival of Babek in July 2004, and prepared the following report that was published in a number of important Azeri and Iranian newspapers (Asgharzadeh, July 2004). In the following pages I first present excerpts of the actual report, then some reactions to the original report followed by the report of the Iranian government's news agency regarding the event. The learning objective from this presentation is twofold: first, to show the extent of the struggle of various ethnic groups in contemporary Iran; second, to show the extent to which the struggle of marginalized groups in Iran is suppressed and misrepresented by the dominant group even in the twenty-first century—the age of global networking, cyberspace connections, and the information explosion.

FESTIVAL OF BABEK: THE LIVING SOUL OF AZERBAIJAN'S HISTORY

Every year in early July the Azeri town of Kaleyber becomes a colorful landscape of anti-colonial resistance against internal colonialism and oppression in Iran. People come from all over Azerbaijan in their hundreds of thousands to a place at the heart of which lies the famous Fortress of Bez, a sacred sanctuary that sheltered a local resistance movement centuries ago. They gather in the town of Kaleyber to pay homage to their ancient hero, Babek Khorramdin, who over twelve centuries ago put up a fierce resistance against the invading Islamic/Arabic forces. Men, women, students, workers, peasants and farmers come to celebrate the birthday of Babek, this legendary figure who has now turned into the living soul of a people's history of resistance and struggle. They pitch their tents around the Fortress of Bez, the stronghold of Babek and his fighters for 23 years; they explore the Qala/Fortress from dawn to dusk; they gather around bonfires at night; they sing, dance, exchange ideas and read poetry.

This magnificent festival is not just about dance and poetry, though. There is more to it than meets the eye. People come here with their musical instruments, songs, dances, and poems to redefine themselves by means of their own culture, their own language, on their own terms. This is about the survival and resistance of an entire people in defiance of an internal colonial force determined to annihilate its very existence. By annihilating their means of communication, their language, their culture, and their historical rootedness the government seeks to annihilate the Azeri people's authentic means of self-definition and self-expression. It is not surprising that the people's slogans attest to their devotion to the language and identity to which they belong:

Azerbaijan is not dead	Azerbaycan ölmeyib
It has not abandoned its identity	Özlüyünden dönmeyib
Azerbaijan is awake	Azerbaycan oyaqdır
It preserves its existence	Varlığına dayaqdır
My mother tongue will not die	Ana dilim ölen deyil
It will not be supplanted by other tongues	Özge dile çönen deyil

The Azerbaijanis come to the *Babek Qalasi* to announce to the entire world that they exist as a people; that they are conscious of their own history and validate their historical heroes; that they are able to define themselves by means of their own culture; to articulate their condition through their own language.

Here the real living history of the people of Azerbaijan comes face to face with the official/national history of the ruling elite, a history fabricated during the Pahlavi era, and reinforced in the Islamic Republic. This is where the culture of resistance explodes through artistic talents, intellectual creativities, and in the songs and poems of the masses of people. The festival becomes a moving, breathing manifestation of history, culture, and all sorts of communal activities, where the latest published books are exchanged; the clandestinely printed articles and pamphlets are distributed; the latest CDs and tapes are sold. Here, songs, poems and ideas of liberation are smuggled from tent to tent. The Iranian government finds all these cultural paraphernalia, musical products and literary activities extremely dangerous. Why? Because they are produced in the forbidden tongue of the people of Azerbaijan, the Azeri-Turkic: an endangered language that the government has openly condemned to death by forbidding it to become a language of education, of instruction, correspondence, and governance.

This year, the Iranian government was determined more than ever to prevent the people of South Azerbaijan from celebrating the birthday of their historic hero. So it brought out its repressive forces to *Babek Qalasi*. Local activists estimate that there were over 40,000 revolutionary guards, Basiji militia, and plain-clothes secret service agents temporarily stationed around the Fortress of Bez, apparently to engage in military exercises. They put up checkpoints at all major roads and alleys leading to the town of Kaleyber. They harassed the pilgrims at every opportunity they got. They confiscated the drivers' registration and car ownership documents. They wrote down the licence plate numbers of the cars carrying passengers and pilgrims. They interrogated the pilgrims inside the cars, buses, and in their tents. They rented, before hand, hotel rooms, hostels, and rental spaces where the pilgrims were going to stay. They marked the open areas around the *Qala* as spaces reserved for military exercises. They pitched large khaki tents in every available nook and cranny.

The government also dispatched groups of religious fanatics to perform the ritual of chest and back beating to mourn the death over 13 centuries ago of Hazrat-e Fatemeh, the daughter of the Prophet Mohammad, the anniversary of whose passing apparently coincided with the birthday of Babek. So the mourners came in black shirts, with mournful faces and long beards. There were thus rituals of mourning, accompanied by shrill chants of the eulogy speakers; the performers of "*shaxsey*" and "*vaxsey*," where the names of Imams and holy figures were chanted in one voice, in an attempt to invoke their sacred memory. In the midst of the commotion and mourning frenzy, a Basiji militia fell down a cliff, and having broken some limbs, drowned in a pool of water underneath.

The pilgrims came, nonetheless. They sought shelter in people's houses, in whatever empty spaces they got, and they pitched their tents among the tents of the military personnel, in the belly of the beast, as it were. In the dead of night, many a pilgrim was taken away, for questioning, interrogation, and who knows what. Some were released later on; some are still gone, without a trace. Various reports indicate the number of detainees to be in hundreds, among whom are women and young students. The government used all the tricks in the bag of all dictatorships to prevent this event from taking place. From intimidation to psychological warfare to open arrest and detention, it used all it could to prevent the Azeris from participating in this festival of commemoration and remembrance. But the tricks did not work; the intimidations, coercions and detentions failed. The people came out to defy the culture of fear, threat, and oppression. And they succeeded.

As usual, the dominant Fars-centric media and press censored the event. This dominant media, particularly its extension abroad, is run by a bunch of pseudo-democrats and pseudo-intellectuals who dismiss the legitimate demands of non-Persian communities as backward, traitorous, and reactionary demands. They brand the democratic struggle of these communities to restore their human rights as inspired by the imperialist powers and ill-intentioned neighbours. They do not see it as problematic that their language (Farsi) has masqueraded itself as the national, official, and mother tongue of the majority of people in Iran. They regard it as perfectly normal to impose their mother tongue on others. But when a non-Persian community asks for its right to education in its own language, that community becomes pan-Turkist, pan-Arabist, or pan-Kurdist. It is perfectly normal for them, for the Persians, that is, to talk about "the greater zone of Iranic culture," to share the latest literary and artistic innovations with other Farsi-speaking groups in Afghanistan, Tajikistan, and elsewhere. But when an Iranian Azeri expresses his/her love for the language, music, and literature developed by his/her co-ethnics in the Republic of Azerbaijan north of the border, this Azeri becomes a separatist, a traitor disloyal to Iran's territorial integrity.

That is how the dominant Farsi-speaking group has always treated non-Persian activists, be it during the Pahlavi era or in the Islamic Republic. And the marginalized, oppressed minority activist has always defended him/herself by confessing that s/he is not a traitor; that s/he too is a human being and has human rights. That is how a leading Azeri poet, Bulut Qarachorlu, had understood the situation and articulated it under the Pahlavi rule:

> Men demirem üstün nejaddanam men
> Demirem elim ellerden başdır
>
> I don't say I belong to a superior race
> I don't say my people is better than others
>
> Menim meslekimde, menim yolumda
> Milletler hamısı dostdur, yoldaşdır
> In my ideology, in my approach
> All peoples are friends and comrades
>
> Ancaq bir sözüm var: men de insanam
> Dilim var, xalqım var, yurdum-yuvam var
> But I have this to say: I too am a human being
> I too have a language, a people, a place I call home
>
> Yerden çıxmamışam göbelek kimi
> Adamam haqqım var, elim-obam var
> I have not sprung from the ground like a mushroom
> I am a person with rights, rooted in my community

The Azerbaijani Festival of Babek is a major decolonizing movement initiated by the people of Azerbaijan in an attempt to resist the Iranian government's politics of assimilation, and cultural/linguistic annihilation of non-Persian communities. It is imperative that Azeri intellectuals and activists articulate this festival to the world as it is, that is, without tarnishing its antiracist spirit. Now more than ever we need to show to the world that this movement is rooted in the legitimate struggle of the Azerbaijani people for democracy, human rights, and the right for self-determination. As such, Azeri writers and intellectuals ought to try and cleanse this movement from undemocratic tendencies, signs and symbols that serve to project negative images to the outside world. The Festival of Babek is a manifestation of the living soul of Azerbaijan's history. It embodies the continuous movement of the South-Azerbaijani people for equality and justice. We are all responsible to carry this movement to its final destination within the guiding principles of democracy, human rights, and antiracist vision (Asgharzadeh, 2004a).

The Dominant Misrepresentation

The above report was published in a number of newspapers and online publications. A clear act of appropriating the event was manifested in a report published by Iranian Cultural Heritage News Agency in July 2004. This news agency affiliated with the Iranian government blatantly falsified the whole event by asserting that people were there to recite Persian poetry and remember ancient Persian customs. Below is the crux of this report:

> Tens of Babak Khorramdin fans, an Iranian national hero resisting Arab Caliphs, gathered in his awesome fort in Kelidar area, near Tabriz, on Friday to mark his symbolic birthday. His staunch followers, mostly Iranian nationalists, had camped in the mountainous castle since last Thursday, reading poetry including Shahnameh (Iran's most famous epic poetry book) and playing traditional music. They also lit up bonfires to follow traditional rituals of ancient Persia. His historical fort, known as the Immortal or Republic Castle, is located 16 km southwest of Kelidar in East Azerbaijan Province and is 2,300 to 2,600 meters above the sea level. Khorramdin was one of the first Iranian to take arms against Arab rulers during their reign over Iran. . . . Khorramdin originally was known as Abdullah Babak. He and his followers promoted a purely Persian religion as an alternative to Islam. During a 20-year rebellion (816–837 AD) they killed many of the Abbasid Caliphate's (750–1258 AD) troops. (News Service: Iran July 12, 2004 8:36 AM)

This act of appropriation and falsification shows that those in positions of power and authority are capable of presenting an upside-down version of reality, no matter how unethical, immoral, and even ridiculous such an act may be. It also shows the importance of having power over the means of publication and dissemination of knowledge. Falsification of this magnitude leaves one to wonder at the degree to which realities can be easily distorted and misrepresented by the dominant group. If a government can present such a false version of reality in this age of Internet technology and satellite television, it would not be difficult to imagine the magnitude of falsifications of this kind when there were no televisions, no media, no press, and no Internet.

There was a time that means of publication and dissemination of knowledge were the exclusive property of the dominant group. Under those conditions, the minoritized groups were completely robbed of their identity, language, history, and culture–if not entirely physically, certainly discursively and textually. The dominant group was able to present an entirely distorted version of the colonized subjects' history, identity, and existence, particularly in texts, signs, and symbols that it left behind as historical sources of reference. In large part, it is the legacy of such appropriations and misrepresentations that Iran's minoritized communities are grappling with today.

While the official sources openly misrepresented the events of Festival of Babek, nonofficial sources entirely boycotted both the Festival and its coverage. Some of them, however, reacted to the published reports in an attempt to discredit them. For instance, on July 15, 2004, Tajikistan Online Forum published a short critique of my report posted by an individual nicknamed Pan-Iranist. The message was titled "in reply to 'Alireza Asgharzade on babek festival' " and argued,

> [Asgharzadeh writes that the Azerbaijanis] "over twelve centuries ago put up a fierce resistance against the invading Islamic/Arabic forces." Over 12 centuries ago there were no "Turks" in that area—so that proves the point that he [Babek] was Iranian. (Pan-Iranist, July 15, 2004, 4:27 PM)

This individual's reply is an echo of the dominant way of thinking in the country. Racialization and biological categorization of the country's inhabitants still constitute the dominant approach to social, cultural, and political issues faced by Iran's citizens. It can be seen that in the original report, it has never been mentioned whether Babek was a Persian or a Turk, or whatever was his DNA and genetic makeup. It has been said that the Azerbaijanis were celebrating the birthday of their ancient hero. They consider this hero a fellow Azerbaijani because he lived in Azerbaijan and struggled till the end of his life there against the invading forces. An invocation of the memory of his anticolonial struggle has been a source of inspiration for the current population's own anticolonial struggle. There is no doubt that the context of Babek's struggle against the caliphate in the ninth century was different from the context in which non-Persian Iranians, and Azerbaijanis in particular, are now engaged in acts of anticolonial and antiracist resistance. However, it is the anticolonial nature of both struggles that brings them together. The Azerbaijanis consider him a fellow Azerbaijani simply because he was one of them, he lived among them, and defended their homeland with them. What is there to be gained by assigning him a racialized Persian/Aryan identity?

Another individual, Farhad, responded to the report on the "Political Dialogue" section of Iran's National Front Web site. This individual too highlighted issues relating to race, DNA, and biology, among other things:

> I am not sure that Azerbaijanis are not Persian. It is my opinion that Azerbaijanis are actually Persians who [have] mixed several languages (some of which is from Central Asian languages of Mongols who invaded Iran in 13th century). Of course DNA tests can easily see whether Iranian Azerbaijanis are actually related to Persians or to Central Asians. Anyone who looks around in Tabriz sees that Azerbaijanis have no physical resemblances to Mongols

(slanted eyes, little body and facial hair) and actually are more like the rest of Iranians (round eyes, hairy body and face, a variety of hair, green, hazel and even blue eyes) and other peoples from the region (Armenians). In other words, the notion of Azeris being of an entirely different nation [mellat] seems to be a false notion. (Farhad, July 13, 2004)

In Farhad's reaction too the dominant racist/racialized view surfaces as the main determining factor in dealing with human and collective rights of millions of minoritized individuals. The author cautions that Azeris genetically may be the same as Persians, a theory that in his view could be determined by a DNA test. However, it does not concern him that no matter what the genetic makeup and DNA of Azerbaijanis may be, they would still be a distinct community with their own language, culture, history, and way of life. The nature of their DNA has absolutely nothing to do with the fact that they speak a language totally different from the dominant Farsi and they demand the right to use that language in schools, universities, press, media, courts, and so on. Even if they had the same DNA as Persians, they would still need to read and write in their own language. Just as speaking an Indo-European language has not prevented the Kurds and Baluchs from struggling for their own ethnic, cultural, and linguistic rights, so too the Azeris would still struggle for the same rights.

In fact, playing the race card has become very fashionable nowadays. In order to create animosity amongst various ethnic groups, the dominant group divides them based on their so-called racial origins. The lion's share of racializing propaganda in this regard is directed toward the Kurdish community that speaks an Indo-European language closely related to Farsi. During his presidency, the reformist president Mohammad Khatami took notions of "Aryan race" and "true owner of Iran" to new heights, particularly in his trips to Kurdistan, where he never failed to remind the Kurds of their Aryan origins that in his view made them "the true owners of Iran" ("saheban-e asli-ye iran"). In his position as the president of a multiethnic and multinational country, Khatami did not realize that by singling out certain groups as true owners of Iran he created resentments and uneasiness among the rest of the populace.

The politics of using the race card and belonging to the same "Aryan race" slogan are major issues that Mustafa Hijri (2001) explores in his interview with Ardashir Mehrdad:

A. *Mehrdad:* . . . Since Khatami was elected as president there has been a shift in the official propaganda towards the Iranian nationalities. A discourse has emerged with clear racist nationalism at its core. It claims that Kurds are Aryans and of the same racial characteristics as the Fars. Not only does this viewpoint deny Kurdish claims for national distinction, but also it aims to put a barrier between them and other nations and thus weakens the national solidarity within Iran. What do you think? Indeed what are your views of the racial viewpoints on the national question?

M. Hijri: I remember when I was in high school, in the previous regime, whenever there was tension between Iran and its neighbors the monarchy suddenly remembered the Kurds, the brave defenders of our borders, "Kurdish heroes." These Kurdish heroes were only fit to die. They had no other rights. Today too after all the developments in the region and especially after the fall of the Soviet Union, and with a dozen new independent nations on our northern border, the Islamic Republic is also banging that same drum. Mr. Khatami too is unfortunately using that rusty weapon. He thinks this will impress the Kurdish people. However, I doubt if such ruses could split the Kurds from other nationalities.

(Hijri, 2001, p. 3)

Given the discriminatory and racist politics of the Islamic Republic, it is no wonder that the Islamic government is playing the race card to seduce different nationalities away from pursuing their legitimate social, cultural, and national demands. The former president, Mohammad Khatami, tried to present a nationalistic image of himself among the Iranians. Like other sorts of Iranian nationalism, his nationalism was also deeply rooted in Aryanism, the Aryan-Persian ownership of the country, and eventually the supremacy of one racial/ethnic group over others. Ethnicities such as Kurdish, Baluchi, Luri, Gilaki, and Mazandarani are looked at by the dominant group as speakers of Iranic languages. And from this linguistic definition the dominant group extrapolates a racial understanding in the sense that if all these groups belong to the same language family, then they must be related racially as well. And from this categorization they propagate the absurd notion that as speakers of an Indo-European language, these diverse ethnic/national groups are and ought to be the true owners of Iran. This line of argument may appeal to the ultranationalist element amongst these otherwise marginalized communities. The majority of people, however, do not buy into this absurdity and continue to struggle for their collective cultural and national rights. This is a fact to which the continuously fierce and bloody struggle of Kurdish community attests:

The people of Kurdistan have sacrificed, and suffered, hugely. We have given tens of thousands of lives in these two decades. We have lost such personalities as Dr Ghasemlu and Dr Sharafkandi and many Kurdish militants. We know that approximately 5,000 pishmargehs from the KDP-I alone have been martyred. Hundreds of Kurdish freedom seekers are in the prisons of the Islamic Republic. If the Islamic Republic believed in the right of the Kurdish people there would have been no need for so much bloodshed and imprisonments. It is totally erroneous to believe that these achievements, and the democratic process, which have been obtained through the blood of committed people, are given as presents by this regime. The Islamic Republic is too weak to be able to give freedom to the people of Iran. I have no doubt that the people of Iran will get their freedom through their own efforts. There are many cultural associations. Books are now being translated into Kurdish and there are now writers who write in Kurdish. They are forever being arrested and tortured but they go on writing. (Hijri, 2001, pp. 3–4)

Amongst Iran's various nationalities, perhaps the Kurdish nationality has been the most persistent and determined in its struggle for national, social, cultural, and political rights. Yet, by all accounts the Kurds are speakers of a language belonging to the Indo-European linguistic family. If there were any truth to the claim of the dominant group that "Iran belonged to the Aryan race," then the language and nationality of the Kurds would have been accorded similar status as those of the Persians. However, the Kurds have been subjected to acts of assimilation, genocide, and cultural annihilation similar to the other nationalities—if not more so. This fact alone clearly shows that the dominant group is using the race card in an attempt to maintain its hegemony over different communities. The Kurdish community is aware of the racist and racializing discourse used by the government to prevent their solidarity with other oppressed nationalities; that is why they continue with their legitimate struggle despite the dominant group's racist propaganda to separate them from the others.

Theorizing the Struggle: Farstoxication, Fars-Strickenness, and Fars-Centrism

The kind of terminologies and concepts employed by marginalized writers, intellectuals, and activists have a central bearing in defining and articulating anticolonial and antioppression struggles. While the use of a plethora of slogans and mottos at the grassroots level helps to identify the nature and direction of a people's struggle, the choice of terms, concepts, words, signs, and symbols to describe a movement is extremely important in the way others perceive the movement and make sense of its objectives. In the majority of cases, usually terms and concepts developed and used at the beginning stages of grassroots movements are adopted or coined hastily and are nowhere near describing the true spirit of these movements. However, as the struggle progresses, the concepts and terminologies mature to present a more objective and thorough image of the struggle.

The struggle of Iran's minoritized communities is a democratic struggle rooted in modern conceptions of human rights, sociocultural freedoms, and the right for self-determination. Nevertheless, this movement has yet to articulate itself through concepts and terminologies in line with the spirit of its antioppression character. Against the backdrop of a lack of democratic conceptualization, Hojjat-ul-islam Abduleziz Azimi-Qadim's (2004) conception of Farstoxication (*Fars-zadegi/Farsa Vurulmaq*) heralds a new era of democratic conceptualizing and theorizing to identify the colonizer as well as the decolonizing movement. Farstoxication is a new term coined by this enlightened clergyman that helps articulate the ongoing struggle of non-Persian communities for social justice and equality in Iran. Hojjat-ul-islam Abduleziz Azimi-Qadim is an Azerbaijani cleric from the city of Ardabil who, in his recent writing, has clearly outlined the ongoing linguistic hegemony of the dominant Farsi-speaking group in Iran. In an article titled "Fars-zadegi: Mari Khosh Khatt-o Khal" ["Fars-Strickenness: A Colorful Charming Snake"], he explains the degree to which non-Persian peoples' languages, histories, even creativities, and imagination have been colonized by the Persian minority in current Iran:

> Ever since we have opened our eyes in Iran, they have told us that we should have one official language. We thought that all countries in the world were run through one (official) language; that only a single language was taught and learned in their schools. We were so mentally stagnated that we thought the purpose of education was learning Farsi. The more they smeared us in Farsi, the more we became suspicious of our own mother tongue. . . . We learned science in Farsi and slang in Turkish. They kept us away from education in Turkish . . . to the extent that we became infatuated with Farsi and disgusted by our own mother tongue. . . . But when we traveled to the Farsi-speaking cities of the country, we saw a completely different picture and realized that essentially our language was condemned to annihilation. We realized that an illiterate Farsi-speaking shepherd expressed himself more comfortably than our Turkic-speaking person with a bachelor's degree. And I as a Turk, because of my Turkic accent, with devastating shame and embarrassments, am only able to approve whatever the Farsi-speaking shepherd says. If we speak with a Turkic accent they tell us, "You better go and correct your accent first." We thus realized that we are condemned to annihilation. (Azimi-Qadim, 2004, p. 1)

The sentiments expressed by Azimi-Qadim are not new. What makes his observation new, though, is the fact that it comes from a member of the ruling clergy, that is, from someone wearing the official clergy garment and acting as a revered member of the ulama community. Ever since the establishment of clerical rule in Iran, the ulama and members of the clergy have become the focus of alluring employment opportunities and glamorous official positions. It is in competing for these high status positions that the clergy from non-Farsi-speaking regions come to feel the sting of language-based discrimination. While the Sunni clergy are automatically excluded from these positions due to their religious beliefs, the Shia clergy receive differential treatment based on their language, accent, and place of birth. The Shia ulama such as Azimi-Qadim have realized that the most lucrative positions go to those who are fluent in Farsi or speak it without an accent—Tehrani accent being the standard.

The non-Persian ulama and members of the clergy realize that when it comes to patriotism, they are as patriotic as the Farsi-speaking clergy—if not more so; when it comes to education, they are as qualified as the ulama from Farsi-speaking areas. Likewise, when it comes to devotion to Islam and Shi'ism, they are as devoted a Muslim as the next person—if not more so. Irrespective of all the right qualifications, however, they are discriminated against when it comes to allocation of prestigious jobs with high-paying salaries and glamorous social status. Why? It is at this point that the reality of language-based racism begins to sink in. The Shia ulama from non-Persian regions come to realize that they can never obtain those glamorous positions because the mastery of Farsi is a determining factor in getting those positions. And since they have not been brought up in a Farsi-speaking environment, they can never speak it like a native speaker. A new language is not something that one may master overnight. It takes a lifetime for one to master a different language. And since the Azerbaijani ulama traditionally have not been schooled in Farsi, it is almost impossible for them to speak it like someone from Tehran, Isfahan, Mashhad, Kerman, or Yazd. Hence, the bitter realization that exclusion, discrimination, and racism can be caused as a direct result of the monolingualism and linguistic domination of one group over others. Awareness, of course, propels action. And the aware ulama, like Azimi-Qadim, are brave and decent enough to take action and resist acts of internal colonialism and oppression.

Hojjat-ul-islam Abduleziz Azimi-Qadim goes on to further elaborate on the ramifications of Farstoxication:

> [K]nowledge is not limited to one language. Education in the mother tongue is not only possible but also preferable. By teaching Farsi to your child, your child will not be related to Tehranis, for s/he is your child. Whether s/he is good or bad, s/he is a Turk and belongs to Turks. However [by forgetting his/her identity], s/he becomes a Persianized Turk, or in my terminology, Farstoxicated. Farstoxication is not a simple problem; it is a crisis. Farstoxication is a cultural aggression against the Turk and Kurd and Baluch. . . . Farstoxication is like a dew of disgrace that tightens the circle of our entrapment with every passing day. Once it was the Pahlavi regime who was forcing us into Farstoxication, but today, in the height of indignity, we ourselves run after Farstoxication. . . . The People of various nationalities must wake up from their deep sleep and free their children from the clutches of this dangerous snake. For tomorrow will be too late and the task will become more difficult. (Azimi-Qadim, 2004, pp. 1–2)

Fars-zadegi is a twin notion to what Jalal Al-e Ahmad had called in the 1960s *Gharb-zadegi*, which meant "plagued by the West," "West-stricken-ness," or Westoxication. In Al-e Ahmad's view, *Gharb-zadegi* was a cultural illness that had stricken many Eastern societies, and Iran in particular. Al-e Ahmad adopted the term from Ahmad Fardid's (d. 1994) lexicon. Fardid was an oral scholar of controversial ideas and character who derived the term *Gharb-zadegi* from his interpretation of the German philosopher Martin Heidegger's (1889–1976) critique of modern technology and the ways in which it was employed. In a book titled *The Question Concerning Technology* Heidegger envisioned that

> the threat to man does not come in the first instance from the potentially lethal machines and apparatus of technology. The actual threat has already affected man in his essence. The rule of Enframing threatens man with the possibility that it could be denied to him to enter into a more original revealing and hence to experience the call of a more primal truth. (Heidegger, 1977, p. 28)

The decadence of the world had already begun in the West, maintained Heidegger, and through Western technology and culture was fast spreading to the East. This was the idea that Fardid borrowed from Heidegger and coined from it his own notion of *Gharb-zadegi* or West-stricken-ness. Western notions of liberalism, democracy, and technology were in opposition to Eastern notions of spirituality and unity of the realm of spirit with that of nature. The West had dominated nature and environment technologically. It was also in the process of dominating the East culturally, through the imposition of its understanding of technology, ethics, and humanity. It was from these ideas of Fardid that Al-e Ahmad built up his own notion of *Gharb zadegi* or Westoxication. In his usage, the term signified a sense of (toxic) contamination as well as a sense of intoxication, where it functioned as sweet, lethal poison:

> A west-stricken man who is a member of the ruling establishment of the country has no place to stand. He is like a dust particle floating in space, or a straw floating on water. He has severed his ties with the essence of society, culture, and custom. He is not a bond between antiquity and modernity. He is not a dividing line between the old and the new. He is something unrelated to the past and someone with no understanding of the future. He is not a point on a line, but an imaginary point on a plane or in space—just like that dust particle. (Al-e Ahmad, 1962/1982, p. 67)

Al-e Ahmad's emphasis is on the Westoxicated creature's disinterest in his/her own culture, society, and community. Such a creature is not entirely uprooted from his/her community; s/he is not separated from her/his means of communication and language. S/he is just infatuated and fascinated by an alien culture and society. The more pronounced this infatuation becomes, the more s/he becomes, in Al-e Ahmad's view, alienated from her/his own community. The Iran of Mohammad Reza Pahlavi era serves as a model for Al-e Ahmad based on which to conceptualize his notion of Westoxication. In this era, the West was looked upon by the ruling elite as a superior civilization that had to be emulated. The underlying explanation for this admiration and emulation was a racist notion that there was supposedly a common Aryan ancestry between Europe's white race and the Persian race in Iran. Following in the footsteps of Europe's nineteenth and twentieth centuries racist theorists, the dominant Persian group was advertising Iran as the origin and birthplace of the European-constructed Aryan race. This supposedly superior race's offspring had taken giant strides toward industrial, technological, and economic progress in the West. And yet, the presumed ancestral home of this supposedly superior race was in shambles. It was a disastrously backward society economically, socially, politically, and industrially.

According to the dominant ruling elite, the main reason for Iran's dismal state of backwardness was none other than the introduction of Islam to the country in the seventh century, which had resulted, among other things, in more than 1,000 years of Arab and Turkic rule over the supposedly Aryan inhabitants of Iran. The Arabs and Turks had kept the country away from the certain advancement and progress that were to be the destiny of Iran's presumably superior Aryan race. The only way to overcome this backwardness was to emulate the West and become Westernized "from the tip of the toe to the top of the head" (Taqizadeh, 1920/1978). As far as the ruling elite was concerned, becoming Westernized meant the blind mimicry of the West, on the one hand, and the purging of such un-Iranic (*anirani*) elements as the Arabs and Turks from Iran's history, on the other. Al-e Ahmad was not able to fully grasp and articulate the underlying racist and supremacist components of the politics of Persianization and Westernization at the time. As a result, his work mainly focused on individual tendencies toward the West as reflected in superficialities such as mode of dress and behavior:

> The west-stricken man chooses the easiest path. He is always ready to "seize the opportunity," and appreciate the moment. . . . He never troubles himself about anything. He can easily shrug off any problem. . . . He is jack of all trades and master of none. . . . The west-stricken man has no personality. He is a creature lacking in originality. . . . The west-stricken man is a gigolo. . . . [He] is the most faithful consumer of western manufactured products. . . . The west-stricken man never takes his eyes off the West. He does not care what happens in his cozy little part of the world, in this corner of the East. If by chance he is interested in politics, he is aware of the slightest shift to the right or left on the part of the English Labour Party and he knows the names of American Senators better than he knows the names of ministers in his own country's government. He knows more about the commentators in *Time* and the *News Chronicle* than he does about his cousin far away in Khorasan. (Al-e Ahmad, 1962/1982, pp. 69–72)

It is this notion of mimicry that Al-e Ahmad cites as the main defining feature of a Westoxicated person. It, however, is not a Bhabhaian (1990, 1994) notion of mimicry with the potential for rupture and disturbance of the colonized order. In Al-e Ahmad's interpretation, it is more like a Fanonian notion of "nauseating mimicry" (Fanon, 1961/1990). It is the mimicry of a person blindly imitating whatever s/he thinks is confirmed and approved by the West. So Al-e Ahmad emphasizes such superficial values as mode of dress, behavior, eating habit, and fashion. It would, of course, have been a different picture had Al-e Ahmad's creature been forced to abandon his/her language for that of the West. However, this had not happened in the Iranian context. So Al-e Ahmad had to focus on superficialities rather than on real defining values such as language and religion.

What would happen if Al-e Ahmad's Westoxicated person abandoned his/her language in favor of a dominant Western language such as English, French, Spanish or Portuguese? Of course, this would give a whole new meaning to the notion of Westoxication. And herein lies the difference between Al-e Ahmad's notion of Westoxication and Hojjat-ul-islam Azimi-Qadim's conception of Farstoxication. Farstoxication takes place in an environment where non-Farsi languages are not allowed to be studied, learned, and used as normal languages of learning and education. The governing apparatus in society sees to it that Farsi receives all the support it needs to supplant other languages.

The government's absolute power is undividedly behind the processes that lead to Farstoxication. It is only by mastering Farsi that a non-Persian individual can secure good government employment; it is only through speaking Farsi that one can have any claim to knowledge and literacy; it is through the mastery of Farsi that one is able to express oneself creatively, artistically, and scientifically. The mastery of Farsi is the key to all privileges in the country, from economic to social to cultural to scientific to psychological. It is in such an environment that the Farstoxicated creature comes into being. S/he comes into being first by learning Farsi, then by replacing it with his/her own mother tongue, and at a later stage by vilifying his/her own language.

In Al-e Ahmad's Westoxication, language plays very little role. The Westoxicated individual may aspire to learn a Western language, but it does not mean that s/he has to abandon her/his own language. The West exerts its hegemony through cultural, technological, and economic means, but it is not actually there to enforce them physically (at least in Iranian case). Farstoxication, on the other hand, is enforced by the government and the ruling elite. The non-Farsi-speaking individual in Iran has no choice but to learn Farsi and try to speak it better than his/her own mother tongue. This process is characterized by sheer force, need, and coercion, whereas Al-e Ahmad's Westoxicated person enjoys a great degree of choice and flexibility in decision.

In the previous chapter, we saw some glaring examples of Farstoxicated, minoritized intelligentsia and the way they were eager to demonize their own ancestors, history, culture, and language. It is important to note that Farstoxication was not limited to the Pahlavi era. Nor is it limited now to the borders of the current Iran. In recent years there have been some cases of Farstoxication that make one wonder how far can a person go in denying her/his language and identity, in order to prove that s/he is Persian—hence Aryan. A glaring case in point is the recent publication of an "academic" work entitled *A Grammar of Iranian Azari, Including Comparisons with Persian*. The book is written by Yavar Dehghani, who has completed it as a PhD dissertation in linguistics at La Trobe University in Melbourne in 1999.

A brief overview of the book and its major arguments will certainly help to shed light on the concept of Farstoxication, on its definition, function, and purposes. In the beginning of the book, Dehghani makes several statements regarding the Azerbaijani language, each of which is enough to send shock waves through anyone with the slightest familiarity with the language academically known as Azerbaijani, Azeri, or Azeri-Turkic. Dehghani starts off his discussions by identifying the name of the language currently spoken in Azerbaijan. Without any academic, methodological, or ethical considerations, he arbitrarily and single-handedly identifies the name of the language as Azari. On first sight, one gets the impression that perhaps by Azari the author means to refer to Azeri, which is currently acknowledged in international literature as an authentic designation to refer to Azerbaijani Turks and their language, Azeri-Turkic. However, in subsequent discussions the author exposes his personal and political agenda by distinguishing between Azari and Azerbaijani.

In Dehghani's view, Azari and Azerbaijani are not one and the same language whose over 40 million speakers believe that they are. According to him, Azari is a language distinctively different from Azerbaijani. As he puts it,

[O]ne of the languages closely related to Azari is Azebaijani which is spoken in the Republic of Azerbaijan. . . . In fact, currently, the difference between these two languages is so great that it is difficult for their speakers to understand each other, or at least to communicate effectively. (Dehghani, 2000, p. 4)

To prove this absurd assertion, Dehghani quotes a passage from a text produced in northern Azerbaijan. He then arbitrarily translates it into what he calls Azari, which is supposed to be the language of millions of people in southern Azerbaijan. Since Dehghani considers himself a supreme authority in the Azerbaijani language, he does not see a need to justify his absurd translation of a passage from a literary text into his invented Azari language. The idea does not even occur to him to compare a literary text produced in northern Azerbaijan with a similar text produced in southern Azerbaijan. As an "expert" in Azeri language, he surely should know that there are thousands of comparable texts produced in southern Azerbaijan particularly after the Islamic Revolution. All he had to do was to glance through a journal such as *Varliq* and select a passage of his choosing for comparison. Since Dehghani is after his own personal/political agenda, he does not carry his "academic research" based on objective academic research methodologies. The crux of his personal and political agenda is to say that "the language of the Republic of Azerbaijan and Iranian Azari are two distinct languages" (2000, p. 6).

Dehghani's amateurish assertion begs the question: why is he trying so hard to prove that the Azeri language spoken by Azerbaijanis on the northern banks of the Araz River is completely different than the Azeri spoken by the same Azerbaijanis on the southern banks of the same river? After all, all one has to do is to pay a short visit to one of many Azerbaijani chat rooms on the Internet and see whether Azeris from north and south speak the same language or two different languages. All you have to do is check the archival material of one of many Azerbaijani e-mail discussion groups and see whether Azeris are using the same language or two different languages to communicate with each other. Dehghani, understandably, does not bother doing any sensible research. He only relies on his own "expertise" as an Azeri along with those of his "informants." The result is a distorted (mis)representation of both the Azerbaijani people and their language. He embarks upon such a dishonest misrepresentation in order to show that the Azeri language spoken in Iran is almost identical with Farsi.

Persian has influenced Azari in every aspect except in case markings and verbs. A large number of Persian words constitute a considerable part of the Azari speakers' vocabulary. In some cases, the only criteria to distinguish between Persian and Azari sentences uttered by those speakers who have had at least a primary education can be Azari verbs and postpositions and certain

phonological properties. For example, in the Azari sentence:
> män bayäd hämisä bäraye kišvär müfid olam . . . "I should always be useful for the country." Only the verb /olam/ is an Azari word, and other elements are borrowed from Persian. (Dehghani, 2000, p. 2)

Dehghani goes so far as fabricating an entirely ridiculous sentence only to show that Azeri is almost the same language as Persian. In fact, what he does is to write a sentence in Farsi, remove the verb at the end of the sentence and replace it with an Azeri verb, then present the entire charade as an authentic Azeri sentence. Here too we can see a clear act of Farstoxication in action. This individual seems to be infatuated with Farsi to the extent that he is willing to present an entirely distorted picture of his own mother tongue in order to prove that his mother tongue is Persian. Throughout his book, not even once does he mention the fact that Farsi has been elevated to the status of "the national tongue" in Iran by force and coercion, that it has become the only language of education and instruction because of the assimilationist agenda of the dominant group and the ruling elite in society. Nor does he mention the fact that Azeri has been a demonized, criminalized, and banned language for the past 80 years, that if Azerbaijanis speak Farsi it is not because they love Persian but because their own mother tongue has been proscribed and Farsi has been imposed upon them.

Farstoxication thus becomes a process through which one's own identity and language are denied so that one may easily associate oneself with the language and identity of the dominant group. It is a colonial act that entails the complicity and open participation of the colonized within the colonization processes. Allured by the economic and social advantages of self-denial, the Farstoxicated creature gnaws at the roots of her/his language, culture, and history as if s/he were the only person on earth with exclusive and absolute authority on that language, culture, and history. S/he is able to do this only because s/he immensely enjoys the political, economic, and coercive support of the dominant group. S/he knows perfectly well that the colonized language has no means of defending itself, that the individuals speaking that language are coerced into silence and are themselves at a point of extinction as a people. The realization of this bitter fact emboldens the Farstoxicated creature to attack the marginalized language and identity ever more fiercely, confident that the dominant group is ready to reward his/her acts of self-denial accordingly.

That is why Azimi-Qadim's initiative to identify this group of accomplices is a bold act of resistance against the colonial enterprise in its entirety. For the dominant group always uses these collaborators to justify its act of annihilating minoritized languages, cultures, histories, and identities. The dominant group says that it is not we the dominant who want non-Farsi languages destroyed; it is the educated scholars and intellectuals from within these communities themselves who believe that such languages are dangerous to Iran's territorial integrity and therefore must be destroyed. "Don't you believe us?" they ask. "Then look at Ahmad Kasravi, Taqi Arani, Rezazadeh Shafaq, Naseh Nateq. . . . Aren't these honorable individuals the most knowledgeable, the most educated and talented within these communities? Well, it's they who believe that Farsi should become the only language throughout the country. Who are we to reject the patriotic demand of the honorable leaders of non-Persian communities?" (see, e.g., I. Afshar 1985, 1989, 1990a, 1990b).

By exposing the central place of collaborators in the processes of colonization and assimilation, Azimi-Qadim exposes one of the deadliest weapons used by the dominant. His articulation of Farstoxication makes it clear that the colonized too bear responsibility for the way acts of colonization and assimilation are carried out. It also signals a warning to collaborators that their complicity in the act of colonization and assimilation does not go unnoticed by the marginalized.

> Our problem is with the Farstoxicated segment of our population who sees civilization and progress as the exclusive province of Persian language. They are oblivious to the fact that their home[land] is plundered, the names of their cities and villages are changed to Farsi, and little by little the language of most of their cities is changing from Turki to Farsi. Today, it is Qazvin, Hamadan and Saveh [that we have lost]; tomorrow it will be Zanjan and Miyaneh, and it won't be long that Tabriz and Ardabil will also lose before this colorful charming snake [Farstoxication]. When that day comes, we are already dead and someone must bury our rotten corpses. Today is our last opportunity to understand that just as being Muslim is not synonymous with being Arab, so too being Iranian should not be synonymous with being Persian. We are Turkic Muslims, we are Turkic Iranians, and so are our children. And we must defend our being Turk and Kurd, just as the people from Yazd (Yazdiha) defend their being Fars. We are Turks and we are Kurds; we won't submit Iran to the Farsi-speaking group, for Iran belongs to all of the ethnic groups living within it. (Azimi-Qadim, 2004, p. 2)

As expected, Hojjat-ul-islam Azimi-Qadim's resistance against the politics of assimilation and Farstoxication has come with a price. Because of writing the above words and consistently resisting the dominant group's colonialist advances, he was put on trial in the city of Tabriz and on August 24, 2004, was sentenced for two years of internal exile from Azerbaijan to Farsi-speaking regions. A report posted on a Web page dedicated to him on April 18, 2006, indicated that Azimi-Qadim was being held in Tabriz prison (http://ezimi-qedim.blogspot.com/). The struggle of this enlightened cleric has breathed new life into the anticolonial movement in Azerbaijan. The presence of ecclesiastic clerics and ulama like him indicates that the ruling theocrats do not see eye to eye when it comes to Iranian nationalism and Fars-centered politics of assimilation. As a matter of fact, from the very beginning the local ulama and clergy have been staunchest supporters of having education in local languages. During the Pahlavi era, when writing in the Azerbaijani language was prohibited, it was the ulama and members of the clergy who conducted their sermons in the Azeri language. The Azerbaijan of the racist Pahlavi period witnessed an enormous output of eulogy literature produced in the Azeri language that was read in mosques and places of worship in the holy months of Moharram, Ramadan, and on other occasions.

Azeri-Turkic is the language of instruction even today in all seminaries and religious schools in Azerbaijan. Since the ulama have not completed their education in the centralized so-called modern schooling system, they are not so well versed in Farsi. After the Islamic Revolution, the government required, of all imams leading Friday Prayers, to read at least one of the two sermons in Farsi. The Azerbaijani imams reluctantly accepted to read one of the sermons in Farsi from a previously prepared text. Even then, their Turkic accent became the butt of jokes throughout Azerbaijan and Iran, an unattractive habit that is a direct result of the politics of monolingualism and linguistic racism. A former imam of Tabriz, Ayatollah Moslem Malakouti, is still remembered for frequently uttering the phrase, "I say this in Farsi so that the Americans will also understand what I say!" Implicit in this anecdote is a view of Farsi as a foreign language in Azerbaijan, that is, a language that is comprehensible to the Americans but not to the local people.

In seminaries the main texts are in Arabic, and the language of instruction is the local language. As such, it is not surprising to see Azerbaijani clerics persistently resisting the politics of Persianization. The extent of their resistance and the degree of their involvement in the antiracist struggle will, no doubt, play a decisive role in the future outcome of the Azerbaijani resistance movement. Similarly, the roles played by other ulama—who are subject to racist exclusions not only because of their ethnicity and language but more importantly due to their religious faith—are giving new dimensions to the decolonizing movement throughout the country.

CONCLUSION

In modern Iran, the banning of non-Persian communities' languages automatically corresponds with the banning of their literatures and means of creative expression, just as their political exclusion corresponds with their literary exclusion. The terrain of discourse and language is a major area where Persian racism and colonialism come face to face with marginalized narratives of resistance. It is in this terrain that the dominant uses its language and discursive means to misrepresent, devalue, and eventually annihilate the other's means of communication and representation. Equally importantly, the marginalized uses language and discourse to repudiate the dominant's construction of an image of the colonized as the Other. The colonized Other uses indigenous languages, narratives, stories, songs, poems, and other discursive means to self-represent, self-express, and self-identify. The dominant uses its privileged sites of language, literature, history, and discourse to deny and eventually destroy the marginalized's language, history, and identity, just as the marginalized uses the same means to resist the power of racist discourse by defining itself in opposition to the misrepresentation of itself by the dominant.

Having found no outlets for expression in the dominant circles, marginalized writers, poets, and intellectuals in Iran have created their own spaces where they challenge the official discourse by providing a counterdiscourse of their own. Through their narratives, they contribute immensely to the discourse and praxis of decolonization. Simultaneously, they put forward new and innovative ideas in terms of reimagining more humane living conditions for themselves and others. Their creative energies have become effective weapons in the fight against linguicide, cultural genocide, assimilation, and Farstoxication. In contrast to the dominant group's politics of privilege, aggression, and inferiorization, the marginalized bodies have used their oral histories, traditions, myths, and stories to validate various territorial, political, and cultural claims against colonialist and hegemonic intentions of the dominant racist order.

The little space that Iran's marginalized communities have created for themselves to articulate their condition has empowered them to desacralize the conventional history; to challenge the role of education in the process of assimilation and Persianization; to interrogate the official/dominant narratives on identity, culture, literature, history, nationality and nation; and to confess the fictional origins of the dominant discourse and praxis on Iranian nationalism. They have shown that self-denial, assimilation, and Farstoxication are disingenuous processes designed by the dominant to damage the life chances of the minoritized. Through their narratives of resistance, they have offered an opportunity for their peoples to rediscover themselves as they really are, to rewrite their history in accordance with their own stories and narratives, and to rearticulate their situation and condition in their own voices and on their own terms. All this has been possible thanks for the most part to the revitalization of marginalized mother tongues. A space that the use of mother tongue has created has proven to be an extremely empowering site of resistance, decolonization, and reclamation of one's self, one's community, as well as its collective rights and freedoms. It is this invaluable site that ought to be celebrated by all decolonizing, antiracist, antioppression movements.

CHAPTER 7

Conclusions: Politics of Assimilation and the Challenge of Diversity

And one of His signs is the creation of the heavens and the earth and the diversity of your tongues and colors; most surely there are signs in this for the learned.

(Quran, Romans 30:22).

INTRODUCTION

The history of civilization in what is known today as Iran goes back over 6,000 years. The available archaeological/linguistic record indicates that from the very beginning the region was characterized with extreme ethnic, linguistic, and cultural diversity. No single ethnic group has ever constituted a definite numerical majority in the country, although at certain historical junctures, certain ethnic groups have obtained majority status based on their control over the political power and socioeconomic resources. Up until 1925, the country had been run in accordance with what one may call a traditional confederative system within which all ethnic groups enjoyed the freedom to use and develop their languages, customs, cultures, and identities. With the beginning of the Pahlavi regime in 1925, the natural trend of ethnic and linguistic plurality was abruptly stopped, and a process of monoculturalism and monolingualism started, which continues to date. The aim of this chauvinistic process has been to present the language, history, culture, and identity of the Persian ethnic group as the only authentic language, history, culture, and identity of all Iranians.

For over 80 years, the role of the central government in Iran has been one of denying and dismissing ethnic and linguistic diversity in the country. Just as the Pahlavi regime focused on annihilation of cultural, linguistic, and ethnic differences in the country, so too the current Islamic Republic has continued with the politics of assimilation, exclusion, and racism. Under the current establishment, gender-based and religion-based oppressions have also been added to a host of exclusionary and racist practices left over from the previous regime. The oppressive politics of the governing apparatuses have always been accompanied by ideological and discursive support of the majority of writers, intellectuals, and thinkers who, due to their belonging to the dominant group, have enjoyed the privileges of monolingualism, mono-culturalism, and racism in the country. The governing apparatuses, the dominant elite, and the Farstoxicated intelligentsia have come together and sustained the structural bases of one of the most racist systems in the contemporary world. This naked racism that feeds on outdated and discredited Aryanist paradigms and racist theories of eighteenth- to twentieth-century Europe has outlived the Jim Crow segregationist system in America; it has survived Nazism, European fascism, and the apartheid regime in South Africa.

This work has explored various aspects of Iran's normalized racism, arguing that the dominant discourse and praxis in Iran is and, since 1925, has been racist. Below are some salient characteristics of this dominant racist discourse and praxis:

1. Persian racism in Iran advocates a racist and racialized view of the world where the so-called Aryan race is seen as a superior race. Using the racist ideas of eighteenth- to twentieth-century Europe as its theoretical/ideological bases, the dominant group exploits the country's resources to promote lavishly funded research and explo-ration regarding the history and existence of this superior Aryan race in Iran. On the other hand, serious works challenging the supremacy of Aryanist historiography not only do not receive any assistance but are not even allowed publication in Iran. A glaring case in point is the his-torian Naser Poorpirar whose recent work on the history of Sasanid dynasty was not permitted to be published in Iran. According to his personal Web site (http://naria.persianblog.com/), the author self-published the book in Singapore and shipped it back to Iran for distri-bution. Ordinarily one would expect that a study critically examining the Orientalist construction of pre-Islamic history of Iran would not encounter any kind of government censorship in the Islamic Republic. Not so. Works like Poorpirar's are not allowed publication simply because they interrogate the Aryan/Fars-centric history of Iran, powerfully exposing its fictional, disingenuous, and dishonest character.

2. Persian racism openly identifies Iran as the land of these so-called Aryans who are in turn identified with the dominant Persian group, its language, culture, and identity. Through this racist process, Farsi becomes the national language and the Persian culture gets identified as the national culture of all Iranians, just as Iran's history gets appro-priated to the advantage of this so-called Aryan race by excluding, distorting, and erasing the histories, stories, and narratives of other ethnic groups. This exclusion takes place in government-sponsored research projects, schoolbooks, university texts, curricula, allocation

of funding, and so on. In short, under the racist order in Iran, to be Iranian becomes equated with being Persian. This kind of racist identification serves to foreignize and otherize those communities who are not Persian and who do not speak an Indo-European language.

3. Drawing on Western racist views, the dominant discourse in Iran equates language with race and tries to fabricate Indo-European language ties for non-Farsi-speaking peoples such as the Azeri-Turks in an attempt to show that over 1, 000 years ago they spoke an Indo-European language and are therefore Aryan. This kind of racist reconstruction of prehistoric (imaginary) languages essentializes race-based and language-based identities and prioritizes them based on a fabricated history of origins, arrivals, and so on, giving rise to the absurd idea about who has come earlier than whom, who has come first, who has come second, who has come last, whose language was spoken earlier than the others, and who, as a result, should have mastery over others. These kinds of nonsensical absurdities serve to create unnecessary competitions among various ethnic/national groups that lead to animosity, mistrust, and lack of cooperation among them, while leaving them vulnerable to be colonized and oppressed by the dominant Persian group.

4. The Iranian racist order openly proscribes non-Farsi languages in the country, banning them from becoming languages of education, instruction, learning, correspondence, and governance. By banning non-Farsi languages, the dominant group violates minoritized communities' identities, subjugates their minds, and brutalizes their spirits. It supplants the indigenous names of geographical landmarks, cities, towns, villages, and streets; appropriates ancient heroes, historical figures, literary figures, scientists, movie stars, popular singers, dancers, artists, and athletes belonging to the marginalized communities. It prevents non-Farsi-speaking communities from naming their children as they wish, using their own indigenous languages, cultures, names, words, signs, and symbols, forcing them instead to use names and symbols approved by the dominant discourse.

5. Using an anachronistic method of analysis, the hegemonic discourse in Iran offers purely racist and racialized interpretations of history, historical events, and classical texts such as the Avesta and the *Shahnameh* of Ferdowsi. It interprets these classic texts in accordance with modern racist theories and notions that were not in existence at the time these texts were written. The anachronistic reading of these texts becomes central to the maintenance of racist order in Iran in that such a reading legitimates the ownership of the country by a single race, just as it privileges a single language, history, culture, and identity. Anachronism gives a historical justification for contemporary oppressions, exclusions, and annihilations in Iran.

6. The dominant group plays the race card to create hostilities among marginalized communities, seeking to prevent the formation of any

semblance of solidarity among them. By identifying some of them as "true Iranians," "real Aryans," and "the authentic owners of Iran," it engenders a policy of divide and conquer, while sowing the seeds of mistrust and animosity among different ethnic groups. At the same time, it prevents a sensible census from taking place based on ethnicity and language, fearing that an ethnic-based and language-based census would reveal the true size and number of both the Persian community and non-Persian communities in the country. Just as such racist notions as "the true owners of Iran," "the real Aryans," and similar mumbo jumbos are emphasized to an inflated and inflammatory degree, so too the real issues and concerns such as the need for "conducting of an ethnicity-/language-based nationwide census," "opening of ethnic studies departments in the universities," and "researching ethnic groups and ethnic relations in the country" are de-emphasized, degraded, and dismissed.

7. The Iranian racist order uses the coercive force of governing organs to marginalize, criminalize, and punish the activists advocating the cause of minoritized communities, labeling them as traitors, secessionists, agents of foreign governments, and so on. In so doing, it refuses the legitimate demands of minoritized bodies for equal treatment, justice, and fairness. It brutally suppresses any ethnic-based and language-based activity, forcefully denying and condemning the right for self-determination of various nationalities.

Thus, sites such as history, historiography, language, literature, and the education system have become main arenas where the battle for domination and subjugation of the marginalized Other is waged. The dominant group uses these privileged sites to maintain its oppressive power base, to legitimate its dominance and privileged status, and to justify its oppression. Simultaneously, the marginalized uses these very sites to question, challenge, combat, and eventually subvert the oppressive dominant order. For instance, in the linguistic battleground, the dominant bans the minoritized languages and uses its language to supplant them. The marginalized, on the other hand, seeks to reclaim and revitalize her/his excluded indigenous language so that s/he is empowered to self-express, self-identify, and self-determine. Just as the dominant uses history to deny a historical rootedness and legitimacy to the marginalized Other, so too the marginalized uses her/his own version of history to reject and repudiate the history that is constructed for her/him by the dominant. The dominant uses the education system to enforce its assimilatory and racist policies. The marginalized redefines the purpose of education and schooling to bring about inclusivity, equity, equality, and fairness for all.

Although the marginalized uses all in its power to fight racism and oppression, it is important to realize that her/his battle is an uphill struggle in which s/he has very little access to strategic sites such as history, literature, language, and the education system. These are the sites that have detrimental impacts on the outcome of the battle between the colonizer and the colonized. And these sites are controlled for the most part by the dominant. If the dominant is left to its devices, there is little chance that the marginalized will eventually eliminate the bases of colonialism, oppression, and racism.

EVALUATIONS, POSSIBILITIES, AND FUTURE DIRECTIONS

What is to be done, then? This study has explored a variety of ways through which ongoing Persian racism can be combated and eventually eliminated in Iran. While addressing certain limitations of this work, the following pages explore a number of important possibilities for positive engagement and transformations for a better future. These important points are simultaneously addressed to the minoritized communities, the dominant group, as well as to international organizations, institutions, and agencies. In addition to highlighting the main discussions in this study, each section also highlights the future directions, research possibilities, and possibilities for democratic change in an Iranian as well as a Middle Eastern context.

Linking the Global and the Local

In recent times the world has witnessed the emergence of a powerful phenomenon known as globalization. The trend known as globalization encompasses diverse, contradictory, and contesting components. While it can be articulated in terms of properties attributed to imperialism, neocolonialism, Americanization, and colonization; it can also be explored in terms of transnationalization, hybridization, and even "localization" (Giddens, 1991; Amin, 1992; Cox, 1948; Sassen, 1998; Asgharzadeh et al., 2007). Notwithstanding its various manifestations, the rapidly emerging processes known as globalization affect the environment, biodiversity, as well as a variety of cultural, linguistic, and religious diversities on earth (Welton and Wolf, 2001; Kingsnorth, 2003; Dei and Asgharzadeh, 2006).

Through globalization, the world is rapidly becoming a very small place. In this small place, in this "global village," cultures rub against cultures, languages borrow from one another, economies depend on each other. As a multifaceted phenomenon, globalization may pose threats to the autonomy of local peoples; it may also provide opportunities to connect and bring together in a coherent manner various oppressed groups, their activities, and their common struggle against oppression. Globalization provokes reaction in the form of powerful worldwide movements. It causes people to join their voices and organize collectively in an effort to question, challenge, and subvert the destruction and oppression created by multinational corporations and endorsed by the ruling elite/governments of nation-states. Such collective movements are manifested through what is termed as "globalization from below," which has given rise to large-scale mass protests in Seattle, Prague, Genoa, Quebec City, Washington DC, and elsewhere, having changed the very meaning of the term globalization itself. Modern communications and Internet technology help to mobilize activists all over the world. These forceful organized mobilizations are challenging corporate globalization through their call for consumer boycotts, "name and shame" publicity campaigns, and for greater solidarity between and among various grassroots movements, women's groups, workers, students, laborers, and indigenous communities all over the world.

By using modern information and communication technologies, various marginalized groups can come in contact with one another and articulate their struggle on their own terms. They can manifest their resistance by celebrating oral, visual, textual, political, and cultural expressions of their existence. Today, the global and the local influence each other in unprecedented ways. No longer can one rely on an essentialized notion of the local without considering the impact of global factors, just as blind reliance on the global is an inadequate way to explore, discuss, and articulate the local. This interconnectivity and interdependence between the local and the global manifests itself in areas having to do with individual and collective rights, articulation of identities, and the identity formation processes.

In an Iranian context, the modern information technology has broken the government's monopoly on information. Marginalized communities have now more access to information relevant to their condition produced by members of their own community, members of other similar communities, as well as international sources. Due to globalization, they are more aware of transformations taking place around the world, particularly in the context of diversity, pluralism, and human rights issues. Marginalized activists in Iran should try and link their antiracist movement to worldwide progressive movements and tendencies. To this end, their movement ought to be articulated in line with universal principles of human rights, antiracist, and antioppression vision. One cannot expect to champion reactionary views and receive support from progressive global forces. As minoritized communities and individuals, people should see to it that their struggle is formulated in a clear and transparent language, a language that supports global human rights and avoids reactionary tendencies.

Seizing the Language, Seizing the Narrative

The central place of language in the process of colonization, racialization, and exclusion cannot be emphasized enough. It is through language that values, desires, and wills for oppression and domination are transmitted, legitimized, and justified. Likewise, it is through language that resistance is formulated, articulated, and presented. In the case of Iran, it has been through the recourse to language that the dominant group has fashioned a distinct "Aryan" identity for itself, while rendering the languages deemed to be non-Aryan as foreign, illegitimate, and savage. If a language is identified as alien and savage, there is no question that its speakers too are considered to be savage, repulsive, and foreign. As such, it is imperative that marginalized communities seize their indigenous languages, honor, revitalize, and use them as a most effective tool against the politics of demonization, assimilation, and annihilation. By seizing the language, one seizes the narrative in resistance against the dominant narratives of oppression. By seizing the language, one secures a space on which to articulate one's condition in one's own voice, a space that dominant language has always denied to the colonized.

During the Pahlavi dictatorship in Iran, minoritized bodies had little space to develop narratives of resistance in their own languages. They were forced to use the dominant Farsi language to combat the domination of that language, a paradox that resonates through all colonial conditions. Can one use the colonizer's language to destabilize colonialism? Can one use the master's tools to dismantle the master's house (Lorde, 1984)? How effective is such a strategy? In Iran of the Pahlavi era, just as in the contemporaneous one, generations of minoritized bodies have used the dominant Farsi language to combat its colonizing structure. Prominent among these writers and poets are such figures as Mohammad-Hossein Shahryar, Golamhussein Saidi, Samad Behrangi, and Reza Baraheni.

Mohammad-Hossein Behjat Tabrizi (1906–1988), better known as Shahryar, can safely be called the father of modern Azeri poetry. In a famous piece entitled *Sehendiyye* (1991) addressed to Bulut Qarachorlu, who criticized Shahryar's choice of writing in Farsi, Shahryar passionately defends his use of Farsi language, claiming,

> Dedin: Azer elinin bir yarali nisgiliyem men
> Nisgil olsam da, gülüm, bir ebedi sevgiliyem men
> Yad meni atsa da, oz gülshenimin bulbuluyem men
> Elimin Farsica da derdini söyler diliyem men
> (Shahryar, 1991, p. 80)

> You said I was an injurious despair of the Azeri people
> Even if so, I am still their undying beloved, my dear
> If rejected by strangers, I am still the canary of my own garden
> I am the voice of my people articulating their pains in Farsi

Shahryar was certainly an eloquent voice of his oppressed people in combating Persian racism. To prove this point, suffice to mention his famous poem titled "Tehran va Tehrani" ["Tehran and Tehrani"] (1967/2003) in which he daringly defends the dehumanization and "donkification" of Turkic peoples in the dominant Persian language:

> Hey you, the Tehrani!
> Be fair! Are you a donkey or am I a donkey?!

However, Shahryar's everlasting fame is not because of his Farsi poems but because of his Azeri works, particularly the masterpiece "Heydar-Babaya Salam!" ("Greetings to Heydar-Baba!") (Shahryar, 1943). Through his poetry, Shahryar revitalized the Azeri-Turkic in Iran, and in turn, was himself invigorated and immortalized in his own language and by his own people. The decolonizing and antiracist impact of his work in Farsi is in no degree comparable to the overwhelming impact of his poetry in the Azeri language. He produced his Azeri works during the heydays of Pahlavi racism, when non-Farsi languages such as Azeri were considered a bunch of gibberish unworthy of writing, literature, and literary creations. Shahryar showed that Azeri was a fine vehicle for the expression of most subtle ideas, images, stories, and experiences. He also illustrated the way the mother tongue could be used to combat the politics of assimilation and annihilation. He accomplished all this not by engaging in violent struggle, not by writing polemics and rhetoric, but by merely using his brutalized and demonized mother tongue. He showed that others too could do the same and, in so doing, challenge the foundation of the dominant racist order.

Reza Baraheni is another Azerbaijani scholar writing in Farsi who has been most outspoken, most daring, and most prolific in trying to produce a nonracist Persian literature. Unlike most writers of his generation, Baraheni's Farsi employs an ordinary language, without trying to artificially omit Arabic and Turkic elements from Farsi. In some cases, he has also tried to introduce certain Turkic and other non-Farsi elements in his fiction and poetry. In a way, he and others like him have tried to "carnivalize" (Bakhtin, 1981) the dominant Persian language, by widening its scope, destabilizing its authoritarian status, and making it more reflective of the linguistic reality in Farsi-speaking areas. In justifying his use of the dominant Farsi language, Baraheni notes,

> I raised my voice, trying to strike back at the enemy who had done all he could to paralyze the language of my entire consciousness. I could not hit back in the language of which I had been deprived through an historical necessity devised by the enemy. I took the sword of the enemy in my hands. The enemy, by imposing his conditions on me, had given me training useful in the combat. The enemy's strongest weapon was his language, his culture, and these I had learned as much as any of the sons and daughters of the enemy. I tried to be the tongue of my oppressed nationality in the language of the oppressor. . . . I tried to sing in the words of the master against the dominion of that very master. (Baraheni, 1977, p. 114)

Try as they could, this group of minoritized writers has not been able to introduce any significant changes by way of decolonizing the privileged status of Farsi. They have not even been able to decolonize their own name— "Turk"—in the Persian language, which continues to be written in its derogatory and colonized form, "Tork." Instead of transforming the Persian language to adapt to their needs and experiences, they have ended up adapting their experiences to an imposed language. In effect, all they have done is to strengthen Farsi, while their own language has been plunging into a state of semideath. Of course, Baraheni, Saidi, and others time and again have emphasized that they had to write in Farsi because they were not allowed to write in their own language. But this is not the point here. The point is the effectiveness of using the master's language to disturb the master's dominant discourse. The experience of Iran's minoritized writers shows that, although such disturbance may be possible to a limited degree, it is nowhere near the disruption that the use of one's own language causes in the dominant discourse, in the colonial order, and throughout the hegemonic system. As such, it is essential to any decolonizing movement to seize the mother tongue, the indigenous language, and through it the narrative in resistance, in self-expression, self-definition, and self-identification.

Building an Inclusive Education System

Iran is a society of diverse nationalities, ethnicities, cultures, and languages. Yet, ever since the establishment of the Pahlavi dynasty in 1925, the dominant approach has been one of denying the existence of difference and diversity in Iranian society. Paralleling other state apparatuses, the education system has nourished the politics of monolingualism and monoculturalism in the country. Although the current Islamic Republic has accepted the multi-ethnic character of Iran's population, this acceptance has largely remained on paper, having failed to translate into any sensible action in the real society and amongst real peoples. Hence there is an urgent need for the current racist, sexist, classist, and exclusionary education system in Iran to be transformed in such a way that it can provide equitable access to students of various ethnic, religious, cultural, gender, class, and regional backgrounds.

The first step to the creation of an inclusive education system in a country such as Iran ought to start by a critique of the dominant discourse on school-ing in the country. It ought to be realized that the purpose of education is learning and acquisition of knowledge, not the Persianization of minoritized bodies and non-Persian communities. In fact, the education system should be empowered in such a way that it can engage in a fully fledged critique of the Persianization processes in the country, which include the Persianization of history in general, and the history of schooling in Iran in particular. Given the extremity of state nationalism during the Pahlavi era and the resultant misrepresentation of Iran's history, unbiased and objective sources on the history of ancient Iran are hard to come by. The dominant official/nationalist discourse asserts that education supposedly occupied a very high place in ancient Iran, enjoying a revered and esteemed status. For instance, there are references to education in the holy book of Avesta where its significance has been frequently emphasized. There are also references to the Jondi Shapour academic center, which supposedly functioned as a major scientific center in the Sasanid period. Apparently this center was destroyed in the course of the Arab conquest of Iran in the seventh century, with all books and scientific knowledge accumulated there having been set ablaze (see, e.g., Frye, 1975; Mackey, 1996).

Nevertheless, it is important to note that ever since the demise of the Pahlavi regime, the dominant Fars-centered historiography, particularly in regards to ancient Iran, has come under heavy criticism and interrogation.

Historians such as Naser Poorpirar have questioned the existence of organized learning centers and even the existence of written materials such as books in the pre-Islamic Iran. According to Poorpirar, the pre-Islamic Iran had not developed an appropriate system of writing so much as to produce even a single book, let alone libraries full of books (Poorpirar, 2001a, 2001b, 2002–2005). Based on Poorpirar's compelling arguments, proper writing systems and instruments developed in Iran only after the arrival of Islam in the seventh century, an observation that is increasingly echoed by other contemporary Iranian historians. For instance, historian Parviz Rajabi notes,

> I believe that we did not even have a proper script to write with, and the Avestan script which is our final invented script with qualities for writing is a product of the initial periods of Islam. The Pahlavi and mikhi [cuneiform] scripts were not suitable for writing. . . . It will be a controversial argument if I say now that we learned writing from the Arabs. This is a point that our researchers have overlooked. (Rajabi, 2003)

It is essential for the Iranian education system to come to terms with its own history and try to present it the way it really was and has been, having cleansed it from various racist and chauvinistic influences. Perhaps a more realistic view of education in pre-Islamic Iran is the understanding that formal education at that time was a purely class-based affair. Only the aristocrats and the clergy—that is, the ruling classes—had access to formal education, which remained entirely inaccessible to the people. A misrepresentated and racist reading of the pre-Islamic history of Iran is conducted due to its effectiveness and relevance for the present racism. A misreading of the past in order to glorify a single race is in itself a clear indication that the education system is used in Iran to deny equal access to students and learners based on their ethnicity, language, culture, place of birth, gender, and other markers of social difference. It is extremely important that the education system is able to cleanse its history from racist interpretations if it is to be of equal value for all students. At the same time, it should interrogate the privileged subject of Iranian official/national history as a whole, so that a more objective learning environment can be made possible for all learners.

In similar ways, the education system must be geared toward instilling an antiracist worldview in students and learners. As a major socializing agent, the educational system can and should play a pivotal role in elimination and eradication of racist acts. By interrogating the relationships between power and knowledge (Foucault, 1980), the educational system should aim at exposing the unjust educational language policies through which the language of a dominant group is portrayed not only as the "national language" of diverse communities but also as the only language of learning and instruction. In contemporary Iran there is a close connection between the ruling elite and the language that is taught and learned in schools and universities, and it should be a major task of the education system to interrogate and expose such connections.

In a diverse society such as Iran, the education system should support multilingualism and multiculturalism, as opposed to monolingualism and monoculturalism. For the minoritized and marginalized groups, it is extremely empowering to read and write in their own mother tongues. A fair and equitable education system should support the right to education of members of different nationalities and ethnic groups in their own languages. Similarly, members of the dominant group should be encouraged to learn languages other than their own, so that a mutual respect may be developed for all languages and their speakers in the country.

The Iranian education system should be reformed in such a way that it is able to fairly and equitably cherish the contribution of all nationalities and ethnic groups for the betterment of general living conditions in society. A democratic education system requires that histories, literatures, and cultures of the marginalized groups be included in the curriculum to the same extent as those of the dominant group. An inclusive curriculum would enable the students to be proud of their identity, history, culture, language, religion, gender, and sexuality. It is this sense of pride and dignity that will translate into their becoming responsible members of the community. Rather than fostering an environment of mistrust, hatred, and animosity, an inclusive education system promotes a spirit of cooperation, sharing, and mutual respect among members of diverse groups and communities. In the words of Skutnabb-Kangas, "Words are weapons. They can be used for control or for sharing, cooperation" (2000, p. 666).

Practicing Antiracism

In diverse societies of our world, any form of positive political, cultural, and economic development would be unthinkable in the absence of a democratically inclusive space. This is due to the fact that individuals have different identities, lived realities, and worldviews, and in order to bring them together we need a guiding framework that manifests high degrees of tolerance, flexibility, and respect for difference. Provision of an inclusive space is the most important condition for the possibility of collective work and solidarity. Given Iran's extremely diverse population makeup, the desired democracy will not materialize unless it is deeply combined with principles of antiracism theory and praxis. The Iranians have always coexisted within a mosaic of different ethnic, racial, cultural, religious, and linguistic groups and communities. It is, therefore, imperative that the country's democracy is based upon principles of antiracism theory and praxis.

There is a very thin line between nationalism and racism. Historical experience shows that an unchecked and unmodified nationalism will inevitably lead to racism, chauvinism, xenophobia, and intolerance. Knowledge of an antiracist stance becomes more pressing given the emergence of various nationalist struggles in many contemporary Middle Eastern societies. One way of guaranteeing the humane and emancipatory character of national struggles is through the incorporation of antiracist principles into the fabric of those struggles. After witnessing the magnitude of human tragedies in what used to be Yugoslavia, in the Balkans, in various parts of Asia, Africa, and the Middle East, one cannot afford not paying attention to the deadly pitfalls of blind nationalism.

A clear and transparent antiracist stance should be the guiding framework for all nationalistic movements seeking to overthrow systems of oppression, bondage, and exclusion. In the absence of clear antiracist guiding principles, national movements will not achieve their liberationist and emancipatory goals. They may be able to overthrow one oppressive system, but they will replace it with their own version of oppression, racism, and exclusion. In a word, an antiracist understanding is central for peaceful coexistence in Iran, in the Middle East, and in the world as a whole. Iran comprises diverse ethnicities, religions, cultures, and languages. In order to live in peace and harmony, all peoples of Iran have to be able to respect such a rich diversity. An action-oriented, antiracist worldview will be most effective in helping to bring about that peaceful coexistence, understanding, sharing, and mutual respect.

Antiracism practices are also extremely vital for the maintenance of solidarity and the spirit of cooperation among diverse marginalized communities. For instance, the case of Azeri and Kurdish nationalities in Iran presents a challenging condition that ought to be carefully studied and influenced by antiracist injections if a dreadful racial/ethnic confrontation is to be avoided in future. These two communities have been in close contact throughout history. After the 1978–1979 revolution and pursuant to the Iran-Iraq war, interaction between the two communities has intensified as many Kurdish families have moved to a number of Azeri-populated cities and towns in western Azerbaijan. A great number of intermarriages have taken place between the two communities, which has strengthened the relationship and interaction between them.

Notwithstanding these strong ties, there are ultranationalist and racist elements within both communities who ache for a confrontation between the two peoples. There is no shortage of racist polemics, epithets, and accusations directed at each community by the zealots of the other. Clearly, the dominant racist order would not mind at all seeing these communities at each other's throats. This is a further reason that the antiracist activists ought to highlight the history of cooperation and brotherhood between the two oppressed nationalities, while trying to neutralize the destructive impact of racist elements within each community. Only a sincere devotion to antiracist principles and their internalization by the community activists, intellectuals, and writers are capable of preventing racist clashes among diverse Iranian communities in general, and the Azeri/Kurdish ones in particular.

In recent years, Internet technology has offered an unprecedented opportunity to engage in free debate and dialogue in cyberspace, particularly for those traditionally deprived of formal means of expression. However, a review of the experience with a number of Internet sites devoted to minority issues shows that most of us are not able to form, develop, and express what is called a free opinion. To engage in a free debate, one should be able to think freely. To think freely, one should be an autonomous individual, having obtained some degree of self-reliance and independent personhood. Otherwise, one cannot express that which one thinks is right, and consequently, one cannot fight for the creation of conditions that enable such an expression. This is what Habermas (1981) has called "the ethic of communication" and "the communicative action." This is the ethic that, first and foremost, compels us to protest against that which limits our freedom of expression. Evidently, in some Iran-related minoritized press, media and Internet discussion groups such an ethic seems to be terribly missing.

In general, the antiracist activists should take the lead in generating transparent and lively dialogues necessary for the building of any kind of solidarity and collective work. If we are to overcome this major obstacle, if we are to build something meaningful and enduring, then we should try to open the lines of communication in such a way that we are not afraid to express our opinions; that we are not scared to critique, interrogate, and resist the racism of not only the dominant group but our own community as well.

If we fail this, the alternative will be a closed, frozen space, where slave mentality, selfishness, fear, and hypocrisy become the order of the day; where and when we create and maintain an environment in which outdated feudalistic norms and values get constantly produced, reproduced, and maintained. Currently we have such a closed space. But we have to gear up our efforts to clean up this space. We have to let the winds of criticism and dissent blow through it from all directions. And if it does not withstand the force of our dialogues and multilogues, then we should give it an extra push to fall faster.

Engaging Class and Class-Based Issues

Iran's leftist groups and organizations have traditionally defended the rights and freedoms of minoritized non-Persian communities. Notions such as Iran as a multinational society, autonomy, self-rule, and the right for self-determination have been introduced to Persian language mainly through leftist, socialist, and communistic literature. It was the general trend during the cold war period that the leftist groups talked about ethnic and national rights of minority communities, and those interested in such rights generally joined these groups to promote their objectives. This trend has drastically changed after the cold war period. Major transformations on global, regional, national, and local levels have transformed the current issue of ethnic relations in Iran. Events, occurrences, and factors such as the demise of Soviet Union and the emergence of independent nation-states such as Azerbaijan, Turkmenistan, and Armenia; the ongoing transformations, war, and ethnic conflict in Iraq and Afghanistan; globalization and the unprecedented developments in information technology, the Internet, satellite TV, coupled with other developments have brought about new consciousness regarding ethnic issues and ethnic rights in Iran, so much so that these issues can no longer be fully articulated through class-based ideologies. As a result, the non-Persian community activists are now developing their own means and mediums of expression independently of the countrywide class-based organizations. And this has led to antagonisms between the two different ideological and theoretical camps.

In recent years we have experienced certain antagonisms within minoritized communities between those on the left and those on the right. There are extreme hard-liners on both sides. Those on the right have ceaselessly tried to demonize "the communists." And those on the left—the extremist variant, that is—have tried to reduce the marginalized communities' diverse cultural, national, linguistic, and social demands to class issues and economic relations. The rightist camp harbors undemocratic views that feed on racism, xenophobia, intolerance, and, of course, antileftism, while the extreme left still fails to realize that the time of economic determinism and class reductionism has long passed; that economic-based oppression is but one form of oppression within a host of racial, ethnic, cultural, gendered, and ideological oppressions; that all oppressions are interconnected and interlocked together; and that no single oppression can be successfully defeated unless all oppressions are equally challenged and fought against.

In his *Prison Notebooks*, Antonio Gramsci (1971) talks about a "transformismo" that at the time seemed to engulf the orthodox Marxists. By transformismo Gramsci meant the ideological movement of the intellectuals from left to center and to right of the political spectrum. After the fall of USSR, this transformismo or transformation has accelerated significantly on a global level. Evidently, the transformismo has reached Iranian circles as well, so much so that the number of traditional communists adhering to what Max Weber and others termed "vulgar Marxism" has been decreasing considerably. Irrespective of this, traditional Marxist analyses still serve as the ideological base for the majority of Iranian leftist groups. Notwithstanding that certain Marxists such as Althusser (1965) have taken pains to reconcile the material structure of orthodox Marxism with its ideological, cultural, and discursive superstructure, Eurocentrism, supremacy of class struggle, "class only" mentality, and "class first" methodology still remain at the core of Marxist analyses in Iran. Increasingly though, many left-leaning intellectuals and activists are beginning to critically appraise the "economism" and "class reductionism" inherent in the classical Marxist tradition. They are beginning to realize that although economic relations are very important in the shaping and structuring of the social life, such relations are, nonetheless, not the only determining factors.

Regardless of their ideological or theoretical stances, having left-leaning activists and intellectuals within anticolonial national movements is indeed a blessing in and of itself. Their active participation in the movement for the national rights of minoritized communities will help guarantee the democratic and humane character of the movement. Leftist groups and individuals have always constituted a democratic and progressive force within any coalition and alliance. The case of the Iranian anticolonial struggles should not be different. With the blessing of their presence, leftist individuals will ensure that various grassroots national movements remain faithful to the principles of antiracism, humanism, and democracy. In their absence, collective works and common struggles will face the danger of diversion from its humanitarian and emancipatory path, gravitating more and more toward narrow-minded nationalism, chauvinism, and racism.

In recent years, the ruling elite in Iran has shown flexibility toward discussions of class issues and class-based oppression in the country. While one may easily be involved in a class-based research in Iran, involvement in an ethnicity-based antiracist research is still a major taboo. Class-based analyses and research in an Iranian context are no longer considered taboo subjects and can be conducted without any kind of ostracization, stigmatization, and limitation. Quite conversely, ethnic-based research and antiracist analyses exploring issues of difference and diversity are considered forbidden subjects, discussion of which may entail huge risks to the researcher. Not only will the researcher not receive any support from the mainstream institutions, organizations, and groups, s/he is extremely marginalized and stigmatized by all parties involved, often labeled as traitor, separatist, foreign agent, and so on. Leftist individuals and groups can help facilitate race-based and language-based research in and about Iran by highlighting the significance of such studies for any democratic development in society.

Feminism versus Patriarchal Nationalism

Nationalist movements have been rightly criticized for their patriarchal and paternalistic characteristics. Indeed, all forms of nationalism carry within them the seeds of paternalism and masculinist worldviews. A meaningful coalition of minoritized activists, in order to be effective, must come to terms with the gender-based oppression and inequality, which is inherent to all cultures, including the marginalized ones. An anticolonial, antioppression coalition, without the active presence and participation of women, will have no democratic character. From the feminist literature we learn that the mere presence or attendance of females in meetings or gatherings is not enough to indicate a nonmasculinist condition. Although representation is very important, inclusion of voices, lived experiences, and particular knowledge are far more significant issues that have to be taken seriously.

The anticolonial and antioppression movements should be able to continuously interrogate their use of masculinist terminologies, ideology, patriarchal speech methods, paternalistic points of reference, along with their overall gender biases. We should strive to cleanse our language, our forms of speech, and methods of writing from the signs and symptoms of patriarchal structures. We must work together to provide an environment in which women, sexual minorities, and other marginalized bodies are enabled to come to voice, that is, to defend their rights and articulate their needs through their own voices. We cannot achieve all these within a narrow-minded, chauvinistic nationalism that preaches the "superiority of our nation's sons" and glorifies father-figure heroes and leaders. The time of that kind of nationalism is over. In fact, the time for any kind of "hero-mentality," for revival, creation, and reproduction of new "superhuman" heroes has long passed. Centering the struggle on heroes and leaders with "superhuman qualities" runs counter to democratic norms. We do not need "supermen"; we need democratic norms and values to safeguard our civil rights, and we need the active presence of women to safeguard our democratically inclusive norms and values.

As far as gender inequality is concerned, a significant change has occurred in recent years that has to do with a wider recognition of the need for the realization of women's rights and freedoms in an Iranian context. Amongst various Iranian political organizations and oppositional groups, the acknowledgment of gender-based inequality has gained wider acceptability and has moved higher on their agenda both inside Iran and in the Iranian diaspora. The current Islamic regime's antifemale policies and praxis have been increasingly criticized and challenged by various women's groups, social activists, commentators, foreign governments, human rights organizations, writers, journalists, intellectuals, and scholars. Ironically, these same organizations, groups, and individuals have virtually remained silent in the face of equally unbearable racist and exclusionary policies toward non-Persian communities.

Equally importantly, while there is now no hostility toward gender-based research and researchers within the dominant circles, ethnicity-based research is considered by the dominant a suspicious activity aiming to destabilize the country. This is true not only with the government apparatuses but also with antigovernment oppositional groups both inside the country and in diaspora. As far as the oppositional groups are concerned, addressing issues around gender inequality is considered a precondition for a future democratic Iran, whereas a mere mention of racial inequality, ethnic-based oppression, and language-based exclusion serves to brand the antiracist researcher/activist a traitor, secessionist, separatist, and agent of foreign governments.

Again, the onus is on feminist activists, women's groups, and other progressive forces to let the larger society know that antiracist activism is a necessary part and parcel of any cohesive antihegemonic movement for human rights, democracy, and the right for self-determination. Just as a truly democratic system would not exist without the realization of gender equality and women's rights, so too such a system cannot come into being in the absence of ethnic, linguistic, racial, and cultural equality. It is the duty of all those yearning for the creation of a democratic society to bring antiracist struggle to the forefront of the movement for equality, justice, and humane living conditions.

Acknowledging Diversity: An Antidote to Fundamentalism

No one can deny the impact that Iran's Islamic Revolution and the resultant Islamic Republic have had on the growth and development of what has come to be known as Islamic fundamentalism. The occurrence of the Islamic Revolution in Iran heralded a new era in the history of both Muslim thought and the Muslim Middle East. For the first time in the modern history of the region, the ruling monarchy of a powerful regional country was overthrown through a violent revolution, as a result of which the political power was overtaken by a group of theologians who from the outset identified themselves with their ideological faith and deep devotion to Islamic fundamentalism. This emergent Islamic autocracy saw to it that the Quranic and sharia law became the law of the land in Iran. The new rulers identified themselves with the motto "Neither Eastern, Nor Western: The Islamic Republic."

By rejecting the Eastern bloc they aimed to reject the (then) Soviet Union and whatever it stood for. By rejecting the "Western" element, they meant to reject the United States of America, to which they referred as "the Great Satan," along with Western notions of democracy, liberalism, feminism, freedom of expression, secularism, and so forth. The new rulers also assigned to themselves the task of what they called "exporting the revolution" to neighboring countries and other Muslim societies. Their rise to power in a major Muslim country such as Iran, and their passionate defense of Islamic fundamentalism coupled with their determination to "export the revolution," breathed new life into various Islam-inspired ideologies and fundamentalist groups throughout the world.

In the early 1980s, having received a green light from the United States and some Arab countries, Saddam Hussein of Iraq attacked the Islamic Republic of Iran, quickly occupying a number of important border cities, towns, and villages particularly in the province of Khuzistan. The ruling theocrats in Iran were quick to appeal to the religious fervor of the populace, chief among them notions such as the centrality of jihad, sacrifice, and martyrdom in Islam (and particularly in its Shia branch), as well as a sense of Iranian pride and the historical duty to defend the motherland.

From the amalgamation of all these highly charged sentiments, a powerful sense of nationalism emerged, feeding on centuries-old Shia literature that portrayed bloody images of Karbala, martyrdom of Imam Hossein and his followers in the late seventh century, and the glory of sacrifice for one's faith and homeland. Millions of youth and men were mobilized and dispatched to the warfront, many of whom fought with the hope to achieve martyrdom and reach the gates of paradise. After eight years of fierce battle that left behind over 1 million dead bodies and a destruction of unimaginable magnitude, the war ended in August 1988. This period of death, destruction, and mobilization was long enough to erode the desire for the democratic living conditions that various nationalities and marginalized communities were hoping to achieve after the downfall of shah's absolute monarchism.

Shi'ism and Islamic fundamentalism became the dominant discourse after the fall of the Pahlavi regime, supplanting all the other rival discourses that had been developed around the principles of proportional representation, recognition of linguistic pluralism, and acknowledgment of ethnic diversity (see also Mojab and Hassanpour, 1995). Islamic fundamentalism served as one unifying master narrative capable of gathering individuals of various ethnic and linguistic backgrounds around it. The stronger it grew, the more capable it became of overshadowing issues of democratic rule, federalism, and pluralism, so much so that it managed masterfully to maintain the language-based racism of the Pahlavi era, while at the same time adding a Shia-based religious component to the emergent Iranian nationalism. Meanwhile, Islamic fundamentalism continued to grow in places such as Afghanistan, Pakistan, Egypt, and Saudi Arabia. This ideological trend received a major boost with the rise to power of the Taliban in Afghanistan in 1996, and reached its climax through the tragedy of September the 11, 2001, in the United States. After this tragic event, the entire world became aware of the deadly extent to which fundamentalism had grown and, hence, the need for solutions to combat this deadly force and reduce its effectiveness.

Islamic fundamentalism triumphed in Iran mainly because it devoured other rival discourses/forces addressing issues of difference, gender equality, ethnic pluralism, and linguistic diversity in the country. Functioning as an all-encompassing master narrative, Shi'ism easily brushed aside the other secular, humanitarian, libertarian, leftist, antihegemonic, and antioppression narratives, marginalizing and silencing their supporters. In the absence of the voices to articulate various democratic rights and freedoms, the intellectual energy was exclusively channeled to the building and articulating of a single totalitarian ideology. This totalitarian master narrative defined itself in terms of Shi'ism; it viewed Islam as the only legal, legitimate, and authentic discourse in the country, and believed that "only the Holy Quran is capable of providing solutions for all the social, political, economic, and scientific problems" (Safavi, 1955, p. 7). Ayatollah Khomeini's famous statement regarding the (in)significance of material necessities and economic infrastructure is still well remembered:

> Some persons have come to me and said that now the revolution is over, we must preserve our economic infrastructure. But our people rose for Islam, not for economic infrastructure. What is this economic infrastructure anyway? Donkeys and camels need hay. That's economic infrastructure. But human beings need Islam. (Cited in Limbert, 1987, p. 15)

Although the revolution of 1978–1979 very briefly managed to shake the foundation of Aryanist mentality in Iran, it could not transform the racist structure of social order that was mainly based on the supremacy of one language—Farsi—and its speakers. As soon as the hallucinatory impact of the revolution subsided, the new rulers clung on to the racist legacy of the old regime, and vigorously continued with the politics of monolingualism and monoculturalism. To the already existing language-based system of apartheid, they added a religious dimension and identified the Persian language along with Shi'ism as the two fundamental markers of Iranian nationalism. Thus, maintenance of Iran's territorial integrity, Iranianness (*Iraniyyat*), and devotion to the nation and motherland came to manifest themselves through the devotion to Persian language and Shi'ism.

The ruling fundamentalist ideology was developed in Iran by supplanting democratic discourses on gender equality, ethnic diversity, and linguistic plurality. By the same token, this ideology can be weakened, destabilized, and subverted by way of readdressing and rearticulating these same democratic principles, that is, gender equality, ethnic pluralism, and cultural/linguistic diversity. In order not to address issues of difference and diversity in the country, the ruling elite continues to fan the flames of Shi'ism, Islamic fundamentalism, and pan-Islamism, the grand superficial narratives that have already proved their inability in bringing racial equality, linguistic fairness, and religious inclusion to Iran's diverse population.

Issues of difference and diversity must be highlighted so that religious-based essentialism and fundamentalism lose their grip on a population characterized by ethnic, cultural, religious, and linguistic diversity. Acknowledging of difference and diversity is not only central to the weakening of fundamentalist ideology, but it is also a most basic requirement for the building of democratic institutions and recognition of human, social, cultural, political, and linguistic rights of local peoples. In an extraordinarily multiethnic, multicultural, and multilingual country such as Iran, any democratization process ought to start with addressing issues of difference and diversity, at the heart of which lie ethnic and linguistic pluralities. Once an alternative discourse is created around these democratic principles, the antidemocratic metanarrative of fundamentalism will have no choice but to give way to a powerful antioppression discourse and praxis.

Middle Eastern Societies and the Challenge of Diversity

The problem of dealing with diversity, ethnic pluralism, multilingualism, and multiculturalism is perhaps the single most important social and political issue throughout the Middle East. The imperial global powers have always preferred to deal with one strong dictator in oil-rich Middle Eastern countries, rather than dealing with democratically elected, decentralized governments accountable to their constituencies. This preference is more pronounced in countries with substantial oil reserves such as Iran, Iraq, Saudi Arabia, and Kuwait. Their support for the shah of Iran and for similar dictators elsewhere are clear examples of this preference. Oil has been a glamorous commodity bringing alluring economic advantages to the ruling elite of the countries that produce it. At the same time, it attracts the attention of global powers to these countries, serving as a plausible excuse for them to bring and maintain hated dictators in power, without any consideration for democratic rights and freedoms of local populations.

For imperial global powers, totalitarian rulers have proved to be reliable assets on at least two major arenas. First, regulating the oil price in such a way that considerations of major oil companies are given precedence over considerations of the welfare of local populations. Second, preventing what has been called the spread of communism, particularly during the cold war period. Dictators such as the former shah of Iran devoted their entire energy to the prevention of the spread of communism within Iran, in the region, as well as on a global level. It is ironic that up until the final moments of his life in exile, the shah of Iran kept believing that it was the American administration that had decided to remove him from power. He also believed that the Americans had made a mistake in removing him from power and replacing his absolutist monarchy with an Islamic Republic. He thought that the Americans were doing all this on the assumption that Islamists were a better deterrent to the Soviets than he was. As he put it in *The Shah's Story,*

> [C]learly all the forces involved had their own reasons for pushing me offstage. Throughout 1978, the oil consortium refused to sign a new agreement with Iran to purchase oil. This coordinated action—or inaction—had incredible significance. I believe they somehow had foreknowledge of the events that were to take place later that year. I also believe that members of the Carter Administration . . . were anxious to see me in favour of this new so-called "Islamic Republic." Their strategy, if indeed they have one, appears to assume that Islam is capable of thwarting Soviet ambitions in the region. I wonder with what? Copies of the Koran to replace tanks? (M.R. Sh. Pahlavi, 1980, p. 221)

The resistance of Afghan Mujahedin against the Soviet-occupying forces during the 1980s showed that the shah of Iran could not have been more wrong in his assessment of the power of the Islamists. The Islamic Revolution that dethroned him in Iran coincided with the occupation of Afghanistan by the Soviet forces, effectively from 1979 to February 1989. With the full support of the Americans, a fierce resistance force was formed in Afghanistan, mobilizing the young Afghans and other willing Muslims along the lines of a fanatical Islamic identity with the idea of jihad against the infidels at its core. It was this army of Mujahedin that eventually defeated the army of the then Soviet superpower in Afghanistan. And it was from this American-backed force and its ideological discourse that the current infamous Al-Qaeda was born. The shah of Iran was wrong in his understanding of the potential and effectiveness of a powerful Islamic force in thwarting Soviet intentions in the region, just as he was wrong about the capabilities and resourcefulness of the Islamist forces that toppled his regime and forced him into exile.

It is quite interesting, though, to see how the minds of handpicked dictators function. Since they are brought to power, retained in power, and removed from power by foreign governments, they cannot fathom the idea of their own people having the ability to bring them down, to say no to the foreign puppet masters, and to manifest revolutionary subjectivity and agency of their own. These dictators who always view the local peoples as "their subjects" can never believe in the possibility of these local subjects being in possession of a greater authority capable of resisting the imperial powers and their installed puppet regimes. From a dictator's viewpoint, there can only be one all-powerful, all-embracing force capable of dethroning dictators and changing their regimes; that force is none other than the American government. Of course, the aim here is not to imply that the U.S. government is and has always been an innocent bystander in various local and national regime changes. Quite the contrary. The United States of America has time and again interfered to remove locally elected leaders in various Southern countries, only to replace them with brutal dictators. As Wills has noted,

> Over time, American leadership substituted for that of Muhammad Mossadeq in Iran, Jacobo Arbenz Guzman in Guatemala, Patrice Lumumba in the Congo, Ngo Dinh Diem in South Vietnam, Rafael Trujillo in the Dominican Republic, Salvador Allende in Chile, Daniel Ortega in Nicaragua, Maurice Bishop in Grenada, and Manuel Noriega in Panama. (Wills, 1999, p. 53)

The overwhelming power of the U.S government to interfere in the affairs of others does not preclude the fact that, irrespective of the wants and desires of that government, the local peoples posses the power to resist oppression. They are capable of deposing regimes such as that of the shah of Iran on their own and independently of the influence of foreign forces. It is a basic defining characteristic of human agency and subjectivity that a people ought to be able to determine its destiny independently of any external, colonial, or coercive imposition. This need for independence and autonomy applies to individual growth and development as well as to collective self-determination. The idea of an external imperial force imposing its demands and dictates on other peoples and communities is in fact very antidemocratic and dictatorial. A clear and transparent definition of democracy ought to be realized in the freedom of a people to self-expression, self-rule, and self-governance. This is as true for nation-states such as Iran and Iraq as it is for various nationalities and ethnic groups living within these nation-states. While the demise of dictators such as Saddam Hussein of Iraq is a cause for celebration—particularly on the part of oppressed Iraqi communities such as the Kurds, Turkmens, and the minoritized Shia majority—such transformations should be accompanied by the active and voluntary involvement of these minoritized communities and local peoples.

Any positive development in acknowledging ethnic and cultural pluralism in any country in the region has positive resonance in other countries throughout the Middle East. This is mainly due to the fact that current borders separating various ethnic groups are not natural boundaries constructed through either historical processes or common consensus. Quite to the contrary. These boundaries are imposed by colonial powers and the dictates of their interests. Major Middle Eastern nationalities such as the Kurds, Azeris, Baluchs, Turkmens, and Arabs have been divided over a number of artificially created nation-states. Understandably, these communities watch very closely any cultural, sociopolitical, and democratic developments taking place in any of the neighboring countries. Such developments deeply influence their future visions and the course of their struggle.

In recent years, the occurrence of major global, regional, and local transformations has deeply disturbed the monotonous existence of the racist order in Iran and elsewhere. The breakup of the Soviet Union in the early 1990s has resulted in creation of a number of independent nation-states along Iranian borders. Some of these independent nations such as Azerbaijan and Turkmenistan have large numbers of their coethnics living as distinct ethnic groups within Iranian borders. The independence of northern Azerbaijan and Turkmenistan has elevated the Azeri and Turkmeni languages to the status of national/official languages in these countries. In and of itself, this major development alone is quite enough to send shockwaves through the structure of the racist order in Iran, which continues to undermine the legitimacy of Azeri and Turkmeni languages by identifying them as backward, "unscientific," and merely primitive local accents.

In similar veins, the neighboring countries of Afghanistan and Iraq have also been witnessing significant sociopolitical transformations, particularly in the area of recognition of ethnic and linguistic plurality in these societies. As a result of these changes, the two previous totalitarian states are now in the process of introducing major sociopolitical developments regarding cultural, ethnic, linguistic, and religious plurality among their populations. For instance, the new constitution of Afghanistan, while adopting the two languages of Dari and Pashto as official/national tongues in the country, has recognized multilingualism as state policy by giving recognition to all local, regional, and national languages to be studied in schools and universities. Likewise, Iraq's interim constitution has adopted Kurdish and Arabic languages as the two official languages in the country, while giving democratic recognition to the use of other local/regional languages. These positive developments, of course, have not gone unnoticed by Iran's various oppressed nationalities such as the Kurds, Azeris, Baluchs, Turkmens, Arabs, and others. As a result, these minoritized groups have now intensified their legitimate demands for cultural, linguistic, religious, and political rights in Iran.

Any democratic development in one part of the Middle East impacts on other parts, and a real democratic change can only be possible in the Middle East if it is envisioned within the context of a greater democratic Middle East, resembling something like the current European Union. A Middle East where various ethnic groups are free to interact with their coethnics within various boundaries and share their collective history, culture, and language would be capable of giving rise to the existence of truly democratic nation-states within itself. The right to self-determination ought to be acknowledged as a democratic human right and entrenched in the constitution of any democratic government. As long as terms such as autonomy and self-determination are demonized and criminalized, there will be no freedom from the clutches of chauvinistic fundamentalism. The way to defeat fundamentalism is not through denying and suppressing our differences but in respecting and celebrating them. And such a respect must be engrained as a fundamental right for self-determination in the constitution of any democratic society, particularly multiethnic and multicultural ones. As Joshua Fishman has astutely observed, "Ethnicity grows stronger when denied, oppressed, or repressed, and becomes more reasonable and more tractable when recognized and liberated" (1976, p. 118).

REFERENCES AND
FURTHER READING

Abdo, N. (1996). *Sociological Thought Beyond Eurocentric Theory*. Toronto: Canadian Scholars' Press.

Abidini, H. (1980). *Sad sal dastan nevisi* [One Hundred Years of Fiction Writing]. Tehran: Tondar.

Abrahamian, E. (1970). Communism and Communalism in Iran: The Tudah and the Firqah-i Dimukrat. *International Journal of Middle East Studies* 1(4): 291–316.

——— (1979). The Causes of the Constitutional Revolution in Iran. *International Journal of Middle East Studies* 10(3): 381–414.

——— (1982). *Iran between Two Revolutions*. Princeton, NJ: Princeton University Press.

——— (1989). *Radical Islam: The Iranian Mojahedin*. London: Routledge.

Abu-Lughod, J. (1987). The Islamic City: Historic Myth, Islamic Essence, and Contemporary Relevance. *International Journal of Middle East Studies* 19: 167–171.

Adam, J., and H. Tiffin (Eds.). (1991). *Past the Last Post: Theorizing Post-Colonialism and Post-Modernism*. London: Harvester.

ADF (Azerbaycan Demokrat Firqesi). (1946). *Shahrivarin 12si* [The 12th of Shahrivar/September]. Tabriz: ADF Publications.

Afary, J. (1996). *The Iranian Constitutional Revolution, 1906–11*. New York: Columbia University Press.

Afshar, H. (Ed.). (1985). *Iran: A Revolution in Turmoil*. London: Suny Press.

Afshar, I. (Ed.). (1985). *Namvare-ye Dr Mahmood Afshar* [Essays in Honor of Dr. Mahmud Afshar]. Tehran: Chapkhane-ye Bahman.

——— (Ed.). (1989). *Zaban-e Farsi dar Azerbaijan: dar bargirandeh-ye bisto-haft maqaleh az neveshteh-haye daneshmandan va zabanshinasan* [Persian Language in Azerbaijan: Containing Twenty-Seven Articles from Scholars and Linguists]. Tehran: Bonyad-e Movqufat-e Dr Mahmud Afshar.

——— (1990a). *Haftad maqaleh* [Seventy Articles]. Tehran: Intisharat-e Asatir.

——— (1990b). *Maqalat-e Iranshenasi* [Articles on Iranology]. Tehran: Mu'asseseh-ye Entesharati va Amuzeshi-ye Nasl-e Danesh.

Afshar, M. (1925). Aghaznameh [The Beginning]. *Ayandeh* 1(1): 5–6.

Agasioglu, F. (2000). *Azer Xalqi* [The Azer People]. Baki: Chashioglu Neshriyyati.

Agger, B. (1992). *The Discourse of Domination: From the Frankfurt School to Postmodernism*. Evanston, IL: Northwestern University Press.

Aghajanian, A. (1983). Ethnic Inequality in Iran: An Overview. *International Journal of Middle East Studies* 15: 211–224.

Ahmed, A. (1992). *In Theory: Classes, Nations, Literatures*. London: Verso.

Ahmed, A.S. (1992). *Postmodernism and Islam*. London: Routledge.

Ahmed, F. (1976). Pakistan: The New Dependence. *Race & Class* xviii(1): 3–22.

Akpinar, Y. (1994). *Azeri edebiyati araştırmaları* [Explorations in Azeri Literature]. Istanbul: Dergah Yayinlari.

Al-Ahwazi Arabs. (2002). An Open Letter from the Ahwazi- Arabs for Freedom and Democracy in Iran to Mr Maurice Copithorne, the Special Representative of the UN High Commissioner for Human Rights (UNHCHR). *Al-Ahram Weekly*, December 19–25, 2002, issue no. 617, Letters to the Editor section.

Albright, M.K. (March 17, 2000). "American-Iranian Relations." Secretary of State Madeleine K. Albright Remarks before the American-Iranian Council, March 17, 2000, Washington, DC. As released by the Office of the Spokesman, U.S. Department of State. Online document: http://www.fas.org/news/iran/2000/000317.htm.

Al-e Ahmad, J. (1962/1982). *Plagued by the West*. P. Sprachman (Trans.). New York: Caravan Books.

—— (1970) *Seh-tar*. Third printing. Tehran: Amirkabir.

—— (1978a). *Dar khedmat va khiyanat-e rovshanfekran* [On the Service and Betrayal of the Intellectuals]. Tehran: Intisharat-e Kharazmi.

—— (1978b). *Gharb-zadegi* [Westoxication / Plagued by the West]. Tehran: Ravaq.

Alexander, M.J., and C.T. Mohanty (Eds.). (1997). *Feminist Genealogies, Colonial Legacies, Democratic Futures*. London: Routledge.

Alexander, Y., and A. Nanes (Eds.). (1980). *The United States and Iran: A Documentary History*. Frederick, MD: University Publications of America.

Algar, H. (1969). *Religion and State in Iran in 1785–1906: The Role of the Ulama in the Qajar Period*. Berkeley, CA and Los Angeles, CA: University of California Press.

—— (Trans.). (1980). *Constitution of the Islamic Republic of Iran*. Berkely: Mizan Press.

Ali, T. (2002). *The Clash of Fundamentalisms: Crusades, Jihads and Modernity*. London and New York: Verso.

Aliev, S.M. (1966). The Problems of Nationalities in Contemporary Persia. *Central Asian Review* XIV(1): 62–70.

Al-Mas'udi, A.A. (1967). *Kitab al-Tanbih wa-l-ishraf*. Bibliotheca Geographorum Arabicorum, VIII. M.J. de Goeje (Ed.). Leiden: E.J. Brill.

Al-Muqaddasi, S. (1906). *Ahsan ut-Taqasim fi ma'rifat ul-aqalim*. Bibliotheca Geographorum Arabicorum. M.J. de Goeje (Ed.). Leiden: E.J. Brill.

Althusser, L. (1965). *Pour Marx* [For Marx]. Paris: Maspero.

Altstadt, A.L. (1992). *The Azerbaijani Turks: Power and Identity under Russian Rule*. Stanford, CA: Hoover Institution Press.

Amanat, A. (1989). *Resurrection and Renewal: The Making of the Babi Movement in Iran: 1844–1850*. Ithaca, NY: Cornell University Press, 1989.

Amin, S. (1989). *Eurocentrism: Critique of an Ideology*. New York: Monthly Review Press.

—— (1992). *The Empire of Chaos*. New York: Monthly Review Press.

Amnesty International. (1987). *Iran: Amnesty International Briefing*. London: Amnesty International Publications.

—— (1990). *Iran: Violations of Human Rights*. New York: AI Publications.

Amuzegar, J. (1991). *The Dynamics of the Iranian Revolution: The Pahlavis' Triumph and Tragedy*. Albany, NY: State University of New York Press.

Anderson, B. (1983). *Imagined Communities: Reflections on the Origin and Spread of Nationalism*. London: Verso.

Ansari, A.M. (2003). *Modern Iran since 1921: The Pahlavis and After*. London: Longman.

Ansari, M. (1974). The History of Khuzistan, 1878–1925: A Study in Provincial Autonomy and Change. Unpublished DPhil Dissertation, University of Chicago, Illinois.

Anzaldua, G. (1987). How to Tame a Wild Tongue. In Russell Ferguson, M. Gever, T.T. Minh-ha, and C. West (Eds.), *Out There: Marginalization and Contemporary Cultures* (pp. 204–211). New York: New Museum of Contemporary Art.

Arani, T. (1924). Azerbayjan ya yek masaleh-ye hayati va mamati-ye iran [Azerbaijan, or a Vital Issue of Iran]. *Farhangestan* 1(1): 247–254.

Arberry, A.J. (1953). *The Legacy of Persia.* Oxford: Oxford University Press.

——— (1955). *The Koran Interpreted.* New York: Macmillan.

Ardebili, A. (1999). Dadnameh-ye Azerbaijan [Azerbaijan's Grievance]. *Tribun* 2(4): 211–345.

Arfa, H. (1964). *Under Five Shahs.* London: John Murray.

Arjomand, S.A. (Ed.). (1984). *From Nationalism to Revolutionary Islam: Essays on Social Movements in the Contemporary near and Middle East.* Albany, NY: State University of New York Press.

Aronowitz, S. (1988). *Science as Power: Discourse and Ideology in Modern Society.* Minneapolis, MN: University of Minnesota Press.

Aryanpur, Y. (1988). *Az Saba ta Nima: tarikh-e sad-o-panjah sal adab-e farsi* [From Saba to Nima: One-Hundred-Fifty Years History of Persian Literature]. Saarbrucken, Germany: Intisharat-e Navid.

Asgharzadeh, A. (1999). Reflections on Debate over Civil Society in Iran. *Qurtulush* 3(8): 14–27.

——— (2000). Notes on Azeri/Turk Dichotomy. *Ildirim* 1(4): 16–21.

——— (2001). The Flagpole. *Journal of Central Asian Literature* 1(1): 41–52. Online document: cenasia-fiction.netfirms.com/asgharzadehsara.html (access date: December 20, 2001).

——— (2002). Linguistic Racism and Its Ramifications: The Iranian Case. *Journal of Postcolonial Education* 1(2): 3–27.

——— (2004a). Islamic Fundamentalism, Globalization, and Migration: New Challenges for Canada. In R. Folson (Ed.), *Calculated Kindness: Global Restructuring, Immigration and Settlement in Canada* (pp. 130–150) Halifax: Fernwood Publishing.

——— (2004b). Book review of N.R. Keddie and R. Matthee (Eds.), *Iran and the Surrounding World: Interactions in Culture and Cultural Politics.* Seattle, WA: University of Washington Press. *The American Journal of Islamic Social Sciences* 21(2): 100–104.

——— (July 2004). Festival of Babek: The Living Soul of Azerbaijan's History. *Durna.* Online document: http://www.google.ca/search?q=cache:nYrJ6UP-F9IJ:www.durna.info/bebek_asgerzade.htm+festival+of+Babek&hl=en.

——— (2005). Book review of Sh. Vatanabadi and M. Mehdi Khorrami (Trans. and Eds.), *Another Sea, Another Shore: Persian Stories of Migration.* Northampton, MA: Interlink Books. *The American Journal of Islamic Social Sciences* 22(1): 128–130.

Asgharzadeh, A., E. Lawson, K. Oka, and A. Wahab (Eds.). (2007). *Diasporic Ruptures: Globality, Migrancy, and Expressions of Identity.* Vols. 1 and 2. Rotterdam: Sense Publishers.

Ashcroft, B., G. Griffiths, and H. Tiffin. (1989). *The Empire Writes Back: Theory and Practice in Postcolonial Literature.* London: Routledge.

——— (Eds.). (1995). *The Postcolonial Studies Reader.* London: Routledge.

Atabaki, T. (1993). *Azerbaijan: Ethnicity and Autonomy in Twentieth-Century Iran.* London: British Academic Press.

Atkinson, J. (1832). *The Shahnameh of Ferdowsi.* London.

Azerbaycan Danishir. (June 28, 2003). *Azerbaijan Speaks..* Online document: http://manifestimiz.persianblog.com/ (access date: July 11, 2003).

Azeri, A. (1955). *Qiyam-e Sheykh Mohammad-e Khiyabani dar Tabriz* [The Revolt of Sheikh Mohammed Khiabani in Tabriz]. Tehran: Bongah-e Safi Ali Shah.

Azeri, F. (Ed.). (1955). *Women of Iran: The Conflict with Fundamentalist Islam.* London: Ithaca Press.

Azimi-Qadim, H.A. (2004). "Fars-zadegi: Mari Khosh Khatt-o Khal" [Fars-Strickenness: A Colorful Charming Snake]. Online document: http://ezimi-qedim.blogspot.com/ (access date: November 25, 2004).

Azizi-Banitorof, Y. (1979). *Dar bareh-ye a'raab-e Khuzestan* [On Khuzestani Arabs]. Tehran: Nashr-e Azar.

———— (1993). *Qabayel va ashayer-e arab-e Khuzestan* [The Arab Ethnicities and Tribes of Khuzestan]. Tehran (self-published).

———— (1996). *Afsaneh-há-ye mardom-e arab-e Khuzestan* [The Legends of Arabs of Khuzistan]. Tehran: Anzan.

———— (2002). *Hoviyyat va tabar-e Arabha-ye Khuzistan* [Identity and Lineage of Khuzistani Arabs]. Online document: http://www.tribun.com/ (access date: October 17, 2002).

———— (2003). *Qomiyyatha va Tovse'e dar Iran* [Ethnicities and Development in Iran]. Online document: http://www.tribun.com/800/811.htm.

———— (November 28, 2002). *Goftogu-ye ruznameh-ye e'temad ba Yusof Azizi-Banitorof, dastan-nevis va pajuhesh-gar-e farhang-e mardom-e arab* [An interview with Yusof Azizi-Banitorof, the Storyteller and Researcher of the Culture of Arab People]. Online document: http://www.tribun.com/ (access date: November 28, 2002).

Bailey, H.W. (1987). Arya. *Encyclopedia Iranica* 2(97): 681–683.

Baker, D. (1978). Race and Power: Comparative Approaches to the Analysis of Race Relations. *Ethnic and Racial Studies* 1(3): 316–335.

Bakhash, Sh. (1978). *Iran: Monarchy, Bureaucracy, and Reform under the Qajars, 1858–1896.* London: Ithaca Press.

———— (1984). *The Reign of the Ayatollahs: Iran and the Islamic Revolution.* 2nd ed. New York: Basic Books.

Bakhtin, M.M. (1980). *The Word in the Novel. Comparative Criticism: A Yearbook* (pp. 213–220). Vol. 2. Cambridge: Cambridge University Press.

———— (1981). *The Dialogic Imagination.* C. Emerson and M. Holquist (Trans.), M. Holquist (Ed.). Austin, TX: University of Texas Press.

———— (1986). *Speech Genres and Other Late Essays.* V. McGee (Trans.), C. Emerson and M. Holquist (Eds.). Austin, TX: University of Texas Press.

Balibar, E. (1994). *Masses, Classes, Ideas: Studies on Politics and Philosophy before and after Marx.* J. Swenson (Trans.). New York and London: Routledge.

Balochistan-e-Raji Zrombesh. (2004). *National Movement of Baluchistan.* Online document: http://www.zrombesh.org/ (access date: December 5, 2004).

Banani, A. (1961). *The Modernization of Iran, 1921–1941.* Stanford, CA: Stanford University Press.

Baraheni, R. (1968). *Tala dar mes* [Gold in Copper]. Tehran: Nashr-e Zaman.

———— (1977). *The Crowned Cannibals: Writings on Repression in Iran.* New York: Vintage Books.

———— (1984). *Tarikh-e mozakkar: farhang-e hakem va farhang-e mahkum* [Masculine History: The Dominant Culture and the Subjugated Culture]. Tehran: Nashr-e Avval.

———— (1989). *Junun-e neveshtan* [The Madness of Writing]. Tehran: Resam.

———— (1998). The Poet as Prisoner: Language and Creative Imagination in Exile. *Reflections,* Summer 1998: 21–24.

——— (June 9, 2006). "Surat-e masale-ye Azerbayjan?/Hall-e masale-ye Azerbayjan?" [The Face of Azerbaijani Problem?/The Solution of Azerbaijani Problem?] *Shahrvand* 16(1077). Online document: http://www.shahrvand.com/FA/ Default.asp?Content=NW&CD=PL&NID=33#BN1077 (access date: June 10, 2006).

Barfield, T.J. (2002). Turk, Persian, and Arab: Changing Relationships between Tribes and State in Iran and along Its Frontiers. In N.R. Keddie and R. Matthee (Eds.), *Iran and the Surrounding World: Interactions in Culture and Cultural Politics* (pp. 61–87). Seattle, WA: University of Washington Press.

Barman, J., Y. Hébert, and D. McCaskill (Eds.). (1986). *Indian Education in Canada. Vol. I: The Legacy.* Vancouver, WA: UBC Press.

Bashiriyeh, H. (1984). *The State and Revolution in Iran, 1962–1982.* New York: St. Martin's Press.

Bayat, M. (1982). *Mysticism and Dissent: Socioreligious Thought in Qajar Iran.* Syracuse, NY: Syracuse University Press.

Beck, L. (1986). *The Qashqa'i of Iran.* New Haven, CT: Yale University Press.

Behdad, A. (1994). *Belated Travelers: Orientalism in the Age of Colonial Dissolution.* Durham, NC and London: Duke University Press.

Behrangi, A. (1999). *Baradaram Samad Behrangi: revayet-e zendegi-ye u* [My Brother Samad Behrangi: A Narrative of His Life]. Tabriz: Nashr-e Behrangi.

Behrangi, S. (1969a). *Kandokav dar masa'el-e tarbiyati-ye Iran* [Investigations into the Educational Problems of Iran]. Tehran: Shabgir.

——— (1969b). Adabiyyat-e kudakan [Children's Literature]. In *Majmueh-ye Maqaleh-ha* [Collection of Essays] (pp. 120–129). Tabriz: Intsharat-e Shams.

——— (1969c). Kechal-e kaftarbaaz [The Bald Pigeon-Keeper]. In *Qesseha-ye Behrang* [Stories of Behrang] (pp. 141–166). Tabriz: Intsharat-e Shams.

——— (1976). *The Little Black Fish and Other Modern Persian Stories.* E. Hooglund and M. Hooglund (Trans.). Washington, DC: Three Continents Press.

Behrangi, S., and B. Dehqani. (1970). *Afsaneh-ha-ye Azerbaijan* [Tales of Azerbaijan]. 2 Vols. Tehran: Nil.

Behzadi, B. (1990). *Farhang-e Azerbaijani-Farsi* [A Dictionary of Azerbaijani-Farsi]. Tehran: Entesharat-e Donya.

Benjamin, R. (2003). *Orientalist Aesthetics: Art, Colonialism, and French North Africa, 1880–1930.* Berkeley, CA and Los Angeles, CA: University of California Press.

Berengian, S. (1988). *Azeri and Persian Literary Works in Twentieth Century Azerbaijan.* Berlin: Schwarz.

Bernal, M. (1987). *Black Athena: The Afro-Asiatic Roots of Classical Civilization. vol. I, the Fabrication of Ancient Greece 1785–1985.* London: Free Association Books; New Brunswick, NJ: Rutgers University Press.

——— (1991). *Black Athena: The Afro-Asiatic Roots of Classical Civilization. vol. 2, the Archaeological and Documentary Evidence.* London: Free Association Books; New Brunswick, NJ: Rutgers University Press.

——— (2001). *Black Athena Writes Back: Martin Bernal Responds to His Critics.* Durham, NC and London: Duke University Press.

Beygi, M.B. (1989). *Bokhara-ye Man Eyl-e Man* [My Bokhara, My Tribe]. Tehran: Agah.

Bhabha, H. (1990) *DissemiNation: Time, Narrative, and the Margins of the Modern Nation.* In H. Bhabha (Ed.), *Nation and Narration* (pp. 291–322). London: Routledge.

——— (1994). *The Location of Culture.* London: Routledge.

Birdoğan, N. (2001). *Shah Ismail Hatai: Yashami ve Yapitlari* [Shah Ismail Khatayi: His Life and Works]. Ankara: Kaynak Yayinlari.

Biruni, A.R. (1879). *The Chronology of Ancient Nations.* C.E. Sachau (Trans.). London: W.H.. Allen.

Blucher, W. (1949). *Zeitwende in Iran.* Ravensburg: Biberach an der Riss.

Boas, F. (1974). *Race, Language, and Culture.* New York: Macmillan.

Bohrer, F.N. (2003). *Orientalism and Visual Culture: Imagining Mesopotamia in Nineteenth-Century Europe.* Cambridge: Cambridge University Press.

Bosworth, C.E. (Ed.). (1971). *Iran and Islam.* Edinburgh: Edinburgh University Press.

Bosworth, C.E., and C. Hillenbrand (Eds.). (1983). *Qajar Iran: Political, Social, and Cultural Change, 1800–1925.* Edinburgh: Edinburgh University Press.

Bourdieu, P. (1977). *Outline of a Theory of Practice.* R. Nice (Trans.). Cambridge: University Press. (Original work published 1972 as *Esquisse d'une théorie de la pratique, précédé de trois études d'ethnologie Kabyle.* Geneva, Droz, 1972.)

——— (1991). *Language and Symbolic Power.* G. Raymond and M. Adamson (Trans.). Cambridge, MA: Harvard University Press.

Bourdieu, P., J.C. Passeron, and M. Saint-Martin. (1994). *Academic Discourse: Linguistic Misunderstanding and Professorial Power.* Cambridge: Polity.

Bower, B. (1991). Race Falls from Grace. *Science News* 38(140): 8–15.

Browne, E.G. (1910). *The Persian Revolution of 1905–1909.* London: Cambridge University Press.

——— (1925–1928). *A Literary History of Persia.* 4 Vols. Cambridge: Cambridge University Press.

Burrow, T. (1973). The Proto Indo-Aryans. *Journal of the Royal Asiatic Society* 1(2): 123–140.

Burton, F., and P. Carlen. (1979). *Official Discourse: On Discourse Analysis, Government Publications, Ideology and the State.* London: Routledge & Kegan Paul.

Caldas-Coulthard, C.R., and M. Coulthard (Eds.). (1996). *Texts and Practices: Readings in Critical Discourse Analysis.* London: Routledge.

Calhoun, C. (1995). *Critical Social Theory.* Oxford: Blackwell.

Cameron, D. (Ed.). (1990). *The Feminist Critique of Language: A Reader.* London: Routledge.

——— (1992). *Feminism and Linguistic Theory.* 2nd ed. London: Macmillan.

Card, C. (1999). On Race, Racism and Ethnicity. In L. Harris (Ed.), *Key Concepts in Critical Theory of Racism* (pp. 257–266). New York: Humanity Books.

Carnoy, M. (1974). *Education as Cultural Imperialism.* New York: David McKay.

Chamberlain, H. S. (1889/1912) *Foundations of the Nineteenth Century.* John Lees (Trans.). New York: John Lane.

Chamberlayne, P., J. Bornat, and T. Wengraf (Eds.). (2000). *The Turn to Biographical Methods in the Social Sciences: Comparative Issues and Examples.* London: Routledge.

Chatterjee, P. (1993). *The Nation and Its Fragments: Colonial and Postcolonial Histories.* Princeton, NJ: Princeton University Press.

Chehabi, H.E. (1990). *Iranian Politics and Religious Modernism: The Liberation Movement of Iran under the Shah and Khomeini.* Ithaca, NY: Cornell University Press.

——— (1997). Ardabil Becomes a Province: Center-Periphery Relations in Iran. *International Journal of Middle East Studies* 29(2): 235–253.

Childe, V.G. (1926). *The Aryans: A Study of Indo-European Origins.* London: Kegan Paul.

Childs, P., and P. Williams. (1997). *An Introduction to Post-Colonial Theory.* New York: Prentice Hall.

Christensen, P. (1993). *The Decline of Iranshahr: Irrigation and Environments in the History of the Middle East, 500 B.C. to A.D 1500.* Copenhagen: Museum Tusculanum Press.

Chubin, Sh., and S. Zabih. (1974). *The Foreign Relations of Iran: A Developing State in a Zone of Great-Power Conflict.* Berkeley, CA and Los Angeles, CA: University of California Press.

Church, K. (1995). *Forbidden Narratives: Critical Autobiography as Social Science.* New York: Gordon & Breach.

Cole, J.R.I., and N.R. Keddie (Eds.). (1986). *Shi'ism and Social Protest.* New Haven, CT: Yale University Press.

Collins, R. (1988). *Theoretical Sociology.* San Diego, CA: San Diego Press.

Cooper, R. (1985). *The Baha'is of Iran.* London: Minority Rights Group.

Cottam, R.W. (1964). *Nationalism in Iran.* Pittsburgh: University of Pittsburgh Press.

Coulthard, R.M. (Ed.). (1994). *Advances in Written Text Analysis.* London: Routledge.

Cox, O. (1948). *Caste, Class and Race.* Garden City, NY: Doubleday.

Curzon, G. (1966). *Persia and the Persian question.* 2 Vols. London: Frank Cass.

Dandamaev, M.A. (1989). *A Political History of the Achaemenid Empire.* Leiden: E.J. Brill.

Dandamaev, M.A., and V.G. Lukonin. (1989). *The Culture and Social Institutions of Ancient Iran.* Cambridge: Cambridge University Press.

Darmesteter, J. (1883). *The Zend-Avesta, Part II: The Sirozahs, Yashts, and Nyayish.* London: Oxford University Press.

Darwin, Ch. (1859). *On the Origin of Species by Means of Natural Selection or the Preservation of Favoured Races in the Struggle for Life.* London: John Murray.

Daryabandari, N. (1989). Zaban-e Farsi, zaban-e moshtarak [Persian Language, the Common Language]. *Iran Nameh* 7(4), Summer 1989: 674–678.

Davidson Kalmar, I., and D.J. Penslar (Eds.). (2005). *Orientalism and the Jews.* Hanover and London: University Press of New England/Brandeis University Press.

Dehghani, Y. (2000). *A Grammar of Iranian Azari: Including Comparisons with Persian.* München: Lincom Europa.

Dehqani, A. (1978). *Hamase-ye moqavemat* [The Epic of Resistance]. Tehran: Jonbesh.

Dei, G.J.S. (1996). *Anti-Racism Education: Theory and Practice.* Halifax: Fernwood Publishing.

——— (1999). Knowledge and Politics of Social Change: The Implications of Anti-Racism. *British Journal of Sociology of Education* 20(3): 395–409.

Dei, G.J.S., and A. Asgharzadeh. (2001). The Power of Social Theory: The Anti-Colonial Discursive Framework. *Journal of Educational Thought* 35(3): 297–323.

——— (2003). Language, Education and Development: Case Studies from Southern Contexts. *Language and Education: An International Journal* 17(6): 421–449.

——— (2004). Farewell to Edward Said. *Journal of Post Colonial Education* 2(2): 3–10.

——— (2006). "Indigenous Knowledges and Globalization: An African Perspective." In A. Abdi, K. Puplampu, and G. Dei (Eds.), *African Education and Globalization: Critical Perspectives* (pp. 53–79). Lanham, MD: Lexington Books.

Dei, G.J.S., and A. Calliste (Eds.). (2000). *Power, Knowledge, and Anti-Racism Education: A Critical Reader.* Halifax: Fernwood Publishing.

Delgado, R. (1995). Words that Wound: A Tort Action for Racial Insults, Epithets, and Name Calling. In R. Delgado (Ed.), *Critical Race Theory: The Cutting Edge* (pp. 159–168). Philadelphia, PA: Temple University Press.

Derrida, J. (1976). *Of Grammatology.* G. Spivak (Trans.). Baltimore: Johns Hopkins University Press.

———— (1994). *Specters of Marx.* P. Kamuf (Trans.). New York: Routledge.

Diakonov, M.M. (1965). *Ashkanian.* Tehran: Aban.

Diba, F. (1986). *Mohammad Mossadegh: A Political Biography.* London: Croom Helm.

Dorraj, M. (1990). *From Zarathustra to Khomeini: Populism and Dissent in Iran.* Boulder, CO and London: Lynne Rienner.

Douglas, W.O. (1951). *Strange Lands and Friendly People.* New York: Harper & Brothers.

DPK (Democratic Party of Kurdistan). (1945). FO/371/45436, November 8.

DuGay, P. (Ed.). (1997). *Production of Culture/Cultures of Production, Book 4.* London: Sage/Open University.

Duranti, A., and C. Goodwin (Eds.). (1992). *Rethinking Context: Language as an Interactive Phenomenon.* Cambridge: Cambridge University Press.

Dustkhah, J. (1970). *Avesta: nameh-ye minevi-ye ayin-e Zartoshti* [Avesta: The Heavenly Book of Zoroastrian Religion]. Tehran: Aban.

Eagleton, T. (1976). *Marxism and Literary Criticism.* Los Angeles, CA: University of California Press.

Eagleton, W. (1963). *The Kurdish Republic of 1946.* London: Oxford University Press.

Edwards, H. (2000). *Noble Dreams, Wicked Pleasures: Orientalism in America, 1870–1930.* Princeton, NJ: Princeton University Press.

Elchibey, E. (1997). *Butov Azerbaycan yolunda* [Towards a United Azerbaijan]. Ankara: Ecdad Yayinlari.

Elgar, H. (1973). *Mirza Malkum Khan: A Study in the History of Iranian Modernism.* Berkeley, CA: University of California Press.

Erfan, A. (2004). Anonymous. In Sh. Vatanabadi and M. Mehdi Khorrami (Trans. and Eds.), *Another Sea, Another Shore: Persian Stories of Migration* (pp. 207–229). Northampton, MA: Interlink Books.

Esposito, J.L. (1990). *The Iranian Revolution: It's Global Impact.* Miami, FL: Florida International University Press.

Ethnologue. (2002). *Languages of Iran.* Online document: http://www.ethnologue. com/show_country.asp?name=Iran (access date: July 14, 2002).

Fairclough, N.L. (1989). *Language and Power.* London: Longman.

———— (1992). *Discourse and Social Change.* Cambridge: Polity.

———— (1995a). *Critical Discourse Analysis: The Critical Study of Language.* Harlow, UK: Longman.

———— (1995b). *Media Discourse.* London: Edward Arnold.

Fairclough, N.L., and R. Wodak,. R. (1997). Critical Discourse Analysis. In T.A. van Dijk. (Ed.), *Discourse Studies: A Multidisciplinary Introduction. Vol. 2. Discourse as Social Interaction.* (pp. 258–284). London: Sage.

Fanon, F. (1961/1990). *The Wretched of the Earth.* 3rd ed. C. Farrington (Trans.). New York: Penguin.

———— (1967). *Black Skin, White Masks.* C.L. Markmann (Trans.). New York: Grove Press.

Farhad, A. (July 13, 2004). Against Internal Colonialism and Oppression in Iran! *Jebhe Melli Iran Political Dialogue.* Online document: http://www.jebhemelli.net/ (access date: July 13, 2004).

Farrar, F.W. (1878). *Language and Languages, Being "Chapters on Language" and "Families of Speech."* London: Longmans, Green & Co.

Farsoun, S., and M. Mashayekhi. (1992). *Iran: Political Culture in the Islamic Republic.* London: Sage.

Farzaneh, M.A. (1998) 'Zaban-e farsi va melli-gerayi-e efrati [The Persian Language and Aggressive Nationalism]. *Azerbaijan Sesi* 2(16): 19–27.

——— (September 7, 2002). Semed Behrengiye hesr olunmush verilish [Radio Program Dedicated to Samad Behrangi]. Vancouver, WA, Radio Odlar yurdu. Online document: http://www.shamstabriz.com (access date: September 7, 2002).

Fathi, A. (Ed.). (1991). *Iranian Refugees and Exiles since Khomeini.* Costa Mesa, CA: Mazda Publishers.

Fawcett, L.L. (1992). *Iran and the Cold War: The Azerbaijani Crisis of 1946.* Cambridge: Cambridge University Press.

Feagin, J.R., and H. Vera. (1995). *White Racism: The Basics.* New York: Routledge.

Ferdowsi, A. (1010/1960). *Shahnameh.* 2 Vols. Moscow: Progressive Publishing.

——— (1967). Religion in Iranian Nationalism: The Study of the Fad'iyan-e Islam. PhD dissertation, Indiana University, Indiana.

——— (1983). Women and the Islamic Revolution. *International Journal of Middle East Studies* 15(2): 284–298.

Field, C. (1939). *Persian Literature.* London: Herbert & Daniel.

Fishman, J.A. (1976). *Bilingual Education: An International Sociological Perspective.* Rowley, MA: Newbury House.

——— (1989). *Language and Ethnicity in Minority Sociolinguistic Perspective.* Clevedon and Philadelphia, PA: Multilingual Matters.

Flood, G. (Ed.). (2003). *The Blackwell Companion to Hinduism.* Oxford: Blackwell.

Folson, R. (Ed.). (2004). *Calculated Kindness: Global Restructuring, Immigration and Settlement in Canada.* Halifax: Fernwood Publishing.

Foran, J. (Ed.). (1994). *A Century of Revolution: Social Movements in Iran.* Minneapolis, MN: University of Minnesota Press.

Foucault, M. (1969). *The Archaeology of Knowledge and the Discourse on Language.* Sh. Smith (Trans.). New York: Pantheon.

——— (1977). *Discipline and Punish: The Birth of the Prison.* A. Sheridan (Trans.). New York: Vintage.

——— (1980). *Power/Knowledge: Selected Interviews and Other Writings, 1972–1977.* C. Gordon (Ed.), C. Gordon, L. Marshall, J. Mepham, and Kate Soper (Trans.). New York: Pantheon.

Fredrickson, G.M. (2002). *Racism: A Short History.* Princeton, NJ: Princeton University Press.

Freire, P. (1974). *Pedagogy of the Oppressed.* New York: Seabury.

Frow, J. (1988). *Marxism and Literary History.* 2nd ed. Cambridge, MA: Harvard University Press.

Frye, R.N. (1963). *The Heritage of Persia.* Cleveland: World Publishing.

——— (1969). *Persia.* 3rd ed. London: Allen and Unwin.

——— (1975). *The Golden Age of Persia.* London: Weidenfeld and Nicolson.

Gabriel, J., and G. Ben-Tovim. (1978). Marxism and the Concept of Racism. *Economy and Society* 7(2): 118–154.

Gandy, O.H. Jr. (Ed.). (1998). The Social Construction of Race. In *Race & Communication* (pp. 5–92). London: Edward Arnold.

Garthwaite, G. (1983). *Khans and Shahs: The Bakhtiyari in Iran.* Cambridge: Cambridge University Press.

Geertz, Clifford. (1973). *The Interpretation of Cultures: Selected Essays*. London: Basic Books.

Georgakopoulou, A., and D. Goutsos. (1997). *Discourse Analysis: An Introduction*. Edinburgh: Edinburgh University Press.

Gershevitch, I. (1967). *The Avestan Hymn to Mithra*. Cambridge: Cambridge University Press.

Ghani, C. (1998). *Iran and the Rise of Reza Shah: From Qajar Collapse to Pahlavi Rule*. London: I.B. Tauris.

Ghirshman, R. (1954). *Iran: From the Earliest Times to the Islamic Conquest*. London: Pelican.

Ghods, M.R. (1989). *Iran in the Twentieth Century*. London: Adamantine Press.

Giddens, A. (1991). *Modernity and Self-Identity: Self and Society in the Late Modern Age*. Stanford, CA: Stanford University Press.

Gobineau, J.-A. (1869). *Histoire des Perses* [History of Persia]. 2 Vols. Paris.

—— (1915). *Essai sur l'inégalité des races humaines* (*Essay on the Inequality of Human Races*). A. Collins (Trans.). London: William Heinemann.

—— (1971). *The World of the Persians*. Geneva: Editions Minerva S.A.

Gökalp, Zia. (1923/1975). *Turkish Nationalism and Western Civilizations*. N. Berkes (Trans. and Ed.). Ottawa: Greenwood.

Goldberg, D.T. (Ed.). (1998). *Racial Subjects: Writing on Race in America*. New York: Routledge.

Goldblatt, D., D. Held, A. Mcgrew, and J. Perraton. (1997). *Global Flows, Global Transformations: Concepts, Evidence and Arguments*. Cambridge: Polity.

Goodell, G. (1986). *The Elemental Structures of Political Life: Rural Development in Pahlavi Iran*. Oxford: Oxford University Press.

Gooya News. (December 27, 2002). *Shovonizm-e Rezakhani hanuz zendeh ast*. [Reza-Khani Chauvinism Is Still Alive.] Online document: http://news.gooya.com/ (access date: December 27, 2002).

Gough, J. (2000). History, Representation, Globalization and Indigenous Cultures: A Tasmanian Perspective. In C. Smith and G.K. Ward (Eds.), *Indigenous Cultures in an Interconnected World* (pp. 89–107). Vancouver, WA: UBC Press.

Gramsci, A. (1971). *The Prison Notebooks: Selections*. Q. Hoare and G.N. Smith (Trans. and Eds.). New York: International Publishers.

Grant, A.C., and J.L. Lei (Eds.). (2001). *Global Constructions of Multicultural Education: Theories and Realities*. Mahwah, NJ: Lawrence Erlbaum.

Gruhi az danesh-amuzan-e Azerbaijani [A Group of Azerbaijani Students]. (August 26, 2004). *Letter to Morteza Haji, the Minister of Education*. Madares-e Mantaqeh 3, Tehran. Online document: http://tomarlar.blogspot.com/ (access date: August 26, 2004).

Gruhi az danesh-amuzan-e Marageh [A Group of Students from the City of Maragheh]. (August 2004). *Nameh beh maqam-e moazzam-e velayat va rahbari* [A Letter to the Venerated Spiritual Leader]. August 17, 2004. Online document: http://tomarlar.blogspot.com/   http://www.durna.info/maraga_rehber.htm (access date: August 26, 2004).

Guha, R. (1988). Section 1: Methodology. In R. Guha and G.C. Spivak (Eds.), *Selected Subaltern Studies* (pp. 35–86). New York and Oxford: Oxford University Press.

Guha, R., and G.C. Spivak (Eds.). (1988). *Selected Subaltern Studies*. New York and Oxford: Oxford University Press.

Gunther, H.F.K. (1927). *The Radical Elements of European History*. G.C. Wheeler (Trans.). London: Methuen.

Habermas, J. (1981). *Theory of Communicative Action.* 2 Vols. T. McCarthy (Trans.). Cambridge: Polity.

Hairi, A.H. (1977). *Shi'ism and Constitutionalism in Iran.* Leiden: E.J. Brill.

Hakimi, M.R. (1979). *Adabiyyat va ta'ahhod dar Islam* [Literature and Commitment in Islam]. Tehran: Daftar-e Nashr-e Farhang-e Islami.

Hall, S. (Ed.). (1997). *Representation: Cultural Representation and Signifying Practices.* London: Sage/Open University.

Halliday, F. (1979). *Iran: Dictatorship and Development.* Harmondsworth, NY: Penguin.

Hamavi, Y. (1866). *Kitab mo'jam al-buldan,* vol. 1 [A Lexicon of Cities]. F. Wustenfeld (Trans.). Leipzig: Brockhaus.

Hamshahri [Tehran's Persian Daily]. (May 27, 2000). Name-yi az Kurdistan [A Letter from Kurdistan]. Tehran: Hamshahri Publications.

Hanson, B. (1983). The Westoxication of Iran: Depictions and Reactions of Behrangi, Al-e Ahmad and Shariati. *International Journal of Middle Eastern Studies* 15: 1–23.

Haqqi, B. (1993). *Lahezati az zendegi-ye Safar Qehremanian* [Moments from the Life of Safar Qahramanian]. Alman: Neshr-e Azerbaycan.

Haraway, D. (1988). Situated Knowledges: The Science Question in Feminism and the Privilege of Partial Perspective. *Feminist Studies* 14(3): 575–579.

Hassanpour, A. (1991). State Policy on the Kurdish Language: The Politics of Status Planning. *Kurdish Times* (New York) 4(1–2): 42–85.

——— (1992a). *Nationalism and Language in Kurdistan, 1918–1985.* New York: Mellen Research University Press.

——— (1992b). The Pen and the Sword: Literacy, Education and Revolution in Kurdistan. In P. Freebody and A. Welsh (Eds.), *Knowledge, Culture and Power: International Perspectives on Literacy as Policy and Practice* (pp. 23–54). London: Falmer Press.

——— (1993). The Internationalization of Language Conflict: The Case of Kurdish. In E. Fraenkel and C. Kramer (Eds.), *Language Contact-Language Conflict* (pp. 107–155). New York: Peter Lang.

——— (1994). The Nationalist Movements in Azerbaijan and Kurdistan, 1941–46. In J. Foran (Ed.), *A Century of Revolution: Social Movements in Iran* (pp. 78–104). Minneapolis, MN: University of Minnesota Press.

——— (2000). The Politics of A-Political Linguistics: Linguists and Linguicide. In Robert Phillipson (Ed.), *Rights to Language: Equity, Power, and Education: Celebrating the 60th Birthday of Tove Skutnabb-Kangas* (pp. 33–39). Mahwah, NJ: Lawrence Erlbaum.

Hay, S.N. (1970). *Asian Ideas of East and West: Tagore and His Critics in Japan, China, and India.* Cambridge, MA: Harvard University Press.

Hayes, C. (1928). *Essays on Nationalism.* New York: Macmillan.

Hedayat, S. (1962). *Seh qatreh khun* [Three Drops of Blood]. 6th impression. Tehran: Amir Kabir.

——— (1980). *Afsane-ye afarinesh: kheymeh-shab bazi dar seh pardeh* [The Myth of Creation: A Puppet Show in Three Acts]. Encino, CA: Ketab Corp.

——— (1984). *Blind Owl and Other Hedayat Stories.* C.L. Sayers (Comp.), R.P. Christensen (Ed.). Minneapolis, MN: Sorayya Publishers.

Heidegger, M. (1977). *The Question Concerning Technology and Other Essays.* L.William (Ed., Intro., and Trans.). New York: Harper & Row.

Heikal, M. (1981). *The Return of the Ayatollah.* London: André Deutsch.

Hekmat, A.A. (1957). Some Aspects of Modern Iran. *Islamic Culture* 31: 90–92.

Henderson, R.C. (1998). Letter to President Khatami, January. Online document: http://www.bahaindex.com/modules.php?name=News&file=article&sid=230 (access date: March 1999).

Hendessi, M. (1990). *Armed Angels: Women in Iran*. London: Zed Books.

Herman, E.S., and N. Chomsky. (1988). *Manufacturing Consent: The Political Economy of the Mass Media*. New York: Pantheon.

Herodotus (1954). *The Histories*. A. de Selincourt (Trans.). London: Penguin.

Heyat, J. (1983). Regression of Azeri Language and Literature under the Oppressive Period of Pahlavi. Paper prepared in advance for participants of The First International Conference on Turkic Studies, Indiana University, Indiana, May 19–22, 1983.

―――― (1990). *Azerbaycan edebiyyat tarixine bir baxish* [A Look at the History of Azerbaijani Literature]. Tehran: Sazman-e Chap-e Khajeh.

―――― (1993) Azerbaycanin adi ve serhedleri [Azerbaijan's Name and Borders]. *Varliq* 15(90–93): 3–13.

Heyat-e Rahbari-ye Jebhe-ye Melli-ye Iran [The Leadership Committee of Iran's National Front] (February 9, 2004). Name-ye sargoshadeh: Janab Aqay-e Morteza Haji, Vazir-e Amuzesh-o-Parvaresh [An Open Letter to Mr Morteza Haji, the Minister of Education]. Published in *Iran-e Emrooz*, February 12, 2004. Online document: http://news.iran-emrooz.de/more.php?id=3041_0_7_0_M (access date: February 12, 2004).

Hijri, M. (2001). *Interview with Mostafa Hijri: Iranian Kurds: Political and Cultural Inequalities and Their Solution*. Translated from Farsi, in *Rah-e Kargar* [The Worker's Way] (169), Winter 2001. Online document: http://www. iranbulletin.org/interview/MOSTAF1.html (access date: February 25, 2001).

Hinz, W. (1964–1973). *The Lost World of Elam*. Columbia: Columbia University Press.

Hitler, A. (1925/1943). *Mein kampf*. R. Manheim (Trans.). Boston: Houghton Mifflin.

Holquist, M. (1992). *Introduction to the Dialogic Imagination: Four Essays by M.M. Bakhtin*. Austin, TX: University of Texas Press.

hooks, b. (1994). *Outlaw Culture: Resisting Representations*. New York: Routledge.

Hoveyda, F. (1979). *The Fall of the Shah*. London: Weidenfeld and Nicolson.

Hulme, P. (1986). *Colonial Encounters: Europe and the Native Caribbean, 1492–1797*. London: Methuen.

HRW (Human Rights Watch). (2001). *World Report 2002*, "*Iran*." New York, 2001. Online document: http://hrw.org/wr2k2/mena3.html (access date: July 14, 2002).

Hunter, S.T. (1992). *Iran after Khomeini*. New York: Praeger.

Ibn Faqih, A.A.H. (1970). *Kitab al-buldan* [A Book of Cities]. Tehran: Bonyad-e Farhang-e Iran.

Ibn Howqal, S. (1966). *Surat al-arz* [Face of the Earth]. J. Shoar (Ed.). Tehran: Bonyad-e Farhang-e Iran.

Iran Newspaper. (May 12, 2006). Cheh konim ta soosk-ha sooskeman nakonand. Special edition for kids section, *Iran Newspaper*, May 12. Online document: http://www.iran-newspaper.com/1385/850302/html/index.htm (access date: May 25, 2006).

Iran-e Emrooz [Iranian Political Bulletin]. (March 15, 2004). Piramoon-e tazahorat-e mardom dar shahrhay-e Kurdestan-e Iran [Regarding Demonstrations in Iranian Kurdish towns]. Online document: http://www.iran-emrooz.net/ (access date: March 15, 2004).

Iraqi Governing Council. (2004). Iraq's Transitional Administrative Law. *Washington Post*, March 8, p. A13. Online document: http://www.washingtonpost.com/ac2/wpdyn?pagename=article&contentId=A39825–2004Mar8&notFound=true.

Irfani, S. (1983). *Iran's Islamic Revolution: Popular Liberation or Religious Dictatorship*. London: Zed Books.

Islamic Republic of Iran (1990). *A Statistical Reflection of the Islamic Republic of Iran*. No. 6, August. Tehran: Markaz-e Amar-e Iran [Statistical Centre of Iran].

——— (1992). *Qanun-e mojazat-e islami: majmue-ye qavanin-e sal-e 1370* [Islamic Criminal Law: Listing of the Laws for the Year 1991]. Ruzname-ye Rasmi [The Government's Official Newsletter].

——— (1995). *Multi-Round Population Survey, 1991: National Results*. Tehran: Markaz-e Amar-e Iran [Statistical Centre of Iran].

Ismael, T.Y. (1982). *Iraq and Iran: Roots of Conflict*. Syracuse, NY: Syracuse University Press.

Issawi, C. (1971). *The Economic History of Iran, 1800–1914*. Chicago, IL: University of Chicago Press.

Istakhri, A.I.I.I.M. (1961). *Kitab al-Masalik wa al-Mamalik* [Book of Roads and Kingdoms]. Cairo.

Jackson, A.W. (1899). *Zoroaster, the Prophet of Ancient Iran*. London and New York: Macmillan.

Jamalzadeh, M.A. (1954). *Farsi shakar ast* [Persian Is Sugar]. Tehran: Gotanbirg.

JAMI (Jebhe-ye azadi-ye mardum-e Iran). (1983). *Gozashteh cheragh rah-e ayandeh ast* [The Past Is the Light on the Path to Future]. Tehran: Agah.

Jasanoff, J.H., and A. Nussbaum. (1996). Word Games: The Linguistic Evidence in Black Athena. In M.R. Lefkowitz and G.M. Rogers (Eds.), *Black Athena Revisited* (pp. 177–205). Chapel Hill, NC and London: University of North Carolina Press.

Jersild, A. (2002). *Orientalism and Empire: North Caucasus Mountain Peoples and the Georgian Frontier, 1845–1917*. Montreal: McGill-Queen's University Press.

Jones, S.W. (1784). *A Discourse on the Institution of a Society for Inquiring into the History of Asia*. Delivered at Calcutta, January 15, 1784. London.

——— (1788). On the Hindu's [*sic*]. *Asiatic Researches* 1: 415–431.

Kabbani, R. (1986). *Europe's Myths of Orient*. London: Pandora Press.

Kalmar, I.D., and D. Penslar (Eds.). (2005). *Orientalism and the Jews*. Hanover, NH: University Press of New England.

Kaseb, A. (1989). *Monhani-ye qodrat dar tarikh-e iran* [The Circle of Power in Iran's History]. Tehran: A. Kaseb.

Kashani-Sabet, F. (1999). *Frontier Fictions: Shaping the Iranian Nation, 1804–1946*. Princeton, NJ: Princeton University Press

——— (2002). Cultures of Iranianness: The Evolving Polemic of Iranian Nationalism. In N.R. Keddie and R. Matthee (Eds.), *Iran and the Surrounding World: Interactions in Culture and Cultural Politics* (pp. 162–181). Seattle, WA: University of Washington Press.

Kashgari, M. (1073/1996). *Divan luget at-Turk*. M. Siyaqi (Trans.). Tehran: Pajuheshgah-e Olum-e Ensani ve Motaleat-e Farhangi.

Kasravi, A. (1925). *Azari ya zaban-e bastani-ye Azerbaigan* [Azeri or the Ancient Language of Azerbaijan]. Tehran: Taban.

——— (1941). *Tarikh-e hejdah Saleh-ye Azerbaijan* [Eighteen-Years History of Azerbaijan]. Tehran: Intsharat-e Amirkabir.

Kasravi, A. (1991). *Dar piramun-e adabiyyat* [On Literature]. Bethesda, MD: Ketab-forushi-ye Iran.

Katouzian, H. (1981). *The Political Economy of Modern Iran: Despotism and Pseudo-Modernism, 1926–1979.* New York: New York University Press.
——— (1999). *Musaddiq and the Struggle for Power in Iran.* London: I.B. Tauris.
——— (2003). Riza Shah's Political Legitimacy and Social Base, 1921–1941. In S. Cornin (Ed.), *The Making of Modern Iran: State and Society under Riza Shah, 1921–1941* (pp. 15–37). London and New York: Routledge.
Kazemi, F. (1980). *Poverty and Revolution in Iran: The Migrant Poor, Urban Marginality, and Politics.* New York: New York University Press.
Kazemzadeh, F. (1968). *Russia and Britain in Persia, 1864–1914.* New Haven, CT: Yale University Press.
Kedar, L. (Ed.). (1987). *Power through Discourse.* Norwood, NJ: Ablex.
Keddie, N.R. (1966). *Religion and Rebellion in Iran: The Iranian Tobacco Protest of 1891–1892.* London: Frank Cass.
——— (1968). *An Islamic Response to Imperialism: Political and Religious Writings of Sayyid Jamal ad-Din "al-Afghani."* Berkeley, CA and Los Angeles, CA: University of California Press.
——— (1983). *Religion and Politics in Iran: Shi'ism from Political Quietism to Revolution.* New Haven, CT: Yale University Press.
Keddie, N.R., and R. Matthee (Eds.). (2002). *Iran and the Surrounding World: Interactions in Culture and Cultural Politics.* Seattle, WA: University of Washington Press.
Khaksar, N. (2004). The Road to Arizona. In Sh. Vatanabadi and M. Mehdi Khorrami (Trans. and Eds.), *Another Sea, Another Shore: Persian Stories of Migration* (pp. 84–91). Northampton, MA: Interlink Books.
Khalaf-Tabrizi, M. (1683/1963). *Borhan-e qate'.* M. Moin (Ed.). Tehran: Ibn-e Sina.
Khamenei, A. (2006). Rahbar-e Mo'azzam-e enqelab dar didar-e nomayandegan-e majles. Keyhan [The Leader of Revolution Receives Members of the Parliament]. Online document: http://www.kayhannews.ir/850308/3.htm#other301 (access date: May 29, 2006).
Khatami, M. (1998). Statement by H.E. Mohammad Khatami President of the Islamic Republic of Iran before the 53rd Session of the United Nations General Assembly, New York, September 21, 1998. Online document:http://www.parstimes.com/history/khatami_speech_un.html (access date: September 21, 1998).
Khomeini, R. (1961). *Kashf ul-asrar* [The Discovery of Secrets]. Qom.
——— (1978). *Resaleh-ye tozih-ol-masael* [Thesis on the Clarification of Dilemmas]. Tehran: Nur.
——— (1981). *Islam and Revolution: Writings and Declarations of Imam Khomeini.* H. Algar (Trans.). Berkeley, CA: Mizan Press.
——— (1999). Letter to People of Kurdistan. *Kurdistan,* November issue, p. 7.
Kingsnorth, P. (2003). *One No, Many Yeses: A Journey to the Heart of the Global Resistance Movement.* London: Free Press.
Klein, C. (2003). *Cold War Orientalism: Asia in the Middlebrow Imagination, 1945–1961.* Berkeley, CA: University of California Press.
Kononov, A.N. (1947). Opit analiza termina "Turk" [On the Analysis of the Term Turk] *Sovetaskaya Ethnografiya* [Soviet Ethnography] 1:40–47.
Koohi-Kamali, F. (2003). *The Political Development of the Kurds in Iran: Pastoral Nationalism.* New York: Palgrave Macmillan.
Koprulu, M.F. (1958). *Azeri edebiyati* [Azeri Literature]. Istanbul: Kurtulus.

Kornfeld , J.S. Dispatch 244, (891.51A/115), August 21, 1923, as cited in Majd, M.G. (2001). *Great Britain and Reza Shah: The Plunder of Iran, 1921–1941.* Gainesville, FL: University Press of Florida.

Kovel, J. (1970). *White Racism: A Psychohistory.* New York: Pantheon.

Kress, G. (1997). *Before Writing: Rethinking the Paths to Literacy.* London: Routledge.

Kusha, H. (1987). Iran: The Problematic of Women's Participation in a Male-Dominated Society. Working Paper No. 136, University of Kentucky, Kentucky.

Lambton, A.K.S. (1969). *Landlord and Peasant in Persia: A Study of Land Tenure and Land Revenue Administration.* London: Oxford University Press.

——— (1987). *Qajar Persia* [Persia under Qajars]. London: I.B. Tauris.

Lefkowitz, M.R., and Guy M. Rogers (Eds.). (1996). *Black Athena Revisited.* Chapel Hill, NC and London: University of North Carolina Press.

Lehtonen, M. (2000). *The Cultural Analysis of Texts.* A.L. Ahonen and K. Clarke (Trans.). London: Sage.

Lenczowski, G. (1949). *Russia and the West in Iran, 1918–48.* Ithaca, NY: Cornell University Press.

——— (Ed.). (1978). *Iran under the Pahlavis.* Stanford, CA: Hoover Institution Press.

Lewis, B. (1998). *The Multiple Identities of the Middle East.* New York: Schocken.

Lewontin, R.C. (1972). The Apportionment of Human Diversity. *Evolutionary Biology* 1(6): 6–12.

Limbert, J.W. (1987). *Iran: At War with History.* Boulder, CO: Westview Press.

Little, D. (2002). *American Orientalism: The United States and the Middle East since 1945.* Chapel Hill, NC: University of North Carolina Press.

Lockhart, L. (1953). Persia as Seen by the West. In Arbery, A.J. (Ed.), *The Legacy of Persia* (pp. 318–358). Oxford: Oxford University Press.

——— (1958). *The Fall of the Safavid Dynasty and the Afghan Occupation of Persia.* Cambridge: Cambridge University Press.

Lockman, Z. (2004). *Contending Visions of the Middle East: The History and Politics of Orientalism.* New York: Cambridge University Press.

Lopez, I.J. (1995). The Social Construction of Race. In R. Delgado (Ed.), *Critical Race Theory: The Cutting Edge* (pp. 191–203). Philadelphia, PA: Temple University Press.

Lorde, A. (1984). The Master's Tools Will Never Dismantle the Master's House. In *Sister Outsider: Essays & Speeches* (pp. 110–113). Trumansburg: Crossing Press.

Lyotard, J.F. (1984). *The Postmodern Condition: A Report on Knowledge.* G. Bennington and B. Massumi (Trans). Manchester: Manchester University Press.

Macfie, A.L. (2000). *Orientalism: A Reader.* Edinburgh: Edinburgh University Press.

Mackey, S. (1996). *The Iranians: Persia, Islam and the Soul of a Nation.* New York: Dutton.

Majd, M.G. (2001). *Great Britain and Reza Shah: The Plunder of Iran, 1921–1941.* Gainesville, FL: University Press of Florida.

——— (2003). *The Great American Plunder of Persia's Antiquities: 1925–1941.* New York: University Press of America.

Malcolm, S.J. (1815). *A History of Persia.* 2 Vols. London: John Murray.

Mallory, J.P. (1989). *In Search of the Indo-Europeans: Language, Archaeology and Myth.* London: Thames & Hudson.

Marcuse, H. (1969). *An Essay on Liberation.* Boston: Beacon Press.

Marshal, P.J. (1970). *The British Discovery of Hinduism in the Eighteenth Century.* Cambridge: Cambridge University Press.

Marx, K. (August 8, 1853/1979). The Future Results of British Rule in India. *New-York Daily Tribune*; reprinted in the *New-York Semi-Weekly Tribune*, issue no. 856, August 9, 1853.

Marx, K. (1904). *A Contribution to the Critique of Political Economy*. Chicago, IL: C.H. Kerr.

Matini, J. (1992). Iran dar gozasht-e ruzgaran [Iran in the Passage of Times]. *Majalle-ye Iran-shenasi* [A Journal of Iranian Studies] 4(2): 233–247.

——— (1998). "Pishnhad" [Suggestion]. *Majalle-ye Iran-shenasi* [A Journal of Iranian Studies] 10(2): 229–238.

Mazrui, A., and M. Mazrui. (1992). Language in a Multicultural Context: The African Experience. *Language and Education* 6(2–4): 83–98.

Mazzaoui, M. (1972). *The Origins of the Safavids: Shi'ism, Sufism, and the Gulat*. Wiesbaden, West Germany: F. Steiner.

McDowall, D.(1996). *A Modern History of the Kurds*. London: I.B. Tauris.

Mehran, G. (1989). Socialization of School Children in the Islamic Republic of Iran. *Iranian Studies* 22(1): 31–48.

——— (2002). The Presentation of the "Self" and the "Other" in Postrevolutionary Iranian School Textbooks. In N.R. Keddie and R. Matthee (Eds.), *Iran and the Surrounding World: Interactions in Culture and Cultural Politics* (pp. 232–253). Seattle, WA: University of Washington Press.

Melville, C. (2000). The Caspian Provinces: A World Apart, Three Local Histories of Mazandaran. *Iranian Studies* 33(1–2): 45–91.

Memmi, A. (1969). *The Colonizer and the Colonized*. Boston: Beacon Press.

Meshkur, M.J. (1996). *Nazari beh tarikh-e Azerbaijan* [A Look at the History of Azerbaijan]. Tehran: Kahkeshan.

Meskoob, S. (1992). *Iranian Nationality and the Persian Language*. New York: Mage Publishers.

Mey, J.L. (1985). *Whose Language: A Study in Linguistic Pragmatics*. Amsterdam: John Benjamins.

Milani, F. (1992). *Veils and Words: The Emerging Voices of Iranian Women Writers*. Syracuse, NY: Syracuse University Press.

Miles, R. (1989). *Racism*. London: Routledge.

Millspaugh, A. (1973). *The American Task in Persia*. New York: Arno Press.

Minorsky, V. (1978). *The Turks, Iran, and the Caucasus in the Middle Ages*. London: Variorum Prints.

Modarres, S. (1993). Amuzesh-e kudakan-e do-zabaneh dar Azerbayjan-e sharqi [Education of Bilingual Children in Eastern Azerbaijan]. MA thesis, University of Tehran.

Mohammedzadeh Sadiq, H. (2004) Azer va Azeri. *Azeri* (5), Fall 2004: 31–40.

Mohanty, C.T. (1991). *Third World Women and the Politics of Feminism*. Bloomington, IN: Indiana University Press.

Mojab, Sh., and A. Hassanpour. (1995). The Politics of Nationality and Ethnic Diversity. In S. Rahnema and S. Behdad (Eds.), *Iran After the Revolution: Crisis of an Islamic State* (pp. 229–250). London: I.B. Tauris.

Mojahedin-e Khalq of Iran. (1982). *At War with Humanity: A Report on the Human Rights Record of Khomeini Regime*. London: MKI.

Mojtahed-Zadeh, P. (1995). *The Amirs of the Borderlands and Eastern Iranian Borders*. London: Urosevic Foundation.

Montagu, A. (1965). *The Idea of Race*. Lincoln, NE: University of Nebraska Press.

Morad, A. (2003). Dard-e mellat-e Turkmen [The Grievance of Turkmen Nation]. *Kar* (Central Organ of the Organization of Iranian People's Fedaian) (209): 5–8.

Morshedizad, A. (2001). *Rovshanfekran-e Azeri va hoviyyat-e melli va qovmi* [Azeri Intellectuals and Their Attitude to National and Ethnic Identity]. Tehran: Nahsr-e Markaz.

Mortazavi, M. (1981). *Zaban-e dirin-e Azerbayjan* [The Ancient Language of Azerbaijan]. Tehran: Movqufat-e Dr Mahmud Afshar.

Motahheri, M. (1984). *Seyri dar afkar-e Ayatollah Motahheri* [A Journey into Ayat. Motahheri's Thoughts]. Tehran: Intisharat-e Nur.

Müller, F. M. (1862). *Lectures on the Science of Language.* Delivered at the Royal Institution of Great Britain in April, May, and June 1861. New York: C. Scribner.

────── (1888). *Biographies of Words and the Home of the Aryas.* New Delhi: Asian Educational Services.

Murti, K.P. (2001). *India: The Seductive and Seduced "Other" of German Orientalism.* Westport: Greenwood.

Myers, A.C. (Ed.). (1987). *The Eerdmans Bible Dictionary.* Grand Rapids, MI: Wm. B. Eerdmans Publishing.

Nabavi, N. (2003). *Intellectuals and the State in Iran: Politics, Discourse, and the Dilemma of Authenticity.* Gainesville, FL: University of Florida Press.

Nafisy, M. (1997). *Modernism and Ideology in Persian Literature.* Lanham, MD: University Press of America.

Nahir, M. (1984). *Language Problems and Language Planning.* Austin, TX: University of Texas Press.

Najmabadi, A. (1990). *Women's Autobiographies in Contemporary Iran.* Cambridge, MA: Harvard University Press.

Nameh-ye Iran-e Bastan [The Journal of Ancient Iran]. (1933). Issue nos. 21–35.

────── (September 1933). Chera ma Bartarim? [Why We Are Superior?]. (35):1–2.

Nash, M. (1989). *The Cauldron of Ethnicity in the Modern World.* Chicago, IL: University of Chicago Press.

Nateq, N. (1979). *Zaban-e Azarbaycan va vahdat-e melli-ye iran* [The Language of Azerbaijan and the National Unity of Iran]. Tehran: Movqufat-e Dr Mahmud-e Afshar.

Nehzat-e Azadi. (1982). *Asnad-e nehzat-e azadi: jarayan-e tasis va bayaniyye-ha* [The Documents of the Freedom Movement of Iran: Process of Establishment and Announcements]. Tehran: Nehzat.

News Service: Iran. (July 12, 2004, 8:36 AM). Khorramdin's Fans Mark His Birthday. Iranian Cultural Heritage News Agency (CHN). Online document: http://www.chn.ir/english/eshownews.asp?no=2078 (access date: July 12, 2004).

Ng, S.H., and J.J. Bradac. (1993). *Power in Language.* Newbury Park, CA: Sage.

Nieto, S. (2002). *Language, Culture, and Teaching: Critical Perspectives for a New Century.* Mahwah, NJ: Lawrence Erlbaum.

Nyrop, R.F. (Ed.). (1978). *Iran: A Country Study.* Washington, DC: American University Foreign Area Studies.

Oberling, P. (1974). *The Qashqa'i Nomads of Fars.* The Hague: Mouton.

O'Brien, M. (1981). *The Politics of Reproduction.* Boston: Beacon Press.

Olmstead, A.T. (1948). *History of the Persian Empire: Achaemenid Period.* Chicago, IL: University of Chicago Press.

Omi, M., and H. Winant. (1993). On the Theoretical Concept of Race. In C. MacCarthy and W. Crichlow (Eds.), *Race, Identity, and Representation in Education* (pp. 3–10). New York: Routledge.

————— (1995). Racial Formations. In P.S. Rothenberg (Ed.), *Race, Class and Gender in the United States* (pp. 12–21). New York: St. Martin's Press.

Pahlavan, Ch. (1989). Zaban-e Farsi va towse'e-ye melli [The Persian Language and National Development]. *Iran Nameh* 7(3), Spring 1989: 507–525.

Pahlavi, A. (1980). *Faces in a Mirror: Memoirs from Exile.* Englewood Cliffs, NJ: Prentice Hall.

Pahlavi, M. (1980). *Pasokh b-e tarikh* [Answer to History]. Tehran: Ketabkhane-ye Saltanati.

Pahlavi, M.R. Sh. (1961). *Mission for My Country.* London: Hutchinson.

————— (1962). *Mamuriyyat baray-e vatanam* [A Mission for My Country]. Tehran: Ketabkhane-ye Saltanati.

————— (1967). *Enqelab-e sefid* [The White Revolution]. Tehran: Ketabkhane-ye Saltanati.

————— (1980a). *Answer to History.* New York: Stein and Day.

————— (1980b). *The Shah's Story.* London: Michael Joseph.

Pan-Iranist. (July 15, 2004, 4:27 PM). *In Reply to "Alireza Asgharzade on Babek Festival."* Online document: http://members.boardhost.com/tajikistan/ (access date: July 15, 2004).

Parsa, M. (1989). *Social Origins of the Iranian Revolution.* New Brunswick, NJ: Rutgers University Press.

Parsons, J. (1767–1768). *The Remains of Japhet: Being Historical Enquiries into the Affinity and Origin of the European Languages.* London.

Phillipson, R. (1992). *Linguistic Imperialism.* Oxford: Oxford University Press.

————— (Ed.). (2000). *Rights to Language: Equity, Power, and Education: Celebrating the 60th Birthday of Tove Skutnabb-Kangas.* Mahwah, NJ: Lawrence Erlbaum.

Phillipson, R., M. Rannut, and T. Skutnabb-Kangas. (1994). Introduction. In T. Skutnabb-Kangas and R. Phillipson (Eds., in collaboration with M. Rannut), *Linguistic Human Rights: Overcoming Linguistic Discrimination* (pp. 1–22). Berlin: Mouton de Gruyter.

Pirnia, H. (1983). *Iran-e bastan* [The Ancient Iran]. Vols. I–III. Tehran: Donya-ye Ketab.

Pishevari, J. (September 5, 1945). *Ruznamemizin Dili* [The Language of Our Newspaper]. *Azerbaycan* 1: 1–2.

————— (December 3, 1946). *Azerbaijan*, p. 1.

Pisyan, N. (1949). *Az Mahabad-e khunin ta karane-hay-e Aras* [From Bloody Mahabad to the Banks of the Aras]. Tehran: Bamdad.

Poliakov, L. (1974). *The Aryan Myth: A History of Racist and Nationalist Ideas in Europe.* E. Howard (Trans.). New York: New American Library.

Poorpirar, N. (2000). *T'ammoli dar bonyan-e tarikh-e iran. Davazdah qarn sokoot! Ketab-e avval: bar-amadan-e hakhamaneshiyan* [Explorations in the Foundation of Iran's History. Twelve Centuries of Silence! Book One: The Coming of the Akhaemenids]. Tehran: Nashr-e Karang.

————— (2001a). *T'ammoli dar bonyan-e tarikh-e iran. ketab-e dovvom: baramadan-e eslam: poli bar gozashte! Bakhsh-e dovvom: Barrasi-ye asnad.* [Explorations in the Foundation of Iran's History. Book Two: The Coming of Islam, a Bridge to the Past. Second Part: Analyzing the Documents]. Tehran: Nashr-e Karang.

————— (2001b). *T'ammoli dar bonyan-e tarikh-e iran. ketab-e dovvom: baramadan-e eslam: poli bar gozashte! Bakhsh-e sevvom: Barrasi-ye asnad va natijeh* [Explorations in the Foundation of Iran's History. Book Two: The Coming of Islam, a Bridge to the Past. Second Part: Analyzing of Documents and the Conclusion]. Tehran: Nashr-e Karang.

——— (2002–2005). *Haq va sabr* [Right and Patience]. Naser poorpirar's personal Web site. Online document: http://www.naria.persianblog.com/ (access date: November 2005).

——— (2004). *Radd-e ketab-e Shahnameh va bozorgdasht-e shaer-e an* [A Rejection of the Book of Shahnameh and a Tribute to Its Poet]. Online document: http://naria.persianblog.com/1383_2_naria_archive.html.

Price, I.M. (1899). *The Monuments and the Old Testament.* London: Eyre and Spottis-woode.

Prime Ministry Files. (May 1934). 102012/3201. Memo no. 41749, May 1934/ 3–10–1313. Tehran: Government Publications.

Qanoonparvar, M.R. (1984). *Prophets of Doom: Literature as a Socio-Political Phenomenon in Iran.* Lanham, MD: University Press of America.

Qarachorlu, B. [Sehend]. (1965). Taleyime sen bax! [Look at My Misfortune!] In Y. Akpinar (1994), *Azeri edebiyati arastirmalari* [Explorations in Azeri Literature] (p. 130). Istanbul: Dergah Yayinlari.

Qazvini, A. (1923). She'r. *Iranshahr.* 2: 103.

Qurtulush. (1999). Open Letter to President Khatami (pp. 53–55). Toronto, January 20, 1999.

Radford, J., and D. Russell (Eds.). (1989). *Femicide: The Politics of Woman Killing.* New York: Routledge.

Rajabi, P. (2003). Interview with Professor Parviz Rajabi. *Hamshahri* (Tehran) September 28.

Rajaram, N., and D. Frawley. (1994). *Vedic Aryans and the Origins of Civilization: A Literary and Scientific Perspective.* Ottawa and New Delhi: World Heritage Press.

Ramezanzadeh, A. (1996). *Internal and International Dynamics of Ethnic Conflict: The Case of Iran.* Leuven: Katholieke Universiteit Leuven.

Ranger, T.O (1968). Introduction. In T.O. Ranger (Ed.), *Emerging Themes of African History* (pp. ix–xxii). Nairobi: East African Publishing House.

Ranking, G.S.A. (1910). *A History of the Minor Dynasties of Persia.* London: Oxford University Press.

Rasmussen, D.M. (Ed.). (1996). *The Handbook of Critical Theory.* Oxford: Blackwell.

Rayisnia, R. (1975). *Do mobarez-e jonbesh-e mashruteh: Sattarkhan va Sheykh Mohammad Khiyabani* [Two Fighters of the Constitutional Revolution: Sattarkhan and Sheykh Mohammad Khiyabani]. Tehran: Intisharat-e Agah.

——— (1990). *Azerbaijan dar seyr-e tarikh-e Iran* [Azerbaijan in the Evolution of Iran's History]. 2 Vols. Tabriz: Nima Publishers.

Razmi, M. (2000). *Azerbaycan va jonbesh-e tarafdaran-e Ayatollah Shariatmadari dar Iran* [Azerbaijan and the Movement of Ayatollah Shariatmadari Supporters in Iran]. Stockholm: Tribun.

Reeves, M. (1989). *Female Warriors of Allah: Women and the Islamic Revolution.* New York: Routledge.

Rendal, G. (1889). *The Cradle of the Aryans.* London: Macmillan.

Renfrew, C. (1987). *Archaeology and Language: The Puzzle of Indo-European Origins.* New York: Cambridge University Press.

Resulzade, M.A. (1920/1996). *Azerbaijan problemi* [The Problem of Azerbaijan]. Ankara: Azerbaycan Kultur Dernegi Yayinlari.

Rex, J. (1999). Racism, Institutionalized and Otherwise. In L. Harris (Ed.), *Racism: Key Concepts in Critical Theory* (pp. 41–55). New York: Humanity Books.

Reza, E. (1981). *Tireh va zaban-e mardom-e Azarbayjan: bekhsh-e 6, Azarbayjan va Aran* [Ethnicity and Language of People of Azerbaijan, Part 6: Azerbaijan and Arran]. Tehran: Sherkat-e Entesharat-e Elmi va Farhangi.

——— (1986). *Iran va Turkan dar ruzgar-e Sasaniyan* [Iran and the Turks in the Era of Sassanian]. Tehran: Sherkat-e Entesharat-e Elmi va Farhangi.

Rezazadeh Shafaq Tabrizi, S. (1924). *Divan-e mirza Abulqasem Aref Qazvini* [The Divan of Mirza Abulqasem Aref Qazvini]. Berlin.

Rezazadeh-Malek, R. (1973). *Guyesh-e Azeri* [The Azeri Accent]. Tehran: Entesharat-e Anjoman-e Farhang-e Iran-e Bastan.

Rezun, M. (1982). *The Iranian Crisis of 1941: The Actors, Britain, Germany, and the Soviet Union*. Wien: Bohlau.

Richard, Y. (1989). The Relevance of "Nationalism" in Contemporary Iran. *Middle East Review* Summer 1989: 27–36.

Richardson, L. (1988). *The Dynamics of Sex and Gender: A Sociological Perspective.* New York: Harper & Row.

Richardson, L., and V. Taylor. (1989). *Feminist Frontiers 2: Rethinking Sex, Gender, and Society.* New York: McGraw Hill.

Ricks, T. (Ed.). (1984). *Critical Perspectives on Modern Persian Literature.* Washington, DC: Three Continents Press.

Ritzer, G. (1988). *Contemporary Sociological Theory.* 2nd ed. New York: Alfred Knopf.

——— (1992). *Classical Sociological Theory.* New York: McGraw-Hill.

Robinson, C.J. (1983). *Black Marxism: The Making of the Black Radical Tradition.* London: Zed Books; Totowa, NJ: Biblio Distribution Center.

Robinson, L. (1989). What Culture Should Mean. *Nation* September 1989: 391–397.

Roosevelt, A. (1947). The Kurdish Republic of Mahabad. *Middle East Journal* July 1947: 247–269.

Roosevelt, K. (1979). *Countercoup: The Struggle for the Control of Iran.* New York: McGraw-Hill.

Roozname-ye Iran [Iran Newspaper] (January 29, 2004). "Yek Tahavol dar Nezam-e Amuzeshi-ye Keshvar" [A New Development in the Country's Educational System], p. 1.

Roshdiyyeh, M.H. (1887/1888). *Amsal-e Loqman* [The Sayings of Loqman]. H. Mohammadzadeh Sediq (Ed.). Tehran: Nashr-e Zovfa.

——— (1905a). *Vatan Dili: Mubtedi Shagirdlere* [The Language of Homeland: For the Beginners]. Tabriz: Agha Ali Metbuesi.

——— (1905b). *Ana Dili* [The Mother Tongue]. Tabriz: Agha Ali Metbuesi.

Ruether, R. (1974). *Religion and Sexism.* New York: Simon & Schuster.

Rushdi, S. (1991). *Imaginary Homelands.* London: Granta/Penguin.

Saad, B.J. (1996). *The Image of Arabs in Modern Persian Literature.* New York: University Press of America.

Sadr, Z. (1997). Kesrat-e qovmi va hoviyyat-e melli-ye Iranian. *Tribun* 2: 11–62.

Safavi, N. (1955). *Jame'eh va hokumat-e islami* [Society and Islamic Government]. Qom.

Sahir, H. (1961/2004). *Habib Sahirin chap olmamish sherleri* [Unpublished Poems of Habib Sahir] (pp. 1–7). Online document: http://www.shamsnews.com/habib-sahir.HTM (access date: August 23, 2004).

———— (1973). *Esir Ellerin Shairi* [The Poet of Captive Peoples]. In Y. Akpinar (1994), *Azeri edebiyati arastirmalari* [Explorations in Azeri Literature] (pp. 138–147). Istanbul: Dergah Yayinlari.

Said, E. (1966). *Joseph Conrad and the Fiction of Autobiography*. Cambridge, MA: Harvard University Press; London: Oxford University Press.

———— (1975). *Beginnings: Intention and Method*. New York: Basic Books.

———— (1979). *Orientalism*. New York: Vintage Books.

———— (1980). *The Question of Palestine*. New York: Times Books.

———— (1981). *Covering Islam: How the Media and the Experts Determine How We See the Rest of the World*. New York: Pantheon; London: Routledge & Kegan Paul.

———— (1983). *The World, the Text, and the Critic*. Cambridge, MA: Harvard University Press.

———— (1986). *After the Last Sky: Palestinian Lives*. Photographs by Jean Mohr. New York: Pantheon; London: Faber.

———— (1988). Foreword. In Guha P. and G.C. Spivak (Eds.), *Selected Subaltern Studies* (pp. v–x). New York and Oxford: Oxford University Press.

———— (1993). *Culture and Imperialism*. New York: Alfred Knopf.

———— (1994a). *Representations of the Intellectual: The 1993 Reith Lectures*. New York: Pantheon.

———— (1994b). *The Politics of Dispossession: The Struggle for Palestinian Self-Determination, 1969–1994*. New York: Pantheon.

———— (1999). *Out of Place: A Memoir*. New York: Alfred Knopf.

———— (August 7, 2003). Orientalism, 25 Years Later. *Al-Ahram Weekly Online*. Online document: http://w3.uniroma1.it/studiorientali/varia/Edward%20Said%20%20Preface%20to%20Orientalism.htm.

Saidi, Gh. (1976). *It's Night, Yes Night!* A. Azad (Trans.). In E. Hooglund and M. Hooglund (Eds. and Trans.) (1976), *The Little Black Fish and Other Modern Persian Stories by Samad Behrangi* (pp. xxiii–xxvi). Washington, DC: Three Continents Press.

Saleh, A.P. (1985). Yaddashtha-yee dar bare-ye zaban-e Farsi. In I. Afshar (Ed.), *Namvare-ye Dr Mahmood Afshar* (pp. 27–58). Tehran: Chapkhane-ye Bahman.

Sanasarian, E. (1983). *The Women's Rights Movement in Iran: Mutiny, Appeasement, and Repression from 1900 to Khomeini*. New York: Praeger Publishers.

Sarkar, J. (1979). [1st ed. 1928]. *India through the Ages*. Calcutta: Orient Longman.

Sarrafi, A. (2003). *Lozum-e amuzesh beh zaban-e madari dar Azerbayjan* [The Necessity of Education in the Mother Tongue in Azerbaijan]. Online document: http://www.durna.se/ (access date: December 20, 2003).

Sartre, J.P. (1961/1990). Preface. In F. Fanon, *The Wretched of the Earth* (pp. 1–37). C. Farrington (Trans.). New York: Penguin. (Originally published as *Les damnés de la terre* [Paris: Présence Africaine, 1961]).

———— (1964/2001). *Colonialism and Neocolonialism*. First published in 1964 by Editions Gallimard: Paris. Translated and published in English in 2001 by London: Routledge.

Sassen, S. (1998). *Globalization and Its Discontents*. New York: New York Press.

Savory, R. (1980). *Iran under the Safavids*. Cambridge: Cambridge University Press.

Sayce, A. (1885). *The Ancient Empires of the East*. New York: Charles Scribners' Sons.

Schlegel, F. V. (1808/1849). *Über die Sprache und Weisheit der Indier Heidelberg, Mohr und Zimmer* [Essay on the Language and Wisdom of the Indians]. E.J. Millington (Trans.) (1849). London: Henry G. Bohn.]

Schneider, J. (Ed.). (1998). *Italy's "Southern Question": Orientalism in One Country*. Oxford and New York: Berg.

Seidman, S. (1994). *Contested Knowledge: Social Theory in the Postmodern Era*. Oxford: Blackwell.

Shaffer, B. (2002). *Borders and Brethren: Iran and the Challenge of Azerbaijani Identity*. Cambridge, MA: MIT Press.

Shaffer, J. (1984). The Indo-Aryan Invasions: Cultural Myth and Archaeological Reality. In J. Lukacs (Ed.), *The People of South Asia* (pp. 64–78). New York: Plenum.

Shahabi, S. (1993). *What Is Happening to Women in Iran?* Gothenberg (self-published).

Shahbazi, A. (1990). *Zohur va soqut-e saltanat-e Pahlavi, jeld 2* [The Rise and Fall of Pahlavi Dynasty, vol 2]. Tehran: Entesharat-e Ettela'at.

——— (1998). *Nazariyye-ye tovte'e, so'ud-e saltanat-e pahlavi va tarikhnegari-ye jadid dar iran* [The Conspiracy Theories, the Rise of Pahlavi Dynasty, and New Historiography in Iran]. Tehran: Moassese-ye motaleat va pajuheshhay-e siyasi.

Shahryar, M.H. (1943). Haydar-Babaya Salam! [Greetings to Heydar-Baba!]. Tabriz: Hasan Taqvimi.

——— (1967/2003). Tehran va Tehrani [Tehran and Tehrani]. Online document: http://www.tribun.com/ (access date: November 25, 2003).

——— (1991). *Kolliyyat-e divan-e Torki* [The Collection of Turkish Divan]. H. Mohammadzadeh (Ed.). Tehran: Entsharat-e Negah/Entsharat-e Zarrin.

Shams Tabriz News. (May 20, 2006). Vije-nameh-ye e'traz beh karikator [Special Edition on Protests against the Cartoons]. Online document: http://www.shamstabriz.com/ (access date: May 28, 2006).

Shawcross, W. (1988). *The Shah's Last Ride: The Fate of an Ally*. New York: Simon & Schuster.

Sheikhol-islami, J. (1989). Zaban-e Farsi neshan-e valay-e qovmiyyat-e irani [Persian Language: The Elevated Sign of Iranian Ethnicity]. In I. Afshar (Ed.), *Zaban-e Farsi dar Azerbaijan: dar bargirandeh-ye bisto-haft maqaleh az neveshteh-haye daneshmandan va zabanshinasan* [Persian Language in Azerbaijan: Containing Twenty-Seven Articles from Scholars and Linguists] (pp. 441–467). Tehran: Boyad-e Moqufat-e Dr Mahmud Afshar.

Shoar, M.R. (1967). *Vajeha-ye farsi dar farhang-e emruzi-ye Azerbayjan: bahsi dar bare-ye zaban-e Azarbayjan* [The Persian Words in Contemporary Azerbaijani Accent: A Discussion on the Language of Azerbaijan]. Tabriz.

Sinfield, A. (1992). *Faultlines: Cultural Materialism and the Politics of Dissident Reading*. Berkeley, CA: University of California Press.

Singh, R. (Ed.). (1996). *Towards a Critical Sociolinguistics*. Amsterdam: John Benjamins Publishing.

Sistani, I.A. (1990). *Negahi b-e Azerbaijan-e sharghi* [A Look at Eastern Azerbaijan]. Tehran: Movqyfat-e Afshar.

Skutnabb-Kangas, T. (2000). *Linguistic Genocide in Education or Worldwide Diversity and Human Rights?* Mahwah, NJ: Lawrence Erlbaum.

Skutnabb-Kangas, T., and R. Phillipson (Eds.). (1994). *Linguistic Human Rights: Overcoming Linguistic Discrimination*. Berlin: Mouton de Gruyter.

Spivak, G.C. (1987). *In Other Worlds*. New York and London: Methuen.

——— (1988). "Can the Subaltern Speak?" In C. Nelson and L. Grossberg (Eds.), *Marxism and the Interpretation of Culture* (pp. 271–313). Urbana and Chicago, IL: University of Illinois Press, 1988.

——— (1999). *A Critique of Postcolonial Reason: Toward a History of the Vanishing Present*. Cambridge, MA: Harvard University Press.

Sprachman, P. (2002). *Language and Culture in Persian*. Costa Mesa: Mazda Publishers.

Stalin, J. (1946). Letter to Pishevari, May 8, 1946. Reprinted in *Araz* (2), 1996: 3.

Statistical Center of Iran (Markaz-e Amar-e Iran). (1988). *Sarshomari-ye Umumi-ye Nofus va Maskan* [National Census on Population and Housing]. Tehran: Markaz-e Amar-e Iran.]

—— (1996). *Iran: Statistics Yearbook 1996*. Tehran: Markaz-e Amar-e Iran.]

Strunk, W.T. (1977). The Reign of Sheikh Khazal ibn Jabir and the Suppression of the Principality of Arabistan: A Study in British Imperialism in Southwestern Iran, 1897–1925. Unpublished PhD thesis, Indiana University, Indiana, August 1977.

Swietochowski, T. (1995). *Russia and Azerbaijan: A Borderland in Transition*. New York: Columbia University Press.

Swietochowski, T., and B. Collins. (1999). *Historical Dictionary of Azerbaijan*. Lanham, MD: Scarecrow Press.

Tabari, A., and N. Yeganeh (Eds.). (1982). *In the Shadow of Islam: The Women's Movement in Iran*. London: Zed Books.

Talattof, K. (2000). *Politics of Writing in Iran*. Syracuse, NY: Syracuse University Press.

Tanaka, S. (1993). *Japan's Orient: Rendering Pasts into History*. Berkeley, CA: University of California Press.

Taqizadeh, S.H. (1920/1978). *Maqalat-e Taqizadeh* [The Essays of Taqizadeh]. Tehran: Entsharat-e Shokufan.

Taraghi, G. (2004). The Wolf Lady. In Sh.Vatanabadi and M. Mehdi Khorrami (Trans. and Eds.), *Another Sea, Another Shore: Persian Stories of Migration* (pp. 130–143). Northampton, MA: Interlink Books.

Tavakoli-Targhi, M. (2001). *Refashioning Iran: Orientalism, Occidentalism and Historiography*. Hampshire and New York: Palgrave Macmillan.

The Cambridge History of Iran. (1968–1986). 6 Vols. Cambridge: Cambridge University Press.

The Constitution of Afghanistan. (2004). Online document: http://www.concourt. am/wwconst/constit/afghanistan/afgan-e.htm (access date: December 10, 2004).

The Constitution of the Islamic Republic of Iran. (1979). Iranology Foundation. http://www.iranologyfo.com/ (access date: October 20, 2003).

Torkman, M. (1996). *Dr. Mohammad Mosaddegh's Letters*. 2nd ed. Tehran: Hezaran Publications.

Trask, H.K. (1993). Lovely Hula Hands: Corporate Tourism and the Prostitution of Howaiian culture. In *From a Native Daughter* (pp. 179–195). New York: Vintage Books.

Turkish Daily News. (2001). *Orkhon Inscriptions. Turkish Daily News*, April 17, 2001, p. 1.

UNCHR (UN Commission on Human Rights). (2002). *Report on the Situation of Human Rights in the Islamic Republic of Iran*. Prepared by the Special Representative of the Commission on Human Rights Mr. M.D. Copithorne, January 16, 2002, E/CN.4/2002/42. http://www.unhchr.ch/huridocda/ huridoca.nsf/Documents?OpenFrameset (access date: January 25, 2002).

Van Dijk, T.A. (1984). *Prejudice in Discourse*. Amsterdam: Benjamins.

—— (1987). *Communicating Racism: Ethnic Prejudice in Thought and Talk*. Newbury Park, CA: Sage.

—— (1988a). How "They" Hit the Headlines: Ethnic Minorities in the Press. In G. Smitherman-Donaldson and T.A. van Dijk (Eds.), *Discourse and Discrimination* (pp. 221–262). Detroit, MI: Wayne State University Press.

—— (1988b). *News as Discourse*. Hillsdale, NJ: Lawrence Erlbaum.

—— (1991). *Racism and the Press*. London: Routledge.

Van Dijk, T.A. (1992). Discourse and the Denial of Racism. *Discourse and Society* 3(1): 87–118.

——— (1993a). *Elite Discourse and Racism*. Newbury Park, CA: Sage.

Van Dijk, T.A. (1993b). Principles of Critical Discourse Analysis. *Discourse and Society* 4(2): 249–283.

——— (2001). Critical Discourse Analysis. In D. Schiffrin, D. Tannen, and H. E. Hamilton (Eds.), *The Handbook of Discourse Analysis* (pp. 352–371). Malden, MA: Blackwell.

Van Dijk, T.A., and W. Kintsch. (1983). *Strategies of Discourse Comprehension*. New York: Academic Press.

Varjavand, P. (2004). Demokrasi va hoquq-e bashar: Tegyir-e shoar-e hezb-e democrat-e Kordestan-e iran [Democracy and Human Rights: The Changing of Democratic Party of Iranian Kurdistan's Motto]. *Mizgerd-e radio Farda* [Farda Radio Roundtable Discussion], November 12, 2004. Online document: http://www.pdk-iran.org (access date: December 24, 2004).

Varliq: Turkce-Farsca ferhengi dergi [Varliq: A Turkish and Persian Cultural Journal]. (1993). Mektublar [Letters to the Editor]. (91–92), Spring 1993: 102–103.

Vatanabadi, Sh., and M. Mehdi Khorrami (Trans. and Eds.). (2004). *Another Sea, Another Shore: Persian Stories of Migration*. Northampton, MA: Interlink Books.

Vaziri, M. (1993). *Iran as Imagined Nation: The Construction of National Identity*. New York: Paragon House.

Vefayi, Z. (2003). *Savad-amuzi elzamen farsi-amuzi nist* [Knowledge Acquisition Is Not Necessarily Farsi-Learning]. Online document: http://Zohreh-vefayi. blogspot.com/http://news.gooya.com/society/archives/000637.php (access date: December 10, 2003).

Vurgun, S. (1952). Yandirilan Kitablar [The Books That Burned]. In J. Heyat (1990), *Azerbaycan edebiyyat tarixine bir baxish* [A Look at the History of Azerbaijani Literature] (pp. 133–135). Tehran: Sazman-e Chap-e Khajeh.

Wa Thiong'o, N. (1986). *Decolonising the Mind: The Politics of Language in African Literature*. London: James Currey.

——— (1993). *Moving the Centre: The Struggle for Cultural Freedom*. London: James Currey.

Warner, A.G., and E. Warner. (1905). *The Shahnameh of Ferdausi*. London: Dryden House.

Weiss, G., and R. Wodak. (2003). *Critical Discourse Analysis: Theory and Interdisciplinarity*. Basinstoke: Palgrave Macmillan.

Wells, H.G. (1920/1931). *The Outline of History*. Vols. I and II. Garden City, NY: Garden City Publishing.

Welton, N., and L. Wolf. (2001). *Global Uprising: Confronting the Tyrannies of the 21st Century: Stories from a New Generation of Activists*. Island, BC: New Society Publishers.

West, C. (1994). *Race Matters*. New York: Vintage Books.

Wilber, D. (1975). *Reza Shah Pahlavi: The Resurrection and Reconstruction of Iran*. New York: Exposition Press.

——— (1981). *Iran Past and Present*. Princeton, NJ: Princeton University Press.

Wills, G. (1999). Bully of the Free World. *Foreign Affairs* (Washington) 78(2), March/April: 50–59.

Wodak, R. (Ed.). (1989). *Language, Power and Ideology: Studies in Political Discourse*. Amsterdam: Benjamins.

——— (1996). *Disorders of Discourse*. London: Longman.

—— (1997). *Gender and Discourse*. London: Sage.

Woods, J. (1976). *The Aqquyunllu: Clan, Confederation, Empire*. Minneapolis, MN: Bibliotheca Islamica.

Wrong, D.H. (1979). *Power: Its Forms, Bases and Uses*. Oxford: Blackwell. www. etnologue.com, 2004.

Xenophon. (430 BC/1992). *The Education of Cyrus, or Cyropaedia*. H.G. Dakyns (Trans.). London: Everyman's Library.

Yalfani, M. (2004). Without Roots. In Sh. Vatanabadi and M. Mehdi Khorrami (Trans. and Eds.), *Another Sea, Another Shore: Persian Stories of Migration* (pp. 92–98). Northampton, MA: Interlink Books.

Yann, R. (1989). The Relevance of "Nationalism" in Contemporary Iran. *Middle East Review* Summer 1989: 27–36.

Yarshater, E. (1985). The Absence of Median and Achaemenian Kings in Iran's Traditional History. *Iran Nameh* III: 191–213.

Yazdi, M.H. (1945). *Arzesh-e masa'i-ye Iran dar jang* [The Value of Iran's Contribution to the War]. Tehran: Bamdad.

Yoshihara, M. (2003). *Embracing the East: White Women and American Orientalism*. New York: Oxford University Press.

Young, L., and C. Harrison (Eds.). (2004). *Systemic Functional Linguistics and Critical Discourse Analysis: Studies in Social Change*. London: Continuum Press.

Young, R.J.C. (1995). *Colonial Desire: Hybridity in Theory, Culture and Race*. London: Routledge.

Yushij, N. (1940/1992). *Majmu'e-ye kamel-e asar-e Nima Yushij: farsi va tabari* [A Complete Collection of Nima Yushij's Works in Persian and Tabari]. S. Tahbaz (Ed.). Tehran: Negah.

Zabih, S. (1986). *The Mossadegh Era: Roots of the Iranian Revolution*. Chicago, IL: Lakeview Press.

Zeka, Y. (1955). *Maqalat-e Kasravi* [Kasravi's Essays]. Tehran.

Zanjani, A. (1974). *Khaterati az ma'muriyathay-e man dar Azerbaijan* [Memoirs of My Assignments in Azerbaijan]. Tehran: Aban.

Zarrinkoob, A.H. (1957). *Do qern sokut* [Two Centuries of Silence]. Tehran: Amirkabir.

Zehtabi, M.T. (1999). *Iran turklerinin eski tarixi* [The Ancient History of Iranian Turks]. "Birnici Cild: En Qedim Dovrden Iskendere Qeder" [Vol. 1, From Earliest Times to Alexander]. 2nd ed. Tebriz: Artun.

Zein, M.F. (2003). *Christianity, Islam and Orientalism*. London: Saqi Books.

Zonis, M. (1971). *The Political Elite of Iran*. Princeton, NJ: Princeton University Press.

INDEX